MURDER
THE
TRUTH

MURDER THE TRUTH

FEAR, THE FIRST AMENDMENT, AND A SECRET
CAMPAIGN TO PROTECT THE POWERFUL

DAVID ENRICH

MARINER BOOKS

New York   Boston

HarperCollins books may be purchased for educational, business, or sales promotional use. For information, please email the Special Markets Department at SPsales@harpercollins.com.

The Mariner flag design is a registered trademark of HarperCollins Publishers LLC.

FIRST EDITION

Designed by Chloe Foster

Newspaper art by seongjin from Adobe Stock

Library of Congress Cataloging-in-Publication Data has been applied for.

ISBN 978-0-06-337290-0

24 25 26 27 28 LBC 5 4 3 2 1

To Liza and Nicholas

A freshening stream of libel actions, which often seem as much designed to punish writers and publications as to recover damages for real injuries, may threaten the public and constitutional interest in free, and frequently rough, discussion.

—Judge Robert Bork,
    concurring opinion in *Ollman v. Evans*, 1984

CONTENTS

AUTHOR'S NOTE

I am biased. I've been a journalist my entire adult life. I believe in my profession's fundamental mission: to inform the public and hold the powerful to account. And based on my experience, I believe that most journalists—though we are by no means immune from mistakes—try to live up to that mission. Yet I recognize that not everyone agrees with me, and I have done my best in this book to understand and fairly portray these opposing perspectives.

This book is based on a variety of sources. I interviewed more than two hundred people, including lawyers, judges, journalists, lawmakers, activists, and those whose reputations were harmed by what they perceived as false or unfair articles, books, and other published statements. I reviewed thousands of pages of court documents and obtained hundreds of pages of other materials through public records requests. And I relied on the previous work of countless journalists, academics, and others in newspapers, magazines, websites, books, podcasts, and elsewhere. Except in cases of people who spoke to me on a not-for-attribution basis, I have detailed my sources at the end of the book.

I tried to talk to everyone who is featured in these pages. A few, told that I was working on a book about legal threats and intimidation, threatened to sue me, as I describe in more detail in the Epilogue. But most agreed to speak openly about their views and experiences. I am grateful for their help.

Guy Lawson was in his office, surrounded by books, notepads, and stacks of files yellowing with age, when one of his teenage daughters called in a panic. It was a warm, breezy evening in June 2017, and the sun was gliding down toward the Catskill Mountains and the Hudson River, due west of Lawson's cluttered workplace. He and his wife had moved to Upstate New York nearly a decade earlier. Art galleries, clothing boutiques, and "locavore" cafés lined his village's leafy streets. Lawson, whose office was above a bright purple storefront peddling pricey bath soaps, knocked the neighborhood as "twee." But he and his wife had twin girls, and the family had needed to escape the exorbitance of New York City.

Lawson was a magazine writer, his wife an entrepreneur. Neither had enjoyed a particularly smooth career trajectory. Lawson was, as he put it, an old-school, anti-authority "punk journalist" whose mission was "holding corrupt motherfuckers to account." He had a bit of a temper and could be impulsive, and for a while, after getting fired from an early job, he'd lived in a crash pad frequented by junkies in Montreal. Once, someone stole virtually his entire wardrobe, which he had to replenish at a charity shop that sold clothes by the pound.

Now, though, Lawson and his wife, Maya Kaimal, were thriving. They'd recently purchased and renovated a beautiful Victorian-style house, built in 1895, with a white widow's walk on top and a towering ginkgo tree out front. Kaimal's eponymous Indian food business was booming. And two years earlier, Lawson had published his third book, *Arms and the Dude*. Part hard-hitting exposé, part fast-paced yarn, it was the true story of three Miami stoners who had become international arms traffickers, supplying the Pentagon with ammunition for its war in

Afghanistan. Much of the action was set in Albania, where Lawson had once been embedded as a war correspondent and which had become an ideal venue for arms dealers thanks to its loosely controlled stockpiles of surplus weaponry. The country struck Lawson as corrupt and borderline feudal, a land where interfamily grudges were sometimes resolved with deadly violence. Yet he had fallen in love with Albania and its people, everyone except what he saw as the thuggish ruling class. Perhaps it was paranoia, but Lawson sometimes mentioned that New York City—a scenic two-hour drive from his riverside village—was home to a sizable population of Albanian expats, some of whom, he imagined, might be willing to settle scores in this country as well.

In 2016, Lawson's tale had been turned into a big-budget film, *War Dogs*, starring Jonah Hill. Lawson hadn't always loved the Hollywood experience—he'd chafed at the feeling of powerlessness as his work was adapted for the screen, and the sense of being sidelined only grew when he was forced to pay his own way to the movie's premiere at the famed Chinese Theater in Los Angeles—but there was little doubt that his career was in flight. A *War Dogs* movie poster and translated editions of his bestselling books graced his office, along with a few pairs of old sneakers, a CD-playing boombox, and an ancient Rolodex.

Lawson was trying to identify his next book project when one of his thirteen-year-old twins called that June evening. She was home alone, and she was crying. "Some creepy guy" had pounded on their door and insisted on seeing her father. Now the man was lurking outside, she reported, the words spilling out of her mouth in an anxious jumble.

Lawson instructed his daughter to remain indoors. He bounded down a carpeted flight of stairs, out the purple door, past the bath-and-body shop, and hustled home on foot. Even at a leisurely pace, the journey would have taken barely five minutes, as the village's shopping district yielded to tidy blocks of colorfully painted Victorians. When Lawson rounded the corner, he saw an unfamiliar car parked in his gravel driveway. A brawny man emerged. He shoved a sheaf of papers into Lawson's hands.

Lawson's adrenaline was pumping. All he could think about was his frightened daughter. "Get the fuck away from my house!" he shouted.

It wasn't until Lawson got inside that he scanned the papers. "A lawsuit has been filed against you," the cover sheet read. The plaintiff was a man named Shkëlzen Berisha. He was the son of Albania's former prime minister and a small but important character in Lawson's book, which had described him as being part of the country's mafia. The suit accused Lawson of libel. In a small font near the bottom of the cover sheet, Berisha's lawyer had typed in his demand: $60,000,000.

Four years later, the clerk of the United States Supreme Court distributed a legal petition to the nine justices for discussion at an upcoming meeting. The justices' so-called conferences are among the most secretive and ritualized proceedings in the US government. Held in an undisclosed room inside the court's neoclassical temple on Capitol Hill, each justice is required to shake the others' hands before taking his or her seat, according to seniority, around a long table. Only the nine are allowed in. No clerks. No secretaries. If anyone needs something, the junior justice—in this case, Amy Coney Barrett, who had joined the court days before Donald Trump lost the 2020 election to Joe Biden—peeks outside the room and asks a waiting staff member to fetch it.

The paperwork that the clerk shared on July 1, 2021, was what's known as a petition for a writ of certiorari. If a party to a legal matter, such as a lawsuit or a criminal proceeding, is unhappy with a lower court's ruling, in certain circumstances he or she can use such a petition to ask the Supreme Court to review and potentially overturn the judgment. These petitions are common—thousands are submitted each year—but few manage to attract the justices' attention. Most years, the court accepts about eighty cases, or roughly 1 percent.

This particular petition was already familiar to the justices. The clerk had circulated it twice the prior month. On both occasions, the justices had punted on announcing a decision about whether to accept the matter for review.

But the Supreme Court's term was just about over, and so was the time for delays. For a cert petition to be accepted, at least four justices had to vote in favor of granting review. In this case—known by its official number, 20–1063—it was clear that there weren't enough votes. The court would reject the petition. A torturous legal odyssey that had begun four years earlier in a quaint Hudson Valley village was about to be over.

Except for one thing. The following morning, when the court published the term's final, fifty-four-page list of orders, a few petitions were denied without explanation. But that was not what happened with 20–1063, otherwise known as *Shkëlzen Berisha v. Guy Lawson, et al.* The court's justices had disagreed with one another about whether they should take the case. It was about to become a rallying cry for politicians, lawyers, judges, and activists who wanted to curb Americans' freedom to question and critique the rich and powerful.

This book is the story of a largely under-the-radar legal movement that is weaponizing the obscure field of libel law—a campaign whose growing momentum has closely tracked the country's increasing flirtations with authoritarianism.

At first glance, libel law might seem an unlikely venue for a battle with high stakes for American democracy. Accusations of libel—publishing or writing something that injures someone's reputation—are nothing new. For a long time, they were settled by duels and other forms of violence. In medieval England, libel was punishable by, among other things, cutting off the offender's tongue. Gradually punishments evolved from mutilations to monetary and sometimes even criminal penalties. People's reputations were at least as valuable as their property. Stealing their stuff was a punishable offense. So, too, should be impugning their characters through lies and deceit. Countless victims—ranging from businesses harmed by false news reports to poll workers or grieving families defamed by extremist conspiracy theorists like Alex Jones and Rudy Giuliani—were awarded money to compensate for the reputational harms they suffered. It was a mark of a well-functioning society that such grievances could be settled at a courthouse, not a dueling ground.

Yet long before a process server showed up at Guy Lawson's house on behalf of a politically connected Albanian, businessmen, companies, and politicians had also been wielding libel lawsuits for a much less benign purpose: to muzzle their critics. What better way to deter people from speaking out than by making it crystal clear that such speech would be greeted with an overwhelming legal response?

Starting in the 1960s, the Supreme Court grew troubled by this dynamic and, in a series of landmark decisions, began making it harder for public figures to prevail in such legal actions. The court concluded that journalists and others shouldn't be held liable when they accidentally got facts wrong about people in the public eye. (If someone was deliberately or recklessly spreading falsehoods, that was a different matter; nobody thought defamatory lies deserved protection.) The theory was that a vigorous, probing press was an essential safeguard of democracy, a key to holding the government and other institutions in check. If a public figure could seek debilitating damages every time a news organization made a mistake, the media would either start to censor itself or be sued into oblivion. Both scenarios ran counter to the First Amendment's guarantee of a free press—and the core American belief in the value of unfettered speech.

For the next half century, even as American politics grew increasingly polarized, there was remarkably broad agreement that the Supreme Court had gotten this right. Its string of libel decisions—beginning with its unanimous 1964 ruling in *New York Times Company v. Sullivan*—was generally regarded with reverence. As recently as 2010, Congress passed a law celebrating the country's commitment to defending Americans from weaponized libel claims. In a barely recognizable act of bipartisan unity, not a single lawmaker voted against the legislation.

And then, in the space of only a few years, that consensus crumbled.

Donald Trump was a crucial catalyst. Beginning in 2016 and continuing through 2024, he relentlessly demonized the media as "evil," "criminals," and "the enemy of the people," applauding violence, threatening to revoke TV networks' licenses, and floating the idea of jailing reporters. There is a long history, of course, of politicians attacking the news media. What set this apart was not just Trump's rhetoric but also his success. He convinced broad swaths of the public that journalism itself was illegitimate, that its articles, fact checks, and exposés were not to be trusted—a belief that was enhanced at times by some journalists shirking their roles as open-minded seekers of truth and instead donning the robes of ideologues. As this distrust took root among millions of Americans, it would become much easier to justify the curtailment of long-standing press freedoms and for politicians, business executives, and others to escape accountability.

But more subtle forces were also at play, including the emergence of a clique of high-powered lawyers who, motivated by a mixture of profits and politics, specialized in attacking journalists and others on behalf of Russian oligarchs, opioid-pushing executives, corrupt politicians, scandal-plagued celebrities, and many others who were the subjects of unfavorable media coverage.

The successes of these lawyers soon inspired hordes of copycats, ushering in a perilous new era in which those who criticized or even scrutinized the powerful often provoked a barrage of legal warfare. An onslaught of letters threatening litigation prompted news outlets to pull punches as they investigated deep-pocketed people and companies. It wasn't just journalists. Members of the public who posted nasty restaurant reviews or complained about local construction projects found themselves in the crosshairs. Libel lawsuits, even those chucked out of court at an early stage, sometimes drove community newspapers and independent bloggers to the brink of bankruptcy. That, in turn, exacerbated a crisis in which thousands of newspapers have vanished and tens of millions of Americans now lack reliable sources for local news—a trend that has contributed to the spread of disinformation, the polarization of politics, and a new era of impunity for elected officials and big companies.

Dozens of lawyers, many with decades of experience, told me that the popularity of these menacing legal tactics has recently surged to unprecedented heights. In such an environment, the safest course often seemed to be to avoid writing about anyone or anything that smacked of controversy—or at least anyone with the inclination and wherewithal to retain aggressive counsel. It was a form of quiet censorship all but inaudible to the American public.

There was one thing standing in the way of these lawsuits and scare tactics becoming even more potent: the Supreme Court's decisions in *New York Times v. Sullivan* and a handful of subsequent cases.

And so, around the time that the first Trump administration began reshaping the federal judiciary and that conservatives sensed a once-in-a-lifetime opportunity to end abortion rights, restrict voting access, and gut federal regulations, a handful of lawyers, judges, and politicians embarked on another quest—one that went far beyond the traditional efforts to complain about and sow distrust toward the media. Their goal was to eviscerate the long-standing Supreme Court rulings that shielded journalists, activists, and everyday citizens when they wrote or spoke critically about important people and institutions, whether it was the president of the United States or a local real estate developer. One of their main methods was to latch onto lawsuits—like Shkëlzen Berisha's against Guy Lawson—that they thought were promising vessels for the creation of new, more palatable precedents.

These advocates were soon joined by a network of pressure groups with a knack for injecting fringe ideas into the conservative mainstream. They cloaked their arguments in the rhetoric of patriotism, fidelity to the Constitution, and protecting the innocent. They claimed that it was virtually impossible to win libel lawsuits and that the high barriers to success incentivized recklessness and were a key cause of disinformation. This argument ignored the plethora of recent successful libel cases, some against disinformation super-spreaders—a trend that suggests the current system works. The true mission of the crusade—whose momentum was poised to grow as Trump returned to the White House—was broader: to neutralize the media and anyone else who might expose the wrongdoing and secrets of those with the resources to wage legal war. To borrow the words of a British lawmaker who was appalled by his country's censorious laws, the leaders of this movement were trying to murder the truth.

The outcome of Berisha's yearslong litigation showed that this campaign's influence had finally reached the highest branches of American government. Following the Supreme Court's action, one of Lawson's attorneys emailed him the news. The result, she wrote with a dash of lawyerly understatement, "portends trouble down the road."

That winding road is the subject of this book.

PART I

THE CONSENSUS

1

CLARENCE THOMAS'S CLEAREST ANSWER

On Monday, September 16, 1991, Clarence Thomas and his wife, Ginni, drove to Capitol Hill from their small home in the suburbs of Northern Virginia. The day was going to be smoldering—the temperature would max out at ninety-six degrees—and even early in the morning the air was muggy, one of those late-summer days in Washington where the sweat starts beading the moment you set foot outdoors. The forty-three-year-old Thomas, in a dark gray suit and plum-colored tie, was not dressed for this weather. Then again, he would be spending most of the day in the cool confines of an air-conditioned stone fortress.

The Thomases arrived at the Russell Senate Office Building and were greeted by reporters awaiting what was to be the fifth and final day of Senate Judiciary Committee hearings into Clarence's nomination to the Supreme Court. Far in the future, when the Thomases had become perhaps the country's most celebrated—or detested—conservative power couple, this sort of hoopla might have seemed routine. But not yet.

The hearings took place in what was known as the Caucus Room, a cavernous space with imposing marble columns and chandeliers dangling from the sculpted ceiling. It had been the venue for famous congressional hearings into Watergate, Pearl Harbor, and the sinking of the *Titanic*. Today, bright lights were arranged at the front to ensure that TV cameras would have a clear view of the nominee and his Senate inquisitors. After shaking hands with a handful of committee members, Thomas sat down, alone, in a leather-upholstered chair before a table draped in green cloth.

Decades later, Thomas would spearhead a campaign to make it easier for the wealthy and powerful to cow the media into submission. But on this sweltering day, he would do the opposite. A long-forgotten portion of his testimony would highlight the near-universal agreement that a vigorous news media—insulated by the Constitution from litigation designed to punish innocent mistakes—was a bulwark of American democracy. It was a view that Thomas and his conservative allies would adhere to for years, even as they grumbled about hostile and biased coverage.

So far, at least, Thomas hadn't faced much difficulty in his confirmation hearings. That was partly because the Democrats who controlled the Judiciary Committee didn't have much to go on; Thomas had left a relatively scant paper trail during his brief time in Washington. A key breakthrough had occurred a decade earlier, in 1980. As a junior aide to Missouri's junior US senator, with whom he'd connected after graduating from Yale Law School, Thomas had paid his own way to attend a conference of Black conservatives in San Francisco. At lunch at the Fairmont Hotel on the final day, he found himself seated next to a young *Washington Post* journalist named Juan Williams. Thomas spouted off about the evils of welfare, going so far as to denounce his sister down in Georgia. "She gets mad when the mailman is late with her welfare check," Thomas fumed. "That is how dependent she is."

After Williams published the blunt remarks—they appear to have been the first time the thirty-two-year-old was quoted in the national media—Thomas claimed not to have realized he was speaking on the record and said that he received hate mail as a result. (The more legitimate complaint surely belonged to Thomas's sister, Emma Mae Martin, who later said that she had been working two minimum-wage jobs at the time that Thomas humiliated her.) Many a public figure, of course, has voiced similar protests when his words sounded worse in print than when they came out of his mouth. But for Thomas, this anodyne event would become the start of a long pattern of maintaining that he'd been maligned by the media.

The irony was that the *Post*'s piece ended up playing to Thomas's advantage. Ronald Reagan had just been elected, and Thomas's published remarks aligned with the president-elect's views of the social safety net. Thomas—a rare Black conservative in those days—was soon slotted into a prominent role overseeing civil rights in the Department of Education. Then Reagan named him to the Equal Employment Opportunity Commission, where he would discourage affirmative action and relax federal enforcement of antidiscrimination laws.

His time at the EEOC would prove formative. By his own admission, Thomas didn't have a very firm grasp on the US Constitution or the American founding. After experimenting in college with left-wing radicalism, he'd veered sharply rightward, but he lacked a cohesive worldview. Thomas used his budget for speechwriters to hire a pair of political theorists from the Claremont Institute, an archconservative think tank in the Los Angeles suburbs. Their job was to lead their boss on discussions about things like the Constitution and the supremacy of God's natural laws—to train him, in essence, to become a proper conservative. "It was sort of a period of just great intellectual development," Thomas would recall.

Another source of that development was a woman named Ricky Silberman, who became an EEOC commissioner in 1984. Thomas's relationship with the White House had been rocky at times, and Silberman, who along with her husband was a well-connected Republican insider, would smooth things over. "If I couldn't work well with someone, she did it for me, calming me down whenever I was too combative," Thomas wrote years later. Silberman and Thomas grew tight; she was with him when he met Ginni, his future wife, at an Anti-Defamation League event in New York. It wasn't long before the lives and careers of Clarence, Ginni, Ricky, and her husband, Larry, became entwined.

Larry had spent nearly two decades in senior jobs in the Nixon, Ford, and Reagan administrations, including as US ambassador to Yugoslavia, gradually morphing from a liberal Rockefeller Republican into a hard-right GOP activist. His final career stop was the federal appeals court in Washington, widely regarded as the country's second most powerful judicial body, to which Silberman scored a lifetime appointment in 1985.

Three years later, Bush won the presidential election, and Larry Silberman spoke to the transition team about candidates to become federal judges. He recommended Thomas. In Thomas's telling, he was initially reluctant to join the judiciary. When Bush's team sounded him out, he derided a judgeship as "a job for old people." His preference was to get rich working in the corporate world. Thomas turned to Silberman for advice, explaining his misgivings about a lifetime assignment. "It's not like slavery, Clarence," Silberman replied. "You can always leave if you don't like it." Thomas soon joined Silberman on the DC appeals court.

The older judge showed his new colleague the ropes. Silberman "became my judicial mentor," Thomas would recall, crediting him with doing "more to give me a judicial philosophy" than just about anyone else. What was more, the Silbermans began introducing Thomas around town, further elevating his stature among Republican brokers of power and influence.

Fifteen months after Thomas became a judge, Thurgood Marshall announced his retirement as the first Black justice on the Supreme Court, a seat he'd held since 1967. The Bush White House drew up a short list of candidates to replace him. Silberman was on it. But it was his mentee who ended up getting the nod.

Thomas had spent weeks preparing for his confirmation hearings. The White House had assigned Mike Luttig—a Justice Department official who would soon become a federal judge himself—the seven-days-a-week task of steering Thomas through a crash course in constitutional law and coaching him on the fine art of deflecting senators' questions.

In the Caucus Room, there were plenty of pointed queries about Thomas's views on civil rights and affirmative action—the nominee's tenure at the EEOC, seemingly devoted to neutering the agency that he helped oversee, had predictably ruffled feathers—but for the most part the Democratic senators on the Judiciary Committee were restrained, perhaps fearful of the optics of attacking a Black nominee with a rags-to-riches life story. Thomas, for his part, responded to the senators' questions as if he were weighing every word. Even to the White House, the judge came across as "wooden." His answers seemed rehearsed—because they were.

Patrick Leahy was the toughest inquisitor, pressing the judge about his views on abortion and *Roe v. Wade*. Thomas was prepared. The trick, as he later put it, was "to say as little as possible," to dodge substantive questions by insisting that to offer a concrete viewpoint risked undermining his impartiality as a judge. (Thomas also claimed that he simply hadn't given much thought to the landmark abortion case.) On Day Five, after three hours of questioning in the morning, the committee adjourned for lunch. When it reconvened, Leahy would ask about a fresh topic. Thomas's answers that afternoon would garner virtually no media attention, even when, decades later, the Supreme Court justice dramatically changed his position.

Twenty-seven years earlier, in 1964, the Supreme Court had heard the case of *New York Times Company v. Sullivan*. Its genesis was a full-page ad that had run in the *Times* in 1960. The civil rights movement was in full swing, and across the South, government officials were doing everything in their power to preserve white supremacy. The ad was a fundraising appeal to support the Rev. Martin Luther King Jr. and to bankroll a voter-registration drive in the South. It ran under the headline "Heed Their Rising Voices," and it criticized unnamed "Southern violators of the Constitution" for their efforts to destroy King. Above a long list of civil rights activists, celebrities, and political and religious leaders who'd endorsed its message, the ad cataloged the ways in which southern officials had "answered Dr. King's peaceful protests with intimidation and violence." The gist of the ad was true: southern authorities were engaged in brutal repression that many observers likened to the tactics of dictators such as Stalin. But some of the details in the ad were exaggerated or wrong. For example, it falsely stated that students protesting at an Alabama state college had been padlocked inside a dining hall "in an attempt to starve them into submission."

The *Times* was a national newspaper, with a circulation of about 650,000, but its readership in the South was minuscule. In 1960, a grand total of 394 copies a day went to subscribers, libraries, and newsstands in Alabama. Yet local journalists there spotted the ad, and a couple of the state's newspapers published pieces about it, bringing it to the attention of a wider audience—including L. B. Sullivan, a city commissioner in Montgomery. The city's three commissioners operated as essentially a mayor-by-committee, and Sullivan's responsibilities included overseeing Montgomery's police force, whose behavior the "Heed Their Rising

Voices" ad had condemned. On April 8, he wrote an angry letter to the *Times* stating that the ad, which had not named him, nonetheless amounted to a personal accusation of "grave misconduct." He demanded a retraction. Less than two weeks later, when no retraction was forthcoming, Sullivan filed a lawsuit in a local court accusing the *Times* and some of the ad's signatories of libel. He sought damages of $500,000.

At the time, it was relatively easy for plaintiffs, regardless of their public stature, to prevail in such cases. Unlike in a criminal trial where the defendant is presumed innocent, the starting point in libel cases, based on centuries of "common law" originating in England, tended to be that what the defendant had written was false. It was up to him to prove otherwise. The result was that "publishing criticism—even truthful criticism—of public officials was a dangerous undertaking for a newspaper," as the First Amendment scholar Samantha Barbas put it. Politicians weren't the only ones taking advantage: powerful industrialists like Henry Ford and James Fisk sought to combat negative press coverage with frivolous but ruinous lawsuits against newspapers.

In the weeks after Sullivan filed his lawsuit, other Alabama officials—none of them named in the ad—followed his lead, seeking a total of roughly $3 million in damages from the *Times*. Such penalties posed an existential threat to the barely profitable newspaper. The goal of Sullivan and his colleagues was clear. They were not trying to hold the *Times* accountable for minor inaccuracies. They were seeking to send a message to it and other influential news organizations: if they aggressively covered the civil rights struggle, if they documented the illegal and at times violent ways that many southerners were fighting to maintain power, they would incur catastrophic costs. The goal was to use libel law as "a state political weapon to intimidate the press," the journalist Anthony Lewis wrote in his 1991 book *Make No Law*.

Why did Sullivan and his colleagues care what papers like the *Times*, with its paltry southern subscribership, wrote about them? Because civil rights leaders had been relying on the national media to provoke outrage among the broader public about southern racism, and this unwanted attention was causing trouble. More protesters were arriving from northern cities. And through legislation and law enforcement, the federal government was taking a more muscular approach to protecting civil rights. More news coverage meant more meddling.

Sullivan, who had smooth pale skin and a receding hairline that exposed a long sloping forehead, was an unapologetic bigot. He had campaigned for his commissionership on a hardline anti-integration platform, and he had railed against the influence of outside "agitators," whether they were student protesters or carpetbagging northern reporters. On more than one occasion, when mobs of Klansmen and other angry whites attacked demonstrators, Sullivan had instructed the police not to intervene until the victims were sufficiently bloodied. "Providing police protection for agitators is not our policy," he explained.

What *was* part of the policy—for Sullivan and his peers across the South—was trying to delegitimize the media as lying "propagandists" and "Commies" who were seeking to indoctrinate and brainwash gullible readers. The *Times*, with its unparalleled influence and small army of reporters, was demonized as the worst of the worst. At least in the South, these antimedia tactics worked. Out-of-state journalists were routinely assaulted. The libel lawsuit had become just another weapon in the same arsenal.

Sullivan's lawsuit went to trial in the Montgomery courtroom of Judge Walter Jones, who maintained segregated seating, was a devout promoter of all things Confederacy, and believed in what he called "white man's justice." (The seventy-two-year-old judge also apparently was a pedophile. He had been arrested for molesting a boy in a local YMCA, and his study was adorned with photos of nude boys.) As the Sullivan trial was about to get underway, some prospective jurors showed up to court in Confederate costumes, toting pistols.

Jones instructed the jury to assume that Sullivan had been injured by the ad. It took the jurors barely two hours to return a verdict against the *Times*. The newspaper was ordered to pay Sullivan $500,000. It was the largest libel judgment in the state's history.

For racist southerners, this was the equivalent of a green light. The courts could be used to scare the press into silent submission. More libel suits followed, including a $1.5 million action against CBS for a segment showing the difficulties Blacks faced registering to vote in Alabama. Over the next few years, southern officials would bring libel suits against the media seeking damages totaling nearly $300 million (roughly $3 billion today). The *Times*, fearing a tidal wave of litigation, barred its reporters from setting foot in Alabama, and its lawyers urged staff not to write articles that detailed the state's institutionalized racism.

The *Times* appealed the verdict for Sullivan. Nobody was surprised when Alabama's highest court rejected the appeal. That left one last hope: the US Supreme Court.

This seemed like a long shot. The Constitution guaranteed people the right to freely express themselves, but there were limits. You couldn't shout "fire" in a crowded theater, for example. Libelous speech was another exception. The Supreme Court did not regard it as protected by the First Amendment, and states therefore were free to come up with their own standards governing what constituted defamation and when people could collect damages.

To handle the Supreme Court appeal, the *Times* hired a renowned Columbia University law professor named Herbert Wechsler. He argued that in an era when government officials like Sullivan were weaponizing libel law, a hands-off approach was dangerously outdated. People had a right to protect their reputations, but the First Amendment barred the government from impeding a free press. The Alabama verdict made it so perilous "to criticize official conduct that it abridges the freedom of the press," Wechsler wrote in the *Times* appeal. "It transforms the action for defamation from a method of protecting private reputation to a device for insulating government against attack." He proposed a new framework: to win damages, a government official should be required to prove that the defendant knew that what he was writing was false.

The Supreme Court accepted the case for review. To prepare, Wechsler, his wife, and a colleague dove into the history of the First Amendment. Its text was short and vague, and the surviving records of the debates among the framers of the Constitution shed little light on precisely what they had intended—ambiguity, perhaps, that was designed to preserve flexibility for future generations to reinterpret the amendment's forty-five words as the world evolved. One clue to at least some of the framers' thinking had emerged during the heated national debate over the 1798

Sedition Act, which penalized criticism of the government. The act's ultimate repeal—and the verdict of history that it ran counter to America's founding ideals—was evidence to Wechsler that, from the outset, the First Amendment was designed to protect citizens' rights to sharply question their government. By rendering and then upholding a libel verdict that was meant to stifle outside scrutiny, Alabama's courts had infringed upon that right.

Despite its long odds, the appeal garnered heaps of attention, in part because the Supreme Court, under Chief Justice Earl Warren, had recently become the country's most powerful champion of civil liberties. At the same time that the court was hearing *New York Times v. Sullivan*, it was also preparing to issue major rulings governing desegregation, school prayers, and obscenity. In one sign of the *Sullivan* case's cachet, Martin Luther King showed up to witness oral arguments in January 1964; one justice asked him to autograph a copy of his book, *Stride Toward Freedom*, about the bus boycotts in Alabama.

Two months later, the court announced its decision. It was unanimous, and it was a stunner: the justices found that Alabama courts had violated the constitutional protections of free speech and a free press.

William Brennan wrote the court's majority opinion on behalf of himself and five other justices. As a starting point, he noted that the case was being heard "against the background of a profound national commitment to the principle that debate on public issues should be uninhibited, robust, and wide open, and that it may well include vehement, caustic, and sometimes unpleasantly sharp attacks on government and public officials." Maintaining that commitment was a central purpose of the First Amendment, and it was the prism through which L. B. Sullivan's libel lawsuit—and the Alabama courts' handling of it—needed to be viewed. Yes, there had been inaccuracies in the "Heed Their Rising Voices" ad, but "erroneous statement is inevitable in free debate," and writers and publishers needed "breathing space" to engage in robust argument and criticism without worrying that a factual slipup could cause financial ruin.

Brennan went on to essentially adopt the framework that Wechsler had proposed for evaluating libel claims by a government official like

Sullivan. He could not collect damages "unless he proves that the statement was made with 'actual malice'—that is, with knowledge that it was false or with reckless disregard of whether it was false or not," Brennan wrote. Deliberate smears were actionable; accidental errors were not. The burden of proof would rest with the plaintiff.

L. B. Sullivan's efforts to intimidate the press had backfired to such a degree that his name would live on as an enduring symbol of American press freedoms.

Brennan's thirty-nine-page majority opinion was just the start. (The three other justices signed on to concurring opinions that espoused even broader interpretations of the First Amendment: that public officials should be barred, even in cases of deliberate falsehoods, from bringing libel claims against their critics.) In the coming years, the justices delivered a succession of rulings that built on the landmark case. In 1967, there was *Curtis Publishing Company v. Butts*, which expanded *Sullivan*'s logic to apply to public figures—business leaders, celebrities, or university presidents, for example—in addition to government officials. "Many who do not hold public office at the moment are nevertheless intimately involved in the resolution of important public questions," Chief Justice Warren wrote in that case. "Our citizenry has a legitimate and substantial interest in the conduct of such persons, and freedom of the press to engage in uninhibited debate about their involvement in public issues and events is as crucial as it is in the case of 'public officials.'"

Seven years later, in *Gertz v. Robert Welch Inc.*, the court further broadened that group to include "limited purpose public figures." These were people who weren't necessarily famous but had injected themselves into a public controversy by, for example, becoming prominent advocates for or against abortion rights. The five-to-four decision even acknowledged that in rare cases, someone might fall under this umbrella involuntarily. (Think of an air traffic controller on duty when a plane crashed.) The logic was the same: people needed to be able to investigate and write about those in the public sphere, even if they accidentally got a fact wrong.

This was hardly the end of libel lawsuits. There were plenty in the years ahead—by some counts, even more than before *Sullivan*. (Private people had to clear a much lower bar to win libel suits; they just had to show that someone had acted negligently, not that they'd known that what they were writing was false.) Some suits succeeded. Many others failed. But *Sullivan* and its successor cases had changed the dynamic. Journalists and publishers now knew that as long as they were making a good-faith effort to ascertain the truth, they were free to dig into the rich, famous, and powerful.

This realization—along with factors like the Freedom of Information Act, which made it much easier to obtain government records—helped usher in a new age of American journalism devoted to exposing malfeasance, questioning authority, and promoting the public interest. Reporters uncovered wrongdoing in Vietnam, the White House, and the Pentagon. It was not a coincidence that the *Washington Post* cracked open Watergate in the years after *Sullivan*; if the burden of proof in a defamation case had still rested with the defendant, and if even honest mistakes had remained punishable under the law, the costs of publishing such a series of investigations might have been prohibitive. (As his presidency circled the drain, Richard Nixon blamed *Sullivan* and had his administration craft legislation that he hoped would supersede the precedent and put the media back in a pen.) Journalists—along with activists like Ralph Nader—dug into the tobacco, auto, and chemical industries, whose top executives knew they were peddling deadly products. And they revealed the crimes, lies, and half-truths of actual and aspiring presidents, senators, governors, Cabinet secretaries, and even Supreme Court justices.

In short, the "actual malice" standard would distinguish the United States, with its tradition of celebrating free speech and expression, from many other democracies, and it would become an indispensable safeguard for American journalists and everyday citizens who hoped to hold their leaders and other powerful actors to account.

Back in the Caucus Room after lunch, Senator Leahy asked Clarence Thomas a series of questions about free speech. Then he turned to the *Sullivan* decision. Did the "actual malice" rule set too high a bar for public figures to win libel cases?

"I guess I haven't looked at it from that standpoint," Thomas replied. "You know, I think all of us who have found our names occasionally in the newspaper would like to feel that we have—"

Leahy interjected with a stab at humor: "Never happened to you, has it, Judge?" Everyone in the room—Thomas most of all—knew what Leahy was alluding to. Ever since Bush had announced his nomination eleven weeks earlier, journalists had been prying into Thomas's career and life story. Much of the coverage had focused on Thomas's rise from poverty-stricken Pinpoint, Georgia, but journalists had also delved into less comfortable territory, like his EEOC tenure, the church he and Ginni attended, and his sister's disclosure to reporters that she'd once had an abortion.

Thomas fiddled with a pen, his eyes darting left to right, as if he were scanning the senators on the dais for guidance as to whether he was about to stumble into a trap. The waves of media scrutiny had been hard for Thomas. But under the bright TV lights, he smiled and shook his head. "Well, as I was telling my wife during this process, no matter how badly it turned out as far as the publicity, I think that the freedom of the press is essential to a free society. And she sort of looked at me, because we were going through the midst of it, sort of, 'Are you out of your mind?'"

At this point, a C-SPAN camera panned to Ginni, who was sitting behind Thomas. She was wearing a patterned blue-green dress, her left leg folded over her right, hands clasped over her knee. As her husband mentioned her apparent impatience with a free press, Ginni flexed her left foot up and down and tensed her shoulders.

Thomas elaborated. Even though he felt like he was getting raked over the coals, a free press—as articulated by the court in *Sullivan*—was paramount. "And I believe that even as I was going through it and even as I am going through it," he said. "I think what the court was attempting to do there [in *Sullivan*] was of course to balance the First Amendment rights, the freedom of the press as we know it, and to not have that in a way impeded by one's abilities to sue the media or to intimidate the media. . . . That is something of course that one could debate, but I think it is a clear demonstration on the court's part that the freedom of the press is important in our society, it's critical in our society, even though individuals may at times be hurt by the use of that right."

"Do you see any need to change that standard?" Leahy asked.

"I at this moment certainly have not thought about changing that standard and have no agenda to change that standard," Thomas answered. "My view, as I've attempted to express here, is that we should protect our First Amendment freedoms as much as possible." He had been testifying for five days, and this was perhaps the clearest response he had given about his position on any specific case.

Less than three weeks later, shortly before the Senate was scheduled to vote to confirm him, word leaked to reporters at *Newsday* and National Public Radio that one of Thomas's former EEOC subordinates, Anita Hill, had accused him of sexual harassment. When the news broke, he and Ginni hid out at the Silbermans' home in Georgetown. Thomas spent hours anxiously pacing around their swimming pool, smoke from his cigars swirling in the autumn sunlight. He and his allies figured that this was Democrats' handiwork, and they blamed the national media for amplifying Hill's salacious allegations.

The Senate decided to postpone its vote and reopen the confirmation hearings. Thomas had already been squirming in the media spotlight; now he nearly lost it. One sleepless night, he lay on the floor, writhing in agony like a man possessed. Another day, Mike Luttig, the lawyer whom the White House had assigned to prepare Thomas for the hearings, visited the judge in his chambers at the appeals court to discuss Hill's accusations. The judge spent fifteen minutes "crying and hyperventilating" about how "these people have destroyed my life," as Luttig later put it. The media attention that Thomas had referred to in response to Leahy's questions now seemed like a warm-up act. TV trucks parked outside the Thomases' home, and photographers trained their lenses through his windows.

The second round of hearings began on Friday, October 11, in the same grand room. Hill spent seven hours describing in lurid detail how Thomas had repeatedly asked her out on dates and, when those entreaties failed, kept bringing up sex in the workplace. That night, Thomas was summoned back before the Judiciary Committee. Larry Silberman had advised him to go in "with all guns blazing," and he did. Thomas famously accused Democrats and their media allies of "a high-tech lynching for uppity blacks." Ginni sat behind him, wiping away tears.

Thomas's allies, led by Ricky Silberman, went on the offensive. She stalked the hallway outside the Caucus Room, buttonholing reporters—sometimes interrupting their interviews with Thomas's critics—to tar Hill as a serial liar. Larry Silberman whispered to conservative writers like David Brock that Hill was a lesbian who was "acting out."

In the end, Thomas would scrape by. The Senate confirmed him fifty-two to forty-eight. But it was more *no* votes than any Supreme Court justice had ever received and the narrowest margin in a confirmation fight in a century.

Thomas emerged from this gauntlet animated by a burning anger toward his perceived persecutors. Chief among those was the media. During the Hill hearings, Thomas had actually received more favorable news coverage than his accuser—one study found that nearly four out of five individuals quoted in TV or newspaper stories had sided with him—but that was not how Thomas experienced it. He understandably dwelled on the negative, whether it was *Time* magazine likening Anita Hill to Rosa Parks or network news anchors interviewing experts who judged Hill's accusations as credible.

In Thomas's estimation, the media had gone from being a core part of a functioning democracy into something akin to a rabid beast. He would soon boast to audiences that he didn't read newspapers, "and I would suggest others do the same." Long before Donald Trump started decrying "fake news," Thomas was doing his part to sow distrust toward the press. The simmering anger would eventually influence how he—and the rest of the conservative movement, which came to view him as a standard bearer—viewed the First Amendment and the freedom of the press.

For now, though, the consensus on the Supreme Court and among most of the American legal profession remained as Thomas had articulated it during the confirmation hearings: the strong protections of *Sullivan* were vital to the American republic—even when they meant that bystanders got banged up in the process.

THE FIGHTER PILOT

Three years after Thomas joined the Supreme Court, the phone rang at Elaine Donnelly's home in Livonia, Michigan, just outside Detroit. It was Thanksgiving weekend of 1994. A Naval lieutenant, Patrick Burns, was on the line. He was calling with what he said was life-or-death information.

Donnelly had no way to know it, but the out-of-the-blue phone call, from a man she had never heard of, was going to change her life. She would soon be immersed in a yearslong libel lawsuit. Many are filed every year, but this one would turn out to be especially momentous: it would showcase how *Sullivan* and its successor cases protected not only the media but also activists and interest groups, conservative and liberal alike—and how those precedents enjoyed unflinching support from judges across the political spectrum.

Burns was phoning Donnelly in the wake of a tragic accident that had just rocked the Navy. A month earlier, an F-14 Tomcat on a routine training flight had crashed on its approach to the USS *Abraham Lincoln* aircraft carrier, off the coast of San Diego. The pilot, Lt. Kara Hultgreen, was one of only two women who had been cleared to fly fighter jets on combat missions for the US military. Now she was dead. Her funeral at Arlington National Cemetery—her flag-draped casket carried on a horse-drawn caisson—was attended by the secretary of the Navy and network news camera crews.

Donnelly knew all about what had happened to Hultgreen. A conservative Republican, Donnelly had first become interested in the issue of women in the military in the late 1970s, when she joined the fight against the proposed Equal Rights Amendment to the US Constitution. Her primary objection to the amendment, which would have guaranteed that women had the same legal rights as men, was that it would open the door to women being drafted into the military. Donnelly didn't want that to happen to her young daughters. It was the beginning of her long crusade against women in combat.

Presidents Reagan and George H. W. Bush appointed Donnelly to federal commissions studying the proper roles of women in the armed forces. She visited military bases nationwide, and she cultivated a network of officers who, like her, viewed women (and gays) in combat roles as threats to the military's ability to fight effectively. Soon she created the Center for Military Readiness. She recruited an advisory board of conservative activists and retired brass who shared her concerns about political correctness emasculating the military. She became known as a sympathetic receptacle for damaging information about women in the armed services.

Donnelly sometimes felt like she was fighting a lost cause. In 1993, the Clinton administration announced that the military was lifting its ban on women flying in combat. The decision had undeniable political undertones. The Pentagon was trying to repair its public image amid the ongoing Tailhook scandal, in which Navy aviators had sexually assaulted dozens of women and then escaped with impunity, thanks in part to a military coverup.

After the policy change, Hultgreen and a younger pilot, Lt. Carey Lohrenz, had been the first women to make it through the elite Top Gun training program. In the summer of 1994, on a tour of the Miramar air base in San Diego, Donnelly happened to meet Hultgreen. Donnelly had been impressed by the pilot's poise and beauty, though she suspected that Hultgreen was the beneficiary of double standards as the Navy hustled women into high-profile combat roles. Hultgreen's death reinforced Donnelly's convictions.

Now here was Patrick Burns cold-calling her. He introduced himself as an aviator who had trained both Hultgreen and Lohrenz. He said the women had not been qualified and that the only reason they'd been permitted to enter the elite fraternity of fighter pilots was that Navy leaders had repeatedly given them extra chances that men never would have received. Donnelly asked Burns if he had documentation to substantiate his allegations. He sent her a detailed letter that explained the Navy's fighter training program and what he claimed were the concessions that had been granted to ensure that Lohrenz and Hultgreen would pass.

Burns struck Donnelly as trustworthy. In January 1995, she wrote to Senator Strom Thurmond, the Republican chairman of the Senate Armed Services Committee. "I am sending you specific information indicating that certain practices designed to assure that women will not fail have now been extended to the demanding and dangerous field of carrier aviation," she wrote, adding that the information she possessed was "highly credible and well-informed." She asked the senator to "put a stop to practices that threaten the lives of our aviators and all personnel serving on the hazardous decks of aircraft carriers."

Weeks later, Burns sent Donnelly another batch of information. This time, he included portions of Lohrenz's and Hultgreen's confidential training records. The materials were incomplete—they left out the fact that Lohrenz's overall training record had been above average—but Donnelly didn't know that. She ran the records by some of her Navy contacts, who agreed that Lohrenz and Hultgreen appeared to have benefited from double standards.

When Donnelly presented her findings to senior Navy officers, they assured her that both women had been fully qualified, and they explained that it was normal for pilots to fail certain exercises, especially early in their training. Donnelly, however, shrugged this off. It wasn't like military brass were going to freely admit to having skewed their stars' performance ratings.

That April, Donnelly's Center for Military Readiness published a report entitled "Double Standards in Naval Aviation." The report, which included some of the training-record excerpts that Burns had secretly provided, claimed that the definition of what qualified someone to fly combat jets "has been radically changed by practices that forgive low scores and major errors in training so that certain people"—women—"will not fail." While the report didn't include Lohrenz's name, its repeated references to "Pilot B"—who, the report said, was aided by "extraordinary concessions and dual-track standards"—were obvious to anyone who knew that there was only one female fighter pilot remaining in the Navy.

Carey Lohrenz came from a military family. Her father had flown for the Marines in Vietnam, and she and her brother (who'd also go on to become a fighter pilot) used to obsess over his silk maps, pretending to be aviators. Fighter pilots, however, were almost always men, and as Lohrenz got older, she began to think that her dream of following her father was unrealistic. Dad, however, wouldn't have it. The family lived in Green Bay, and each summer they attended the famed EEA air show in Oshkosh, Wisconsin. Pilots and aviation enthusiasts would mingle on the tarmac. Lohrenz's father spotted a member of the WASPs—the legendary corps of female pilots who transported aircraft for the military during World War II—and told Lohrenz to go over and introduce herself. She did, and her hopes were rekindled.

After college, the six-feet-tall Lohrenz enlisted in the Navy, graduated from officer candidate school with honors, and received her commission. Next, she aced primary flight training, finishing third in her class of forty-five and landing on the Commodore's List. The performance allowed Lohrenz to choose what kind of aircraft she wished to fly. She chose jets, completed additional rounds of training, and in 1993 received the designation of naval aviator.

Thanks to the Clinton administration's decision to lift the ban on women flying in combat, Lohrenz—call sign: "Vixen"—was selected to pilot the F-14 Tomcat, the Navy's premier fighter jet. She and Hultgreen became useful symbols of the military's newfound progressivism. To the irritation of some of their male colleagues, they were feted by military publications, their hometown newspapers, and TV networks; the Navy even used Lohrenz's face on a recruiting poster. "A plane doesn't know if a man or woman is flying it," she told the *Green Bay Press Gazette*, which ran a profile of her. Another time, she explained to a military publication, "I think we've opened some doors, and the more exposure we get, the more people see that women can do this."

After completing additional training, Lohrenz and Hultgreen had been assigned to a squadron attached to the nuclear-powered USS *Lincoln*, part of the Navy's Pacific Fleet. Landing a 54,000-pound, $38 million, supersonic war machine on a carrier was a terrifying thrill, especially at night or when the swells of the Pacific caused the carrier to seesaw wildly. The jets came tearing in at 150 miles per hour, and being even slightly off target could kill dozens of people on the flight deck. Because of the difficulty and danger, only a select few—the best of the best—ever were given the opportunity to land on a carrier. Lohrenz would successfully do it well over one hundred times. "You don't get that by being lucky," she told me.

On the afternoon of October 25, 1994, the twenty-six-year-old Lohrenz was preparing for her latest training flight. She was about to rev her engines on the runway at the Miramar air base when her aircraft's radio crackled. She was told to stand down. Hultgreen's F-14 had crashed.

The two women had been close, and coming to terms with Hultgreen's death was hard enough for Lohrenz. Donnelly's report made things worse. Conservative publications like the *Washington Times* ran front-page articles about it. A summary of the report was included in the *Early Bird Brief*, a daily news digest that was faxed to US military locations all over the world—including onboard the USS *Lincoln*.

"I walked into the ready room, and everyone had a copy of it," Lohrenz said, her voice shaking as she recounted the experience nearly three decades later. She felt like everyone thought she was unqualified. Her self-confidence began slipping away. The *Lincoln* was steaming toward the Persian Gulf, and Lohrenz's performance in training exercises deteriorated. The day before her squadron was scheduled to begin patrolling the no-fly zone above Iraq, she noticed that another pilot was in her slot on the flight schedule.

"Skipper wants to see you," an officer told her. She was grounded.

Lohrenz was sent back to Miramar. She had a stint in human resources, then a job overseeing the base's recycling program. "I can tell you a lot about the price of cardboard," Lohrenz glumly told a *Newsweek* reporter in 1997.

One day, she got a phone call from a pioneering aviator, Rosemary Mariner, who had been a leading advocate of lifting the ban on women flying combat missions. Mariner explained that Lohrenz was being smeared, and unless she did something to stop it, she could kiss her career goodbye. "You don't know how bad this is," Mariner warned. "You need help."

She gave Lohrenz the phone number for Susan Barnes, a lawyer who had repeatedly sued the military on behalf of female service members. After reviewing Lohrenz's personnel records, Barnes convinced Lohrenz that she had a strong legal case. So, in 1996, Lohrenz sued Donnelly and the Center for Military Readiness for defamation. (She also sued the *Washington Times*, which quickly agreed to a settlement.) The complaint consisted of two main arguments. First, Donnelly had used incomplete records to wrongly portray Lohrenz as unqualified. Second, Lohrenz had paid a heavy price. She would never again fly a fighter jet. None of this would have happened, Lohrenz argued, were it not for Donnelly's relentless pursuit of a retrograde agenda.

Donnelly learned about the lawsuit when a man showed up at her front door to serve her with court papers. Scared and angry, she viewed the litigation as an attempt to silence her. She shelled out $10,000 to retain lawyers (her total legal bill would ultimately exceed $600,000), who moved to dismiss the lawsuit. They insisted that her report had been accurate. But even if there were errors, they said, Donnelly had acted responsibly. Her information had come from a source inside the Navy, and she had vetted it with other sources. She had good reason to believe it to be true. That was important because Donnelly's camp argued that for the purposes of this lawsuit, Lohrenz was a public figure. To win damages under the *New York Times v. Sullivan* standards, she therefore would need to prove that Donnelly knew or should have known that what she was publishing was false—that she had acted with actual malice.

Was Lohrenz really a public figure? She was not a politician or a celebrity or a billionaire. Yet by dint of becoming one of the first two female fighter pilots, she had emerged as a potent symbol—of progress or peril, depending on your perspective. At the Navy's urging, she had spoken publicly in favor of women serving in combat.

There was no doubt that it was in the public interest for people like Donnelly, regardless of whether you agreed with their politics, to be able to freely question and criticize the military. Wasn't it therefore fair game to investigate the credentials of someone whom the Pentagon was holding up as a model? What if that person's reputation was pulverized in the process?

More than six years would elapse between when Lohrenz filed the lawsuit and a federal judge ruled on Donnelly's motion to dismiss it. By then, after settling for a job in Florida ferrying VIP passengers in C-12 turboprops, Lohrenz had given up on her dreams and resigned from the Navy.

Lohrenz's lawyer, Susan Barnes, knew there was a chance that the judge hearing the case would conclude that her client was a public figure and would therefore dismiss the lawsuit because Lohrenz hadn't established that Donnelly had acted with actual malice. In that case, there would be an appeal, and for that Lohrenz's team wanted advice from someone with experience in high-profile libel litigation.

Barnes turned to a First Amendment scholar and law professor named Rod Smolla. After reading some of the court filings, Smolla told her that he'd be happy to join the team—for free. His law students could help with research and other tasks.

Smolla had long been an academic star—he was the author of the definitive treatise on the First Amendment and libel law—but lately he had escaped the ivory tower and entered the national spotlight. He had defended *Hustler* magazine's right to run a satirical interview about Jerry Falwell having drunken sex with his mother and a Klansman's right to burn a cross in certain circumstances. His profile as a staunch defender of the First Amendment was high enough that CNN offered him a gig as the young cable channel's in-house lawyer, and journalists would travel down to Williamsburg, Virginia, to participate in his mock Supreme Court sessions.

But Smolla was beginning to rethink his allegiances. Before becoming a professor, he had worked at a large corporate law firm, and if he'd continued on that path, he'd probably have been earning ten times what he was making in academia. Instead, his credit cards were maxed out, and he was "financially destitute." "The idea of making some money on a case was attractive," he wrote.

Just as Lohrenz's career was unraveling in 1995, Smolla had agreed to work on a multi-million-dollar lawsuit against the publisher of a book, *Hit Man: A Technical Manual for Independent Contractors*, that had served as a guide for a killer in a triple homicide. In 1999, Smolla's side won. In addition to collecting roughly $500,000 in fees, he wrote a book about the case, *Deliberate Intent*, which the cable channel FX turned into its first original movie. Free speech advocates—until then, Smolla's steadfast allies—had been appalled by the First Amendment implications of a publisher being held liable for murder. "Rod Smolla is a turncoat," wrote Adam Liptak, who at the time was a lawyer for the *New York Times* (and now is its Supreme Court correspondent). "He did grave damage to the cause of free speech."

Henceforth, Smolla would be a go-to lawyer for people looking to sue publishers and news organizations for libel, which was why, three years after the *Hit Man* victory, he'd been an obvious person for Barnes to contact.

Smolla joined Lohrenz's team in 2002. Shortly afterward, a federal judge ruled that she was, in fact, a public figure. She'd known that she was entering the public fray when she decided to become one of the first female fighter pilots, and she had trumpeted that barrier-breaking role to the media. That meant she had to prove not only that Elaine Donnelly's report was false but also that she had acted with reckless disregard for the truth. Seeing no evidence of that, the judge tossed the case.

Donnelly felt vindicated. A judge had recognized her constitutional right to dig into Pentagon policies. She and her husband celebrated with a champagne-soaked dinner at the Lark, a French restaurant near Detroit that was considered one of the best in America.

Lohrenz felt like she'd been violated. But coming on the heels of his *Hit Man* triumph, Smolla hoped to get the suit reinstated on appeal. He told her that she had "the best, strongest case I've ever seen." His plan was to argue to the federal appeals court in Washington—the same body on which Clarence Thomas had briefly sat before ascending to the Su-

preme Court—that Lohrenz hadn't done anything to merit being classified as a public figure.

Donnelly framed the fight as one of censorship versus free speech, of
the rights of citizens "to question the party line." She believed the law
was on her side. There was the 1974 *Gertz v. Robert Welch* decision, in
which the Supreme Court had acknowledged the possibility that someone could become a public figure without meaning to—an involuntary
limited-purpose public figure, to be precise. And in 1985, the same DC
court that would now hear Lohrenz's appeal had ruled on a similar case
called *Dameron v. Washington Magazine, Inc.* Merle Dameron had been
an air traffic controller who was on duty when a plane crashed. He'd
done even less than Lohrenz to seek out the spotlight. But that didn't
change the fact that journalists needed leeway to investigate his role in
a crash that left ninety-two people dead. The appeals court had deemed
Dameron a public figure, and the Supreme Court, by refusing to hear
his appeal, had essentially affirmed the judgment. How was Lohrenz's
situation any different?

Oral arguments were scheduled for September 2003. A hurricane was
headed for the capital, and Smolla drove to DC ahead of the storm. He
checked into a hotel near the federal court and then watched as Hurricane
Isabel snapped trees, downed electrical lines, and caused record-breaking
storm surges. Court, however, would be in session. Smolla drenched his
dress shoes as he waded through the flooded Judiciary Square into the
hulking court building.

A panel of three formidable judges would hear the case. There was Judith Rogers, a Clinton appointee and former DC attorney general. There
was John Roberts, who two years later would become the chief justice
of the Supreme Court. And there was Larry Silberman, the mentor of
Clarence Thomas.

As Smolla stood at a lectern presenting his argument, Roberts and Silberman repeatedly interrupted. How did he square his argument with the
Gertz and *Dameron* decisions? Smolla knew all about that latter case; his
father had been an air traffic controller, so another controller's potential
culpability for a plane crash had been of keen interest. Smolla responded
that the court's earlier decision had been wrong: Merle Dameron should

never have been deemed a public figure because he lacked any sort of high profile or access to the media that would have enabled him to defend himself against false claims in the press. Silberman retorted that *Dameron* was settled precedent. Back and forth this went. It occurred to Smolla that he'd been on his soggy feet, getting poked and prodded by the judges, for quite a long time.

Three months later, the court issued its unanimous decision. "Lohrenz's contention that she was, in effect, an anonymous Navy pilot, rings hollow," Rogers wrote for herself, Roberts, and Silberman. By choosing to become a combat pilot at a time of intense public debate over the role of women in the military, Lohrenz had opened herself up to scrutiny. What's more, the court ruled, Donnelly had conducted due diligence and had noted in her report that some Navy officials disagreed with her findings. In short, it might not have been fair, but she was not legally responsible for the damage to Lohrenz's reputation. Rogers and her colleagues concluded that "no reasonable juror could find by clear and convincing evidence that Donnelly or [the Center for Military Readiness] acted with actual malice."

Donnelly rejoiced with another fancy dinner. Lohrenz felt like her life was ending. "I didn't know how I was going to go on," she told me, and began to cry.

Smolla was surprised by the outcome, but he probably shouldn't have been. Yes, Lohrenz was a sympathetic plaintiff whose career had been destroyed. But *Sullivan* and its progeny—as well as the values they embodied—had become something approaching American gospel. That was in large part because they served people—not just journalists—of all political persuasions. Indeed, Donnelly was just the latest in a long line of conservative beneficiaries.

There were Republican politicians accused of smearing their Democratic rivals. There was the *New York Post*, the conservative tabloid, accused of defaming the Nation of Islam. And there were Rowland Evans and Robert Novak, syndicated conservative columnists who'd written that a Marxist professor had a reputation as an activist, not a scholar. The professor, Bertell Ollman, sued. In 1984, a federal appeals court, repeating the famous language from *Sullivan* about the country's "profound national commitment" to robust debate, decided that the lawsuit should be dismissed.

Ken Starr, who would later gain fame investigating Bill Clinton, wrote the majority ruling. But there was a concurring opinion by an even stauncher conservative, Robert Bork. Just three years later, Democrats would torpedo his Supreme Court nomination, branding him as a right-wing radical. So it was telling that rather than simply sign on to his fellow Republican's decision, Bork instead composed a love letter to *Sullivan*. In it, he denounced "a freshening stream of libel actions, which often seem as much designed to punish writers and publications as to recover damages for real injuries [and] may threaten the public and constitutional interest in free, and frequently rough, discussion."

Lohrenz had one last chance. In 2004, Smolla appealed to the Supreme Court. He asked the justices to consider "whether a plaintiff who has not sought publicity . . . may nonetheless be forced to accept the disabilities of public figure status through sheer dint of her voluntary military service to her country."

Clarence Thomas and his eight colleagues discussed Smolla's petition at their closed-door conference on a Thursday in May. Here, if they had wanted to seize it, was an opportunity to at least entertain the notion that the precedents protecting press freedoms should be reined in.

Four days later, they rejected the appeal. They wouldn't hear the case. If Thomas or any of his fellow justices disagreed with that decision, they kept it to themselves.

3

FUNDING EVIL

One evening in September 2010, a group of about fifty people gathered in a Senate hearing room. The walnut-paneled chamber, with sky-high ceilings and the seal of the United States carved into a wall, was not far from where Clarence Thomas had barely survived his confirmation hearings nineteen years earlier. Eight years in the future, it would be the venue for a similar showdown involving Brett Kavanaugh. This night, Room 226 of the Dirksen Senate Office Building was the site of a party.

The crowd nibbled hors d'oeuvres on paper plates. "Hello, my name is" stickers identified the guests: senators, congressmen, top federal officials, and a petite woman with rust-colored hair and rimless glasses. "I think this is really the culmination of what America is known in the world to be," she intoned in an Israeli accent. "This is a country where you are free to think and say whatever you want to say."

Rachel Ehrenfeld had just passed a federal law. The story of how she did it highlights the breadth of support that the *Sullivan* decision enjoyed as recently as last decade.

The saga had begun around 6 a.m. on a bone-chilling Friday in January 2004. Ehrenfeld was awoken by the screeching sounds of an incoming fax. She was a researcher and an author—a leading authority on the financing of extremism, she'd coined the term "narcoterrorism" to describe the pivotal role the drug trade played in funneling money to bad guys—and her apartment in midtown Manhattan contained both her bedroom and office. She pulled the message out of the fax machine. It was a letter from some lawyers in London. She didn't recognize their names, but their client was well known to her: Khalid bin Mahfouz, a billionaire Saudi sheik.

Ehrenfeld had been watching bin Mahfouz for years. His family owned a network of giant banks and other companies, and *Forbes* pegged his net worth at roughly $3 billion. He traveled in a private Boeing 767 with gold-plated bathroom fixtures. More important, media and government reports over the years had repeatedly described his financial support of Osama bin Laden and al Qaeda.

Ehrenfeld's latest book, *Funding Evil: How Terrorism Is Financed— and How to Stop It*, had been published the previous year in the United States, and it had mentioned bin Mahfouz a few times. She'd noted that he had been accused of depositing tens of millions of dollars into terrorists' bank accounts and that a foundation he controlled had sponsored al Qaeda and other terrorist organizations. This explained the letter she was staring at early on this icy morning. The Saudi's lawyers warned that unless she publicly apologized for what she'd written about bin Mahfouz, paid an unspecified sum to a charity of his choice, and covered his legal expenses, he would sue her and seek a "substantial award of damages."

Ehrenfeld was confident in the accuracy of what she'd written. The book was based on government documents, court filings, and news reports. She wasn't speculating or even making accusations for the first time—she was pulling stuff from countless public sources and weaving it together into a coherent whole. But she also knew that the book's veracity wasn't necessarily enough to spare her an enormous headache. This was especially true since bin Mahfouz's attorneys were threatening to sue her not in New York but in London.

In the United States, thanks to the *Sullivan* decision, it was up to the plaintiff in a libel lawsuit to prove that the information at issue was false; truth was an absolute defense. For public figures, of course, the threshold was even higher: they had to prove that the writer knew or should have known that what was being published was wrong. In the UK, however, the opposite standards applied. The default presumption was that the defamatory statement was false; the defendant had to prove its accuracy. It didn't matter if the plaintiff was a public figure.

These rules had made British courts a popular destination for what came to be known as "libel tourists"—Russian oligarchs, Holocaust deniers, Hollywood stars, and sundry rich individuals, often with only tenuous connections to the UK, who flocked to London to file lawsuits against writers from around the world. So common were these suits that London earned the nickname "a town called sue." The chilling effect was profound. For example, after London's *Sunday Times* reported on allegations that cyclist Lance Armstrong was using performance-enhancing drugs in 2004, the Tour de France winner sued. The *Sunday Times* apologized and paid him £300,000, and the rest of the British media was scared into silence. Armstrong—who in 2013 finally admitted to doping—was allowed to keep competing for nearly a decade. It didn't always take litigation to achieve the desired results; threats, in the form of sternly worded letters from solicitors who specialized in libel cases, were often enough. One editor of a national UK newspaper reportedly was told by his board of directors: "Don't take on the oligarchs; we simply cannot afford it."

Wealthy Saudis had become especially adept at this game. The British publisher of *House of Bush, House of Saud*, by Craig Unger, canceled publication of the 2004 book in the wake of such warnings. Bin Mahfouz was perhaps the most prolific, having sued or threatened litigation against dozens of publishers and writers. Until now, all of them had backed down. His personal website maintained a gleeful running tally of the writers from whom he had extracted public apologies. He was like the Middle Eastern version of Alabama's L. B. Sullivan, having realized that litigation was a reliable way to deter actual and prospective critics.

This appalled Ehrenfeld. A big reason that she'd migrated from Israel to the United States in the mid-1980s was that she adored the US Constitution—especially its guarantees of freedom of speech and the press. As a PhD student in Israel, she'd become fascinated with American liberty. Her dissertation was about forced treatment of drug-addicted criminals, and she traveled extensively to better understand different countries' laws and attitudes toward such compulsory treatment. From there, she expanded her focus to consider the countries' conceptions of individual freedoms. The more she'd learned about the First Amendment, the more she loved America. "Americans don't understand the importance of free speech and freedom of expression," Ehrenfeld told me. "This is what makes the United States different. This is the most important right we have in this country." There was no way she was going to voluntarily add herself to bin Mahfouz's list of vanquished writers.

After receiving the threatening fax, she called a New York lawyer named Daniel Kornstein. His résumé ranged from working on an early Army court martial related to the My Lai massacre to representing a best-selling author in a free-speech case brought by a murderer. Kornstein and Ehrenfeld had met years earlier at a mutual acquaintance's dinner party, and given his First Amendment experience, her situation seemed right up his alley. Kornstein agreed to represent her. Ehrenfeld also enlisted British lawyers to warn bin Mahfouz that if his threats continued, she would sue him and reveal more damaging information about his connections to terrorism.

The strategy failed. In June 2004, bin Mahfouz sued Ehrenfeld for defamation in London's High Court of Justice. The complaint said that online bookstores had sold twenty-three copies of *Funding Evil* in the UK. It wasn't clear how bin Mahfouz could have known that, unless he or his representatives were the ones who had placed the orders.

Kornstein and Ehrenfeld decided that they wouldn't dignify the lawsuit with a response. She wouldn't even show up in court.

Unfortunately for her, the case was assigned to Judge David Eady. Before becoming a judge, he had sued media companies for libel and invasion of privacy on behalf of the rich and famous. From the bench, his repeated rulings against media companies had established "a formidable body of case law on which public figures can rely when they wish to gag the media," as Britain's *Daily Telegraph* put it. Eady was not pleased by Ehrenfeld's refusal to show up or respond to the lawsuit. If defendants in libel actions got the idea that they could simply ignore such actions, it would undermine the clout of Britain's legal system. In December 2004, he issued a default judgment, essentially banning the book in Britain and ordering Ehrenfeld to pay more than $220,000 in damages and legal fees.

Ehrenfeld had no intention of paying—and thanks to some creative legal thinking by Kornstein, she was convinced she wouldn't have to. They filed a lawsuit in New York federal court, seeking a ruling that the British judgment was unenforceable in the United States. Why? Because if bin Mahfouz had sued in America, the action would have been tossed out of court, thanks to *Sullivan*. The stakes, Kornstein wrote in a court filing, were nothing less than "whether American journalists, investigative reporters and independent authors will have the freedom to write and publish—and whether the American public will have the freedom to read and learn—the facts about the funding of international terrorism." He concluded: "This case should be the last stop on Sheikh Mahfouz's 'libel tour.'"

Bin Mahfouz amassed a who's who of American law firms to represent him in the United States. One of his counselors was Steve Brogan, the managing partner of the giant law firm Jones Day, whose other clients had included the bin Laden family. Jones Day argued that it was entirely proper for bin Mahfouz to have sued Ehrenfeld in England and that it was Ehrenfeld, by suing in the United States, "who has been misusing the courts."

Before long, Ehrenfeld had racked up about $200,000 of out-of-pocket legal expenses—roughly what she could have paid to make bin Mahfouz go away in the first place—and the court fights were consuming most of her time. "I'm not reporting," she complained. "I'm doing fundraising to pay my lawyers." In any case, publishers had suddenly grown wary of working with her, a development she attributed to the never-ending litigation.

More bad news followed. In 2006, a federal judge dismissed Ehrenfeld's suit because the court didn't have jurisdiction over bin Mahfouz. The next year, another court decided that this was a matter of state, not federal, law. "They are burning books now in England, and we are sitting here doing nothing," Ehrenfeld told the *Weekly Standard*. Just before Christmas in 2007, a state court dealt Ehrenfeld a final defeat. New York lacked jurisdiction over bin Mahfouz because he hadn't "transacted business" there. The judge wrote that her hands were tied. If people didn't like the law, their complaints "should be directed to the legislature."

Rory Lancman was looking for a way to make a splash. He was halfway through his first term in the New York State Assembly, where he represented Queens. That sounded impressive, but he was one of 150 legislators, and the risk of vanishing into obscurity was high. Lancman was thirty-eight, and he hoped this job would be a launchpad for a successful political career. He wanted a high-profile issue to champion.

In early December, Lancman was leafing through *Jewish Week* magazine and came across an editorial headlined "Last Stop on the Libel Tour." It was about Ehrenfeld's case, which at the time was still pending before the state court. The case had "monumental and far-reaching implications," the magazine explained, "and the very future of free expression and public participation for all US journalists, authors and their publishers hangs in the balance."

It dawned on Lancman: he could introduce a bill in Albany to protect New Yorkers from such libel tourism. As he began pondering this possibility, the court dismissed Ehrenfeld's suit—and practically invited the legislature to empower judges to block foreign libel judgments. Lancman did the political math. Memories of 9/11 remained fresh. Who would oppose a bill to make it harder for terrorism-linked Saudis to sue Americans for exposing their activities? No one. *I found a winner*, Lancman thought.

He contacted the number two Republican in the state senate, who jumped on board, meaning this would be a bipartisan initiative. Staffers worked up the bill's language. It would block overseas libel judgments from being enforced in New York unless a state court concluded that the laws in the other country "provided at least as much protection for freedom of speech and press . . . as would be provided by both the United States and New York constitutions."

In January 2008, Lancman convened a press conference on the steps of the New York Public Library to unveil the "Libel Terrorism Protection Act"—a name meant to ensure that nobody forgot that the legislation was designed to protect someone who had exposed terrorist financing. The bill will help "maintain New York's place as the free speech capital of the world," Lancman declared, flanked by legislators, lawyers, and the library's famous marble lions. Ehrenfeld was there, too, bundled up against the cold. For the first time in a while, she felt like she wasn't alone.

Unlike the court fight, which had dragged on for what seemed like an eternity, the bill breezed through the legislature. Lancman's calculations had proven correct: everyone supported the First Amendment and holding terrorist-linked financiers accountable. "I didn't need to twist arms," he recalled. The state assembly and senate overwhelmingly passed the bill, and the governor signed it on May 1, 2008. It became known as Rachel's Law.

After years of getting kicked around in the courts, Ehrenfeld sensed that momentum was suddenly on her side. She began pushing lawmakers in other states. Six soon enacted similar laws shielding journalists and others against Britain's draconian libel regime.

In Washington, liberal Democrats and conservative Republicans proposed multiple federal versions of Rachel's Law, but the bills stalled in the Senate. To get them dislodged, Ehrenfeld hired a lobbyist named Brett Heimov. He introduced her to congressmen and to staffers for senators including Patrick Leahy, the chairman of the Judiciary Committee, and Jeff Sessions, the panel's top Republican. Over and over, Ehrenfeld and Heimov watched the surprise wash over the faces of lawmakers and their aides when they heard that a British judge had awarded damages against an American citizen even though her book wasn't on sale in the UK.

Yet while Leahy's staff was supportive, the Vermont senator himself was focused on other matters. To get the bill through the Senate Judiciary Committee, a key waystation before the full chamber could vote on it, they needed the chairman's support. Finally, Ehrenfeld and Heimov got a group of Vermont librarians to write to Leahy and push him to move the legislation. The next day, Leahy was on the phone, trying to organize a markup of the bill to get it ready for a vote. "We're gonna get this done," the senator promised.

Now came the sausage making. Ehrenfeld was steering things. She and Kornstein peppered congressional aides with comments on specific language in the evolving legislation. When words were tweaked, everyone agreed that Ehrenfeld needed to sign off. It wasn't an act of kindness.

She was so fiery, persistent, and blunt that if she objected, it might scuttle the whole thing.

By now, bin Mahfouz was dead—felled at sixty by a heart attack in Jeddah—but British officials took up the campaign to kill the bill. Judge Eady delivered a speech slamming it as an ill-considered act of American hegemony. Another time, members of Parliament came to the United States. In a meeting in Kornstein's office, they warned that the law would harm US-Anglo relations. Kornstein picked up a copy of Ehrenfeld's book and asked if any of them had read it. None had. The MPs were endorsing censorship of something they hadn't even looked at. At the end of the meeting, Kornstein, with a wry smile, handed each lawmaker a copy of *Funding Evil* to take with them back to Britain, where the book remained banned.

Rallying around Ehrenfeld, conservatives publicly celebrated free speech and the *Sullivan* decision. In the media, on the House and Senate floors, and even in the text of bills, Republicans praised the court's 1964 ruling. It "reflects the fundamental value that Americans place on promoting the free exchange of ideas and information," read one version of the proposed legislation, sponsored by thirteen Republicans and two Democrats. Conservative writers in the *Wall Street Journal*, *Commentary* magazine, and *Human Events* embraced *Sullivan* as a bulwark against libel tourism in America.

In the summer of 2010, the latest version of the SPEECH Act (an acronym for "Securing the Protection of our Enduring and Established Constitutional Heritage") was put to a vote. The Senate approved it unanimously. Sessions, the far-right Alabama senator, and his aide, the further-right Stephen Miller (who would go on to become a top aide to Donald Trump), issued a news release explaining how the just-passed bill would prevent "a dangerous chilling effect on the exercise of First Amendment rights." Days later, the House followed suit in a unanimous voice vote. Heimov called Ehrenfeld at home in New York. "It's done," he reported. President Barack Obama signed the bill in the Oval Office.

It was an extraordinary achievement. Ehrenfeld had gone from fighting for her survival to engineering a new federal law—one that had garnered universal support in a capital not known for its bipartisan unity. In September, aides to Leahy and Sessions reserved a Judiciary Committee hearing room for an evening engagement. Ehrenfeld paid for the catering. Leahy's office presented her with a framed original of the law, signed by the president. Drinks and food in hand, guests listened as speakers praised Ehrenfeld and lauded their accomplishment.

"I think this is something to celebrate," Sessions said. He was wearing a dark gray suit and red-and-blue-striped tie, and he snapped his right hand up and down as he spoke. The law ensures "that in America, a free citizen, subject to our classical historical rules of libel and slander, can speak or write freely. I really believe that's important."

Five and a half years later, Sessions would hop onstage at a windswept rally in Alabama and become the first senator to endorse Donald Trump for president.

PART II

THE SHIFT

TRUMP'S BIZARRE VOW

Two days before he picked up Jeff Sessions's endorsement in Alabama, Donald Trump had arrived in Fort Worth, Texas, for another rally. After placing second in the Iowa caucuses at the start of February 2016, he'd won the next three contests. Super Tuesday, in which voters in eleven states would cast their votes for their party's nominee, was looming, and Trump was campaigning in Texas—home to his rival Ted Cruz—looking for a knockout.

The rally was in the sprawling Fort Worth Convention Center, whose indoor arena could seat up to thirteen thousand. The campaign had billed this as a major event. Trump would be joined onstage by Chris Christie, the New Jersey governor who weeks earlier had dropped out of the presidential race and tonight would be endorsing his former nemesis.

For eight months now, Trump had been holding enormous rallies, and one of their few predictable features was just how unpredictable they were. This night would prove no exception. After dispensing with perfunctory promises to build a wall and renegotiate international trade deals, Trump turned his attention to Marco Rubio, the Florida senator who along with Cruz was his chief competitor for the Republican nomination. At one GOP debate, Rubio had been visibly sweating, and Trump, like any good insult comic, pounced. Rubio, Trump asserted, was "a nervous basket case" who had been "putting on makeup with a trowel . . . just trying to cover up the sweat." He reached inside the lectern, pulled out a water bottle, and began spraying it all over the stage. "It's Rubio!" Trump bellowed, before flinging the plastic bottle aside.

The crowd cheered and hooted and waved TRUMP placards. The candidate seemed to feed off the audience's energy, like a storm gaining power as it churns through warm waters.

After a while, Trump turned to one of his favorite targets. "I'll tell you what," he declared. "I think the media is among the most dishonest groups of people I've ever met. They're terrible." Trump licked his lips. "Believe me, if I become president, oh do they have problems. They're going to have such problems. And one of the things I'm going to do— and this is only going to make it tougher for me, and I've never said this before—but one of the things I'm going to do, if I win, and I hope I do, and we're certainly leading, is I'm going to open up our libel laws, so when they write purposely negative and horrible and false articles, we can sue them and win lots of money." Wild applause. "So, we're going to open up those libel laws, folks, and we're going to have people sue you like you've never got sued before."

It was a bizarre vow, apparently the first time a major presidential candidate had used the reform of libel laws in a stump speech. In any case, there was no need to "open up our libel laws" to hold reporters to account for writing purposely false articles. The "actual malice" standard covered that; there was no legal protection for someone writing something defamatory that they knew to be false. Plus, this wasn't a law that the president or Congress could tinker with. It was a question of the Supreme Court's interpretation of the First Amendment.

It was easy to dismiss Trump's threat as the confused rant of someone whose career had been defined in part by threatening and sometimes filing libel lawsuits, generally without success. There was his failed $500 million action against the *Chicago Tribune* for criticizing his planned skyscraper. There was his fruitless $5 billion suit against the journalist Tim O'Brien, who Trump claimed had understated his wealth. There were his threats against TV networks and newspapers and investment firms and competing casino and hotel companies. Of the seven libel lawsuits that Trump and his companies had filed at this point, they'd won only once, when a defendant failed to appear in court. If libel standards were substantially loosened, a serial suer like Donald Trump stood to be a big beneficiary. (On the other hand, looser libel laws also could hurt

Trump, who sometimes got sued for defamation. Just a few months after the Texas rally, his lawyers moved to dismiss a libel lawsuit against him—and a New York court agreed, citing cases like *Gertz v. Robert Welch*. Other times, Trump was not so lucky. In 2024, a jury awarded the writer E. Jean Carroll $83 million in damages from the former president, finding that he had defamed her after she accused him of rape.)

Yet there was more to Trump's libel rhetoric than financial self-interest. Demonizing the media was another way to whip his devotees into an us-versus-them furor. It also helped delegitimize one of the few remaining institutional constraints on politicians, at a time when he was facing the most aggressive press coverage of his life. Trump, as was his wont, would be taking things further than previous generations had dared, but he was following a playbook scripted by some of the Republican Party's past leaders.

Nearly fifty years before the rally in Fort Worth, Vice President Spiro Agnew had stepped up to a similar lectern on a stage in Des Moines. He was ostensibly there to address the Midwest Regional Republican Committee, but the real purpose went far beyond the audience in that Iowa ballroom.

It was November 1969. Days earlier, Agnew's boss, Richard Nixon, had delivered a major address about the war in Vietnam. Agnew and other White House officials regarded the so-called Silent Majority speech—which was intended to rally the country around the president's decision to keep fighting in Vietnam—as "the most important address of his administration." Some seventy million people had tuned in, and that was where the problems had begun. After the speech ended, the three major TV networks hadn't returned to their previous programming or simply summarized the president's words. Instead, they reviewed it through a critical, analytical lens, well aware of the tendency of presidents—and this president in particular—to bend the truth. They called in experts to assess the validity of Nixon's claims and political rivals to question the wisdom of Nixon's plans.

Today, in an era of round-the-clock punditry, this seems quaint. At the time, it felt cutting-edge. The media was beginning to radically alter how

it covered major news events and politicians. The long-standing approach
of reporter-as-stenographer, dutifully regurgitating whatever officials
served up, was falling out of favor. In its place was a newfound desire to
hold power to account, in part by providing readers and viewers with
more context and fact-checking. "Interpretation replaced transmission,
and adversarialism replaced deference, as core values of reporting," as
one media observer, Matthew Pressman, later put it.

Nixon was furious. He viewed the TV networks as having deliberately
undercut his ability to speak directly to the American people. The White
House also smelled an opportunity to hammer the media elites. That was
why Agnew had been dispatched to Iowa.

All three broadcasters carried Agnew's speech live. He was dressed in
a dark suit and darker tie, speaking behind a brown lectern with a gray
microphone. "I think it's obvious from the cameras here that I didn't
come to discuss the ban on cyclamates [an artificial sweetener] or DDT
[a pesticide]," Agnew intoned, to knowing laughter. Instead, he wanted
"to focus your attention on this little group of men who not only enjoy a
right of instant rebuttal to every presidential address, but, more importantly, wield a free hand in selecting, presenting, and interpreting the
great issues in our nation." He was referring to the anchors and producers of the three network news programs: "a tiny, enclosed fraternity of
privileged men elected by no one." Agnew went on like this for nearly
thirty minutes.

The speech was front-page news. Nixon called it "a turning point" for
his presidency, noting that the White House switchboards had been over-
whelmed and that praise-filled telegrams had poured in from all over the
country. The speech was later described as "the Magna Carta of the liberal
media critique."

In the ensuing decades, politicians of all stripes griped about the
media—continuing a tradition that dated to America's founding. Jimmy
Carter and Ronald Reagan. Dan Quayle and Sarah Palin. The Clintons
and the Bushes. But Newt Gingrich was perhaps the most enthusiastic
practitioner. In 1994, as he led the Republican takeover of Congress, he
continuously pummeled the "elite media," even barring his hometown

Atlanta Constitution from campaign events as retribution for a political cartoon. "Spiro Agnew with Brains," *Newsweek* called him.

Eighteen years later, Gingrich was seeking his party's 2012 presidential nomination. He'd lost badly in Iowa and New Hampshire and was running low on money. In this do-or-die moment, he reverted to his old strategy. At a debate just before South Carolina's crucial primary, a CNN moderator asked about his acrimonious divorce. Gingrich was ready. "I think the destructive, vicious, negative nature of much of the news media makes it harder to govern this country . . . and I am appalled you would begin a presidential debate on a topic like that," Gingrich hissed. "I am tired of the elite media protecting Barack Obama by attacking Republicans!" His supporters leapt to their feet, chanting "Newt, Newt, Newt!"

Gingrich handily won the South Carolina primary, and the upset was widely attributed to his media bashing. "The thing that struck me was what conservative audiences reacted to, even more than attacks on Obama, was attacks on the media," Gingrich later explained.

Donald Trump had toyed with running for president himself in 2012. It is hard to imagine that he didn't notice the success of Gingrich's strategy.

As 2016 progressed, Trump's attacks intensified. The "dishonest press" became "the most dishonest people ever created by God." Reporters were "crooked," "disgusting," "bad people." His campaign revoked press credentials for out-of-favor outlets.

When Republicans gathered in Cleveland for their convention, a huge billboard, splayed across the top of a building downtown, advised: "DON'T BELIEVE THE LIBERAL MEDIA!" Similar signage appeared on taxis and posters around Cleveland that week. The ads—paid for by the Media Research Center, whose goal was "to expose and neutralize the propaganda arm of the Left: the national news media"—paired nicely with Trump's rhetoric when he accepted the nomination and, once again, slammed the "elite media."

This felt different than the time-honored tradition of politicians grousing about the news. Trump was going much further than Agnew had in scolding the broadcast networks or Gingrich had in swiping at debate moderators. This was a blitzkrieg that cast journalists, at times in highly personal terms, as America's enemy, and it would only get worse after Trump won the White House. Like acid dripping onto a sheet of metal, his attacks would begin corroding the longstanding consensus among politicians and judges that media-protecting precedents like *Sullivan* were vital if imperfect pillars of American democracy.

Gingrich, for one, recognized just what Trump was doing. "He wants to be very aggressive, to make sure that his supporters routinely discount any kind of news media attack," he noted. Other commentators got it, too. "The media has become for the Right what the Soviet Union was during the Cold War—a common, unifying adversary of overwhelming importance," one journalist wrote in the conservative *National Review*. Another, in *Politico*, called 2016 "the year that media loathing became a standard in politics, rather than an anomaly."

It was also the year that such loathing became a standard in the courts. Three weeks after Trump's Fort Worth pledge to make it easier to sue the media, a jury in Florida returned a verdict that highlighted the destructive power that such lawsuits could have.

5

STARTING A REVOLUTION

A. J. Daulerio was in Montana when the package—a thin envelope without a return address, containing nothing more than a DVD—arrived at his New York office. It was September 2012, and Daulerio was the top editor at Gawker, the swashbuckling network of websites whose modus operandi was to offend the sensibilities of the rich, famous, powerful, and power-hungry. For weeks, rumors had been circulating online about an unauthorized sex tape featuring the wrestler Hulk Hogan. A few gossip sites had run items on it, even teased readers with stills from the video. Now someone had sent Gawker thirty minutes of grainy black-and-white footage of Hogan and an unidentified woman.

Daulerio was in Missoula to catch a Pearl Jam show. He was an obsessive follower of the band, which he'd seen perform all over the country. This gig promised to be unusual: it was Pearl Jam's only appearance that year outside of a music festival, and the concert was doubling as a fundraiser for Montana's first-term Democratic senator, Jon Tester, who was locked in a tight reelection battle. Eddie Vedder and company were playing at a smallish venue on the University of Montana campus. Tickets had sold out in fifteen minutes.

By some standards, Daulerio was one of the most notorious journalists of the internet age. Gawker had a reputation for breaking news and shattering norms and being downright mean. So did Daulerio. He'd started out as a traditional reporter, working his way up from a local newspaper in his native Pennsylvania to a couple of niche business publications in New York. He got his big break at Deadspin, Gawker's sports blog, where he produced a mix of juicy scoops—exposing the rickety finances of pro baseball and basketball teams and revealing Brett Favre's alleged sexual harassment, for example—and a constant patter of dick pics and click-bait. During Daulerio's tenure as Deadspin's top editor, its traffic nearly quadrupled. *GQ* credited him with transforming it into "the raunchiest, funniest, and most controversial sports site on the Web." In 2011 he was promoted to be the editor of Gawker itself.

Daulerio was a mess. He'd been abusing substances—alcohol, coke, Adderall, acid, Xanax, you name it—for years. "I didn't treat anything seriously," he later said. Not his relationships, not his job, nothing. "I was basically just like one of those guys that even when I was making a lot of money, I was still broke all the time." Now, at what would become a fateful moment for Gawker and the entire media industry, he was 2,300 miles away, screaming at Eddie Vedder, who was onstage in a short-sleeved flannel shirt and skinny jeans, battling a cold and swigging from a champagne bottle. "It's not every day you get to do a benefit for a candidate you believe in," Vedder rasped to the cheering crowd.

The concert lasted two and a half delirious hours. Pearl Jam rocked a twenty-nine-song set, including many of its staples and a smattering of politically themed covers. An hour in, Vedder performed a melodic rendition of "Know Your Rights" by the Clash. "These are your rights," he sang, tilting the microphone stand toward the crowd. "You have the right to free speech—provided, of course, you're not actually dumb enough to try it."

Daulerio, it turned out, was definitely dumb enough to try it. He, his Gawker colleagues, and many others were about to pay an awful price.

Eighteen months earlier, an Oxford law student named Aron D'Souza had gone out to dinner in Berlin with the hard-right tech billionaire Peter Thiel. The pair had known each other since 2009, when D'Souza had given Thiel a tour of Oxford. D'Souza was one of those young men with a knack for ingratiating themselves with the powerful. "What's the biggest problem you face?" he had asked Thiel as they strolled the ancient campus.

"There's this terrible outlet writing all this terrible stuff about me,"

Thiel had replied. D'Souza always researched people he was about to meet for the first time, and so he had known what Thiel was referring to: Gawker. A couple of years earlier, the website had reported that he was gay. That would have been bad enough—Thiel had come out to a lot of people, though not publicly—but Gawker was pioneering a uniquely skeptical form of writing about tech titans like Thiel, who had grown accustomed to a generally docile press marveling at their latest inventions. That wasn't Gawker's style. The website seemed hell-bent on piercing his self-created image as a visionary. Gawker had documented his hedge fund's financial struggles and tax avoidance and his fringe political and philosophical theories. (Among many other things, Thiel had seemed to complain about women getting the right to vote, and he had written that he "no longer believe[d] that freedom and democracy are compatible.") Thiel thought that Gawker's coverage was causing investors to pull money out of his hedge fund and discouraging others from putting money in.

Just as alarming, Gawker's mode of reporting seemed to be spreading. As the tech industry gained economic and cultural clout, other news outlets—from rival upstarts to established newspapers—were beginning to cover Silicon Valley more aggressively, with an eye toward holding its companies and leaders to account, much as reporters might write about Wall Street or the White House. (Part of this might have been a reaction to Gawker's years of needling rival tech reporters as "toothless.") The result, it was becoming clear, would soon be a new era of intense scrutiny for the men atop what was fast becoming the world's most powerful industry. Someone needed to nip this in the bud.

Thiel had taken to warning that Gawker's style menaced not just him but all of Silicon Valley. "I think they should be described as terrorists, not as writers or reporters," he growled in 2009. At one point, he asked staffers to hire private investigators to dig into the personal life and finances of Gawker's founder, Nick Denton. (The efforts apparently came up empty.)

After their campus tour, Thiel and D'Souza had kept in touch, and they both happened to be in Berlin in April 2011. They met for dinner at Tim Raue, a Michelin-starred restaurant around the corner from

Checkpoint Charlie. Over a seven-course tasting menu and some very expensive Riesling, Thiel resumed his grumbling about Gawker. "Why don't you just sue them?" D'Souza asked. Thiel said that would just attract more attention—the last thing he wanted. The idea, D'Souza told me, hit him out of the blue: What if Thiel recruited someone else to sue Gawker? Thiel could bankroll their litigation through an intermediary, while remaining in the shadows. "Basically run a proxy war," he suggested. D'Souza didn't realize it—he was no expert in American history or constitutional law—but he was in essence proposing a clandestine version of the strategy that L. B. Sullivan and his Alabama colleagues had perfected back in 1960: trying to bankrupt a bothersome media company through waves of costly litigation.

Thiel lit up. He spent the rest of the dinner excitedly talking about the possibilities. It was nearing midnight, and the restaurant was about to close. The pair decamped to a nearby hotel bar. Thiel asked D'Souza what it would cost to crush Gawker. D'Souza was twenty-five years old and had no idea. "Ten million," he guessed. That was nothing for Thiel.

"Aron, come work with me," Thiel said as they parted ways around 2 a.m. "Let's do this." Then and there, D'Souza agreed. Two months later, after collecting his diploma from Oxford, he flew to his native Australia, dropped off his stuff, hopped a flight to New Zealand, sat down with Thiel, and put their plot in motion. It was codenamed MBTO, an acronym for Manhattan-based terrorist organization, which was how they viewed Gawker.

The two men briefly discussed bribing employees to sabotage Gawker, bugging its offices to collect dirt, or even hacking the company's computers. They eventually decided that a legal approach would be better. The first step was to hire a lawyer. D'Souza interviewed a bunch of Brits, but they lacked the entrepreneurial spirit and creativity that the mission would require. Then someone mentioned a Hollywood lawyer named Charles Harder.

D'Souza had never heard of Harder, which was a selling point. "You don't want a superstar," D'Souza explained to me, sitting in his basement office in London on a sunny autumn afternoon. "You want someone who wants to make his name."

Harder, who was in his early forties, was a Los Angeles native and registered Democrat. He'd spent his early years as a lawyer at the firm of Lavely & Singer. It was dominated by the notorious Hollywood hatchet man Marty Singer, who often was the first stop for celebrities engulfed in scandal. Harder considered Singer to be "a mentor of sorts," but he hadn't enjoyed the job. "It wasn't much fun, the stress was constant, the hours were too long, and workload too heavy," Harder told me via email. In 2008 he left to join a larger, cushier LA firm, Wolf Rifkin Shapiro. Harder's specialty was making sure brands didn't use his clients' names or images without authorization. (He represented Clint Eastwood in a lawsuit against a furniture store that was selling "Eastwood" chairs, and he sued a company for using Sandra Bullock's image to advertise diamond-encrusted watches.) Lean and perma-tanned, with sandy hair and a Brooks Brothers–style wardrobe, Harder looked the part of LA lawyer. He wasn't particularly well-known—one writer described him as "another cog in the Hollywood machine"—but he was respected. At one point, Oxford University Press had asked him to help write and edit a book on entertainment law.

One day in early 2012, D'Souza called Harder to introduce himself. He said he was representing some very rich individuals who hated Gawker. Would Harder be interested in exploring legal avenues for destroying the site? Singer's law firm had represented people who'd been attacked by Gawker, and Harder had formed what he described as "a strong negative impression" of the outlet. On the phone, he immediately began brainstorming. D'Souza loved it. This guy was brimming with creativity, ambition, and an instinct to go "straight for the jugular." Plus, Thiel liked the idea of having an LA lawyer, as opposed to someone in New York or Silicon Valley, in the driver's seat. It would add an extra layer of anonymity. If anyone caught on to what D'Souza was doing with this lawyer, they'd probably suspect the operation was being run to benefit someone like Rupert Murdoch.

Harder was hired. Now it was his job to help figure out how to take down Gawker.* He and his team spent months poring over press

---

* Harder denied that the goal was to kill Gawker. "The assignment was to find people with meritorious claims against Gawker and offer our help," he told me.

clippings and legal filings, trying to identify potential points of weakness. Could they pursue a fraud or patent case? An action brought by the shareholders of Gawker's holding companies? An attempt to force out Nick Denton? Ultimately the conclusion was that they would need to win a crippling verdict. And that meant finding a plaintiff—someone who had been severely harmed by a Gawker website—to serve as a vehicle for retribution.

For as long as he'd been a journalist, Daulerio had been hooked on scoops. He loved the competitive chase for news, the adrenaline rush followed by the dopamine hit of being first to reveal something to the world. ("He needs the next story like an addict needs their next fix," Denton said in 2011.) The Hulk Hogan sex tape wasn't exactly Watergate, but it struck Daulerio and his colleagues as fair game. For years Hogan had been boasting about his sexual exploits. Plus, Gawker operated under the basic principle that if the site received information, it should be published.

Gawker's lawyers gave the green light to post the video, so long as they kept it short. Daulerio asked a video editor to cut it into a "highlight reel," and, to accompany the 101-second film, he wrote an essay about the public's obsession with celebrity sex. "I was very enthusiastic about writing about it," Daulerio later said. "I thought it was newsworthy."

On October 4, 2012, a week after the DVD had been delivered to Gawker's offices, the website posted Daulerio's essay and the video, about nine seconds of which displayed a naked Hulk Hogan having sex with what turned out to be his best friend's wife. "Even for a Minute, Watching Hulk Hogan Have Sex in a Canopy Bed Is Not Safe for Work but Watch It Anyway," yelled the headline. The post became "a blockbuster," garnering about seven million page views.

Hogan's longtime lawyer, David Houston, had been working for weeks to prevent the video from being published. He'd persuaded other websites not to post it. Now Gawker had gone and done it. He sent the site a cease-and-desist letter, demanding that the video be taken down. A lawyer for Gawker responded that it was newsworthy and would remain online.

By then, Harder knew all about the sex tape. He and D'Souza had a crew of about twenty employees reading every single item that Gawker had ever published, scouring them for potential causes of action. As soon as Harder saw Daulerio's post, he recognized the opportunity. The publication of the explicit video struck him as a flagrant violation of Hogan's privacy. And Daulerio's piece was quickly racking up page views, which would make it easier to argue that it had damaged Hogan's reputation. He pinged D'Souza. It was the middle of the night in Australia, but D'Souza had set up his phone to alert him whenever Harder or Thiel messaged him. *Bingo*, Harder wrote. *This is it.* D'Souza agreed.

Harder phoned Houston, told him he represented someone with an interest in pursuing Gawker, and volunteered to help on a lawsuit. Houston accepted the offer.

A week later, Harder, Houston, and Hogan stood on the sidewalk outside the federal courthouse in Tampa, facing a cluster of reporters and camera crews. They had just filed a lawsuit seeking $100 million against Gawker for invading Hogan's privacy. "The actions of the defendants cannot be tolerated by a civil society," Harder declared. Hogan posed behind him in a black T-shirt, bandana, and sunglasses, a tough-guy pose etched on his mustachioed face.

The following three-plus years would be war. Harder and his team viewed the lawsuit, which ended up being moved to state court in Florida, as a vessel not only to compensate Hogan but also for a broader blitz against Gawker. They deposed its employees. They reviewed its internal documents, which they obtained through the discovery process. They contacted the subjects of nasty articles and volunteered to help them sue. When Harder learned that Gawker had unpaid interns, he helped organize a lawsuit seeking back pay and damages. Thiel's team would secretly sponsor about a half dozen lawsuits against Gawker, D'Souza told me.

Daulerio, Denton, and Gawker's lawyers had an inkling as to what Harder was doing. When they accused him in court filings, Harder at times seemed to dissemble. Asked whether he was using discovery to amass materials for other potential suits against Gawker, Harder replied that the allegation was "unsupported by any evidence." (This is what journalists call a "nondenial denial.") He also claimed that Gawker's financial resources were "exponentially greater" than Hogan's, which might have been accurate but didn't account for the billionaire lurking in Hogan's corner.*

After years of toiling in the backwaters of Hollywood, Harder sensed that this case—not just the Hogan suit but the overall plot against Gawker— was his moment to make a name for himself. Part of it was the money. Harder was making at least $500 an hour, and the hours were extensive. Yet he didn't feel like he was being compensated sufficiently by his current employer, Wolf Rifkin Shapiro, where, he told me, he was often "one of the biggest rainmakers."

It wasn't long after D'Souza initially contacted him that Harder told him that he was toying with venturing out on his own, just checking that D'Souza and his clients would stick with him. (They would.) Harder sounded out a colleague, Jeffrey Abrams, and the pair soon got serious about opening their own little law firm. Like Harder, Abrams specialized in so-called right-of-publicity litigation, going after companies and individuals that used celebrities' names or likenesses for commercial purposes without authorization. Abrams knew another lawyer, Doug Mirell, who had spent the past thirty-plus years at the giant law firm Loeb & Loeb. The two ran in the same circles: Mirell had recently been representing the estate of Marilyn Monroe, while Abrams had been working on behalf of Marlon Brando's. Their kids attended the same LA private schools. So Abrams pitched Mirell on creating a boutique law firm focused on representing A-list celebrities in publicity cases.

The three men met for breakfast at a diner in LA. Mirell didn't know much about Harder, but he seemed bright and ambitious. The catch was that if they started their own firm, Harder would be taking the Gawker litigation along with him. This was suboptimal for Mirell. He wanted no part in attacking the media. He'd initially been heading for a career in journalism, having been editor in chief of his college newspaper and written for the *Hollywood Reporter*. Even after becoming a lawyer, his

---

* Harder told me that he didn't recall bringing lawsuits against Gawker based on information gathered during the Hogan discovery process. "But even if we had, I'm not aware of any law or rule that prohibits it." He added that Gawker outspent Hogan's side by at least 25 percent.

allegiances were clear. At Loeb & Loeb, he had defended news organizations against aggressive plaintiffs. On the other hand, Gawker's conduct
toward Hulk Hogan struck Mirell as "rather outrageous," he told me.
And the Gawker case would be the exception; Mirell's understanding
was that most of the firm's work would be focused on publicity rights.
He was in.

The law firm of Harder Mirell & Abrams opened its doors in early
2013. Pretty quickly, it became clear that Mirell and Abrams's concep-
tion of their plan had been imprecise at best. Harder imported from his
old firm a couple of high-profile right-of-publicity cases, but he seemed
mostly focused on suing Gawker. "He was growing rich off this conspiracy regardless of the outcome," the author Ryan Holiday wrote in his
book about the Gawker case. "His law firm is built around" Peter Thiel.
Thiel himself would later describe Harder's shop as a purpose-built legal
vehicle: "We set up a whole law firm to bring cases against Gawker."
(Harder said that was inaccurate.)

The Hogan case crawled toward trial. Gawker wasn't the type to back
down. Not realizing that Hogan was endowed with essentially infinite resources, the site's lawyers set out to chisel him down with endless motions
and appeals. "It was obvious they were trying to bankrupt him through
the litigation process," Harder told me. "What they didn't realize is they
were bankrupting themselves." As Thiel's side gained access to the company's internal records and deposed Gawker's employees under oath, the
case grew stronger. There were plentiful examples of employees acting
callously. Daulerio, for example, had posted a video of a young woman
having sex—or perhaps being raped, it was hard to tell—in the bathroom of a sports bar. When the woman's friend begged to have the video
removed, Daulerio initially refused, suggesting that the woman should
just move on. (He later acquiesced.)

It was Mirell who was called in to handle the deposition of Daulerio
in September 2013. Neither Daulerio nor most of his colleagues were
taking the case seriously. They'd been sued before, and lawsuits had in-
variably seemed to get thrown out of court or settled. Nobody thought
there'd be a trial. Daulerio's deposition, in a nondescript Manhattan conference room, had been grinding on for hours by the time Mirell asked

a fateful question. Could Daulerio imagine a scenario "where a celebrity sex tape would *not* be newsworthy?"

"If they were a child," Daulerio responded.

"Under what age?" Mirell asked.

"Four."

"No four-year-old sex tapes," Mirell said. "OK."

Daulerio was exhausted and grumpy, and he'd meant it as an exasperated joke. As far as he could tell, the deposition had gone fine. But the flippant remark would be his undoing.

The trial began in the Pinellas County Courthouse near St. Petersburg, Florida, in March 2016. The case had been assigned to a judge, Pamela Campbell, who was a darling of the religious right; years earlier, she'd gained prominence representing the parents of Terri Schiavo as they unsuccessfully fought against having their comatose daughter's feeding tube removed. In pretrial rulings in the Gawker case, Campbell—who had the dubious distinction of having her decisions reversed on appeal more than any other judge in the county—had routinely sided with Hogan. "We kind of hit the jackpot with the judge," Thiel later boasted.

The first step was jury selection. "Time for the real main event!" Hogan taunted on Twitter. "I AM going to slam another Giant! Hogan vrs Gawker!" Hundreds of prospective jurors were given a twelve-page questionnaire. "This case involves images depicting sex and nudity, and the use of profanity," it cautioned. "Would receiving and viewing this type of content affect your ability to serve as a fair and impartial juror in this case?" It took four days to whittle down the crowd to a jury of six, plus three alternates.

D'Souza had come to Florida to witness what he hoped would be history. He knew his side had more resources and was better prepared than the ragtag Gawker crew. Harder and D'Souza had run two mock trials. They'd commissioned demographic and sociological surveys of the population around St. Petersburg to understand the mindset of the jury pool. They'd dumped $500,000 on audiovisual bells and whistles for the trial. One day during jury selection, D'Souza was standing at a courthouse urinal when Nick Denton walked in. D'Souza loved that

Denton had no idea he was peeing next to the man who had master-minded this war.

Opening statements got underway on the first Monday in March. It was a balmy morning, the sky a cloudless blue, as Hogan, Harder, and the rest of his posse marched toward the beige, blocky courthouse. Camera crews and reporters were packed outside. Hogan was dressed all in black, right up to his signature bandana, which the judge had permitted him to wear on the condition that it was monochromatic. (The bandana was "a self-confidence thing," Hogan claimed, because he was embarrassed by his baldness.) Hogan had just made a difficult decision: he was go-ing to have a different lawyer, Shane Vogt, address the jury for his side's opening. Harder had been at the center of the pretrial action, but Hogan doubted that a slick, tan Hollywood lawyer, especially one who had never tried a case in front of a jury, would be the right fit for a Gulf Coast jury. Vogt, by contrast, had been born and raised in nearby Tampa, where he'd been a local basketball star. (His parents had even gone to high school with Hogan.)

The wood-paneled courtroom had low ceilings with florescent light-ing. The judge sat before a polished, dark stone backsplash affixed with a metal seal depicting a blindfolded, scale-toting Lady Justice. Vogt (pro-nounced "vote") approached the lectern and told the jurors that Gawker was intent on hurting Hogan. "Their motivation wasn't some higher public purpose," he intoned. "It wasn't the truth. It was money. It was power."

Gawker employees had belatedly recognized the high stakes. Hogan was seeking $100 million in damages; the entire company was valued at $83 million. Feeding employees' existential worries, Denton two months earlier had needed to sell a slice of Gawker to drum up cash to cover the legal bills. To avoid a potential doomsday scenario, Gawker had to per-suade the jury that, no matter how distasteful they found the sex tape, no matter how rude Gawker had been in writing about celebrities and others, this wasn't a fight over morality. It was about the degree to which America protected your right to speak freely—and "to hold elites ac-countable," as Denton told his staff before the trial began—even when doing so might offend people.

Hogan had built his career around a macho public persona, Gawker's lawyer, Mike Berry, said in his opening statement. In books, on TV shows, and in interviews Hogan had alternately boasted about his sex life and sworn fidelity to his wife. That made it legitimate for Gawker to delve into his private affairs. The only reason Hogan was now trying to declare his life off-limits was because "he didn't like what Gawker had to say." Plus, Berry pointed out, Gawker didn't make money off Daulerio's piece; the site didn't run ads on articles like this one that were deemed "not safe for work." Denton's mother was a Holocaust survivor, Berry noted. "Mr. Denton grew up with parents who've seen firsthand what happens when speech is suppressed," he said.

The next day, Hogan took the stand. He testified that the video had "completely humiliated" him. When jurors were shown a clip of him on a TV show pulling down his pants and exposing his butt, Hogan insisted it was just "part of the show." Why had he gone on Howard Stern's radio show and joked about the video days after Gawker published it? "I had to be an entertainer," Hogan maintained. What about when he boasted on another radio show about the size of his penis? Hogan acknowledged he'd been exaggerating and said he was simply in character. "I do not have a ten-inch penis," he conceded. A couple of jurors snickered. Others grimaced. Daulerio put his hands to his face, trying not to laugh.

Things, it seemed, were going Gawker's way. Then, on Day Three, Vogt played a video for the jury. He and a consultant had stitched together clips from Daulerio's deposition two and a half years earlier. When the jurors watched Daulerio saying that he'd draw the line for a sex tape with a four-year-old, some gasped; one dropped the notebook he'd been writing in. Daulerio, sitting on a bench behind his lawyers, didn't betray any emotions, but he could feel the jurors shooting daggers at him. Even Denton inched away from him. When the court went into recess, everyone filed out. Daulerio was alone.

This was not an easy time for him. The previous year, he'd felt the world closing in. His life had seemed to consist of waking up, chain-smoking cigarettes, doing drugs, reading nasty stuff about himself on the internet, waiting to get a phone call from his lawyers, then going to bed. The next day would be the same. The drugs caused his tongue to turn black, and he was vomiting and wetting the bed. "I was starting to fall apart physically," he recalled. In October 2015, he'd checked into a rehab facility in Florida for a couple of months. Now, in March 2016, he was in court. "It was like having reconstructive knee surgery and then joining a roller derby league," he said. He found himself looking around the courtroom, trying to focus on the terrible trial, which was easier than contemplating his terrible sobriety.

A few days after jurors watched his videotaped deposition, Daulerio was called to the stand. Walking into court that day, his hair spiked, his face clean-shaven, a sense of doom hung over him. He knew he was about to be filleted.

Vogt asked him about his comment about four-year-olds. Daulerio said it was a sarcastic joke. "You think that's a funny topic to joke about?" Vogt demanded.

"No, not at all," Daulerio managed.

At another point, he said the Hogan video had been newsworthy because people—including Hogan himself—were already discussing it in public. Gawker had the video that everyone was chattering about. Yes, maybe it was mean to post it, "but that is the job of a journalist—to put information out there that's fair and accurate," he said. When Vogt asked whether video of Hogan's penis was newsworthy, though, Daulerio acknowledged it was not. "I included images of his penis because that's sometimes what happens when two people have sex," he snapped. Jurors were appalled.

After nine days of trial, it was time for closing arguments. Hogan's lawyers went first. Denton, Daulerio, and their colleagues are "up there in New York sitting behind a computer playing God with other people's lives," one told the jury. Gawker's team warned about the chilling effect of lawsuits like Hogan's, in which "powerful celebrities, politicians, and public figures would use our courts to punish people. We will all be worse off as a result."

Around lunchtime, the jurors retired to deliberate. They didn't think Denton or Daulerio felt remorse. "It's all about the almighty dollar to them," one juror later said. They wanted not only to punish Gawker but also to send a loud message, "where it makes an example in society and other media organizations," another juror explained. It took them less than six hours to figure out how. Shortly before 7 p.m., the foreman announced the verdict: the jury had found for Hogan and awarded him $115 million in damages—$60 million for emotional distress and the remainder for "economic injury." The former wrestler sobbed and hugged his lawyers.

D'Souza was watching an online video feed of the trial from Australia, where it was Saturday morning. He uncorked a bottle of champagne. Then he called Thiel, who was "ecstatic."

Exiting the courthouse, Hogan and his team were mobbed by reporters. Local TV stations shoved microphones in the face of the lawyer David Houston. "This is not only his victory today," Houston said, gesturing toward Hogan, "but also anyone else who's been victimized by tabloid journalism." Hogan wore dark sunglasses, but dried tears remained visible on his weathered cheeks.

Harder grinned as he posed with the lawyers and his client in the warm Florida air. He would later claim that he, too, had soaked his collar with "tears of joy." The whole team headed to the nearby Vinoy resort to celebrate their landmark victory.

For Daulerio and the rest of Team Gawker, things went from bad to worse. Three days after the verdict, the jury tacked on $25 million in punitive damages. The jurors awarded $100,000 in damages against Daulerio personally, even though the judge had told them that he had no assets and owed $27,000 in student loans.

Denton vowed to appeal, and he expressed confidence that the verdict would be overturned or at least that the eye-popping damages would be greatly reduced by a higher court. His confidence was understandable. Two other courts had previously ruled that the sex tape was protected by the First Amendment, but the judge—the oft-reversed Pamela Campbell—had barred the jury from hearing about that. And a batch of newly unsealed documents suggested that Hogan had known he was being recorded while having sex, contradicting his sworn testimony. The jurors weren't told about that, either.

But there was a big problem. Florida law required Gawker to pony up at least $50 million of the damages before it could file its appeal. Gawker didn't have that much cash at its disposal. The site tried to put up its stock as collateral, but D'Souza had prepared for this eventuality. Working with bankruptcy lawyers, he'd discovered that Gawker's physical stock certificates were in the Cayman Islands and that offshore securities weren't eligible to serve as collateral in Florida courts. And D'Souza had previously instructed his lawyers to jettison a legal claim that would have triggered Gawker's insurance coverage, which applied in the case of certain lawsuits. Now the site was on its own, its financial armor stripped away.

It was checkmate. In June, Gawker filed for bankruptcy protection. In August, Denton did, too. Two weeks later, Gawker was sold to Univision. The thirteen-year-old website would henceforth cease to exist. "It is the end of an era," Denton mourned in Gawker's final article, decrying Harder and company's "act of destruction."

D'Souza flew to California to see Thiel. The billionaire had his chef fetch a bottle of fine wine from the cellar, and they ate lobsters that had been flown in from Japan. Thiel had paid D'Souza "very, very handsomely" for his work, and he'd invested millions in the young man's various startups (including an alternative to the Olympics that would allow athletes to use performance-enhancing drugs). "Thanks, Peter, for making my life," D'Souza told him.

Hogan, however, was still owed $140 million. Harder and his colleagues turned their attention to Daulerio, who had left Gawker and had not declared bankruptcy. Hogan's camp asserted that Daulerio was now personally liable for the $115 million that the jury had awarded in compensatory damages. Daulerio, sober for nine months, briefly relapsed. Hogan's lawyers spent hours deposing him about his finances. They learned he had $1,505.78 in his Chase checking account. One morning in August, Daulerio woke up to find a message from the bank saying that a hold of more than $200 million had been placed on his account. More than five decades earlier, L. B. Sullivan's lawyers had used similar tactics to pressure defendants in libel cases, confiscating their land while verdicts were on appeal.

Less than a week before the 2016 election, lawyers for what was left of Gawker agreed to a $31 million settlement to resolve the litigation. (A couple of other lawsuits that Harder had filed against Gawker were also settled.) Daulerio, sober again, was free.

The war was over. Harder didn't know it yet, but his and Thiel's triumph would accomplish more than killing Gawker. The result would soon be visible in courthouses and newsrooms across America.

VANQUISHING THE DARK SIDE

I n May 2016, as he locked up the Republican nomination and began turning his attention toward the general election, Trump picked up an important new backer: Peter Thiel. Thiel had long flirted with extremism, such as when he questioned the compatibility of freedom and democracy. He had come to believe that an outsider like Trump would present a healthy shock to mainstream politicians—and that he could win. Thiel explained to Aron D'Souza that part of his reason for betting on Trump was what he'd learned from the surveys they'd commissioned around St. Petersburg before the Gawker trial. They showed an electorate that was sick of the media, felt disrespected by coastal elites, and longed for old-fashioned American values. Absent the Hulk Hogan case, "Peter would have never thought about the mindset of people on the Gulf Coast of Florida and therefore would never have backed Trump," D'Souza told me. Thiel's support was important to Trump, and not just because he would end up donating more than $1 million to his campaign. It signaled that Trump was acceptable in some exclusive Silicon Valley circles.

Two weeks after his support for Trump became public, *Forbes* reporters Ryan Mac and Matt Drange outed Thiel as the secret financier of the conspiracy to kill Gawker. It was surprising that his role had remained under wraps as long as it had; even before the verdict, Thiel had been unable to resist dropping hints to acquaintances about what he was up to. Now he fessed up publicly. "I saw Gawker pioneer a unique and incredibly damaging way of getting attention by bullying people even when there was no connection with the public interest," Thiel explained.

Until this point, Charles Harder hadn't known the identity of the man whom he'd been referring to as "our mystery benefactor." Now he made a pilgrimage to Thiel's home, where he was presented with "a really nice chess set" to commemorate his role orchestrating Gawker's demise.

The revelation that a billionaire had single-handedly destroyed a media company was terrifying to some, inspiring to others. Nobody was mistaking Gawker for a run-of-the-mill news organization. It crossed lines, it was nasty, it reveled in recklessness. Yet it also produced valuable journalism and social commentary. Now, thanks to Thiel, there was a battle-tested game plan for wealthy individuals to achieve vengeance against outlets that subjected them to aggressive coverage.

As it turned out, Trump was one such wealthy individual. On the morning of March 21, three days after the Gawker verdict and hours before jurors awarded the additional $25 million in damages, he had arrived at the *Washington Post*'s headquarters for an hour-long interview with the newspaper's editorial board. The discussion started with Trump bragging about how his planned hotel on Pennsylvania Avenue was ahead of schedule and under budget. Then it veered into foreign policy. Eventually the *Post*'s publisher, Fred Ryan, piped up. "You've mentioned that you want to 'open up' the libel laws. You've said that several times."

"I might not have to, based on Gawker, right?" Trump interrupted. "That was amazing."

"What presidential powers and executive actions would you take to open up the libel laws?" Ryan asked. Trump launched into a soliloquy about how the press treated him unfairly. Ryan tried again. "But how would you fix that?" he asked.

Trump wouldn't be pinned down, even as other *Post* journalists asked him increasingly specific questions about *New York Times v. Sullivan* and the actual malice standard. Trump kept marveling at how Hogan had prevailed—an experience that ran counter to Trump's years of futile litigation and threats. "I must tell you that the Hulk Hogan thing was a tremendous shock to me because—not only the amount and the fact that he had the victory—because for the most part I think libel laws almost don't exist in this country, you know, based on everything I've seen and watched and everything else." He sounded impressed—and a little jealous.

Before long, D'Souza began hearing from other very rich people who didn't like how they were being portrayed in the media. "A lot of people have approached me about doing it all over again," he told me. This time the targets would be major news organizations like the *New York Times* or *Washington Post*. D'Souza said he'd heard from folks worth a few hundred million, as well as some A-list celebrities, about setting out on such missions. After D'Souza disclosed the likely price tag, their interest tended to cool. Taking down the *Times*, he estimated, was a $100 million endeavor—a figure at which even a minor billionaire might flinch.

Harder, too, was fielding phone calls. In August 2016, he was visiting his father when he received a voicemail. He read the automatic transcription and turned to his dad: "It says it's a call from Melania Trump!" Harder thought it might be a prank, but when he listened to the message, he recognized her voice. Harder called her back. Melania wanted to sue the *Daily Mail* for a recent article that suggested she had once been a high-end escort. Harder figured that Thiel—now firmly ensconced in Trump's orbit—must have recommended him to Melania. (It was also possible that Hulk Hogan made the connection; the wrestler had known Trump for years.)

Harder took the case. After the British tabloid refused to remove the article, he sued. The Gawker case had put Harder on a national stage; now his work for the wife of the Republican presidential nominee was going to cement his status. He was no longer just a cog in the machine. The *Hollywood Reporter* called him "arguably the highest-profile media lawyer in America." (On the cover of his self-published memoir, Harder used that quote but omitted the word "arguably.") Harder began spending lots of time with the Trumps, riding in their motorcade on the way to and from airports and then flying with them and their Secret Service detail. Trump won the election, and mediation sessions with the *Daily Mail*'s lawyers were held in the Trump Tower offices that had until recently been occupied by the presidential campaign. The tabloid soon agreed to pay Melania $2.9 million and to issue a prominent retraction and apology. Harder, who had voted in the 2016 Democratic primary, switched his California voter registration to nonpartisan.

Harder's law partners, Doug Mirell and Jeffrey Abrams, also were under the impression that Thiel was the one who had connected him and the First Family. And they were anxious. They sat down with Harder in a conference room in their Beverly Hills offices to try to get on the same page. After congratulating him on his success with Melania, they asked if he expected this to morph into Harder representing the president. If so, there needed to be some bright lines. It was acceptable if the firm worked on, say, a lawsuit about a tenant in a Trump building not paying rent. What was not acceptable was taking cases that involved Trump's character or credibility, which both men viewed as indefensible. Mirell and Abrams left the meeting thinking that Harder accepted their position.*

They were wrong. The *Daily Mail* victory yielded a small flurry of new work from the First Family, including counseling Jared Kushner as allegations swirled about potential collusion with Russia and representing the president against Stormy Daniels and *People* magazine, whose reporter wrote that Trump had forcibly kissed her back in 2005.

One morning in January 2018, Mirell was driving to work when he heard on NPR that Trump had sent a threatening letter to a publisher demanding that it halt the forthcoming book *Fire and Fury* by Michael Wolff. Critics decried the president's attempt to quash a yet-to-be-published book as an Orwellian violation of the First Amendment. "Trump is stealing a page out of Richard Nixon's playbook," the historian Douglas Brinkley said. NPR didn't say who had sent the letter on Trump's behalf, but Mirell had a bad feeling. When he arrived at work, he logged into the firm's computer system and, sure enough, found the letter. (Trump's aides later said the president had hired Harder "to crush the media.")

Then and there, Mirell decided that he no longer trusted Harder—and therefore couldn't remain his business partner. "I'm out of here," he informed Abrams, and began updating his résumé. The following afternoon, Mirell received validation in the form of an email from a long-time corporate client. "We can't, in good conscience, continue to work

---

* Harder disputed that, saying his partners simply had been "uncomfortable with a blanket representation of Mr. Trump against the news media."

with a firm that represents a racist, misogynist, and xenophobe. When people choose to work with him, they are helping to enable hate," the message read. "Effective today, Harder Mirell & Abrams LLP no longer represents [the company] or any of its subsidiaries."

Mirell, who hadn't yet informed Harder of his plans to leave, angrily forwarded him the email. "Wow, very sorry about that," Harder responded. (Harder told me that the company that fired the firm, "like Mirell's other clients, paid the firm very little money, was extremely left-wing politically, and obviously ultra-sensitive. It did not bother me that the client chose to leave, or that Mirell left soon after.")

Abrams, who had previously voiced concerns about Harder's work for Trump and was eyeing a new career, soon left, too. The firm was renamed Harder LLP.

Over the next few years, Harder would pocket at least $4.4 million in fees from the Trump campaign and its Make America Great Again PAC. The attorney would begin to describe himself in almost messianic terms. His role, he wrote in his memoir, was "to act as a force for good and to conquer evil." He said he supported the First Amendment and "responsible media," but he viewed his job as vanquishing "the Dark Side" of journalism.

A pattern would soon emerge—one that would show up not only in Harder's portfolio of clients and cases but also in those of other lawyers who specialized in pursuing defamation lawsuits on behalf of the rich and powerful. There would often be a couple of cases with sympathetic clients. It was easy to cringe at a tabloid tarring someone as a prostitute or a secretly recorded sex tape being leaked to a boundary-pushing website. Helping such clients arguably fit within the good-versus-evil worldview that Harder liked to espouse. But those cases tended to be the exceptions. Lawyers like Harder were often plying their craft on behalf of unsavory individuals, and they were doing so in ways that, if they succeeded, would help their clients escape accountability for their past misdeeds and potentially continue to engage in terrible behavior. ("You act like you know my firm's clientele, but you don't know them at all,"

Harder emailed me. "On the contrary, you are cherry-picking the few controversial clients and presenting them as if they were the norm. They were not the norm—they were the exception to the norm.")

For example, in the fall of 2016, Harder was hired by Fox News president Roger Ailes and his wife to threaten *New York* magazine, which was in the process of exposing how Ailes had engaged in sexual harassment and intimidation of female employees—allegations that would lead to his ouster from the cable network he had created. Harder warned *New York* that Ailes might sue and that the magazine therefore must preserve documents, emails, and other records related to its reporting about the Fox president.* It was the type of threat that, especially when it was promptly leaked to the media, put other news organizations on notice that they should be careful about digging into Ailes.

Not long after, *New York Times* reporters Jodi Kantor and Megan Twohey were working on an investigation into Hollywood mogul Harvey Weinstein's history of sexual harassment and assault. Weinstein hired Harder, who dashed off another round of threats. In an eighteen-page letter to the *Times'* in-house counsel, David McCraw, Harder warned that lying, vengeful women were tricking the newspaper into defaming a good man. "My client would likely incur more than $100 million in damages from your false story," Harder wrote. "Should you publish it, he would have no alternative but to hold NYT legally responsible for those damages."

The *Times* published its piece, which helped ignite the #MeToo movement. Weinstein ended up in prison.

Harder told me that he dropped Weinstein as a client "as soon as I practically could" after he realized the extent of his behavior. Yet even after the *Times* published its bombshell—which quoted prominent actresses accusing Weinstein of sexual misconduct and revealed, among other things, that he had reached settlements with at least eight women to resolve sexual-harassment and other claims—Harder declared in a public statement that the piece was "saturated with false and defamatory

---

* Harder said he only wrote that one letter for Ailes, at a time when he was maintaining his innocence.

statements. . . . We sent the *Times* the facts and evidence, but they ignored it and rushed to publish. We are preparing the lawsuit now."* There was no lawsuit. The real audience for his bluster might have been *The New Yorker*, which was putting the finishing touches on its own devastating investigation. Indeed, only days earlier, Harder had written to the magazine, accusing the reporter Ronan Farrow of "an irresolvable conflict of interest" because Weinstein's company had worked with Woody Allen, who was accused of sexually assaulting Farrow's sister. "Mr. Farrow is entitled to his private anger," Harder wrote, "but no publisher should allow those personal feelings to create and pursue a baseless and defamatory story from his personal animus."

Harder sometimes did more than threaten. He sued, too—often targeting independent journalists and those working for relatively small publications. There were multiple lawsuits against a blogger on behalf of a Florida investor whom the Securities and Exchange Commission would later charge with fraud. There was a suit against a reporter for *The Deal*, a finance publication, on behalf of an investment firm that was having problems with regulators. (Harder tried to use a subpoena to unmask the reporter's sources.)

And in January 2017, shortly before Trump was inaugurated, Harder filed a $15 million lawsuit against the award-winning website *Techdirt* on behalf of Shiva Ayyadurai, who claimed to have created the world's first email program. In a series of articles, *Techdirt* had called out Ayyadurai's "bogus" assertions to have invented email, which had existed in various forms before he came along. Harder had previously sued Gawker for its pieces debunking Ayyadurai's legacy; that suit had settled along with the rest of Harder's Gawker litigation. On the same day that settlement was announced, Harder had filed the complaint against *Techdirt*.

Techdirt's founder and editor, Mike Masnick, exuded a renegade, irreverent vibe online, but he was scared. "This is not a fight about who

---

* Harder claimed to me that the *Times* investigation was "largely based on a 7-year-old letter by a plaintiff's lawyer trying to get the most money she could for a client," accusations that Harder said had been refuted. That greatly understates the breadth of the *Times*' reporting.

invented email," Masnick wrote to readers. "This is a fight about whether or not our legal system will silence independent publications for publishing opinions that public figures do not like. And here's the thing: this fight could very well be the end of *Techdirt*, even if we are completely on the right side of the law." That apparently was what Ayyadurai—who at the time was mounting a long-shot campaign for a US Senate seat in Massachusetts—was hoping; he tweeted that *Techdirt* "need to be shut-down for their FAKE NEWS."

Techdirt had an insurance policy that covered the website if it got sued for libel, but the protection kicked in only after the policyholder paid a hefty deductible. *Techdirt* faced out-of-pocket legal costs in the ballpark of $25,000. Masnick told me that he struggled to make payroll. Just as worrisome, he found himself in the unaccustomed position of walking on eggshells. "Each time I write a story, I have to think, *Will I get sued over this?* no matter how sure I am about what I am writing," he said. Indeed, would-be litigants suddenly began coming out of the woodwork, threatening to sue unless *Techdirt* deleted or modified articles. The stress at times was so overpowering that Masnick couldn't write. The volume of stories on *Techdirt* declined by a third.

A judge eventually dismissed Ayyadurai's lawsuit, but Harder appealed, and another twenty months of legal wrangling ensued before a settlement was reached in 2019. Fourteen old articles would be updated with a link to Ayyadurai's website. No money changed hands. Yet *Techdirt* would pay a steep price. Its libel insurer refused to renew its policy. Masnick lined up a new package, but its premiums and deductible were about four times as expensive—a penalty that *Techdirt* would continue paying into the indefinite future.

The experience scarred Masnick, who years later still struggled to speak about the personal toll the case had exacted. Yet he had realized from the outset that he was fortunate to possess years of experience, a loyal audience, and excellent lawyers. Plenty of upstart journalists "are facing these same chilling effects every single day without the kind of support structure that we've had," he told an audience in 2017, doing his best to choke back tears. "In some sense, as horrible as this has been, we are actually in a lucky position compared to so many others."

A COUPLE OF WORKHORSES

T hanks to Hulk Hogan and Melania Trump, Charles Harder had become famous. In late 2016, the journalist Jason Zengerle branded him as "perhaps the greatest threat in the United States to journalists, the First Amendment, and the very notion of a free press." This was a bit hyperbolic—in part because Harder was by no means the only lawyer seeking to weaponize libel laws. His success against Gawker had helped set in motion a transformation in which libel law would go from being a backwater to a bustling growth business.

The week before Trump first vowed to "open up" libel laws, New York University held an alumni event in Washington, DC, entitled "Women in and of the World." Onstage, sitting before a purple, NYU-branded backdrop, five female graduates shared stories of how they'd climbed toward the top of their respected professions. There was a Broadway producer. A senior official in a federal agency. Two directors of think tanks. Then it was the last speaker's turn.

"My name is Libby Locke," she began. "So, I am a defamation lawyer. What does that mean? I sue the media for a living." She flashed a big smile and laughed. "The defamation business is booming these days!" She laughed again.

Locke had reason to be happy. Less than two years earlier, she and another lawyer, Tom Clare, had founded their own law firm that specialized in suing people and news organizations for libel. Locke had been only thirty-five; her rise had been rapid. This partly reflected the fact that she'd known from early on that she wanted to be a lawyer. Nor had it hurt that she'd had a distaste for the media for quite some time as well. Locke traced it to a Capitol Hill internship after her junior year at NYU. Her job included compiling press clippings for Senator Daniel Patrick Moynihan. "You see the news being made throughout the course of the summer, and you see the difference between what actually happens and how it gets reported," she told the NYU audience.

A quintessential overachiever, Locke liked to tell the story of how, as a junior at the same Georgia high school that Marjorie Taylor Greene attended a few years earlier, she had scoured a book of college rankings to find the best schools willing to admit students before their senior year. The highest-ranked school was NYU. She arrived in New York at age seventeen and split her time between schoolwork, the diving team, and roaming the city. After a year postgraduation as a paralegal at a giant New York firm, she enrolled in the night program at Georgetown University's law school. Classmates remembered her as sharp, serious, and driven, the type who sat at the front of lecture halls and whose frequent participation sometimes induced eye rolls. "From the moment we met, it was very clear that she was one of the sharpest people in our class," one friend said. "She seemed like she had something to prove to others," another student observed. Among the mostly liberal class, Locke was a rare outspoken conservative. She became president of the law school's Federalist Society chapter.

Locke married one of her Georgetown classmates, a Marine named Spencer Fisher. After a clerkship with a federal judge in Mississippi, she landed a job at the giant international law firm of Kirkland & Ellis. That was where she met Tom Clare.

Tall, slim, and handsome, with graying hair and a pilot's license that he'd had since college, Clare was nine years older than Locke and a Kirkland partner. He generally handled two types of cases. One was run-of-the-mill business litigation. The other was taking on the media.

Clare had gotten into this latter line of work by way of his mentor, a senior Kirkland partner named Tom Yannucci. Yannucci was not always the most organized, and so the hyperdiligent Clare, who stood ramrod straight, was an ideal complement. Clare was a bit bland—"a piece of white bread," a colleague called him—but he was a workhorse, sometimes billing about three thousand hours a year. Plus, Yannucci and Clare were both "double domers," having received their undergraduate and law degrees from Notre Dame. (Clare had even married his college girl-friend on the university's campus.)

In addition to being chairman of one of the world's richest, most pow-erful law firms, Yannucci was a minor legend of the media bar. Clare worked with him on high-profile defamation cases, including one that culminated in their client, Chiquita Brands, receiving more than $10 million and a series of front-page apologies from the *Cincinnati Enquirer* (whose reporter later pleaded guilty to breaking into Chiquita's voice-mail system). Yannucci taught Clare about using threatening letters to get publishers large and small to back off from negative pieces. When that didn't work, Yannucci's squad would sometimes write to the com-mittees that handed out journalism prizes, urging them not to bestow awards for articles that investigated his clients. Clare excelled at this type of work—he could crank out intimidating letters at lightning speed—and it captured his professional heart.

Locke quickly gravitated toward Clare, who took her into his orbit. (She also worked with lawyers such as Ken Starr, the former judge and independent counsel who had joined Kirkland.) Clare was impressed with her drive; she sometimes billed more than 2,500 hours a year, and she twice returned weeks early from maternity leave "because of her dedication to her work and clients," as Clare and Locke later told me. Early on, the pair teamed up on a case defending an insurance company as it tried to avoid paying out on homeowners' policies after Hurricane Katrina. Then he invited her to work with him on a media case. "I was hooked," Locke recalled. She took on more cases, utilizing the tactics that Yannucci had taught Clare and that Clare now taught Locke. Her profile on Kirkland's website listed achievements including having "deterred" *Vanity Fair* from running a long article and having used a "letter-writing campaign" to persuade *The Dr. Oz Show* not to air a segment it had already recorded. "I fell in love with this practice," Locke told the NYU audience. It was the "perfect intersection of law, media, and politics."

The problem was that media law at Kirkland was far from a priority. The firm made hundreds of millions of dollars a year representing blue-chip

companies, and some of those companies owned newspapers and TV networks, and the last thing Kirkland needed was Clare and Locke suing or
threatening such clients. What was more, some partners distrusted Locke,
noting her propensity to needlessly rev up clients in the apparent hopes of
getting them to file lawsuits that had slim chances of success. Others resented what they saw as her competitive and territorial behavior, including
bad-mouthing her perceived rivals to Kirkland partners. (When I asked her
about this, Locke said that considering her subsequent success, "the joke is
on those who thought so little of my work and the practice.")

One night in 2013, Clare and Locke went out for beers after work. By
then, rumors were swirling inside the firm that they were having an affair.
The pair told me that the rumors were false: "As is unfortunately the case
for many professional men and women who work together, less talented female lawyers started to speculate and gossip that there must be a romantic
relationship." Regardless, associates were complaining to senior partners
that the supposed relationship was creating the impression that the way to
get ahead at Kirkland was to cozy up to your superior, especially since Clare
was often responsible for reviewing Locke's performance. "It was really
eating away at the idea that we're a meritocracy," one partner said.*

Accounts differ about what happened next. Several people said that lawyers on Kirkland's management committee decided that they had to draw
a line: either the relationship ended, or Clare or Locke would have to leave
Kirkland. Clare and Locke denied that either of them was asked to leave.
But, they said, "Kirkland did retaliate against Libby after these rumors
surfaced, including by removing her from several of her cases while allowing Tom to remain on his. . . . We found this incredibly hypocritical given
the incestuous nature" of other romantic relationships among Kirkland
lawyers. (Showcasing their smashmouth tactics, Clare and Locke rattled
off the names of nearly twenty Kirkland lawyers who they said were in
relationships with colleagues, though my understanding is that few if any
had their performances reviewed by the people they were sleeping with.)

---

* Locke said that while some Kirkland attorneys were great, she was surprised by the "serious
lack of quality in lawyers at all levels" of the firm. The bigger threat to a meritocracy, she
and Clare said, was "Kirkland's hiring, retaining, and promoting associates who were politically connected, including family members of judges."

In any case, over drinks that night, the two attorneys discussed a new possibility, one that would give Locke a fresh start and resolve their frustrations with missing out on defamation assignments because of what they saw as Kirkland's rigidity. "What if we were to do this on our own?" Locke blurted. They could start their own law firm. She wasn't entirely serious—or was she? They fantasized about which of their colleagues they'd like to take with them, had a laugh about it. It slowly dawned on them that maybe this wasn't the worst idea.

It didn't take long for Locke to go all in. Both of her parents had been entrepreneurs—her father had started a small insurance brokerage, and her mother had a business breeding Labrador retrievers—so it felt natural. Clare was more risk-averse, though he eventually got on board. When they were picking out a town house for their offices in Alexandria, Virginia—a DC suburb near where both lived with their spouses and children—they negotiated a six-month escape clause in the lease. "Tom thought we were going to be standing in the bread line, and I thought we were going to be wildly successful," Locke would reminisce.

On their last day at Kirkland, the pair had farewell drinks at the Old Ebbitt Grill, on the ground floor of Kirkland's offices and across the street from the Treasury Department and White House. Locke had written something for the occasion, in which she predicted that her Kirkland colleagues would soon be jealously watching their new venture soar and that she wouldn't hire many of her former colleagues "because their work wasn't good enough." The lawyers in the crowded bar gaped at her.

Clare Locke LLP opened for business in March 2014. Kirkland issued an internal memo wishing them well and saying it would partner with Clare Locke on some existing client matters.

But things got off to a rocky start. Clare Locke's employees woke up early one morning to find a short email from Locke's husband, Spencer Fisher, in their inboxes. *I have discovered that Tom and Libby's relationship exceeds the confines of a corporate partnership*, he'd written.* This

---

* Fisher wouldn't answer my questions about the email. He praised Locke as "not only a brilliant lawyer, but also a compassionate and giving person [with] a strong sense of ethics and responsibility."

had set off quite the controversy—"Holy fucking shit!" one recipient exclaimed to their spouse after reading the message, while others wondered if they should even show up to the office that day—and not just for purposes of water-cooler gossip. Both owners had insisted to employees that they were not an item, assurances that Clare repeated as he tried to calm the waters the day of Fisher's email. Some of the firm's lawyers told me that they probably wouldn't have joined Clare Locke had they known about the founders' relationship, which they said eroded trust and made it harder to communicate candidly with their bosses.

Around the time of Fisher's email, Clare's wife kicked him out of their Virginia home. In a divorce filing, she accused him of engaging "in an improper relationship with another woman" and of having "basically deserted and abandoned the marriage relationship." (In his own filing, Clare denied abandoning the marriage.)

Some of Locke's colleagues quickly came to dislike her office demeanor. In 2015, an administrative employee informed Clare and Locke that she was leaving the firm, in part because of Locke's treatment of subordinates. (Among other things, Locke had criticized the employee in a performance review for not being in the office enough as she tended to her mother, who was dying of breast cancer.) Locke commissioned an examination of the employee's computer, which turned up text messages in which the employee had complained to a friend that Locke was crazy. Clare Locke fired off a formal cease-and-desist letter warning the ex-staffer of litigation if she continued questioning Locke's sanity—an escalation that stunned lawyers at the firm.

The good news was that, freed from the constraints of a giant law firm, Clare and Locke could pursue the types of cases they wanted. Eight months after the firm opened, it landed a client who would vault the lawyers into the national spotlight and allow them to claim that they were defending victims of the malicious media, in much the same way that Charles Harder had won justice for someone whom a reckless tabloid had branded as a prostitute.

On the morning of November 19, 2014, *Rolling Stone* magazine had published an explosive article on its website. Headlined "A Rape on

Campus," it purported to tell the harrowing story of a University of Virginia freshman named "Jackie," who claimed to have been gang-raped at a frat party two years earlier. The nearly nine-thousand-word "special report"—which was teased on the cover of *Rolling Stone*'s December issue, alongside a wild-haired photo of the rock star Dave Grohl—painted an ugly picture of UVA. Several parties in particular bore the brunt. One was the fraternity Phi Kappa Psi, where the rape had supposedly taken place. Another was Nicole Eramo, a dean who oversaw the school's sexual misconduct board. *Rolling Stone* depicted her as more interested in preserving UVA's reputation than cracking down on what the magazine dubbed "the campus rape epidemic." To ram the point home, the article included an illustration of Eramo smiling while an unidentified woman—presumably a rape victim—held her head in her hands and protesters waved signs saying things like Stop Victim Blaming.

Shortly after its publication, the article began to unravel. *Rolling Stone*, it turned out, had relied almost exclusively on Jackie, whose hole-ridden account the magazine had barely fact-checked. Seeking to restore trust, *Rolling Stone* enlisted a team from Columbia University's journalism school to do a postmortem. Their report documented a stunning breakdown of basic journalism standards. The magazine retracted the article and apologized to readers.

Even before that happened, defamation lawyers had been circling. Rod Smolla signed on to sue *Rolling Stone* on behalf of Phi Kappa Psi; he eventually secured a $1.65 million settlement. One of Eramo's friends knew Clare from his days at Kirkland, and within a week or two of the article's publication, she had hired Clare Locke. In the spring of 2015, the firm filed a lawsuit seeking $7.5 million in damages. "A case like this comes along once in a lifetime," Clare excitedly told colleagues.

Given the high profile of *Rolling Stone*'s screwup, the lawsuit instantly elevated the stature of the young law firm. "We were the first to file a lawsuit against *Rolling Stone*," Locke boasted to the audience at NYU. In October 2016, the trial was held in the redbrick federal courthouse in Charlottesville, Virginia, less than a mile from UVA's campus. Barely seven months had passed since the Gawker case in Florida showed everyone that an angry jury could doom a media company. In other words, the stakes were high.

The trial ran more than two weeks. Near the end, Clare addressed the ten jurors. The flawed article was not an accident; it was the result of *Rolling Stone*'s preordained agenda. "Once they decided what the article was going to be about, it didn't matter what the facts were," he said. His point was that even though the court had deemed Eramo a public figure, *Rolling Stone* had acted with reckless disregard for the truth—enough to constitute "actual malice" under *New York Times v. Sullivan*. The lawyer for *Rolling Stone* countered that it was not unreasonable for the magazine to have believed Jackie's account. After all, even UVA administrators had taken her allegations seriously. But there was no disputing *Rolling Stone*'s long list of factual and procedural errors, so thoroughly catalogued by the Columbia journalists.

After twenty hours of deliberation, the jurors returned with a verdict: *Rolling Stone* was liable for defaming Eramo. And a few days after that— barely twenty-four hours before Donald Trump won the presidential election—the jury ordered the defendants to pay Eramo $3 million in damages. Clare Locke's first trial had ended in a resounding victory. "It feels very good to have a jury of Nicole's peers come back and vindicate what we have known from Day One, and so we are very pleased," Locke told a local TV station.

Here was a vivid illustration of the *Sullivan* framework in action. As a public figure, Eramo had to clear a high bar to prevail in court. Yet she and her lawyers had overcome that hurdle by presenting clear evidence that *Rolling Stone* had acted with, at the very least, recklessness. And a jury had awarded her millions of dollars. The system worked.

Going forward, Clare and Locke would publicly define their practice around having defended someone whom an irresponsible magazine had wrongly accused of covering up a brutal rape. But that was only one case. Much of Clare Locke's business wasn't nearly as palatable.

8

A FORM OF EXTREMISM

In October 2013, Cherri Foytlin and Karen Savage wrote a piece for the *Huffington Post* about a scientific consulting firm called ChemRisk. Crews cleaning up the vast Deepwater Horizon oil spill in the Gulf of Mexico were getting sick, and the energy giant BP, which was responsible for the catastrophe, had hired ChemRisk to investigate whether the illnesses were linked to unsafe exposure to chemicals. The consulting firm had concluded that the exposures were well within legal limits and that BP wasn't to blame for any sicknesses.

Foytlin had spent years as a features writer for a small newspaper in Louisiana. Shortly after the 2010 spill, BP had invited her and other journalists on a brief boat excursion to admire the great job the oil company was doing to clean up its mess. Sure enough, the Gulf and the nearby wetlands appeared mostly oil-free; the only remaining signs of trouble in the small area they toured was the occasional reed with a trace of black goo.

Foytlin figured she should talk to some people who weren't on the oil company's payroll. She returned a week later without BP's chaperones. A local fisherman agreed to take her out on the water to see the carnage for herself. Unlike BP's tour, this one revealed an oil-drenched wasteland. The chemical stench burned Foytlin's eyes. The Gulf waters were smooth, a thick layer of oil calming any disturbances. There were no signs of life—not even insects. Finally, the fisherman spotted something in the water, and he steered the craft toward a pelican. The creature was smothered in oil. The fisherman scooped it into the boat, and he and Foytlin watched it die. When they returned to shore, they buried the bird on the beach, and the burly fisherman recited a quiet prayer. They both cried.

That night, as her six children slept, Foytlin scrubbed oily grime off her skin and out of her hair. She couldn't stop thinking about what she'd just seen, and she couldn't shake a gnawing feeling of guilt. *What have you done to stop this?* she asked herself, staring into the bathroom mirror. *How are you going to be able to look your kids in the eye?*

Thus began Foytlin's transformation from a traditional reporter into an environmental activist. Soon, she walked from New Orleans to Washington, DC—more than 1,200 miles—to raise awareness about the ongoing effects of the oil spill. In the capital, she happened to meet Karen Savage, who was there urging federal officials to do more.

Savage was a middle school math teacher in Boston's Roxbury neighborhood. She, too, was outraged by what she saw as the tendency of big companies to jeopardize future generations' ability to inhabit Earth. Not long after meeting Foytlin, Savage was researching the aftereffects of the Deepwater Horizon disaster, and she read that BP had hired an independent consulting firm to make sure cleanup workers weren't being endangered. She looked up the study that ChemRisk had produced and reached out to one of its authors to arrange an interview. A ChemRisk spokesman, Richard Keil, joined the call, and he hardly let the author speak. At the end of the interview, Keil retroactively tried to prevent Savage from quoting anything that had been said. To Savage, this was a red flag. So was the fact that Keil appeared to have previously done work for BP. *So much for ChemRisk being independent,* she thought.

Further research soon revealed what struck Savage as a pattern of ChemRisk skewing science to help polluters. A 2005 article in the *Wall Street Journal*, for example, had detailed how the consulting firm had sought to cast doubt on scientific research about the health dangers posed by drinking water tainted by a type of metal called chromium-6. (ChemRisk's client was the utility PG&E, which was being sued by residents of a California town—a legal battle immortalized in the movie *Erin Brockovich*.)

Savage thought this was newsworthy. Foytlin was a guest blogger for the *Huffington Post*, and they wrote a piece together for the site. Their article questioned the credibility of ChemRisk's research. They quoted an outside expert critiquing the firm's methodology in the BP study. And, referring to the consulting firm's chromium-6 work, they described how "ChemRisk has a long, and on at least one occasion fraudulent, history of defending big polluters using questionable ethics to help their clients avoid legal responsibility for their actions."

Foytlin and Savage didn't expect the article to attract much notice. But that evening, Keil sent an angry letter to the *Huffington Post* demanding a retraction and warning that he was looping in ChemRisk's "libel counsel . . . for any and all corrective measures they might seek to take." An editor at the site forwarded the message to Foytlin. She replied that there was nothing inaccurate in what she and Savage had written. The *Huffington Post* kept the story online.

Six months passed, and nothing happened, and Foytlin and Savage basically forgot about the matter. But ChemRisk did not forget. It hired Clare Locke. In April 2014, a month after the law firm was founded, it filed a defamation lawsuit on ChemRisk's behalf against Foytlin and Savage. Neither woman had been sued before. Foytlin had just walked to her car to retrieve gifts for her daughter, who was celebrating her tenth birthday, when she was greeted by a stranger who handed her a bunch of documents and told her she'd been sued. Another man tried to serve Savage in her eighth-grade classroom in Boston.

Foytlin and Savage were both single mothers. Neither had money to hire a lawyer. So they were unprepared when, not long after the suit was filed, a representative of ChemRisk wrote to Foytlin and asked her to come at a certain date and time to the Frog City truck stop and casino, near her home in Rayne, Louisiana, and to please bring all of her electronic devices to be handed over to the lawyers. ("Even the can opener?" Savage joked when she heard this.) Foytlin and Savage consulted a law professor at Loyola University in New Orleans, and he advised them to ignore the letter and to not go to the truck stop, with or without a can opener.

I met Foytlin and Savage in the fall of 2023, when they were attending a climate rally in downtown Manhattan. A large band of protesters had stationed themselves outside the Federal Reserve Bank of New York and were banging drums, waving signs, and chanting "tax the rich." The police blared a recorded message warning that the protesters would be arrested if they didn't clear the sidewalk. Nobody budged. The police began handcuffing people and escorting them to waiting buses. Savage took photos, and Foytlin yelled at the cops. She was wearing a jean jacket, and her long hair was braided in a thick ponytail. She told me she'd been arrested more than a dozen times since she became an activist. I asked her which was scarier: being arrested or being sued. Foytlin didn't hesitate. Getting arrested, she said, was predictable. It would mean a day or two away from her family. Getting sued had been much worse. The scariest thing was her financial vulnerability. Would ChemRisk and its lawyers try to take her house?

Savage felt similarly. She had four kids and had been living paycheck to paycheck. One of her children had asked if ChemRisk was going to seize their stuff. "We don't have anything for them to take," she replied.

"But you just got a new bed!" the child exclaimed. It wasn't even a bed—it was just a mattress—and Savage assured the child that not even Clare Locke or ChemRisk would waste their time trying to snatch it away.

Unable to afford a lawyer, it was up to Foytlin and Savage to respond to the lawsuit. Savage spent hours drafting court motions and laboring to mimic the idiosyncratic formatting that she saw in legal briefs that she looked up online. Eventually, a mutual acquaintance directed them toward an attorney named John Reichman. He immediately sensed that the lawsuit was "an attempt at intimidation," he told me. "They wanted to make an example out of Cherri and Karen. Rather than pick on the *Wall Street Journal*, which would be lawyered up . . . they figured this would be easy pickings." ChemRisk's goal, Reichman believed, was to deter anyone who might consider criticizing the company in the future.

ChemRisk's lawsuit was filed in state court in Massachusetts. This would prove to be a strategic mistake—and Foytlin and Savage's salvation.

Massachusetts had what is known as an anti-SLAPP law. In the 1980s, two professors at the University of Denver had coined the phrase "strategic lawsuits against public participation," or SLAPPs, to describe cases that were aimed at punishing people who spoke out on matters of public concern. The two professors had firsthand experience. George Pring, a lawyer, had defended environmental activists whom polluters had sued for speaking out. Penelope Canan had been threatened with litigation for criticizing a publicly funded research program. They quickly realized that this was part of a much broader trend; thousands of such suits had been filed since the 1970s, for offenses like writing a letter to the editor, circulating a petition, or speaking at a school board meeting. The goal of such lawsuits wasn't necessarily to prevail in court. It was to scare people from speaking their minds, thus stifling public debate—a phenomenon, they wrote in their 1996 book *SLAPPs*, that "has potentially grave consequences for the future of representative democracy."

Since then, quite a few states, including Massachusetts, had passed laws to discourage such litigation. Among other things, the laws made it easier for defendants to get the suits dismissed—they only had to show that they had a reasonable factual basis for what they had written—and required plaintiffs to cover their opponents' legal bills in certain circumstances.

In 2015, Reichman filed a motion to have the ChemRisk suit thrown out on SLAPP grounds. He argued that Foytlin and Savage had a solid basis for everything they'd written. A judge rejected the motion. Reichman appealed. The following year, Massachusetts' Supreme Judicial Court agreed to reconsider the ruling. Nearly two years had passed since ChemRisk had sued. Now the tide was perhaps turning in Foytlin and Savage's favor.

ChemRisk's lawyers seemed to feel the shift. Two days after the high court decided to hear Reichman's SLAPP motion, Clare Locke submitted paperwork to terminate the lawsuit, saying it no longer made business sense to pursue it. It was like a baseball team trying to cancel a game just as their opponent was poised to score the winning run. Foytlin and Savage sought to prevent ChemRisk from backing out; they wanted the company to have to pay Reichman's bills, and they hoped to fish around in its files during the discovery process. A judge sided with them: the case wouldn't be terminated until the higher court had ruled on the SLAPP motion.

That ruling came on Valentine's Day in 2017, a month into the Trump administration. The court wrote that Foytlin and Savage had clearly

articulated why they had believed—and continued to believe—that
what they'd written was accurate. They had included citations to academic publications and newspaper articles that had said largely the same
thing and yet had not provoked lawsuits from ChemRisk. The seven-
judge panel booted ChemRisk's lawsuit and invited Reichman to recover
his legal fees from ChemRisk. (He ultimately negotiated to collect about
$150,000.)

Free speech advocates cheered the ruling. "This is a terrific decision,
and it comes at a very important time, given the Trump presidency," an
American Civil Liberties Union official said. "This is an era when the
right to petition and the right to speak are going to need a lot of protection."

Foytlin and Savage were just relieved that it was over. "I was really
tired," Foytlin told me. "It's like carrying something very heavy for a
very long time." To celebrate, she took her kids bowling.

The defeat was nothing more than a speed bump for Clare Locke, which
was coming off its big *Rolling Stone* victory. The firm would line up
plenty of other clients.

There were abusive corporate executives and secretive hedge fund
kingpins. There was the fashion mogul and sexual predator Peter Nygard.
There was Elon Musk when he was accused of trying to have sex with
subordinates. (Clare Locke represented both Musk and one of the young
women he'd pursued.) There were Russian oligarchs, including the notorious Oleg Deripaska (more on him later).

There was the Sackler family, on whose behalf the law firm threatened
reporters and publishers who were revealing the family's role in spawning
the opioid epidemic. After Clare Locke learned that the journalist Patrick
Radden Keefe was working on a book about the Sacklers, based in part on
an article he'd written for *The New Yorker* two years earlier, Tom Clare
sought to torch his credibility with the magazine and his book publisher,
Doubleday. A fifteen-page letter to *The New Yorker* accused Keefe of "ignoring essential facts and creating a biased narrative." The magazine had
a fact-checker comb through all of Clare's allegations, which it concluded
lacked merit. But in a letter to Doubleday, Clare cited that fact-checking

exercise to suggest that the original article was wobbly. The tactics failed; Keefe had the Sacklers dead to rights, and Doubleday's lawyers were unfazed. The ensuing book, *Empire of Pain*, became an acclaimed bestseller. "I felt really lucky, because I have this rock-solid institutional support," Keefe told me.

There was Idaho billionaire Frank VanderSloot, a Republican mega-donor and, for many years, a staunch opponent of gay rights. (Among other things, he'd helped pay for billboards protesting a television station's plans to air a film about same-sex parents. The billboards said the government should not be "spending our tax dollars to bring the homosexual lifestyle into the classroom and introduce it to our children as being normal, right, acceptable, and good and an appropriate lifestyle for them or anyone else to be living.")* In 2012, after VanderSloot emerged as a leading donor to Mitt Romney's presidential campaign, *Mother Jones* magazine wrote a profile that described him as antigay. Lawyers at VanderSloot's health-products company, Melaleuca, demanded a retraction. The magazine rejected that request, but it did publicly correct some significant errors in the piece.

VanderSloot wasn't satisfied. He hired Clare (who at that point still worked at Kirkland & Ellis) and, shortly after Romney lost the election, filed a lawsuit in Idaho against *Mother Jones*. The magazine had libel insurance, but the out-of-pocket deductibles were significant, especially for a nonprofit on a shoestring budget. "It used to be that lawsuits were supposed to set the record straight," Monika Bauerlein, a top editor who was named as a defendant, told me. That's not what this was; *Mother Jones* had issued a correction and even offered VanderSloot the opportunity to share his thoughts with the magazine's readers. (He declined.) The litigation, Bauerlein said, seemed engineered "to inflict pain and make a public statement."

After seeing what had happened to Gawker, Bauerlein recognized that fighting the suit was risky. Maybe they should just cough up the $75,000 that VanderSloot was seeking. "Their strategy was to put us in a position

---

* VanderSloot later acknowledged that "gay people should have the same freedoms and rights as any other individual."

where the safest thing for us to do was disavow our reporting," she explained. But caving to billionaires wasn't in her DNA, any more than it had been in the *New York Times*' genes when a different bully, L. B. Sullivan, had sued over the Martin Luther King ad. *Mother Jones* would fight.

Finally, after more than two years of legal maneuvering, a state judge threw out the lawsuit on *Sullivan* grounds: VanderSloot was a public figure, and there was no evidence that the magazine had deliberately or recklessly manipulated the facts.

Regardless, the damage was done. *Mother Jones* had to shell out more than $600,000 to cover its legal bills, which it paid for out of a fund earmarked for new journalism projects. When it came time for *Mother Jones* to renew its libel insurance, the magazine's broker approached forty-two different insurers. Forty refused to even offer a quote. Ultimately, the magazine found an insurer, but its annual premiums more than doubled to $75,000, even as the amount of coverage dropped by a third. Its deductible soared to $150,000. "Even the most short-lived, frivolous case is a significant financial hit, because we have to pay all the costs under that deductible," Bauerlein said.

When the judge dismissed the lawsuit, she criticized *Mother Jones* for what she said was "mudslinging advertised as journalistic fearlessness." That was enough for VanderSloot and Clare Locke to declare victory. "My client has been totally vindicated," Clare asserted. For his part, VanderSloot announced the creation of the "Guardian of True Liberty Fund," which he said he was seeding with $1 million to finance other lawsuits against the media.

Finally, there was the strange case of Zambian banker Rajan Mahtani, who faced allegations (which he denied) of involvement in various crimes. A website called Zambia Reports was regularly posting items about Mahtani's supposed misdeeds. Mahtani hired Clare Locke, which in 2015 asked the website's hosting company to shut it down on the grounds that "it was continuously involved in character assassination," as Mahtani put it at the time.

When that didn't work, Clare Locke threatened to sue Zambia Reports, and in 2017, the website's publisher, James Kimer, agreed to remove hundreds of posts about Mahtani. It wasn't hard to understand why Mahtani wanted to silence Zambia Reports. Kimer was a Washington-based public relations executive who seemed to be operating Zambia Reports on behalf of a client. Mahtani and his allies suspected it was one of his political rivals.*

But what Clare Locke did next had nothing to do with Zambian politics. The law firm turned its attention to a website called OffshoreAlert. It had been founded decades earlier by the journalist David Marchant, who had dedicated his career to digging up documents about things like wealthy people and institutions hiding money. Marchant had built an automated system to alert him to interesting court filings and other official documents as soon as they appeared in online databases. These obscure records often provided insight into government investigations in parts of the world that weren't renowned for their transparency. They therefore were valuable to the lawyers, accountants, investigators, and investors who subscribed to OffshoreAlert.

Back in 2012, Marchant had received a notification about a new US government filing in federal court in Detroit. It pertained to a request for information that the Justice Department had received from the Zambian attorney general in connection with a criminal investigation into Mahtani. Marchant skimmed the document and then posted it, along with a single sentence summarizing its contents.

Years passed. Then, on March 13, 2018, Marchant received an email from Joseph Oliveri, a lawyer at Clare Locke. The subject line was "Time-Sensitive Legal Correspondence—Action Required." Oliveri said he was writing on behalf of Mahtani, "a Zambian businessman and philanthropist, regarding false and defamatory statements" published about him on OffshoreAlert. Oliveri said that those statements "appear to originate" in defamatory articles on Zambia Reports, which that site had removed under legal pressure. Oliveri demanded that OffshoreAlert immediately

---

* "I firmly reject that allegation," Kimer told me.

take down the Mahtani-related document from its website. Otherwise, he said, "Dr. Mahtani will take action to enforce his legal rights, including through legal action in all relevant jurisdictions and countries."

This was the kind of threat that years earlier would have terrified Marchant. Virtually from the moment OffshoreAlert had gone live back in 1997, he'd been besieged by legal threats. He'd been sued multiple times. At first, the threats and lawsuits had taken a severe toll. He'd burned hundreds of thousands of dollars on legal fees, which in some years exceeded his site's revenue. "I would get a knot in my stomach, and it would not go away," Marchant told me. He'd felt himself sliding into paranoia. Once, when a post had upset some powerful Russians, Marchant had been so rattled that he'd crashed on a friend's couch for a few nights. He'd been scared to turn on his car.

After a while, though, Marchant had realized that this was all part of an ugly game. Rich guys like Mahtani hired fancy lawyers to send threatening letters, and a certain percentage of those letters were likely to be received by journalists or others who didn't have the money or time or guts to fight back. They would cave. And that would make it worth it.

One source of respite came in 2010 with the passage of the SPEECH Act. Marchant had repeatedly faced lawsuits in foreign jurisdictions. Now, for the most part, he didn't need to bother responding. It was a huge relief—and he sent Rachel Ehrenfeld a letter to express his gratitude. The law "has made my life a lot easier and, as a result, OffshoreAlert can go about its business of professionally and responsibly exposing serious financial crime," he wrote. "So . . . thanks!"

By the time Clare Locke contacted him, Marchant's patience had long since expired. "To be crude about it, you want to take me on, you're fucked basically," he happily told me. "One thing I've learned is that you can't give them a millimeter. You can't be conciliatory because they'll trample all over you. So I treat them like shit." By which he meant two things. First, he would send responses drenched with sarcasm. Second, he would post the correspondence on his website, along with a link back to the original piece that had elicited the threat in the first place. "If you write me a dick letter, I'm going to publish it, and everyone's going to think you're a dick," he explained.

A couple of hours after Oliveri sent his email, Marchant responded. He noted that Clare Locke had no legal basis for demanding the removal of a document written by the US government and posted on a public US government website. In any case, Marchant pointed out, the statute of limitations for any libel claim on a post from 2012 had long since expired. He added: "Feel free to follow through on your threat to sue. I look forward to not only defeating your client but also reporting about the case to our worldwide readership." Then he posted the whole exchange online.

Marchant had called the lawyers' bluff. He never heard back from Mahtani, Oliveri, or anyone else at Clare Locke.

After moving into the White House, Trump amped up his attacks on the press and renewed his calls to loosen libel laws. He had a powerful incentive to do so. He and his staff were often lying, and reporters were calling them out. Just about every major US news organization was investigating whether the Trump campaign had colluded with the Russian government to illicitly win the election. You could agree or disagree with the way the media was handling the norm-busting Trump presidency, but there was no question that the coverage was aggressive and at times hostile. Inside the White House, delegitimizing the media became an existential priority.

In February 2017, Trump called journalists "the enemy of the people," to raucous applause from conservatives at a conference outside Washington. "The fake news doesn't tell the truth," he thundered. "It doesn't and never will represent the people, and we're going to do something about it." Less than three hours later, the White House blocked the *New York Times* and other news outlets from attending a press briefing in the West Wing. That was just the start. Trump would publicly ponder revoking TV networks' broadcast licenses, applaud violence against journalists, and reiterate his pledge to make it easier to sue the media, calling existing libel laws "a sham and a disgrace."

In April 2017, Trump's chief of staff, Reince Priebus, was a guest on ABC's Sunday morning talk show. He was asked about Trump's vow to open up libel laws. "I think it's something that we've looked at," Priebus responded. "How that gets executed and whether that goes anywhere is a different story."

Even if Trump lacked the power to do much, the White House's flirtation with a media crackdown put the issue of libel laws in the spotlight. Libby Locke began hearing from reporters, TV bookers, and conference organizers who wanted her to weigh in on the debate. She was a natural choice. There weren't all that many lawyers out there who'd been in the headlines for successfully suing the media and were willing to argue that Trump was right and *New York Times v. Sullivan* was wrong. Rod Smolla had nuanced views. Harder didn't—almost from the moment he won the Gawker suit, he'd been telling people he thought the Supreme Court should abandon *Sullivan* and the actual malice doctrine—but for all his ambition and good-versus-evil bravado, he was a bit camera-shy. Locke was not.

The afternoon after Priebus made his comments, CNN aired a short debate about libel laws. Locke was there to take the president's side, rolling out talking points that she and Clare had honed during the *Rolling Stone* trial.

"Libby, you say the White House has a point here when it comes to wanting to change libel laws," the CNN anchor Pamela Brown asked. "Why?"

"That is absolutely right," Locke answered. "Let's be clear: The First Amendment is important. It guarantees a free press but doesn't guarantee a consequence-free press. The media has a megaphone that can harm and damage a person's or company's reputation with one news story."

The segment lasted only a few minutes, but Locke managed to unfurl a multifaceted critique of *Sullivan*, which she said had encouraged news organizations to act recklessly because they had no fear of losing a lawsuit. "They can say things with impunity and ruin people's lives and reputations." She went on: "These kinds of protections are what allow them to run amok. There's less of a fear in newsrooms and editing rooms for making sure you get it right."

Locke had witnessed a huge series of blunders at *Rolling Stone*, but the verdict against the magazine and its reporter belied her claim about the media enjoying impunity. (So did the fact that she had built a thriving law firm that sued and threatened news outlets.) Locke didn't cite any evidence to back up her assertion that news organizations or bloggers or anyone else acted recklessly because they viewed *Sullivan* as a get-out-of-jail-free card. Yes, reporters sometimes were sloppy or irresponsible. They sometimes wrote biased articles or harmed innocent people's reputations. But was this a product of thinking they were legally invincible? A simpler explanation was that journalists are humans, and humans make mistakes.

The other guest on the CNN show was the *Washington Post* columnist Erik Wemple. He was known for his willingness to call out reporters and news outlets for their mistakes, including *Rolling Stone* in the UVA case. Wemple's wife happened to be the *Mother Jones* reporter whose article about Frank VanderSloot led to Clare Locke's lawsuit against the magazine, but he respected Locke as a smart, ambitious, "take no prisoners" lawyer. This, however, was the first time he'd heard anyone claim that *Sullivan*'s actual malice standard incentivized recklessness. It struck Wemple as nonsense. "I don't think you understand how carefully we do take our job to get things straight and to protect people that we're writing about," he told Locke on CNN.

In the years ahead, Locke would keep banging this drum, blaming *Sullivan* for what many conservatives viewed as the media's descent into "fake news"—an argument that would soon begin to resonate with a very powerful audience. Six years later, Wemple still remembered how he felt after hearing Locke initially voice this claim. "I thought she was very out there," he told me. "This to me was certainly a form of extremism."

COORDINATED CAMPAIGNS OF HARASSMENT

t was a powerful combination. The president of the United States was attacking the media in incendiary terms. And two upstart law firms—Harder LLP and Clare Locke—seemed to be getting results by taking (or at least threatening to take) people to court for what they wrote. Inspired by their successes, lawyers and their clients all over the country would soon join the rush, inundating the media and many others who publicly criticized the powerful with a flood of libel lawsuits and an even greater deluge of legal ultimatums.

Trumpists and other conservatives led the charge, galloping down a path that had been cleared decades earlier by L. B. Sullivan and his Alabama brethren and had now been retrodden by Harder, Clare, and Locke.

Joe Arpaio—the former sheriff of Maricopa County, Arizona, who had once orchestrated the arrests of journalists who investigated his real estate dealings—sued the *New York Times* for about $150 million in 2018 for an opinion piece that called him "a truly sadistic man." Two months later, he sued CNN, the *Huffington Post*, and *Rolling Stone* for saying he was a convicted felon, when in fact he was only convicted of a misdemeanor. Both lawsuits were dismissed thanks to *Sullivan* and the actual malice standard.

Don Blankenship, a disgraced coal company executive and failed Senate candidate, sued sixteen news organizations and journalists for defamation for falsely saying he, too, was a felon. Like Arpaio, Blankenship had actually been convicted of a misdemeanor and sentenced to a year in prison for conspiring to violate mine-safety standards after an explosion at a West Virginia coal mine killed twenty-nine people. A procession of federal judges ruled against Blankenship, finding that there was no evidence that the journalists deliberately got the facts wrong.

Jason Miller, Trump's former spokesman, sued Gizmodo, which had been part of the Gawker empire, for $100 million for accurately reporting that Miller had been accused in a court document (filed by another former Trump aide) of drugging a woman with whom he was having an affair. Miller was represented by Shane Vogt, the Tampa attorney who had taken Hulk Hogan's lawsuit to trial. Federal judges repeatedly ruled against Miller, finding that even if the allegations in the court documents were false, it was fair game for Gizmodo to have reported what was in an official legal filing.

Devin Nunes, the California congressman who would go on to lead Trump's social media company, and his family filed a series of lawsuits against the media for reporting on, among other things, his family farm's apparent employment of undocumented migrants. He was represented by a lawyer named Steven Biss, a regular suer of news outlets. Other clients would include people who stormed the Capitol on January 6, the former Trump adviser Michael Flynn, and the far-right paramilitary group 1st Amendment Praetorian.

Who was footing the bill for these failed lawsuits? Biss, who suffered a devastating stroke in 2023, didn't respond to my interview requests. Neither did Jesse Binnall, the Trump lawyer who took over some of Biss's cases. Nunes's family members said in depositions that they had paid only minimal legal fees; his brother acknowledged that he had "no idea" who was financing the litigation. "We are all trying to figure out who's paying for all of this," a prominent media lawyer told me. "I think there is an organized effort on the right to harass the media."

While conservatives were behind a disproportionate share of defamation cases, liberal figures and institutions were part of the trend, too. Justin Fairfax, the lieutenant governor of Virginia and a fast-rising star in Democratic politics, sued CBS News for reporting that women had accused him of sexual assault. (He vehemently denied the allegations.) Federal judges on two courts dismissed Fairfax's suit on *Sullivan* grounds; there was no evidence that CBS had acted with reckless disregard for the truth. Fairfax, unsatisfied with the outcome, began publicly complaining about the First Amendment being overly permissive toward the media.

Climate scientist Michael Mann waged a yearslong legal assault against the conservative magazine *National Review* for running a blog post that accused him of "molesting" data. Mann's goal was not only to get the magazine to retract the post. "There is a possibility that I can ruin *National Review* over this," he emailed an acquaintance shortly after the piece ran. "Going to talk with some big-time libel lawyers to see if there is potential for a major lawsuit here that will bring this filthy organization down for good."* *National Review* spent millions of dollars defending itself before the suit against the magazine was finally tossed in 2021. (The litigation was allowed to continue against the man who'd written the blog post, and in 2024 a jury awarded Mann $1 million in damages.)

When Claudine Gay, the president of Harvard University, faced accusations of plagiarism, Harvard hired Clare Locke to act as "defamation counsel" and send letters to the *New York Post* warning that if the tabloid went ahead with a planned article about the allegations, it would "subject the paper—and each of the individuals involved in the decision to publish—to legal liability for defamation." (Gay eventually conceded that she had used "other scholars' language without proper attribution," and she resigned as president.)

And when Democratic lawyer Marc Elias, who had been challenging Republican voting restrictions, didn't like a *New York Times* piece that showed how his law firm had received hard-to-trace "dark money" from liberal nonprofits, he, too, lashed out at the First Amendment. "If the media is not going to be pro-democracy, then it probably is time for the courts to revisit New York Times v Sullivan (as conservative lawyers suggest)," he tweeted. (Elias later claimed that the tweet had been a "test" designed to elicit a reaction from journalists.)

These threats, lawsuits, and tantrums usually ended in embarrassing defeat, even if the targets had to endure years of gargantuan legal bills.

---

* Mann's lawyer, John Williams, told me that his client wrote the email in the heat of the moment and that the litigation was not intended to be protracted. "The purpose was really not to create pain," he insisted.

But the rise of Charles Harder and Clare Locke had also contributed to the spread of another class of legal warfare, aimed at small news organizations and independent journalists. And it was exacting a much higher toll.

Jared Strong was in his cubicle in the newsroom of the *Carroll Times Herald* in western Iowa when the tip came in. A source told him that the recent arrests of two high school girls for vandalizing a car stemmed from a love triangle involving a local cop. Strong, who had grown up an hour south of Carroll, had arrived in this farming community in 2010 after several years at the *Des Moines Register*, which he'd joined straight out of Iowa State University. The *Register*, owned by the newspaper chain Gannett, was shrinking; the layoffs and buyouts were depressing. The *Times Herald*, by contrast, had been owned by the same family for nearly a century. It was still luring readers with robust coverage of local sports, the government, crime, and births and deaths, and it was making respectable money from advertising and classifieds. "It was like stepping back in time" to an era when newspapers were thriving, Strong told me.

Strong, who had a bushy head of light brown hair and a passing resemblance to Seth Rogen, was the paper's crime and courts reporter, but his role was broader: he'd been recruited by the paper's owner to do ambitious investigative reporting and feature writing. There was an eclectic mix of stories. Every day he'd check in with the police department, the county sheriff, and the local court to see what was happening. In 2016, for example, he'd overheard on the police scanner something about a guy trapped in a chimney. He arrived at the scene, just in time to witness the fire department extracting a naked, soot-coated man, who claimed to have gotten stuck while playing hide-and-seek. "I've been a crime reporter for a while now, and you see some crazy things, although I don't think I ever thought about seeing a naked man emerge from a chimney," Strong remarked to a local TV station.

But there was tougher fare, too, like the high school basketball star accused of rape. The reaction to that story was negative; readers objected to the *Times Herald* detailing an alleged sexual assault in a family-oriented newspaper. That was around the time Strong realized his "big

city" journalism might not be all that popular in increasingly conservative Carroll County, which had supported Trump over Hillary Clinton by
a two-to-one margin. The *Times Herald*'s publisher, Doug Burns, could
feel the hostility, too. Starting around 2015, national politics had seeped
into this small town; now it seemed like more and more of his neighbors
viewed the media—him!—as the enemy of the people.

The county sheriff's office in particular found Strong to be a pest, especially when he published pieces about how the department was using
GPS trackers and digging through curbside garbage bins as they investigated drug dealers. It was easy to understand why local law enforcement
would want to discourage this type of reporting. Years before George
Floyd's murder in Minneapolis, public outrage about police violence was
already swelling, and many departments were on the defensive. Carroll's
police department was not immune from complaints, including that it
had failed to share exculpatory evidence with lawyers for people accused
of crimes and that it had hired an officer who'd been accused of threatening to kill his ex-girlfriend and daughter.

Not long after he joined the *Times Herald*, Strong was summoned
for a meeting with the sheriff and his two deputies in an underground,
concrete-walled conference room in the county courthouse. They berated
him for not being as deferential to the cops as Strong's predecessor on the
beat had been.

Yet Strong was not wired to back off. So, when a source in the local
law enforcement community contacted him in the summer of 2017 with
the tip about the cop being in a love triangle, he set out to nail down
the details. The police officer in question turned out to be a twenty-six-
year-old named Jacob Smith. Strong reached out to Smith's girlfriend,
who had met the officer when he responded to her call about someone
trying to break into her car in a Walmart parking lot. They'd started
sleeping together, even though she was still in high school. Next, Strong
confirmed that a nineteen-year-old woman had had a fling with Smith—
and that the high schooler had retaliated by carving a swastika and the
word "slut" into her rival's Ford Fusion. Through government documents and interviews, including with the officer's ex-wife, Strong also
discovered that Smith had been fired from his previous job in another

Iowa police department following infractions such as sending Facebook messages to a sixteen-year-old girl.

It didn't take long for the Carroll police department to learn about what Strong was working on. The police chief called Burns, the newspaper's publisher, and urged him to abandon the story. The age of consent in Iowa was sixteen. Was it really so bad that a cop was having sex with a seventeen-year-old? "People shouldn't judge," the chief, Brad Burke, told Burns. "How do we pick what's right and what's wrong when life is changing every day?" For good measure, the chief implied that his cops could pull over the paper's staffers anytime they wished.

Under Burns's leadership, the *Times Herald* had received its share of angry feedback, even threats, and not just because of Strong's article about the alleged basketball rape. Burns, the third generation of his family to own and publish the paper, wasn't easily swayed. He told the police chief that he trusted Strong and that a cop having sex with a high schooler was a legitimate news story.

Strong eventually approached Officer Smith. Smith had heard his law enforcement colleagues grumbling about Strong, but he agreed to meet the reporter in nearby Graham Park. The caveat was that Smith insisted that the conversation be off-the-record, which meant that Strong couldn't publish anything that Smith told him, unless he could get the information from other sources. In the park, Smith questioned the motive and reliability of his ex-wife, whom he suspected of being Strong's source. But he did not deny the bulk of the information that Strong presented him with.

Then, five days later, Smith quit the police force; it turned out that the chief had threatened to fire him if he didn't step down on his own. The next day, after some frenzied last-minute fact-checking—going back to sources, rereading documents, making a final round of phone calls to seek people's comments—the *Times Herald* published Strong's story on the front page. "Carroll Cop Who Courted Teenage Girls Resigns," the headline read. The article quoted Smith's ex-wife calling him "a pedophile and a predator." And it noted that Smith had "declined to talk publicly about the situation."

Smith learned of the story from a local jailer whom he was friendly with. He went to a nearby Casey's convenience store to pick up a copy. He saw his photo—smiling and in his police uniform—and read the piece with gritted teeth. "I was infuriated," he told me.

The following morning, Strong was in the *Times Herald*'s eight-person newsroom when Burns emerged from his office. "Well, it finally happened," the publisher announced. He had just received a terse email from a local lawyer saying he had filed suit against Strong and the newspaper for defaming Smith. Later that day, someone from the county sheriff's office, which had long been unhappy about Strong's coverage, formally served the paper and Strong with the lawsuit. It described the article, and the ex-wife's "pedophile" comment in particular, as "malicious." Smith's "reputation has been destroyed, his character and integrity forever castigated in the public eye, and his employability as a law officer severely damaged if not totally ruined," the complaint said. That all might have been true, but thanks to Strong's fastidious fact-checking, the article was accurate.

This was hardly the first time that law enforcement had used libel lawsuits to deter or retaliate against journalists. There was L. B. Sullivan's litigation in Alabama, of course. But there were numerous recent examples, too. A pair of police in Tuscaloosa sued *Buzzfeed News* for an article that—as a federal judge ruled in throwing out the case after more than three years of legal warfare—accurately and responsibly depicted their controversial roles handling a rape allegation against a well-connected Alabaman. In Texas, a small newspaper was similarly dogged by long-running litigation over a piece that alleged that a local cop had gone to bat for his son after he was pulled over. A lawyer involved in that case told me that it grew so acrimonious that a police vehicle at one point had trailed an attorney for the newspaper up to the county line in what appeared to be an attempt at intimidation.

The lawyer who brought the Carroll suit was named Jim Van Dyke. He'd grown up in Iowa and lived in Carroll since 1974, building a practice focused largely on personal injury and family law. He'd previously handled Smith's divorce; now he agreed to take this case on contingency, meaning he'd get paid only if Smith received money. After filing the lawsuit, Van Dyke went on the local radio station to attack Strong and his reporting. Six months into the Trump presidency, resentment toward the media, at least in many red states, was running high. Anyone who heard the radio segment would have gotten the distinct impression that Strong was guilty of journalistic malpractice. "The petition is based upon the limits of free press, and we certainly believe that Jared Strong went beyond those limits when he used many unreliable sources and many inaccurate and untrue statements," Van Dyke asserted. He claimed that Smith, during the meeting at Graham Park, had told Strong that what he was writing was false. Van Dyke attached to the lawsuit a printout of the article on which Smith had marked with a yellow highlighter all of the supposed "untruths."

Strong and his colleagues were rattled. "We're in trouble, huh?" a worker in the paper's printing room asked him after hearing Van Dyke's radio interview. Strong kept making his daily rounds at the police station and the courthouse to check on the latest news, but he could feel the police officers and sheriff's deputies glaring at him. Whenever he and his colleagues considered writing a hard-hitting story, lurking in the back of their mind was the question, *Will this get us sued again?* "It just weighed on us constantly," Strong said. Like a tiny parasite, Van Dyke's radio interview wormed its way inside Strong's psyche and was growing into something dangerous. Some days he would cut out of work early and go home. He had a machine shed in the back where he liked to tinker with old cars and engines. Out there, he'd pound beers and morosely listen to Van Dyke's interview on repeat.

For years, the *Times Herald* had managed to avoid the declines in advertising that had felled its rivals and had made it all but impossible for many Americans to keep informed about what was happening in their communities. More than 2,500 newspapers in the United States have stopped publishing in the past two decades, a rate of about two per week. Most counties in the United States are no longer home to any daily papers, and many surviving outlets have been gutted by layoffs and other cost cutting. Seventy million Americans live in what researchers have dubbed "news deserts."

This is not merely academic. When no one is monitoring city council or school board meetings, studies have found that civic engagement withers, politics polarize, and taxes go up. As staffing at local newspapers declines, mayoral races become less competitive, and voter turnout wanes. Misinformation spreads. Politicians and other public figures are rarely held to account for lies and misdeeds. Today, state legislators, city council members, and small-town mayors—not to mention companies that pollute or mistreat workers or sell dangerous products—are operating with a degree of invisibility and impunity that they have not enjoyed in a century.

Now that trend was starting to catch up with the *Times Herald*. Revenues were declining. And following the publication of Strong's article, virtually anyone with a connection to the police department canceled their subscriptions. Some local advertisers—the newspaper's lifeblood—began yanking their business. On top of that the paper was now going to have to shell out for defense lawyers. (The *Times Herald* had libel insurance, but before it kicked in, the newspaper had to cover a six-figure deductible.)

Burns and his family had been running the newspaper since the Great Depression. He knew that if he didn't prevail in this lawsuit, his career and family legacy were toast; he'd have to sell the *Times Herald*. Yet when Smith's side dangled the possibility of a roughly $40,000 settlement, Burns said no. He believed in the importance and accuracy of the story. Plus, if he caved, he worried it would set a precedent in which people could essentially extort small news organizations. "This was the proverbial hill you're willing to die on," Burns said.

In September, Strong got another tip. A longtime Carroll police officer, Sandy March, told him that she'd just been fired. She said she wanted to share some important information. That weekend, they met at Swan Lake State Park on the outskirts of town and walked through the woods and along the lake. The scent of algae hung in the air. March said the Carroll police had covered up a crime committed by a local businessman, but she was on the fence about whether she was comfortable divulging the details. It might help her gain comfort, she explained, if Strong could tell her who had alerted him to the love triangle months earlier. Strong politely refused, and he and March parted ways.

Over the coming days, Strong sent her a bunch of text messages, hoping to draw her out so she would reveal more about the coverup she'd referred to. March ghosted him. Strong began trying to figure out the circumstances of her firing. Then he got an out-of-the-blue email from Burke, the chief of police. "Jared," it read. "Officer Sandy March has not been terminated and never was. She was never asked to resign. She met with you over the weekend at my request." Strong sat at his desk in stunned silence. He was flabbergasted—and a little embarrassed that he hadn't detected the ruse.* (March was fired for real months later for what the police department said was insubordination.)

Trying to trick a reporter into outing a source was not a conventional use of police resources, and it was a telling example of the tactics the Carroll cops were willing to deploy to defend themselves. Burns suspected that the police department was seeking to plant false information in the *Times Herald* to discredit the outlet. He looked into the possibility of suing the police for violating his and Strong's civil rights. "It felt like they were treating us like criminals," Burns told me.

In normal times, the *Times Herald* would have written an article about this misuse of power. But with the lawsuit hanging over the paper's head, there was no appetite to take another swing at the police. The *Times Herald's* lawyers urged Burns "to be exceedingly cautious," and so the failed sting operation remained under wraps for the time being.

In March 2018, Strong was summoned for a sworn deposition. It took place in a small conference room inside a local law office. Strong, his lawyers, Van Dyke (Smith's attorney), and a court reporter crowded around a rectangular table. Strong's heart was racing, and he worried that he might sweat through his polo shirt. It didn't help that he was nursing a hangover, having stayed up late the previous night stress-drinking.

Van Dyke asked Strong why his original article had mentioned that Smith was being financially supported by his wife. "You were attacking Jacob Smith in any way you could find, weren't you, Mr. Strong?"

Strong said no. "My wife makes more money than I do," he pointed out.

Van Dyke demanded to know why the article about Smith's resignation

---

* Burke said in an email that some of my information about him was incorrect. He would not elaborate but warned that if I got facts wrong, "legal action may be necessary."

got such prominent play. "This wound up on the front page of the paper because of the titillating or salacious nature of the allegations, didn't it, Mr. Strong?"

"The vast majority of locally produced articles that we have appear on the front page of the newspaper," Strong answered.

"Especially the titillating or salacious ones," Van Dyke repeated, citing Strong's 2016 article about the basketball player accused of rape. "The ones involving sex go above the fold on the front page, but the ones involving routine matters are buried, aren't they?" He added: "Can we agree that sex sells papers?"

"What do you mean by 'sells papers'?"

"Boosts circulation."

"That's false," Strong replied. And it was. One thing that had gradually dawned on Strong during this monthslong ordeal was that accountability journalism might be in the public interest, but it wasn't in the newspaper's. Whenever the *Times Herald* ran a piece of investigative reporting, the fallout was swift. Subscribers canceled. Advertisers got squeamish. "These stories always cost us more than they got us—every time," Strong told me.

The following spring, a local judge dismissed Smith and Van Dyke's lawsuit, saying the *Times Herald*'s reporting was shielded by the *Sullivan* precedent and the First Amendment. "The article at issue is accurate and true, and the underlying facts undisputed," the judge wrote. He noted that the ex-wife's "pedophile" comment was a constitutionally protected opinion.

But the victory was expensive. The *Times Herald* had racked up huge legal bills and had lost revenue from fleeing subscribers and advertisers. In 2019, Burns decided to print the paper only twice a week, instead of five times. The litigation wasn't the only factor, but it was a big one. Burns created a GoFundMe page begging for money to keep the paper afloat. The plea generated some national attention. "Small newspapers like ours, we're kind of the last vestige for collective or common truth, or trust," Burns told the *Washington Post*. "Pretty much everything in our paper, you're one or two degrees of separation away from personally, so you know it to be true because you were there—you were at the game, or you see an obituary, and it's somebody you were connected to." The appeal yielded about $100,000.

It wasn't enough. In 2022, Burns had to sell his family's paper to cover its debts—it was either that or simply close the outlet. He had been internalizing the *Times Herald*'s mounting financial pressures to such an extent that he contemplated suicide. Selling the newspaper wasn't much of a salve. "It was the worst day of my life," he said.

The *Times Herald* became part of a larger media company, based in a different part of Iowa, and the newspaper's focus shifted. Features and soft news were in; investigative reporting was out. Strong, who had left the paper the year before the sale, looked back with a mix of nostalgia and sadness. "We spent so many years doing accountability journalism," he said. "It did not pay off at all."

Around the time that Doug Burns was raising funds online, another newspaper, this one seven hundred miles to the southwest in Colorado Springs, was confronting its own legal dilemma.

The Gazette had been around since 1872, when the same railroad tycoon who had founded Colorado Springs decided to launch a newspaper. Originally named *Out West*, *The Gazette* grew along with its hometown, which became Colorado's second-largest city. The newspaper was a community fixture, covering staples like local government and sports, but also some of the institutions—including the military and religious groups—that made the Springs unique. (The city is home to the Air Force Academy, among other military installations, and James Dobson's Focus on the Family.) Over the years, *The Gazette* picked up a pair of Pulitzer Prizes, the highest honor in journalism, as well as hundreds of other awards.

But when Conrad Swanson arrived at *The Gazette* in 2017, a haze of controversy was lingering over what had long been a proud, ambitious newsroom. Five years earlier, the conservative billionaire Phil Anschutz had purchased the paper, his latest in a series of media acquisitions and part of a broader pattern of local and regional newspapers being gobbled up by wealthy individuals and conglomerates. Initially journalists had cheered the deal; Anschutz's deep pockets meant *The Gazette* would be able to continue investing in serious journalism. Soon, though, the mood curdled. Some reporters perceived Anschutz's handpicked publisher and editors as toadies, watering down investigations and producing flawed stories to advance the owner's business or political interests. There was a widely panned package of stories in 2015 that railed against Colorado's legalization of marijuana—but didn't mention that one of the authors was an antidrug activist. A year later, a monthslong investigation into a Republican Senate candidate was supposedly neutered on the orders of *The Gazette*'s publisher; the reporter who wrote the story quit in disgust. At various other points, *Gazette* editors diluted or killed articles that reflected poorly on the grand Broadmoor Hotel, which Anschutz owned. More journalists resigned.

Swanson, whose roughly $42,000 salary was barely enough to cover the rent for the small apartment that he and his wife rented next to a Mexican restaurant, picked up on the sour vibes. But he was happy to be at *The Gazette* after years at a smaller paper in Kansas. He was twenty-eight, his beat was City Hall, and he was on his way up the journalism ladder.

One day in the spring of 2019, his editor, Vince Bzdek, came to Swanson with a possible lead. Bzdek had heard from one of his old fraternity brothers, Bill Rudge, who owned a house in a Colorado Springs development called Gold Hill Mesa. The house had been new when Rudge and his wife had bought it, but it quickly began exhibiting serious problems— and, the couple told Bzdek, they suspected it was a sign of deeper trouble at Gold Hill Mesa. Bzdek, a Colorado native who'd joined *The Gazette* in 2016 after years at the *Washington Post*, smelled a story. He sidled over to Swanson's desk. "Do you want to look into this?" he asked.

Swanson had never heard of Gold Hill Mesa, though he soon realized that he'd regularly driven past it. Its history was entwined with Colorado Springs' origins as a gold-mining town. Starting around 1905, the area had been the site of the thrumming Golden Cycle Mill. Sitting at the foot of the Rockies, it processed up to 1,500 tons of ore per day, which trains had transported from the nearby Cripple Creek mines, as well as from farther-flung locales. The mill's refining process used arsenic and other chemicals to separate precious metals from mere rocks. The mill then pumped the leftovers—what would eventually amount to fourteen million tons of toxic dregs known as mine tailings—into a vast earthen basin that, by the time the mill closed in 1949, was brimming with two hundred feet of slurry. This was Gold Hill.

It was a barren landscape. Nothing grew. Few structures stood, aside from the abandoned mill's cement smokestack. Wind whipped dust and debris into populated areas and a nearby creek. By the 1990s, the Colorado Springs real estate market was heating up. Gold Hill stood in the city's west side, just off the interstate. A development company persuaded the city to classify the eyesore as an urban renewal site, making it eligible for millions of dollars in annual tax benefits. The plan was to build 1,400 homes and 700,000 square feet of retail and office space with sparkling views of the snow-capped Pike's Peak and other nearby mountains.

When they approved the building plans, local regulators primarily focused on ensuring that the dangerous chemicals left over from the mill were buried at a sufficient depth that they wouldn't endanger children or animals. An initial plan, later reversed, even called for a ban on planting gardens or fruit trees, out of fear that the roots would burrow below the thick layer of clean soil that developers had trucked in as a buffer. What regulators and other city officials hadn't considered, at least not as closely, was the possibility that building a sprawling residential development atop a pile of mine tailings might pose structural problems, not just chemical ones.

By the time Bzdek shared the tip with Swanson at *The Gazette*, Gold Hill Mesa had blossomed into a bustling, picturesque community of nearly five hundred houses, many painted in pastel hues. The project's developers were seeking clearance to add hundreds more homes and commercial and community spaces.

Swanson's first step was to speak to Bill Rudge and his wife, Hannah Polmer. They met at a Starbucks miles away from Gold Hill Mesa. Sitting outside so that other customers couldn't eavesdrop, the couple unfurled their story. In 2012, they'd bought their dream home in Gold Hill Mesa for $485,000: four beds, three baths, a wraparound porch, geothermal heating and cooling, and easy access to hiking and biking trails.

The house had even been featured in the city's annual Parade of Homes, which showcased the area's coolest new builds.

But, the couple told Swanson, the allure had faded shortly after they moved in. Their utility bills, which were supposed to be much lower than in their 1920s-era previous home, were instead sky-high. One afternoon, Rudge went down to the basement in his socks and was alarmed to find the carpet soaked. Underneath, the cement floor was warped and cracked, like an enormous, leaky jigsaw puzzle. They began noticing other problems around the neighborhood. Fractured foundations. Water seeping up through the street. Soil seeming to recede or sink around houses. They hired a lawyer and some engineers, whose tests concluded that their house was sinking because the mine tailings below it were shifting. After failing to persuade Gold Hill Mesa to buy back their home, they sued the developers for fraud. They also complained to local officials. "I need the City to assure me that the land is safe," Polmer emailed the mayor of Colorado Springs in 2015.

The response was swift, and not at all what the couple had expected: what felt like a coordinated campaign of harassment. People in the community falsely accused them of throwing rocks at construction workers, trying to run over their neighbors, and attacking a builder—accusations that in one instance culminated with Polmer being charged with third-degree assault. (The charge was dismissed.) Another time, the police showed up at Rudge's law and mediation practice to question him about a stolen construction sign. The homeowners' association repeatedly dinged them for what seemed like rinky-dink violations. Gold Hill Mesa circulated flyers urging citizens "to defend and protect your property value and the reputation of the neighborhood" from "a small handful" of agitators who were stigmatizing the development. Neighbors began ostracizing them. Clients deserted Rudge's legal practice. (A spokeswoman for Gold Hill Mesa told me that Rudge, Polmer, and their lawyers were the ones intimidating neighbors, by encouraging them to join a class action lawsuit against the development.)

Having burned roughly $300,000 on legal expenses, Polmer and Rudge agreed to settle their lawsuit in 2016 in exchange for, among other things, Gold Hill Mesa buying back their home—at a price well below what they'd paid four years earlier. As part of the deal, they promised not to disparage the development. But as far as they were concerned, speaking truthfully wasn't disparagement. It was honesty. Polmer's mother had disappeared during Hurricane Katrina, and when Polmer had traveled to New Orleans to search for her, she'd witnessed what can happen when shoddy infrastructure meets natural disaster. (Her mother was among the hundreds who died.) Now she worried that Gold Hill Mesa was trundling down a similar path, and she felt dutybound to expose this public danger.

Polmer and Rudge shared with Swanson a portion of the voluminous public records they had collected during years of litigation and research. Swanson then set out to learn more. He spent months studying engineering papers and court records, submitting requests for government documents pursuant to the state's Open Records Act, and knocking on doors around Gold Hill Mesa. Using a detailed map of the development that he obtained from the city, he marked the dozens of properties where he'd confirmed the existence of problems such as crumbling foundations.

Before the story was published, Swanson exhaustively checked his facts. He created a footnoted Google document with links to the public records and other materials that substantiated each point in the article. And he discussed his findings with Gold Hill Mesa officials and invited them to comment. The conversations struck him as civil and substantive, and he incorporated their responses into the story.

Unbeknownst to Swanson, Gold Hill Mesa was already maneuvering to derail the story. The company had long worked with one of the world's largest law firms, Hogan Lovells, which had a small office in Colorado Springs. That same office also represented some of the companies controlled by Phil Anschutz, the paper's owner. The Hogan Lovells attorneys sought an "informational meeting" with Bzdek and *The Gazette*'s publisher, Chris Reen. In the eyes of the newspaper's leaders, they had little choice but to accept a meeting with the law firm that was also representing their boss. One of the Hogan Lovells lawyers, John Cook, came to *The Gazette*'s office and warned Bzdek and Reen against publishing Swanson's article. Bzdek told me that he resented what struck him as an attempt at intimidation.*

The Gazette didn't back down. Swanson's article was published on the front page on a Sunday in August 2019. The piece revealed that city planners and engineers had belatedly recognized the possibility that the mine tailings that comprised Gold Hill might shift under the weight of the development. Because the mill's refining operation had required lots of liquids, underground pockets of Gold Hill remained wet, increasing the risk of sliding—especially if there were an earthquake. Already, some homeowners—not just Rudge and Polmer—were noticing damage. Their foundations and pipes were breaking, groundwater was invading their basements, and roads were oozing water even when it didn't rain. And according to court documents that Swanson dug up, Gold Hill Mesa officials had been aware of these concerns for years but had brushed them off as the result of shoddy construction by independent builders. The piece acknowledged that there were unresolved debates about whether and to what extent the concerns about Gold Hill Mesa's stability were valid, but Swanson reported that city planners had decided to pause the next stage of development until more testing could be done.

The piece enraged Gold Hill Mesa. "*The Gazette*'s original article was fundamentally flawed and based on incorrect facts," the company's spokeswoman, Heather Kelly, said. Her evidence? Swanson had cited minutes from a local government meeting that noted that twenty-four Gold Hill Mesa homes were experiencing problems. Gold Hill Mesa claimed that the minutes were inaccurate and that the twenty-four homes were located elsewhere in Colorado Springs. The problem with this argument was that Swanson's article had clearly acknowledged that there was a dispute about the accuracy of the minutes, which in any case were only a small part of his reporting. Swanson had other hard evidence

---

* Gold Hill Mesa's spokeswoman, Heather Kelly, denied that the goal was to intimidate. "To the contrary," she wrote in an email to me, "this meeting was scheduled with the consent of both parties and was intended to correct inaccuracies and resolve conflicts fairly." She also said the in-person meeting took place after the story ran, which was not Bzdek's recollection.

of homeowners reporting trouble. And nobody disputed that local officials had paused construction to further study the development's safety.

Gold Hill Mesa, of course, had a strong incentive to minimize the
concerns: it was easy to imagine prospective homebuyers balking if there
were questions about the site's stability. More broadly, the development
was controlled by a Seattle-based company, Hadley Properties, which
owned hotels, skyscrapers, resorts, housing developments, and indus-
trial parks around the United States, as well as finance and construction
companies. The last thing Hadley needed was a journalistic colonoscopy.
With so many properties and so many potentially aggrieved parties, who
knew what a muckraker like Swanson might turn up?

Two days after *The Gazette* published his article, Swanson was copied
on an email to the newspaper's publisher. It was from a Colorado Springs
lawyer named Richard Hanes, who said he was writing on behalf of "a
number of property owners in the Gold Hill Mesa development that are
incensed over reporter Conrad Swanson's irresponsible and libelous recent articles." (Hanes acknowledged to me that he didn't have multiple
clients; he was doing a favor for his son, who happened to own a house
in the development.) The letter incorrectly claimed that "there is not a
single house in Gold Hill Mesa that is *sinking, heaving, and flooding*,"
using the words *The Gazette* had written to describe the conditions of
multiple homes. "The false statement is defamatory and is damaging to
Gold Hill Mesa owners' property values," Hanes asserted. He concluded
by demanding that *The Gazette* retract its piece and "immediately cease
and desist from publishing further articles about alleged conditions in
Gold Hill Mesa."

Neither Swanson nor his editor had any intention of complying with
this final demand. Other stories were already in the pipeline. One revealed that the Colorado Geological Survey, a state agency, had warned
city planners months earlier that an analysis of satellite images showed
that parts of Gold Hill Mesa had sunk more than three inches over a
six-year period. That could be enough to crack buildings. This wasn't
Swanson's opinion. It was the conclusion of Jonathan Lovekin, a senior
CGS engineering geologist who had spent much of his career surveying
Colorado's mines and studying the risks of landslides and shifting soil.

Lawyers soon intensified the pressure. *The Gazette*'s outside counsel, Steven Zansberg, had replied to Hanes's letter, defending Swanson's reporting and noting that it was largely based on documentary evidence and public statements by state and local officials. Now Hanes sent back a fiery response, accusing Zansberg of being "intellectually naïve" and Swanson of engaging in "yellow journalism at its worst." Hanes declared that *The Gazette* had exhibited "a reckless disregard for the truth"—essentially warning that it was vulnerable to damages under the actual malice standard.

Days later, another threat arrived at *The Gazette*, this one from an in-house lawyer at Gold Hill Mesa who claimed that "the recently published articles contain significant materially false information." The letter noted that Gold Hill Mesa had hired a Denver law firm "to evaluate potential litigation." The letter put *The Gazette* on notice that, because of the possibility of litigation, it should retain all records—story drafts, emails, notes, voicemails, text messages, calendar entries, and more—that pertained in any way to Swanson's reporting. Gold Hill Mesa followed up with a press release announcing its hiring of a "'bet-the-company' trial firm with extensive experience in complex litigation to investigate potential claims against *The Gazette*."

This was right out of the SLAPP playbook that George Pring and Penelope Canan had described two decades earlier, in which real estate developers and others used the threat or reality of costly litigation to scare those who aired public grievances. "They're doing this not to win lawsuits but to chill speech and to be part of this campaign to delegitimize the free press," Zansberg, *The Gazette*'s lawyer, told me about such threats. (He was speaking in general, not about Gold Hill Mesa specifically.) Only three months earlier, in June 2019, Colorado's governor had signed a bipartisan law to deter the filing of such SLAPPs, but that only applied to actual litigation, not the sort of saber-rattling that Gold Hill Mesa was now engaged in.

From Swanson's standpoint, the threats seemed effective. Almost immediately, he told me, he noticed a change in the newspaper's attitude toward his reporting. His previous articles had skated into the paper, and he'd exchanged hardly a word with Chris Reen, the publisher, who rarely got involved with the reporting or editing of articles. Now Swanson was called to Reen's office, and phrases, sentences, and entire paragraphs were chopped at the publisher's behest. Bzdek continued to support Swanson's reporting, but he acknowledged to me that it was unusual and suboptimal for Reen to have inserted himself into the editing process. "There was a high concern with us being careful with that story," Bzdek said.

Swanson wasn't thrilled, but he figured it was only natural for his editors to be more cautious in the wake of the legal warnings. Plus, the paper published a couple more of his Gold Hill Mesa stories, including one that quoted unnamed residents complaining about damage to their houses and neighborhoods and expressing fears that speaking publicly "could bring them legal troubles and scorn in the neighborhood."

Swanson had a bunch of additional leads. He had learned through a public records request that Gold Hill Mesa officials were secretly in close contact with the Colorado Springs officials who were supposed to be regulating the development, coordination that outside experts said raised red flags about a lack of independence. Separately, Swanson had confirmed that some properties at Gold Hill Mesa, including Rudge and Polmer's home, had been falsely advertised as having received environmental certifications that they'd never actually received. Swanson typed up drafts of the articles. Bzdek spiked them. He viewed them as "ancillary" compared to the more ambitious Gold Hill Mesa stories that he wanted Swanson pursuing. Swanson, however, felt that the legal threats had spooked his superiors.

The Gazette wasn't the only one receiving warnings. Hogan Lovells repeatedly sent letters threatening to sue Polmer for defamation, potentially seeking millions of dollars, if she kept spreading "false rumors" about the housing development. Two of the letters specifically complained that Polmer was in frequent contact with the Colorado Department of Public Health and Environment about her concerns with Gold Hill Mesa—the type of petitioning of the government that is explicitly protected under the First Amendment. The letters left Polmer and Rudge "scared to death and pissed off at the same time," as he put it. He had been a happy-go-lucky athlete; now he began drinking heavily. Shell-shocked and traumatized, Polmer could no longer even manage to cook dinner.

Meanwhile, taking advantage of the state's public records law, the Hogan Lovells attorneys sought access to communications between Swanson and Colorado Geological Survey employees like Jonathan Lovekin. This was well within Gold Hill Mesa's rights, but deliberately or not, the request for records served as a reminder to CGS employees about the perils of speaking out about potential public dangers. The lawyers also asked for a meeting with Lovekin and a colleague. CGS officials feared it was an attempt by Gold Hill Mesa "to improperly avail themselves of your expertise to advance their client's position in ongoing or potential litigation," as they put it in an internal email.

By then, Swanson had been offered a job by the *Denver Post*. He left the Springs in November 2019. (Polmer and Rudge also moved out of town to escape what they described as ongoing harassment.)

The ambitious articles that Bzdek cited as a rationale for having killed Swanson's other stories never materialized. Indeed, going forward, Gold Hill Mesa found *The Gazette's* occasional pieces to be softer—or, as an executive put it, "way more fact-based"—than the exposés that Swanson had authored. Richard Hanes, one of the lawyers who'd threatened *The Gazette*, was also satisfied. "They stopped writing," he told me. "That's all we wanted them to do."

Less than two months after Swanson left, *The Gazette* invited Gold Hill Mesa to sponsor a community forum that the newspaper was hosting. The development company accepted, though it publicly warned that litigation against *The Gazette* remained a possibility. "Our attorneys are still there in the wings, waiting and watching," a spokeswoman noted ominously.

After another round of testing, Colorado Springs allowed Gold Hill Mesa to resume construction of houses and other buildings. The city even agreed to kick in millions of dollars in taxpayer financing to help defray the costs.

CLARENCE THOMAS CHANGES HIS MIND

O n the morning of February 19, 2019, around the time that Vince Bzdek first suggested that Conrad Swanson look into Gold Hill Mesa, the Supreme Court published a fifty-eight-page document listing the justices' latest batch of orders. These weren't traditional rulings in which the nine justices had voted on the merits of cases. Written in a boxy Courier font, double-spaced to make the case numbers and legalese slightly more legible, these were decisions of a more procedural nature: whether the justices would accept or reject cases for review; whether pleas for injunctions, writs of habeas corpus, or other judicial interventions would be granted or denied; whether parties to pending cases would be given extra time to file briefs or present oral arguments. Most of the time, to most of the queries, the answer was no. Writs were rejected and requests denied, generally without explanation. The court on this chilly Tuesday granted a single petition for a writ of certiorari— meaning it agreed to hear the case, which involved the Clean Water Act. It rejected well over four hundred others.

The final case in the court's long list of orders was entitled *Kathrine Mae McKee v. William H. Cosby, Jr.* It had been a long time coming, rooted in an incident that took place more than forty years earlier. The case's dispensation was going to become a public coming-out party for a movement that until now had resided on the political fringe.

Kathy McKee had arrived in Los Angeles in 1963, when she was fourteen. She was escaping Detroit and a dysfunctional family, and she dreamed of becoming an actress, inspired by Doris Day and Elizabeth Taylor. Recognizing the long odds of breaking into Hollywood, she soon decamped to Las Vegas. One night, she got locked out of her hotel room and spent hours wandering casinos in the city's seedy downtown. She saw a sign seeking go-go dancers. McKee was tall, slender, and beautiful and was hired on the spot—her first gig. At the time, hotels in Vegas had policies against hiring Black showgirls, and so the pale-skinned McKee told prospective employers that she was white. (She also said she was twenty-three.) She eventually landed a job as the lead showgirl in a regular burlesque revue at the Silver Slipper casino.

One night, McKee struck up a conversation with the man next to her at a blackjack table. It happened to be Sammy Davis Jr.'s father, and he insisted on introducing her to his son. Davis was smitten. The following evening, Davis and his entourage showed up at the Silver Slipper to see McKee perform, and he then escorted her backstage for the Rat Pack's show at the Sands casino. McKee couldn't believe that she was hanging out with Davis, Frank Sinatra, and their pals. Before long, Davis invited McKee to go on the road with him and become his "mistress of ceremonies." Naturally, she said yes. At nightclubs and concert halls all over America, she would don a glittering evening gown, introduce Davis and his guest acts, disappear backstage for a wardrobe change, re-introduce Davis after an intermission, bring him a drink, receive a couple of kisses onstage. "I was Sammy's road wife," McKee would say. "He had an open marriage, and we were lovers."

It was a magical time for McKee, who suddenly saw all sorts of previously locked doors swinging open. She dated stars like Tony Curtis and Richard Pryor, with whom she appeared on one of the first episodes of *Saturday Night Live*. She acted on prime-time TV shows, including *Sanford and Sons*, and starred in the 1971 film *Quadroon*, whose posters depicted McKee in a low-cut yellow dress and promised "the shocking truth about the passion slaves" of New Orleans. That same year, she scored a onetime role on the short-lived *Bill Cosby Show* (not to be confused with the longer-running *Cosby Show*). She and Cosby became friends and went out to occasional dinners along with Cosby's wife, Camille.

In June 1974, McKee accompanied Davis to Michigan to perform at the Pine Knob amphitheater. After the show, they bumped into Cosby backstage. McKee was planning to stay in Detroit a few extra days to see family, and so when Cosby proposed that they get together, she was game. He suggested that she grab some ribs from Checker Bar-B-Q and then meet him at the elegant Hotel St. Regis, where he was staying. From there, the plan was to go to a party that Cosby's friend was throwing on a boat in the Detroit River. McKee admired and trusted Cosby but wasn't attracted to him. As far as she was concerned, their relationship was platonic.

She brought the ribs to the hotel. She rode the elevator up and knocked on Cosby's door. He was wearing a bathrobe and wool cap. He took the bag of barbecue out of her hand and set it down on a table. He shut the door. Then, according to McKee, he grabbed her. He spun her around so that her back was to him. He pulled up her dress and yanked down her underwear. Still standing by the door, he raped her. Decades later, McKee remembered a vile stench emanating from Cosby, like a demon had suddenly possessed him and released the essence of a dead man.

It was over quickly, McKee said. She raced to the bathroom and locked the door. She wondered if Cosby was going to get a gun. She made a plan: sprint to the door, flee down the hallway. But when she cracked the bathroom door open, there was Cosby, blocking her exit. "Come on," he barked. McKee drove him to the boat party.

McKee worried that if she reported the rape to the police, or otherwise spoke up, it wouldn't go well. She wouldn't be believed, or she'd be blamed, or she'd be blacklisted, or maybe she'd even be killed. It hadn't been worth the risk, she told me. And so for the next four decades, she kept the rape to herself.

In November 2014, McKee was in Lathrup Village, a suburb of Detroit. Her mother had died weeks earlier, and McKee was grieving. At home one night, she turned on CNN. The talk turned to Cosby. After years of rumors about him being a sexual predator, more of his alleged victims were mustering the courage to publicly accuse him of rape and assault. And for the first time, the media was beginning to take the allegations seriously.

A big part of the reason was Gawker. In 2014, the website—which was more than a year into its legal battle with Hulk Hogan and Charles Harder—began cataloguing old instances of Cosby facing accusations of sexual misconduct. The headline of its initial piece, written by Tom Scocca, asked: "Who Wants to Remember Bill Cosby's Multiple Sexual-Assault Allegations?" The answer, the piece noted, was: very few people. Scocca explained that, going back nearly a decade, numerous women had accused Cosby of drugging and assaulting them. A handful of news organizations had written up the accusations, but they hadn't gained any traction. Cosby remained a sought-after comic, garnering praise and awards. "Basically nobody wanted to live in a world where Bill Cosby was a sexual predator," Scocca wrote. "The whole thing had been, and it remained, something walled off from our collective understanding of Bill Cosby."

Here was Gawker at its best: dredging up damning information that the rest of the media was content to let lie. And Scocca was just getting started. He kept unearthing accusations and scolding the media for ignoring what deserved to be a scandal. Eventually more women came forward, and the rest of the media, including the feisty New York *Daily News*, woke up.

Which was why the anguished McKee, having turned on CNN to distract herself from thinking about her mom, was now learning that she was far from the only woman who said she'd been attacked by Cosby. "That was the first time I realized he did this to people other than me," McKee said. She perceived the reporters and anchors on CNN as being overly deferential to the man they referred to as "America's Dad." It seemed to McKee that they were treating Cosby as if he were actually Cliff Huxtable. It nauseated her—and it convinced her that the time had finally come for her to speak up.

McKee by now had built a successful career as a casting director. She recognized that her rich trove of connections—most of all, the fact that she'd been Sammy Davis Jr.'s girlfriend—might lend her accusations extra credibility. McKee called Nancy Dillon, the *Daily News* reporter who'd been writing about Cosby, and recounted what had happened in the Detroit hotel room. Dillon's story was published on December 22,

2014. "Exclusive: Bill Cosby Accused of Raping Ex-girlfriend of Sammy Davis Jr.," the headline screamed. "I just felt that now I'd be safe with the other women in a group, and I'd come forward and support them and say, 'Yeah, it happened to me also,'" McKee explained in a *Daily News* video, with a picture of Davis and the rest of the Rat Pack on the wall behind her.

By then, more than a dozen women had accused Cosby of sexual assault, including in the same year that McKee said she was raped. To fight back, Cosby hired Marty Singer, the Hollywood attack dog who had been Charles Harder's mentor. Singer's strategy was to annihilate the credibility of Cosby's accusers. A half-dozen ex–Los Angeles Police Department detectives were dispatched to dig up dirt. Another part of Team Cosby's strategy was to threaten women with defamation lawsuits—a tactic that apparently helped explain why so many rape allegations had remained under wraps for so long.

Soon after the *Daily News* story about McKee went online, Singer fired off a letter to the tabloid's general counsel. He savaged the "malicious defamatory article," accused the *Daily News* of engaging in "reckless conduct," and assailed McKee as a liar. Singer noted—accurately but without context—that McKee had once described Cosby as among a group of "wonderful, lovely men" and had touted her work with him on a promotional website. Those fond words, Singer asserted, contradicted her rape claims. What's more, the lawyer wrote, McKee was an admitted liar: she had once told an interviewer about how, as a teenager in Vegas, she'd fibbed about her race and age to get jobs. "To say that Ms. McKee is not a reliable source is a gross understatement," Singer opined.

The letter was marked "confidential" and said that "Publication or Dissemination Is Prohibited." Yet within hours, it was leaked to the *Hollywood Reporter*—presumably part of a Singer strategy to let other would-be accusers and journalists know what they would face if they aired fresh accusations. News outlets began including snippets from the Singer letter, questioning McKee's trustworthiness, in follow-up articles about her allegations.

Even as she did more media interviews, McKee somehow didn't learn about what Singer had written until nearly a year later, in November

2015, when an acquaintance mentioned it to her and suggested that perhaps she should hire a lawyer. McKee had spent enough time in and around Hollywood to know all about Singer—"He was a henchman," she told me—and she was furious to hear that he'd called her a liar. McKee happened to be on her way to New York to work on a documentary, and one night she went out to dinner at Serafina, an Italian eatery, with a cousin named Bill Salo. Salo was a lawyer, and McKee told him about Singer's letter. Might she be able to sue Cosby for having smeared her?

Salo agreed to help. He'd done some defamation work earlier in his career. Most of it involved situations like a guy at a country club badmouthing a stockbroker, who then threatened to sue, claiming that he'd lost out on clients because the whole country club had turned against him. Cases like this tended to settle quickly. Salo's hunch was that he and McKee could wring a settlement out of Cosby, too.

McKee's lawsuit was filed in federal court a month later, just before Christmas. It accused Cosby, through his lawyer, of lying about her "to damage her reputation for truthfulness and honesty" for the sake of casting doubt on her rape allegations. The complaint added that the statements in Singer's letter were made "with reckless disregard for the truth and/or actual malice toward Ms. McKee."

From the start, it was a bizarre case. There was no question that Cosby and Singer had used underhanded tactics to try to tar an accuser. On the other hand, Singer's letter hadn't actually accused McKee of lying about Cosby raping her; it had simply said she had a history of lying about other things (namely, her race and age). And that was true, if irrelevant. Singer was using that fact to make an argument that McKee shouldn't be trusted, but while that conclusion was at best dubious, it was also a matter of opinion. And expressing opinions based on accurate facts did not give rise to a defamation claim. As Cosby's lawyers responded in a court filing, "This is a constitutionally protected opinion about the *Daily News*' journalism; it is not defamation of Plaintiff." They moved to have the lawsuit dismissed.

In early 2017, a federal judge, Mark Mastroianni, granted that motion. Singer and Cosby had the First Amendment right to voice their perspective about McKee's credibility and the *Daily News*' integrity, and the views they'd expressed were grounded in generally uncontested facts that had been disclosed in the letter. "As a result, the statements are protected by the First Amendment and are not actionable," Mastroianni wrote.

That was the crux of his opinion. But there was one other matter that the judge weighed in on. It was a minor issue—Mastroianni confined it to a couple of footnotes—but it would take on great importance in the years ahead. For the purposes of determining whether McKee had been defamed, he wrote, he had to determine whether she was a public figure under the standards established by *New York Times v. Sullivan* and the Supreme Court's subsequent libel decisions. Without fully explaining his reasoning, Mastroianni concluded that McKee was, indeed, a public figure, at least in the limited sense that she had inserted herself into the ongoing fracas surrounding Cosby by speaking publicly about the alleged rape. That meant that even if Singer's letter was defamatory—and Mastroianni had already concluded that it was not—McKee would have had to prove that Cosby and Singer had acted with actual malice.

This might have been the end of the matter. McKee had paid a price for speaking out, though it was less severe than she'd originally feared, and Cosby by then had been criminally charged with sexual assault. (A court would overturn his subsequent conviction.) But Salo was convinced that his cousin had been defamed and that Mastroianni, whom President Obama had nominated to the bench in 2013, had railroaded McKee. "This is outrageous," he told her. But, he added, "Don't worry. I've had some positive results with appeals."

Not this time, though. In October 2017, a three-judge panel on the US Court of Appeals in Boston upheld Mastroianni's ruling. The judges agreed that Singer's heavily footnoted letter had set forth "the non-defamatory facts" on which he was basing his opinions, "thereby immunizing them from defamation liability."

But while Mastroianni had relegated the public figure question to the footnotes, the appeals court addressed it head-on. By speaking up following "decades of silence," and after many other women had come forward with allegations against Cosby, McKee had "thrust herself to the forefront of this controversy, seeking to influence its outcome." Unlike someone who was involuntarily dragged into the public spotlight, "McKee deliberately came forward and accused Cosby of rape in an interview with a reporter, thereby engaging the public's attention and inviting public scrutiny of the credibility of her allegations." She was a "limited purpose public figure." That meant McKee would have needed to prove that Singer and Cosby had defamed her with reckless disregard for the truth. And, the appeals court concluded, there was no evidence to suggest that was the case.

Salo had to call McKee, again, to break the bad news—and to vow to try once more. "This is a longer shot, but we're going to appeal," he told her.

Salo had a mixed record as a lawyer. He had previously won settlements for quite a few clients. But he'd also been suspended for a year from practicing law in New York after he was accused of misappropriating funds; Salo said it was an innocent mistake that occurred while he was suffering from posttraumatic stress disorder following 9/11. When it came to McKee's case, Salo told her that the judges had been biased against her, perhaps because she was a Black woman.

McKee felt like Cosby was victimizing her again—with the help of a growing group of judges who wouldn't even let her have her day in court. "How can he keep getting away with this?" she fumed to Salo. "It seems like they're favoring him over me."

There was one last place for McKee and Salo to turn: the Supreme Court.

Salo had never asked the Supreme Court to hear a case, and filing a petition for a writ of certiorari is a technical, specialized task. Even the font (12-point Century) and paper type (60 pounds) and size (6½ inches by 9½ inches) are prescribed. He and McKee needed help. They turned to Time's Up, a newly created group devoted to helping sexual assault victims. Could someone there connect them with a lawyer who had experience drafting so-called cert petitions?

They were in luck. Someone at Time's Up worked with Sandra Bullock, who'd previously hired a lawyer to go after a company that was using her likeness to sell blingy watches, and lately that lawyer had made a name for himself in the world of defamation: Charles Harder. Salo was

soon on the phone with Harder—who only weeks earlier had been trying to intimidate news organizations on behalf of Harvey Weinstein—to
see if he'd be willing to help McKee. "I inquired if they might be able
to pay something," Harder told me. When the answer came back no, he
agreed to take the case anyway. If McKee ended up winning money in a
settlement or from a jury, Harder would get a cut.

Salo had heard of Harder, who had killed Gawker and now represented the Trump family. "They call him the Darth Vader of the media business," he explained to me.* Over the phone, Harder impressed
him as "a really nice guy," though Salo was puzzled as to why he had
agreed to get involved. "He never really told me why he wanted to get
on this," Salo said. Harder would later say that he'd been "honored" to
represent a sexual assault victim. But in addition to possibly wiping away
some of Weinstein's taint, the case also presented an opportunity to advance his views on libel law. In the fall of 2016—months after his victory
against Gawker and more than a year before Salo and McKee were on his
radar—Harder had begun echoing Trump's calls to loosen the country's
libel protections by reconsidering the *Sullivan* decision. "I think the actual malice standard is too stringent," he told the *Hollywood Reporter*
that September. Two months later, he noted, ruefully, that "there are a
lot of celebrities and public figures who don't bring lawsuits because the
standard is so high."

Now here was a case that Harder could use to make a *Sullivan*-
undercutting argument to the Supreme Court, whose nine justices were
the only ones with the power to actually change the actual malice standard. Harder deputized one of his underlings, a lawyer named Dilan
Esper, who had prepared numerous Supreme Court petitions, to handle
most of the work. Esper and Salo met at an Irish bar in Manhattan; Salo
incorrectly assumed that Esper was Irish and that he therefore would
enjoy such an establishment. After correcting that misimpression, Esper
explained that when you were trying to get the Supreme Court to hear

---

* That was not quite how Harder saw himself. "I'm the media's Luke Skywalker," he wrote
in his memoir.

your case, you had to settle on a single question—the sexier, the better, in his estimation—for the justices to resolve. Esper and Salo got to work. The final petition was eleven pages. Gone was the debate about whether Cosby (via Singer) had defamed McKee. Now it all hinged on a profound constitutional question, which the men had spent weeks workshopping: "Whether a victim of sexual misconduct who merely publicly states that she was victimized (i.e. '#metoo'), has thrust herself to the forefront of a public debate in an attempt to influence the outcome, thereby becoming a limited purpose public figure who loses her right to recover for defamation absent a showing of actual malice by clear and convincing evidence." The lawyers had even debated whether to include the hashtag. Ultimately they decided that it was a clever way to remind the justices that this was a great hot-button topic for them to wade into.

They filed the petition with the Supreme Court on April 19, 2018. It asked the justices to narrow the scope of who qualified as a public figure, a category that had been gradually growing ever since the court created it. At the heart of the lawyers' argument was that McKee was a private person who'd told journalists that she'd been raped by someone who happened to be famous. Surely that alone should not allow people, including her attacker, to defame her with impunity.

It was tempting to automatically take McKee's side. She was a rape victim calling out a powerful man, and there was no question that she deserved justice. But there were problems with the argument her lawyers were making. First of all, McKee was a little famous. There were her numerous on-screen acting credits, as well as her romantic relationships with A-list celebrities. It was that fame that had led McKee to speak out in the first place—she realized that she was more likely to be taken seriously than people without name recognition—and it was what had led the *Daily News* to make a big deal about her allegations (and for media outlets worldwide to follow suit). This was not the typical profile of a private person. Yes, Cosby was accused of heinous crimes, and yes, Marty Singer seemed to have cynically exploited the protections of the First Amendment in order to smear his client's accuser. But what mattered under the Constitution was the principle, not the popularity of the speaker. McKee had used her celebrity status to shift the public debate, which meant she forfeited some of her rights to recourse if she were defamed.

Of course, even if the justices decided that McKee was not a public figure, that didn't change the fact that, according to two different federal courts, she hadn't actually been defamed. The facts in Singer's letter were accurate and were simply providing the basis for his opinions. And so the odds of the court agreeing to hear McKee's case seemed slim.

Even so—and despite the fact that the Supreme Court rejects more than 99 percent of the cert petitions it receives, generally without explanation—Salo was optimistic. "If we win this case, every law student from now to eternity is going to be reading your name," he told McKee, who was beginning to realize that her lawsuit had ceased being primarily about her.

Cosby's lawyers waived their right to reply to McKee's petition. This was a common way to exude a too-cool-for-school vibe, to signal to the justices that they shouldn't bother closely examining a meritless petition. It didn't work. In June 2018, the court asked Cosby's side to file a response. This was the first sign that the court might—*just might*—be preparing to seriously consider taking the case. Cosby's lawyers submitted their reply a month later, urging the court to reject McKee's petition.

The court set a date in late September 2018 for the justices to talk at one of their regular conferences about whether to accept the case. Four days before the appointed day, the discussion was rescheduled for early October. When that day approached, it was postponed again. The same thing would happen another ten times, dragging into 2019. Something was clearly afoot. If the court was going to simply reject the petition, McKee's lawyers figured, it would've done so by now.

What felt less encouraging was that President Trump's latest nominee to the Supreme Court was at that very moment being publicly accused of sexual misconduct. The same week that the justices had been scheduled to begin considering the McKee petition, Christine Blasey Ford had testified about Brett Kavanaugh's alleged role in a sexual assault back when he was in high school. The Senate was preparing to narrowly confirm Kavanaugh just as the court was scheduled, for a second time, to discuss the case. And the petition was due to be considered at other internal conferences in the weeks after Kavanaugh was sworn in as the Supreme Court's 102nd associate justice in early October. Harder and Esper wondered whether the justices might be reluctant to accept a high-profile sexual assault case as they welcomed their new colleague, who'd just gone through a grueling public exploration of his conduct as a hard-drinking teenager.

At least four justices needed to vote to accept a case. Harder and Esper surveyed the possibilities.

Elena Kagan felt like a potential ally. Many years earlier, as a professor at the University of Chicago, she'd written a piece in an academic journal that questioned aspects of the *Sullivan* decision and critiqued its successor cases. And during her Supreme Court confirmation hearings, she'd been hard to pin down on the topic. She'd voiced support for *Sullivan* but also noted "that people who did nothing to ask for trouble, who did not put themselves into the public sphere, can be greatly harmed by—when something goes around the internet and everybody believes something false about a person, that is a real harm. And the legal system should not pretend that it is not."

Chief Justice John Roberts also seemed like a plausible yes vote. In 1985, as a lawyer in the Reagan White House, he'd written a short memo expressing his personal views on libel law. He suggested that perhaps it should be easier for public figures to win in libel cases, though he thought punitive damages should be off-limits; plaintiffs should be able to collect damages only to compensate them for harm that they'd suffered. That, Roberts wrote, "would strike the balance about right, and would satisfy the First Amendment concerns of *Sullivan*."

Neil Gorsuch, who'd joined the court in 2017, was a wild card. During his confirmation hearings, he'd noted that *Sullivan* and the actual malice standard had "been the law of the land for, gosh, fifty, sixty years," but he stopped short of endorsing them. Stephen Breyer was another toss-up; presumably he wouldn't want to overturn *Sullivan* outright, but maybe he'd be amenable to reining in who qualified as a public figure. At the very least, it wasn't impossible that he'd be curious enough to accept the case and hear the arguments.

Finally, Clarence Thomas. He was a dedicated "originalist," whose devotion to the plain text of the Constitution—and his antipathy toward the liberal Warren Court, whose many landmark rulings included *Sullivan*—had only strengthened over time.

Perhaps more important, so had his disgust with the media. "I harbor a lot of resentment toward your industry," he'd snapped at a journalist who requested an interview in 2001, adding that the treatment he endured during his confirmation hearings was worse than anything the Ku Klux Klan could have inflicted. Over the years, that anger had twisted and hardened and grown inside him—to such a degree that by 2007, when Thomas published his memoir, he was remembering (or perhaps concocting) slights and errors by the media that had not occurred.

For example, Thomas recounted in *My Grandfather's Son* how, shortly after he joined the EEOC, he had granted his first interview to Ernie Holsendolph, a young reporter at the *New York Times*. (Thomas's memoir repeatedly misidentified him as "Holzendorf.") "To my surprise, what appeared in the *Times* was an article consisting mainly of quotes from people who disapproved of my views, none of whom knew me," Thomas wrote. The truth was that the 905-word story had quoted the former EEOC chairman and another commissioner at the time, who both had politely disagreed with Thomas's positions on affirmative action. Their critiques comprised less than three hundred words. The rest of the piece was devoted to Thomas's perspective. Thomas, in his memoir, went on to claim that an EEOC aide had told him that the reason the story was so negative (it wasn't!) was that "Holzendorf" had been ordered by his editors to make Thomas seem controversial. Holsendolph denied that ever happened.

This pattern repeated. Thomas wrote that in the frenzied period before his confirmation hearings, he and Ginni had stopped going to church "to spare our congregation the ordeal of being harassed by reporters." He wrote that he'd "been told that at least one article falsely suggested that the members of the church we were then attending engaged in such extreme religious practices as handling poisonous snakes and speaking in tongues." That appeared to be a reference to an article in the *Los Angeles Times* by a veteran journalist named David Savage. The article quoted Gordon Klooster, the parish administrator of Thomas's church, saying that "sometimes you will hear a prophecy or someone speaking in tongues," though Savage noted that it was "not on a regular basis." The article hadn't said anything about snakes.

And at another point, Thomas complained that after Bush nominated him, reporters had traveled to Georgia to interview his sister, Emma Mae Martin. In what he described as "especially contemptible" behavior, he accused reporters of "plying her with kind words and a few hundred dollars" to say that she'd had an abortion, which Thomas claimed was false. These were potentially career-destroying accusations, which Thomas presented no evidence to support. The journalists who wrote the stories were well regarded and denied paying Martin.

Thomas had perceived his treatment at the hands of the media as a destabilizing experience that, aside from nearly torpedoing his Supreme Court nomination, had left him teetering on the psychological brink. His allies had retaliated by smearing Hill. Now, decades later, Thomas and his fellow justices were weighing whether to hear a case in which another famous Black man was accused of having defamed his alleged victim. It is hard to imagine that Thomas missed the parallels.

At the same time, the president of the United States had declared war on the media and was pushing for libel laws to be loosened. Thomas and his bride, as he often referred to Ginni, were very much in Trump's orbit. The Thomases and the Trumps dined together. In fact, just as Thomas was mulling McKee's petition, Ginni went to the White House to lobby Trump to install more far-right activists in his administration. "It is unusual for the spouse of a sitting Supreme Court justice to have such a meeting with a president," the *New York Times* drily noted.

A month later, on February 19, the waiting ended. The Supreme Court published its long list of orders. When it came to *McKee v. Cosby*, nine words brought the yearslong case to a close: "The petition for a writ of certiorari is denied." Harder, Esper, Salo, and most of all Kathy McKee had lost.

But there was an enormous asterisk. Clarence Thomas had submitted an opinion outlining his thinking on the matter. He started by briefly describing the case. He listed the reasons that McKee felt she'd been wronged—first by Cosby (via Singer) and then by federal judges. And then he announced that he agreed with his colleagues: the Supreme Court should not entertain her appeal. If McKee was a victim of injustice, neither Thomas nor the other eight justices saw it as their responsibility to intervene.

But Thomas was just getting started. He was going to use this opportunity to make a much broader argument: that at some point in the future, the court should find a more "appropriate case" with which to reconsider *New York Times v. Sullivan*. Thomas's argument had nothing to do with McKee or Cosby, who weren't mentioned again in the ensuing twelve single-spaced pages. His thesis was, in some ways, simple: the text of the First Amendment said nothing about libel, and the court in *Sullivan* (and the subsequent cases that had broadened the actual malice standard to encompass public figures as well as public officials) had constructed a self-serving rationale for protecting certain types of defamatory speech. "None of these decisions made a sustained effort to ground their holdings in the Constitution's original meaning," Thomas wrote.

By his logic, the only way to interpret the First Amendment (or any other part of the Constitution) was to consider the intent of the men who had written it. At the time that the Bill of Rights was ratified in 1791, Thomas wrote, to win damages in a libel case a public figure typically needed to prove only that a false statement had subjected him to "hatred, contempt, or ridicule." A victim didn't even need to prove that his reputation had been harmed, much less that the defamer had acted with reckless disregard for the truth. This was by design, Thomas said, because the traditional understanding in British and American law was that defaming a public figure was even worse than defaming a normal citizen; after all, the public figure's livelihood hinged upon public trust.

Before the *Sullivan* decision, libel had been a matter of state law, not federal. That was where Thomas thought it belonged. If some states wanted to protect people's rights to speak falsely about a public figure, that was their prerogative. But there was no reason for the Supreme Court to dictate state policy in a way that went beyond what the framers of the Constitution had written. "We did not begin meddling in this area until 1964, nearly 175 years after the First Amendment was ratified," Thomas concluded. "The States are perfectly capable of striking an acceptable balance between encouraging robust public discourse and providing a meaningful remedy for reputational harm."

This, of course, contradicted history—as well as Thomas's endorsement of the *Sullivan* decision back in 1991. The whole reason Justice Brennan and his colleagues had created the actual malice standard in the first place was that Alabama and other southern states were manifestly *incapable* of striking an acceptable balance. With the blessing of state courts, local officials like L. B. Sullivan had realized that by seeking overwhelming financial penalties when the media made even trivial mistakes, they could effectively prevent national news organizations from writing about the civil rights movement. That, the Supreme Court had decided, violated the First Amendment's prohibition on the government "abridging the freedom of speech, or of the press."

Thomas's focus on the framers' original intent in this case felt arbitrary. Judge Robert Bork was one of the intellectual fathers of originalism, and back in 1984, in his opinion in *Ollman v. Evans*, he had anticipated— and sought to preempt—the argument that Thomas was now making. While not much was known about the "precise intentions" of the men who wrote the First Amendment, Bork noted, there was no question that they'd placed a premium on protecting freedom of expression. "Perhaps the framers did not envision libel actions as a major threat to that freedom," he went on. "But if, over time, the libel action becomes a threat to the central meaning of the First Amendment, why should not judges adapt their doctrines? Why is it different to refine and evolve doctrine here, so long as one is faithful to the basic meaning of the amendment, than it is to adapt the Fourth Amendment [which prohibited unreasonable searches and seizures of people's property] to take account of electronic surveillance?" Bork asked, before ticking off another couple of examples. "I do not believe there is a difference."

In other cases, Thomas had embraced an expansive view of the First Amendment, standing up for corporations' rights to donate to political campaigns and striking down local laws that regulated outdoor signs, for example. It would have taken a creative legal mind to justify those stances based on the forty-five words of the First Amendment.

Thomas was writing only for himself. No colleagues signed on to his opinion (or wrote their own). But his words carried weight. For the first time in decades, a justice had written an opinion calling for the reconsideration of one of the court's most hallowed decisions. And Thomas wasn't just any justice. Since Antonin Scalia's death in 2016, he had become perhaps the foremost figure in the conservative legal movement, certainly in the federal judiciary. It wouldn't take long for his denunciation of *Sullivan* to reverberate loudly.

Superficially at least, McKee made an attractive case study in the excesses of the *Sullivan* regime. Here was a sexual assault survivor whose hands were tied when she tried to seek justice against the man who allegedly raped her and then called her a liar. "I am confident that the Supreme Court . . . never intended for someone like Katherine [*sic*] McKee to be classified as a public figure," wrote Rod Smolla, who fifteen years earlier had unsuccessfully asked the Supreme Court to make it easier for borderline public figures like Carey Lohrenz to win libel lawsuits. "I endorse the call by Justice Thomas for a re-examination" of *Sullivan* and its successor cases.

Amul Thapar, a prominent conservative judge on the federal appeals court in Cincinnati, hailed Thomas's opinion as inspired. "Justice Thomas doesn't criticize *New York Times v. Sullivan* simply because it is unsupported by the text of the Constitution and American history," he wrote in his hagiographic book about Thomas, *The People's Justice*. "Justice Thomas is committed to applying the law's meaning, but he is not blind to the struggles of the people before him," he concluded. "He speaks out for rape survivors like . . . Kathy McKee."

Except that he hadn't. Thomas didn't want the court to even hear McKee's case. McKee was livid. There was only one justice on the Supreme Court whom she'd feared would not give her a fair shake: Thomas. She had despised him ever since watching his confirmation hearings and observing how he handled Anita Hill's allegations. *I've seen men like that,*

she'd thought to herself at the time, glued to the TV. Her mind had flit-
ted back to Cosby and the secret that she'd been keeping for nearly two
decades at that point.

Now McKee felt like she was being victimized once again. Thomas
and his colleagues had refused to hear her case—and Thomas then had
the temerity to use her to advance his ideological agenda. She had no
interest in becoming a cause célèbre for the conservative movement. "It
was," she said, "a slap in my face."

PART III

THE MOVEMENT

THE OLIGARCHS' REVENGE

The day after the Supreme Court turned down Kathy McKee's appeal, Libby Locke arrived at a TV studio to film a segment on the country's most watched cable news show, Fox News' *Tucker Carlson Tonight*.

Ever since her victory against *Rolling Stone*, appearances like this had become routine for Locke, whose law firm had cemented itself as the country's marquee defamation shop. It was a lucrative niche; Clare and Locke generally charged more than $1,200 an hour, and that was often on top of tens of thousands of dollars in fixed fees. To threaten a lawsuit, the firm sometimes required clients to cough up another $100,000 or so, lawyers told me. Some of Clare and Locke's colleagues estimated that the two founders were personally taking home well over $10 million apiece per year, an extraordinary windfall even by the standards of the legal industry's exorbitant paydays. "They probably make more money than [partners at] any other law firm in the country," one of their business contacts told me admiringly.* Lower-level employees at the firm were doing just fine, too. One Clare Locke associate earned enough to buy himself an Aston Martin.

By now, the romance between the two founders was out in the open. They had been married in August 2017; one of their firm's first recruits, Megan Meier, had agreed to officiate the wedding at the elegant Four

---

* This was a slight exaggeration. Top partners at the richest US law firms sometimes pulled in more than $20 million a year.

Seasons hotel in Georgetown. Yet some colleagues' concerns about office dynamics had only deepened. Clare was widely regarded as calm, courteous, and risk-averse. He had a black belt in Tae Kwon Do and had been on Notre Dame's varsity fencing team, and a colleague told me that he "takes seriously the art of war"; being gratuitously nasty to your adversaries was not constructive. Locke was different. She was more entrepreneurial than her husband but also could be impetuous and antagonistic. Once, at a legal conference at a resort in Virginia, she stunned some panelists when she shouted from the audience to express her views about the *Sullivan* ruling. Some of her colleagues worried that her bombastic demeanor needlessly alienated lawyers who represented media companies. Clare seemed to acknowledge his wife's hot temperament. "We like to joke that ours is a story of fire and ice," he once said.

In November 2017, shortly after the newlyweds returned from their honeymoon in the Seychelles, Locke had been a featured speaker at a Federalist Society convention, where she complained about the inability of plaintiffs to unmask journalists' confidential sources. "How are you supposed to prove as a defamation plaintiff that the journalist knew what they were writing was false if you don't have access to the identity of their sources?" she asked. "It's really problematic." Sources often insist that their names not be published because they fear for their jobs or safety. State legislatures and federal courts have regularly recognized the sanctity of confidential sources, in part because forcing journalists to reveal their identities would often make it impossible to get them to speak in the first place—an outcome that would keep countless crimes and other misdeeds out of public view.

The next year, after Christine Blasey Ford accused Brett Kavanaugh of sexual assault, Locke had leapt to his defense with opinion pieces in the *Wall Street Journal* that lamented how public figures have limited recourse when their reputations are harmed. That was the first time Tucker Carlson had her on, and she described how hard it can be to win defamation cases. "Fifty years ago, you would have been a liberal hero for doing what you are doing, and I'm sure now they mock you," Carlson gushed.

Months later, in January 2019, she returned to discuss the case of a high school student, Nick Sandmann, who'd been in a face-off with a Native American activist at a rally near the Lincoln Memorial. Footage of the encounter had gone viral, and countless people, including Democratic lawmakers and quite a few journalists, had pilloried Sandmann as a racist. When it turned out that Sandmann, who'd been wearing a red MAGA hat, and his classmates hadn't instigated a fight, they became symbols, at least on Fox News, of liberals sullying conservatives as bigots.

"What's their recourse?" Carlson asked.

"Well, they can bring defamation claims," Locke replied. "They should hire experienced defamation counsel, someone not just an experienced lawyer, but someone who knows this area of the law, and who can really evaluate legal claims. It's what we did in the UVA case." Carlson wrapped the segment by praising Locke as "one of the most successful lawyers in this small but important field."

On the law firm's internal Slack channel, Locke's colleagues applauded her appearances. "Rock star!" one commented. Others posted emojis featuring the law firm's logo or Locke's smiling face. Privately, though, some were grimacing. They worried that large companies—potentially lucrative clients—wouldn't want to associate with a firm whose owner was comfortable on a show that often trafficked in xenophobia and lies. (It didn't help matters internally when, not long after she appeared on another Fox News show, *The Ingraham Angle*, Clare Locke hired the husband of one of the show's producers.)

The day after the *McKee* opinion, Locke was back on Carlson's show. This time the topic was the actor Jussie Smollett, who had just been indicted for staging a hate crime against himself. The Smollett saga presented the latest opportunity for Carlson and his guests to follow Trump's lead and rip the mainstream media. In just the past few days, the president had endorsed Sandmann's libel lawsuit against the *Washington Post*. He'd suggested "retribution" against broadcast networks after a *Saturday Night Live* skit lampooned him. And he'd slammed the *New York Times* as "a true ENEMY OF THE PEOPLE," falsely claiming the newspaper hadn't sought comment before publishing an article about investigations into the president.

A Stars and Stripes montage fluttered on a screen behind Locke. Her expertise in the Smollett case derived, apparently, from her suit against *Rolling Stone*, which also involved someone fabricating, or at least exaggerating, criminal allegations. Now she blamed the media for having assumed that Smollett was telling the truth when he claimed to have been attacked. "There was no stopping and thinking about, 'Does this smell right?'" Locke scolded.

"Why would reporters fall for [the Smollett hoax] before everyone else?" asked Carlson, as an image of the illuminated US Capitol glimmered over his shoulder.

"That's a great question, Tucker," Locke replied, arching her eyebrows and leaning back in her chair. It was a chance to pivot to her real passion. "It's exactly why Justice Thomas was correct in raising yesterday in the Supreme Court why we need to rethink that *New York Times v. Sullivan* standard . . . which has insulated the media from liability in these cases."

"I totally agree," Carlson said, shaking his head.

"An informed electorate is important," Locke stated somberly, "and the media is responsible for helping the American electorate be properly informed."

"That's right," Carlson said, "and we're falling down on the job, I would say. Us being the media."

If Locke was truly concerned about the media properly informing the American electorate, it was hard to understand her repeated appearances on Fox News' prime-time programs, which often peddled blatant disinformation. A more important goal of her anti-*Sullivan* advocacy, it seemed, was insulating clients from unwanted media attention.

As if to illustrate this, about an hour before her segment with Carlson aired on Fox News, Locke's husband had received an email from Ken Vogel, an investigative reporter at the *New York Times*. He was working on a story about an operative who had links both to Trump's 2016 campaign and to the Russian oligarch Oleg Deripaska. In the 1990s, Deripaska had amassed a multi-billion-dollar fortune in the aluminum industry as he outmaneuvered rivals who were racing to seize state-owned assets. It had been a "corpse-filled struggle," rife with murders and corruption. Deripaska was suspected by the US government of ties to organized crime, of money laundering, and of ordering a contract killing. More recently, he'd emerged as a character in Special Counsel Robert Mueller's investigation into Russian interference in the 2016 election. (Deripaska denied wrongdoing.)

Now he was one of several Russian oligarchs whom Clare Locke represented. Vogel had learned about the firm's work for Deripaska a month earlier, in January 2019, when Clare sent an unsolicited letter to the *Times* to complain about its coverage. "Mr. Deripaska has retained our firm to conduct a review and analysis of the Times' and other media publications' biased and misleading coverage of Mr. Deripaska and to ensure fairness and balance in all future reporting," Clare wrote. "With this letter, the Times is on notice that, should it continue its biased and misleading reporting, it could be liable for the catastrophic economic damages Mr. Deripaska and [his companies] would incur as a result of its negative, misleading, unfair, and biased reporting."

And so, on February 20, as Vogel was working on a story about Deripaska, he sent Clare a list of ten questions. The goal was to make sure that the *Times* was getting its facts right and to offer Deripaska and his advisers an opportunity to add any context or comments. Clare replied that he would try to get the questions to the right person. Then . . . silence. Neither he nor any other Deripaska representative followed up. This would become a pattern. Clare, having threatened the *Times* over its coverage of a client, now refused to provide information to help ensure the accuracy of its articles.

With its work for Deripaska, Clare Locke was toeing a fine legal line. A federal law, the Foreign Agents Registration Act, was designed to protect the United States from covert foreign influence. The law required people working on behalf of overseas governments, organizations, and individuals to register with the Justice Department if they were engaging in political activities or trying to influence the public. This included "taking part in perception management efforts or acting as a public relations counsel." Once registered, representatives had to disclose exactly what they were doing on behalf of their foreign clients and how much they were being paid.

This was clearly on Clare's mind when Vogel emailed him "in your capacity as a public relations representative for Oleg Deripaska." Clare responded six minutes later that "I am not (and never have been) his public relations representative—and I do not act in that capacity."

But Clare soon decided that perhaps it would be prudent to check whether he and his firm were required to register with the government. In the spring of 2019, Clare Locke wrote to the Justice Department to seek guidance. The law firm explained that it had not been hired by Deripaska to lobby Congress or influence public opinion; its mandate was limited to pursuing potential litigation, including by sending "demand letters" to US media outlets.

This was an awfully narrow interpretation of what Clare Locke was actually doing. The letters it wrote to outlets like the *Times*—on behalf of Deripaska and many others—often warned of possible litigation, but that was hardly their only or even primary purpose. They were also intended to influence the way journalists wrote about the Deripaskas of the world—and, by extension, to influence the way the public perceived them.

Trump's Justice Department, however, was satisfied by Clare Locke's explanation. "Based upon the representations in your letters, we have concluded that [Clare Locke] is not currently obligated to register under the Act," a senior official in the department's National Security Division responded. That gave Clare free rein to continue menacing journalists on behalf of a notorious Russian oligarch.*

In any given year, the *Times* receives dozens of threatening letters from lawyers trying to sway the newspaper's coverage. Like other national news organizations, the *Times* has a robust legal department, with many years of experience fielding such missives. The paper takes these letters seriously but is rarely intimidated by them.

Scott Stedman did not have that luxury. His journalism career dated to 2017 when, as a senior at University of California, Irvine, he had started

---

* After Russia invaded Ukraine in 2022, Clare said that his firm no longer represented Deripaska.

blogging. Stedman was a news junkie, but he was not impressed by the mainstream media's coverage of the Mueller investigation and Russian interference in the presidential election. Maybe he'd give reporting a try. That year, George Papadopolous, a foreign policy adviser to the Trump campaign, was in the headlines because of his interactions with people linked to Russian intelligence agencies. Stedman sent messages to dozens of foreign consulates asking if they'd had contact with Papadopolous. To Stedman's surprise, the British government confirmed that its officials had met with him. Stedman published the scoop on his blog. It began getting noticed on social media. Then the BBC picked up the story, which set off a round of media coverage. Stedman's journalism career was off and running.

After graduating—his grades had taken a drubbing as he devoted most of his waking hours to his guerilla journalism rather than his schoolwork—he set up in his parents' ranch-style house on a tidy Southern California cul de sac. He named his online publication *Forensic News*. The goal was to mine public documents and financial records to expose secrets. He offered readers a way to donate to help pay for his reporting, and enough money eventually was coming in—about $3,000 a month—to allow him to pay his few bills and to commission occasional articles from other aspiring journalists.

Stedman's investigative techniques—an ability to track down obscure government documents, to plumb the depths of off-brand social media networks, to follow the money—were surprising for a fresh-out-of-college rookie. But they were part of his family heritage. His father, John Stedman, had spent three decades in the Los Angeles Sheriff's Department, largely focused on chasing terrorists. Scott Stedman spent his youth surrounded by law enforcement and intelligence types, learning some of their tradecraft through osmosis.

In June 2019, a *Politico* article caught Stedman's attention. It reported that the Senate Intelligence Committee, which was investigating Russian election interference, was trying to track down an Israeli and British security consultant named Walter Soriano. It wasn't entirely clear why the investigators wanted to talk to him. *Politico* described him as "virtually a ghost." Stedman set out to find him.

He soon picked up a breadcrumb trail. It concerned the airport in the Russian city of Sochi. Ahead of the 2014 Olympics there, the airport was being built by companies controlled by Oleg Deripaska; Soriano's company had won a contract to provide security. Stedman unearthed records from a small-claims court in the Russian city of Krasnador that documented the previously unreported connection, which, given the sensitivity of the Olympic assignment, suggested that Soriano enjoyed close ties not only to Deripaska but also to the Kremlin.

Stedman and another reporter, Jess Coleman, published a 3,700-word story outlining their findings. It described Soriano as a "covert operative for Russian and Israeli elite." More stories and a podcast episode followed. They painted a picture of Soriano as an important enabler of oligarchs like Deripaska and Israeli power players like Benjamin Netanyahu, and as someone whose companies specialized in sophisticated electronic surveillance and hacking.

The pieces weren't always bulletproof. Stedman sometimes presented a pile of circumstantial facts as evidence of a conspiracy. His language could be overheated. Yet there was no denying that he was shedding light on some very murky corners of the business and geopolitical worlds—and, in Soriano, a shadowy man who had such a strong interest in keeping his operations under wraps that he had apparently managed to scrub the internet of any photos of himself.

Not surprisingly, Soriano resented these American journalists nosing around in his affairs. When I spoke to Stedman in January 2023, he told me that right off the bat, Soriano's lawyer had threatened to sue. This didn't come as much of a surprise. Stedman knew that Soriano regularly went after journalists who wrote critically of him, filing suits in Israel, Ireland, and Britain in an often-successful operation to keep himself and his companies out of the public eye. Yet to the twenty-three-year-old Stedman, there was something validating about receiving a threat like this; it signaled that his work was having an impact. At the end of the first major article, he and Coleman noted that Soriano had warned of a libel lawsuit. "We will not delete this story under any circumstances," they vowed.

In May 2020, Stedman was working on another piece about Soriano, this one in partnership with a law student named Robert DeNault. This article described the connections between Soriano, Deripaska, and a network of Israeli hacking and surveillance companies that had paid people including Michael Flynn, Trump's disgraced national security adviser. Stedman reached out to Soriano's lawyer, Shlomo Rechtschaffen, who again threatened to sue and demanded that he cease his reporting. Stedman also contacted representatives of Deripaska to see if they would like to comment for the upcoming article.

A few days later, Stedman received a three-page letter from Tom Clare, who said he was responding on Deripaska's behalf. Clare started off by saying that the allegations Stedman had sought responses to "are false." He then noted that it would be impossible for Deripaska to respond substantively "without understanding the actual sources of these false claims." Therefore, Clare wrote, "you must provide him with your sources and any documentation (public or otherwise) you claim supports them." A failure to do so "would demonstrate a reckless disregard for the truth and be supportive evidence of actual malice." After Libby Locke had called for the unmasking of confidential sources at the Federalist Society convention, here was her husband demanding that a young, independent journalist do so—or risk litigation. Clare concluded his letter by putting Stedman "on written notice of the significant risks you take by publishing false claims about Mr. Deripaska" and instructing *Forensic News* to retain all communications and documents related to Stedman's reporting in case there was a lawsuit.

Stedman couldn't contain himself. "Oleg Deripaska is now being represented by a top DC defamation lawyer known for his aggressive tactics in attempting to kill stories," he tweeted. "Won't be silenced."

That elicited another letter from Clare, who denied trying to silence Stedman and insisted that he'd only been asking for sources that were in the public domain. Someone at Clare Locke even dug up an old item that Stedman had posted on Reddit in which he called on journalists to "be more transparent" and to rely less on anonymous sourcing.

Stedman and DeNault published their piece on June 16. It featured rare photos of Soriano, which Stedman had received from someone with access to a Soriano relative's social media account. The article cited

Clare's and Rechtschaffen's denials—as well as the legal threats. "To date, no lawsuit has been initiated," the article deadpanned.

Four weeks later, a lawsuit was initiated.

Soriano sued *Forensic News*, Stedman, Robert DeNault, Jess Coleman, and others in the High Court of England and Wales. The suit accused them of making dozens of defamatory statements about Soriano in articles, the podcast, and hundreds of tweets and Facebook posts. In addition to libel, the complaint alleged that Stedman and his colleagues had violated British laws against the misuse of private information, harassment, spreading "malicious falsehoods," and improperly handling personal data. This last claim was especially edgy. It relied on a law designed to protect UK consumers from having their data exploited, such as by ads surreptitiously tracking which websites they visited. Soriano argued that Stedman and the others had handled the businessman's "data"—information and photos that the journalists had come upon through their reporting—in an unfair and inaccurate manner. In addition to monetary damages, Soriano asked for an injunction barring the defendants from continuing to harass him or invade his privacy with future articles.

Stedman and his colleagues wouldn't learn that they had been sued for nearly three months. But about two weeks after the lawsuit was filed, there was a warning sign: Twitter, apparently reacting to legal demands from Soriano, suspended Stedman's account, which had tens of thousands of followers. To regain access, the social media company told him that he would have to delete the Soriano images. Stedman grudgingly complied. It was a clear indication that Soriano and his allies were trying to muzzle the journalist—and that they just might succeed.

Stedman then did something that inadvertently exacerbated his predicament. Still not knowing he'd been sued, he announced that *Forensic News* would let readers donate money in pounds and euros, not just dollars. It seemed like a logical way to appeal to supporters outside the United States. But that was enough for Soriano and his lawyer to argue in court that, at least for the purposes of determining its compliance with the data-protection act and other laws, *Forensic News* was technically "established within the United Kingdom."

Stedman finally learned of the lawsuit in October 2020. His father was getting home from work one evening when a man got out of a car and rushed toward him. John Stedman instinctively moved his hand to his holstered gun, only to learn that the process server was looking for his son. "You almost got shot, dude!" the older Stedman reprimanded the man, who eventually tracked down Scott and presented him with the lawsuit. "This is from Mr. Soriano," he said.

Despite all the warnings, Stedman hadn't expected this to happen; he'd figured that Soriano's lawyer, Shlomo Rechtschaffen, had just been trying to scare him with the legal threats. Yet the fact that he'd been sued in England gave Stedman some early confidence. Not only were he and *Forensic News* based in California, but he'd never even set foot outside the United States. "I'm an American citizen," Stedman said. "I thought the First Amendment applied to me." On the other hand, he understood that Britain's libel laws—even after Parliament, embarrassed by waves of bad publicity following Rachel Ehrenfeld's crusade against libel tourism, had altered them in 2013 to make them less plaintiff-friendly—had earned London its reputation as the "town called sue." And adding to his anxiety, Stedman suspected that Soriano was just a cutout through which Deripaska and other oligarchs were trying to crush journalists, much as Peter Thiel had used Charles Harder and Hulk Hogan to annihilate Gawker.

Stedman announced on Twitter that he needed a lawyer. He soon received an email from a partner at the international law firm Gibson Dunn & Crutcher in London. "Your tweet," read the subject line. "Saw it," the lawyer wrote in the email's body. "Feel free to contact me if serious." So Stedman did, and Gibson Dunn soon agreed to take the case without requiring any upfront payments. It felt to Stedman like a minor miracle.

The first test came in January 2021, when a British judge, Robert Jay, had to rule on whether to let some or all of the lawsuit's allegations proceed toward trial. Jay allowed the libel claims to stand, concluding that the English courts were an appropriate venue because Soriano was "a British citizen whose personal and business interests lie principally within this jurisdiction." But he threw out other "fanciful" claims, including of spreading malicious falsehoods and of harassment. He also struck down the data-protection claim, noting that *Forensic News* had received a total of three donations denominated in pounds sterling and that it was therefore hard to argue that the news organization or Stedman was bound by British laws.

This was a big win for Stedman and *Forensic News*, especially because the SPEECH Act that Rachel Ehrenfeld had muscled through Congress a decade earlier served as a powerful fortification against the one surviving libel claim. That law, the Gibson Dunn lawyers noted in a court filing, likely "renders unenforceable" any libel judgment issued in the UK.

The victory, however, proved fleeting. Soriano's team appealed. A three-judge panel heard arguments and, in December 2021, issued its ruling. The court noted that nearly 2,500 people in England and Wales had read at least one of *Forensic News*' pieces about Soriano. And Stedman's decision to accept pound-denominated donations was the equivalent of him soliciting business in the UK, even if only a few Brits had contributed money, the court ruled. The data-protection claims were reinstated.

It was a landmark decision, expanding the reach of the data-protection law to people and publications with virtually no connections to the UK or Europe. Using the law "to silence journalists is expressly not what Parliament's intention was," a British lawmaker said. "It's all part of trying to murder the truth"—a description that applied not just to this court ruling but to the broader weaponization of libel and other laws to stifle criticism of the wealthy and powerful. By potentially dodging the SPEECH Act—which shielded Americans from overseas libel lawsuits, but not necessarily those regarding the misuse of someone's data—the ruling armed men like Soriano with a potent new weapon to attack anyone who dug into their affairs.

Adding insult to injury, the court ordered Stedman and his colleagues to pay Soriano more than £85,000 to cover some of the costs of his appeal. It was more money than Stedman had ever had.

For years, Stedman had struggled with occasional panic attacks. Now, as he faced growing legal and financial jeopardy, they grew worse.

One evening in December, he was returning home from a walk. He couldn't shake the feeling that he was wasting his twenties dealing with this fight. He was getting more and more upset with himself and his limited options. As he walked in the door, the spiral intensified. He felt his heart rate spike. His face went numb. Pain radiated through his chest. His father rushed him to the nearby Providence St. Jude hospital. Medical staff quickly determined that he was having a severe panic attack. At 3 a.m., Stedman took a selfie from the hospital bed. He was wearing a blue gown, his hair tousled. He looked wiped out.

Stedman's parents were alarmed. It wasn't just the increasingly frequent and severe panic attacks, which sometimes were accompanied by their son vomiting and shaking uncontrollably. Stedman was withdrawn. He wasn't sleeping. All he wanted to talk about was the lawsuit. Even so, his father urged him not to give up. "You're in the right," he told Scott. "Don't ever think of backing down when you're in the right."

Legal expenses piled up, slowly at first and then with gathering speed, like snow after the first layer coats the ground. His lawyers at Gibson Dunn were donating their time. But Stedman and his codefendants had to foot the bill for the British barristers who handled court appearances. And Stedman wanted to depose witnesses in the United States; he hoped to both impeach Soriano's credibility and rake up information that would prove that his reporting had been accurate. Those witnesses needed to be subpoenaed, and each subpoena cost a few thousand dollars, which came straight out of Stedman's rapidly dwindling savings.

Soriano hired Marty Singer's law firm to pursue Stedman and his colleagues for the £85,000 the court said they owed. In March the journalists received the latest threatening letter, this one from a Singer lawyer named Andrew Brettler, demanding that they cough up the money. "Should you ignore this demand, you will be proceeding at your own peril," Brettler warned.

The financial pressures exacerbated Stedman's anxiety problems, which made it harder for him to focus on producing articles, which made it harder to raise money. Round and round this cycle spun. On top of that, after the court's ruling in late 2021, Robert DeNault and Jess Coleman— with whom Stedman had written the offending articles—were wobbling.

They felt that they should probably settle the lawsuit; there was no clear path to victory, and, even if one existed, it would likely take years to get there. They had careers to look after.

Stedman disagreed. He believed in the principle of free speech, and he was stubborn. Plus, Soriano's lawsuit and Deripaska's legal threats were beginning to attract attention. Here were two rich and powerful businessmen, supported by rich and powerful lawyers, gunning for an upstart journalist. In the spring of 2022, shortly after Russia invaded Ukraine, a federal commission invited Stedman to testify at a Capitol Hill hearing about Russians' exploitation of western legal systems. He would be appearing alongside Bill Browder, the prominent anti-Putin activist and author.

Around this time, Stedman began noticing a troubling trend. He relied on social media to publicize *Forensic News*. Now, every time he posted something, his feed would immediately be overrun by what appeared to be coordinated attacks from online trolls.

His most aggressive and persistent tormentors included accounts called "Stedman Watch" and "Objective Journalism." In addition to a steady stream of insults, innuendo, baseless accusations, and photoshopped images of Stedman with coins for eyes, they posted links to multi-million-dollar verdicts that juries had handed down against media companies and reporters, including in the Gawker and *Rolling Stone* cases. Stedman Watch, in particular, had Soriano's fingerprints on it, at one point posting a screenshot of an email sent to Soriano seeking comment for an upcoming article. Other times, various accounts claimed that Stedman's father had left his job in the LA sheriff's department in disgrace and that unethical behavior ran in the family. Stedman very much doubted it was a coincidence that Rechtschaffen had once asked him whether John Stedman was his father.

It was the type of sustained abuse that has caused more than a few veteran journalists—including those whose employers have systems in place for dealing with these ambushes—to wilt. The cacophony crescendoed as Stedman was about to testify before the so-called Helsinki Commission. On the cross-country flight to Washington, Stedman checked his phone, scrolled through the latest hateful messages, and could feel the panic building inside him. "It's hard to just push it away," he told me. He wanted to go home and hide.

Instead, on April 6, he appeared in a Senate hearing room before the lawmakers and other officials who sat on the commission. He was wearing a blue suit and tie, and he placed a *Forensic News* water bottle on the table next to him. "Over the last eighteen months, I've lived the increasingly too common life of an investigative journalist who splits his time between researching and writing articles and tending to a defamation lawsuit," Stedman testified. He described the repeated legal threats he'd received on behalf of Soriano and Deripaska. "This is what lawfare looks like," he said, holding up a stack of correspondence from Tom Clare and others. "It is designed to suppress, stall, scare critical coverage of the Russian elite and their neighbors."

The effectiveness of those suppression tactics soon became clear. Soriano's team persuaded DeNault and Coleman to concede defeat. The settlement required them to publicly acknowledge that their stories about Soriano were "based on circumstantial and inadequate evidence." They went on to say, "They cannot attest to the truth of the allegations published in *Forensic News*' reporting and unreservedly apologize for this reporting and for the distress caused to Mr. Soriano as a result." It was a coup for Soriano, who could now trumpet the disavowals in court. Stedman felt blindsided, betrayed, and alone. *Forensic News* had been so close to becoming a real thing, with a permanent staff and actual offices. Now those hopes were fading, and his world felt like it was unraveling. Unable to bear any more online abuse, he quit Twitter, his primary means of recruiting subscribers and telling the world about his work.

He began taking long walks on the beach, sipping coffee, trying to ground himself, and contemplating whether he should give up and move on with his life. A not-much-younger version of him would have viewed this as an unconscionable act of weakness—he had written as much at the end of one of his first articles about Soriano. But Stedman was staring at a life in debt, his reputation ruined, his health ragged. He worried that Soriano was having him surveilled. He operated under the assumption that his phone and computer had been hacked. He couldn't tell if he was being prudent or paranoid. This was no way to live.

In March 2023, Stedman folded. He agreed to take down his articles about Soriano and to delete any social media posts about him. With a few keystrokes on his WordPress publishing account, Stedman erased years of relentless reporting.

The final indignity: as part of the settlement, Stedman was forced to contact certain news outlets that had written about *Forensic News*' reporting. "I kindly request that you immediately remove all references to Mr. Soriano on your website," Stedman wrote in one such email to David Marchant of OffshoreAlert, which had posted a couple of legal filings related to Soriano's litigation. In an attached document, Stedman noted that "third parties should not rely upon [the articles] for any of their own current or future published work." (Marchant replied tartly that he would not take down the documents.)

In July 2023, after both sides had agreed to the settlement but before they had fully executed its terms, the online trolls restarted their abuse. And someone removed the license plates from Stedman's Hyundai Sonata and replaced them with a pair of stolen plates. Was he being set up? "Stedman stated he is involved in high-profile litigation in London due to his journalism work," read a police report about the incident. "And does not know if this incident is somehow related, but wanted that information documented."

Stedman didn't see how he could go on with journalism, at least not for the time being. He got a job as a researcher at a nonprofit. "I'm looking forward to utilizing my skills in a fresh way and living a little bit more of a private life," he explained on social media. *Forensic News* "will be indefinitely dormant as I start this new journey."

TRIGGERING A FEDERAL JUDGE

L arry Silberman was cranky. It was the morning of September 14, 2020, and the judge and two of his colleagues on the federal appeals court in Washington, DC, were about to hear oral arguments in an important First Amendment case. Covid was raging, and so court was in session virtually. Silberman, who was about to turn eighty-five, had long since taken "senior status," and he only sat on the court about a third of the time that it was in session. But he was on this morning, and like so many others in the first year of the pandemic, he appeared to be having trouble navigating the Zoom videoconferencing setup. Lawyers in the digital meeting room overheard him mutter "bullshit" as he leaned in toward his computer's camera, his glowering face and bald head all that was visible.

In the nearly thirty years since his friend Clarence Thomas had ascended to the Supreme Court, Silberman's stature in conservative circles had only grown. A big part of it was his myriad rulings in service of Republicans and right-wing causes, whether it was helping the Reagan administration wriggle out of the Iran-Contra scandal, making it harder for Bill Clinton to wriggle out of the Monica Lewinsky scandal, or laying the legal groundwork for one of the Supreme Court's most important decisions against gun control.

But Silberman's status as a conservative folk hero was about more than how he ruled from the bench. In his time, he had been the rare federal judge who was also an unabashed ideological activist. During the Clinton administration, he and his wife, Ricky, had pushed the conservative journalist David Brock to pursue the "Troopergate" scandal in the hopes of taking down the Democratic president. He had opposed the renaming of military bases that honored Confederate leaders. He had been a behind-the-scenes adviser to the *Wall Street Journal*'s hardline editorial page. He even denounced the Supreme Court as "a largely illegitimate institution" because he perceived its justices as straying from the original (conservative) meaning of the Constitution. (Paradoxically, he also argued that other judges "who take political positions jeopardize the whole judiciary.")

Part of Silberman's schtick was bashing the media, a pastime he had picked up years before Clarence Thomas. John Yoo, who clerked for Silberman in the early 1990s (and would gain notoriety with his "torture memos" in the George W. Bush administration), had flirted with a journalism career, and he periodically tried to soften Silberman's views toward the media by inviting reporters to stop by the judge's chambers for lunch. Silberman would start off on an aggressive note, asking the guest to defend the news industry against allegations of liberal bias, and wouldn't let up. Yoo attributed Silberman's attitude to his time in the Nixon administration, when he'd watched a hostile press corps topple the president.

In 1992, just as Yoo's clerkship began, Silberman had delivered a keynote speech at the Federalist Society's annual gathering in Washington. The group was not as powerful as it would later become in the first Trump administration, for example, it exerted near total control over the White House's judge-selecting machinery—but it was still influential. Silberman was a rock star with this crowd, and his performance didn't disappoint. He attacked two longtime federal judges who'd questioned Thomas's fitness for the Supreme Court. Next, he trained his sights on the media. "The American working press has, to a man and a woman, accepted and embraced the tenets of judicial activism," he asserted. He complained that judges were often swayed by their desire for praise in the media, including for having "grown in office," which Silberman said was code for having moved to the left. He dubbed this the "Greenhouse effect"—a reference to Linda Greenhouse, the Supreme Court reporter for the *New York Times*, whom Silberman claimed was the journalist whose praise judges coveted most.

(There was one judge whom Silberman thought was immune from this phenomenon. "Clarence Thomas has, for some time, resolutely refused to read all but a couple of newspapers," Silberman said. "There will be, I would bet my shirt, no journalistic hole bored in his ozone level.") A *Wall Street Journal* columnist hailed it as a "landmark" speech.

The irony was that for all his moaning, Silberman was savvy at using the media to advance his agenda. It wasn't just with David Brock and the *Journal*'s editorial page. He and Ricky (who died in 2007, a month shy of their fiftieth wedding anniversary) had cultivated fruitful and very leaky relationships with journalists all over Washington, everyone from conservative stalwarts like William Safire to rank-and-file political reporters at outlets like the *Times* and the *Washington Post*.

Yet Silberman, like Thomas, went to great, and at times dishonest, lengths to frame himself as the media's victim. In 2004, for example, the *Los Angeles Times* published an article about his history as a partisan warrior. Silberman later claimed to an interviewer that the newspaper had refused to give him time to offer a comment and that one of the article's authors had "confessed" that the *Times* was in cahoots with Senate Democrats. The authors, David Savage and Tom Hamburger, each told me that this was nonsense.*

Now, on a pleasant September day in the middle of the pandemic, Silberman had an opportunity to vent his years of boiling anger toward the media. He was preparing to have his say on a case with potentially great ramifications for the legal protections enjoyed by journalists and anyone else who investigated or criticized the powerful.

Two and a half years earlier, the anticorruption group Global Witness had published a report about a suspicious oil deal in Liberia. The report was written by an idealistic lawyer and activist named Jon Noronha-Gant. He had been fascinated by Liberia for years, living in the West African nation on and off as he fought for the rights of prisoners and people whose homes were threatened by the clearcutting of forests. "I fell in

---

* Savage was the same reporter whose article about Clarence Thomas's church the justice had later mischaracterized.

love with the country," he told me, though it was a complicated place. Ravaged by years of civil war, Liberia was trying to create an economy essentially from scratch. Corruption remained rampant.

In 2009, Noronha-Gant had arrived at Global Witness. His job was to dig into government and corporate wrongdoing in Liberia, and, working with local nongovernmental organizations, he soon produced some high-impact reports. There was an exposé about illegal logging permits decimating the country's rainforests, which prompted the government to cancel the contracts and arrest the former head of the Forestry Development Authority. Another investigation, in 2011, explained how the state oil company had bribed Liberian legislators to ratify contracts that would give foreign energy companies the rights to drill for oil off Liberia's Atlantic coast.

Not long after that report, the drilling rights for a rectangular area known as Block 13 had come on the market. ExxonMobil won the bidding, agreeing to pay $120 million. It was a multipart transaction, apparently designed to keep some distance between Exxon and the previous owner of the drilling rights, which had been tainted by corruption allegations.

The transaction's complexity and size caught the attention of Noronha-Gant, a slim man who wore his thick, dishwater-blond hair brushed back from his high forehead. He and a colleague began fanning out to their contacts in Liberia and the oil industry, searching for hints of improprieties. Had any money changed hands between Exxon and the Liberian government or the company that had previously held the drilling rights? Noronha-Gant kept drawing blanks—and making more phone calls. Finally, in 2017, a breakthrough: a source, angry about the way the Exxon deal had come together, claimed to have bank records proving that government insiders had received large payments following the completion of the Exxon deal. The source eventually provided transaction-by-transaction statements from an account at an African bank. They showed that in May 2013, Liberia's state oil company, Nocal, had paid $35,000 apiece to six government officials who had been on the committee that negotiated the Exxon deal. One of those officials was Christiana Tah, Liberia's attorney general.

Noronha-Gant's immediate thought was that these might be bribes. For most Liberians, $35,000 would have been a windfall; it was more than what the country's highest-paid minister earned in a year. What was more, the money appeared to have come from the same Nocal bank account that had just received millions of dollars from Exxon in connection with the Block 13 transaction. And years earlier, when members of the Liberian legislature were bribed to support other offshore drilling deals, those payments had also come from a government bank account.

Over the next few months, Noronha-Gant tracked down additional details about the Exxon transaction and the history of Block 13. In early 2018, he reached out to Tah and the other recipients of the $35,000 payments: "We believe that the payment made . . . to you was most likely a bribe, paid as a reward to ensure that [Block] 13 was negotiated successfully." Tah responded that these were bonuses, not bribes, and that they'd been approved by Nocal's board of directors to employees "who performed exceptionally in conducting the negotiations on the Exxon contract." She emphasized that the payments had not come from Exxon and that smaller payouts had gone to countless other Nocal employees, including drivers, janitors, and secretaries. "Do you mean to tell me that Exxon was so desperate that it even bribed drivers?" she asked. She was "appalled" that Noronha-Gant had the nerve to accuse her of a crime. "I will not sit by and allow you to defame my good name," she warned.

Tah had a solid reputation, but Noronha-Gant was not convinced that the payments were aboveboard. His source provided him with years of bank records, which showed that aside from some small Christmas bonuses, there was no sign of comparable payouts to high-ranking Liberian officials on other occasions. Noronha-Gant wrote up his findings; the $210,000 in total bonuses were just one of the deal's many unusual hallmarks, ultimately taking up a couple of the report's forty heavily footnoted pages. Among those to review the piece before it was published was Nicola Namdjou, Global Witness's general counsel. She dialed back some of the wording and arranged for outside lawyers to review it to make sure it was legally sturdy—a standard move by publishers when they're preparing to run something controversial.

The report—*Catch Me If You Can: Exxon's Complicity in Liberian*

Oil Sector Corruption and How Its Washington Lobbyists Fight to Keep Oil Deals Secret—was published in March 2018. It was carefully worded. Global Witness took great care not to accuse Tah or her colleagues of having received bribes. The report referred to the bonuses as "unusual, large payments," which they undoubtedly were. It noted the history of bribery allegations involving Liberian oil deals. And it urged officials in Liberia and elsewhere to further investigate. But the report also acknowledged that it "cannot prove that these payments were improper" and that "there is no evidence that Exxon itself directed or knew about payments to officials." And it quoted Tah and other Liberian officials denying that they had been bribed and defending the integrity of the transaction.

Global Witness sent copies of the report to the US attorney general and the chairman of the Securities and Exchange Commission, urging them to look into whether Exxon had violated anticorruption laws. Thanks to all the lawyering and caveated language, Noronha-Gant wasn't worried about the fact that Tah kept saying publicly that Global Witness had falsely accused her of accepting bribes. He didn't expect things to escalate.

Tah regarded herself as a force for good in Liberia. She and her child had fled the country in 1990 as its civil war raged. They settled in the United States, where Tah had previously attended college and graduate school. She'd been lured back to Liberia in 2009, when she was nearly sixty, to help her country rebuild as part of a newly elected reformist government. As attorney general, she'd attacked public corruption—it was her Justice Ministry that had prosecuted the forestry officials for the illegal logging permits that Global Witness had exposed. Tah had long had a positive view of the organization, which had made it all the more baffling to her when it had seemed to turn on her. She felt like Noronha-Gant had shrugged off her and others' denials about receiving bribes and just plowed ahead without considering how the report might harm her hard-won reputation.

In 2014 Tah had returned to the United States, and she was trying to build a career as a consultant and business adviser. Now some of her international work began drying up, which she blamed on the publicity around Global Witness's report. "It hurt me professionally," she explained. "I felt like I needed to seek redress."

Decades earlier, Tah had received a law degree at Yale, and now she asked one of her friends there if he knew of a good defamation lawyer. The friend referred her to an acquaintance, who directed her to someone else, who suggested Rod Smolla, who'd made his name as a prominent First Amendment scholar before making his name, again, as a lawyer who sued publishers.

Tah called Smolla and asked if he'd be interested in taking her case. Smolla read *Catch Me If You Can* and then traveled to Maryland to meet her. He recognized that the report hadn't literally accused Tah of taking a bribe, but that sure seemed like the implication. Tah insisted to Smolla that she hadn't been bribed, and, given her credentials as a reformer, Smolla had little trouble trusting her. "I believe the courts will see you are honorable people who were trying to move Liberia out of corrupt times," he told his new client. He agreed to work on contingency, meaning he would get a substantial cut of any settlement or damages.

The fact that Smolla was willing to take this case reflected just how far he had traveled since his earlier days as a champion of press freedoms. A generation earlier, in the mid-1980s, he'd written a book, *Suing the Press*, which documented the "explosion" of libel cases brought by celebrities, politicians, and businessmen. Smolla took pains not to reveal much about where he stood on the balance between free speech and a person's right to protect her reputation. But on the final page, Smolla tipped his hand: "The libel explosion does chill the courage of the press, and in that chill all of us suffer, for it threatens to make the press slavishly safe, pouring out a centrist, spineless paste of consensus thought. All of us lose if we permit the trivialization of free speech." Now he was going to pursue a case that arguably would do exactly that.

In September 2018, about six months after Global Witness published its report, Smolla filed a defamation lawsuit against the organization on behalf of Tah and another former Liberian official, Randolph McClain, who'd also received a $35,000 payment. Each sought about $6 million in damages for their "extreme personal anguish and humiliation." Tah insisted to me that the suit wasn't about money, and she said she didn't know how Smolla had come up with that very large sum. ("It was a round figure that struck me as where cases like this would typically come out if the plaintiff won," Smolla explained.)

The lawsuit, filed in federal court in Washington, DC, did not dispute the specific facts in *Catch Me If You Can*. Instead, it took issue with its implications. The report "conveys to ordinary reasonable average readers the defamatory imputation" that Tah and McClain accepted bribes in exchange for approving the Block 13 transaction. The phrase "unusual, large payments" was merely a euphemism for bribery. Smolla's proof? A few media outlets had interpreted the report that way. (The complaint didn't mention that other reputable news organizations had correctly read the Global Witness report as simply flagging "irregular payments.") Smolla argued that the overall tenor of *Catch Me If You Can*—everything from its words to the color of its headlines—was meant to insinuate corruption. Based on Tah's and others' denials, the organization had reason to doubt that the bonuses were bribes, yet it went ahead and published the report anyway. That was actual malice.

The problem with this argument was not just that Global Witness hadn't accused anyone of bribery. A presidential committee in Liberia soon followed the report's recommendation and began looking into the $35,000 payments. It found that while they were not bribes, they were nonetheless illegal and should be swiftly returned if the recipients wanted to avoid criminal charges for "economic sabotage and misuse of public money." To Noronha-Gant and Namdjou, that validated their work. They had exposed hundreds of thousands of dollars' worth of improprieties in an impoverished country that needed every penny it could get.

To defend Global Witness, Namdjou hired the law firm Ballard Spahr, which had worked with the nonprofit in the past. The lead attorney was Chad Bowman. A former journalist, he had represented many news organizations in libel lawsuits—including before the same federal judge, Rosemary Collyer, who'd be hearing this case. In November 2018, Bowman asked her to dismiss the suit. In addition to pointing out that the underlying facts weren't in question, he noted that the plaintiffs were public officials. He invoked *Carey Lohrenz v. Elaine Donnelly*—the case that Smolla had argued years earlier on behalf of the female fighter pilot—to remind the court that "those who have chosen to engage in public endeavors or participate in public debate accept a greater risk of critical public comment and scrutiny." As former government officials, Tah and McClain clearly met those criteria. Bowman pointed out that courts had previously ruled that hearing a public official's denial of wrongdoing does not constitute knowledge that a statement might be false, because public officials sometimes lie. In any case, the report had quoted Tah and other officials and had acknowledged that there was no proof that the $35,000 payments were improper, even though Liberia later concluded that they were.

It would be months before a ruling. Behind the scenes, Namdjou and Bowman floated a possible compromise. Global Witness was willing to publish an addendum clarifying that the report had not meant to suggest that Tah or McClain received bribes. Smolla shot that down, insisting that any settlement would have to involve Global Witness forking over a substantial amount of money. That clarified things for Namdjou: This was not about setting the record straight. It seemed to be about money and vengeance.*

In the meantime, the long hours that Noronha-Gant was spending helping Bowman and his team to prepare for a possible court date left him with less time to investigate wrongdoing in Liberia. His gnawing anxiety wasn't helping. He was especially scared that he might be forced to reveal the identities of his sources, which could put them in real danger. His fears soon had consequences. When sources came to him with new information about the corrupt history of Block 13—information that, in Noronha-Gant's estimation, was potentially explosive—he felt obligated to warn them that their names theoretically could become public as part of the legal proceedings. He didn't expect that to happen, and

---

* Smolla said he didn't recall settlement discussions. He said his motivation was purely to win for his clients.

he would fight to prevent it, but could he guarantee their protection? He could not. Predictably, that put a quick stop to the sources sharing information. "I basically talked them out of it," he told me.

In 2019, a little more than a year after Smolla had filed the lawsuit, Judge Collyer, who'd been appointed by George W. Bush, ruled on Bowman's motion to dismiss. She concluded that a reader easily could have interpreted *Catch Me If You Can* as accusing Tah and McClain of bribery. That was defamatory. The question then became whether Global Witness had acted with actual malice. And on this front, the judge wrote, she regarded the lawsuit's evidence as "weak." There was no sign of Global Witness acting in "bad faith," of Noronha-Gant or his colleagues molding the facts to fit a preconceived storyline. "Plaintiffs do not allege facts supporting a culture of reckless reporting and disregard for the truth at Global Witness," she wrote. In short, the lawsuit's allegations "are insufficient to overcome First Amendment protections for speech." The motion was granted, and the lawsuit dismissed.

Bowman knew this was not the end of the fight. He warned Noronha-Gant and Namdjou that an appeal was all but certain. By now they suspected that Smolla was hoping to provoke a constitutional reckoning. They were right. With the federal judiciary having shifted to the right under Trump, Smolla had a chance to use Christiana Tah's lawsuit for more than simply attacking Global Witness. He could also take a swing at the *Sullivan* precedent.

Smolla filed his appeal barely two weeks later. It would be heard by a three-judge panel on the federal appeals court in DC, the same body that had decided *Lohrenz v. Donnelly*. And one of the same judges who'd heard that case back in 2003 would also be presiding over this one seventeen years later: Larry Silberman.

There had been a time, decades earlier, when Smolla was petrified of appearing in court. The first few cases he'd tried, he sweated through his suits and worried he was having a heart attack. But he'd eventually beaten down the anxiety and come first to enjoy and then to be addicted to the adrenaline rush. He'd long since forsaken prewritten speeches, or even detailed notes, in favor of speaking extemporaneously.

The oral arguments in *Tah v. Global Witness* would be no different—except that they'd be occurring digitally. Smolla was standing at the dining room table in his home in Wilmington, Delaware. A painting of him arguing before the Supreme Court hung nearby. It was a warm, clear day in September 2020, and Smolla had asked his neighbor not to let his groundkeeper mow the lawn for an hour. His wife had taken their noisy dog out for a walk.

Smolla explained to Silberman and his two colleagues—Sri Srinivasan and David Tatel—that Judge Collyer had erred by concluding that there wasn't evidence of actual malice. "From the very beginning, Global Witness was fixated on a story that was going to be alleging that Exxon facilitated or was complicit in bribery," he said. "They turned a blind eye to any contrary evidence and engaged in deliberate avoidance of the truth." Smolla's proof was the blanket denials that Tah and her colleagues had sent in response to Global Witness's questions about whether they'd received bribes.

At this point, Silberman interjected for the first time in what was about to become a feisty fifty-two minutes of argumentation—what's known as a "hot bench." The standard that this very court had established in the *Lohrenz* case, the judge reminded everyone, was whether the publisher (whether it was Elaine Donnelly and her Center for Military Readiness or Jon Noronha-Gant and Global Witness) had obvious reasons to question the accuracy of what it was writing. Silberman made clear that he thought there was ample evidence that the defendants in this case harbored such doubts. After all, *Catch Me If You Can* had conceded that Global Witness lacked evidence that the $35,000 payments were improper or that Exxon had known about them. "What do you make" of those acknowledgments? Silberman asked Smolla.

"We think that statement helps us tremendously, Your Honor," Smolla replied. "We think it's speaking with a forked tongue. On the one hand, what is overwhelmingly communicated here is that they've got the goods on Exxon, and they've got the goods on these officials, and they did it. And then they admit in the very same document that they don't know if they did it."

Silberman cut in again: "Isn't it stronger than that, counsel?" Global

Witness had said it had "no evidence" connecting Exxon to the payments. That was worse than simply not knowing if these were bribes, the judge asserted.

"Absolutely, Your Honor, it *is* stronger than that," Smolla said, allowing himself to be led like a purebred at a dog show. "And I think that is in itself enough to cross the threshold" for surviving a motion to dismiss. "It is at least plausible, given what they have said themselves, that this was communicated with reckless disregard for truth or falsity."

Bowman was sitting in his office on the twelfth floor of Ballard Spahr's suites on K Street in downtown Washington. His mother's old Smith-Corona typewriter was perched on a shelf, and the National Cathedral's gargoyle-studded bell towers were visible in the distance. Bowman had more than fifteen years of legal experience under his belt. It was obvious to him that Silberman had already made up his mind; he was all but instructing Smolla on how to frame his arguments. When it was his turn, Bowman braced for impact. He managed to speak for twenty-two seconds before Silberman interrupted to declare that the only thing that mattered here was whether Global Witness had "obvious reasons to doubt the story." And how could you interpret the report's statement about Exxon not being aware of the payments as anything other than an admission that Global Witness doubted its own findings? "Why isn't that injurious to your position on actual malice?" Silberman barked.

Namdjou and Noronha-Gant were both listening to a livestream of the hearing from their homes in England. They were beginning to think Silberman was either confused or playing dumb. The fact that Exxon hadn't known about the payments was not some damning confession. It didn't mean that the $35,000 payments were kosher; it just meant that Exxon hadn't been specifically aware of them. After all, in Liberia's previous oil deals, bribes had come from a government bank account, not from a private company.

Noronha-Gant and Namdjou were furiously zapping messages back and forth via WhatsApp with mounting alarm about Silberman's hostile questioning. Their concerns only grew when the judge asserted that there had been "no secrecy" surrounding the payments to Tah, McClain, and the others. "This is all public. Bribes take place in the dark of the night!"

Silberman snapped. "People don't normally advertise it publicly." Actually, the only reason the payments were public was that Noronha-Gant had found a source who took a giant risk by sharing secret bank records and that Global Witness had then published its report. Bowman, however, didn't immediately correct Silberman, who kept pelting him with questions without letting him respond.

"It's undisputed you have no evidence connecting Exxon to these payments, none at all," Silberman went on. "Why isn't that per se actual malice? Why isn't there objective reasons to doubt the truth of the implication? It's public, and according to your view, Exxon is spreading bribes around like Johnny Appleseed."

Bowman, having repeatedly failed to get a word in, was growing exasperated. "Your Honor, Exxon doesn't need to be the bribe payer," he explained, trying to keep his voice steady. He reminded the judges that in 2007 bribes had been paid by the government to Liberian legislators. In the more recent deal, "the money was paid as part of the transaction, and it was expressly tied after the transaction as for a job well done."

Silberman, who many years earlier had a stint as an investment banker, now cited his own experience. "Under that theory, as an ex-banker, I can tell you every investment banker that takes his share of the transaction in a sale of a corporation . . . would be guilty of bribery."

"It's slightly different, Your Honor, when they're public servants who are not supposed to necessarily receive bonuses," Bowman explained. He tried to get back to his main point, which was that Global Witness had sought and included responses from Tah and the others. The group had explained its factual basis for calling for an investigation, including that bribes and corruption "are not inherently improbable in Liberia when you're dealing with the disposition of state assets."

"We should just assume that Liberia is corrupt?" Silberman interjected.

"I wouldn't say that, Your Honor," Bowman retorted, no longer hiding his frustration. "However, this particular oil concession did have a history of corruption." A few minutes later, Silberman again claimed that Global Witness's letters to Tah and others, and the responses that he had received, constituted evidence of the group acting with actual malice. Bowman sensed that he had one last chance to make an impression on the other two judges. The fact that the report included the officials' denials, he said, reflected "an intent to portray fairly a complex factual situation, a situation that Global Witness struggled with."

Going into the hearing, Bowman had known that Silberman had a reputation as a brawler. He was rumored to have once had a physical fight with another judge about affirmative action. (Silberman later clarified that he had simply told the other judge that he'd been "tempted to punch him in the nose.") Yet Bowman had never been on the receiving end of such a judicial browbeating.

Silberman clearly was against Global Witness. But what about his two colleagues? Bowman figured they either were aligned with Silberman and letting him speak on their behalf, or Silberman was bludgeoning Bowman in an attempt to convince them about the weakness of Global Witness's defense. Bowman hoped it was the latter—and that the other two judges wouldn't be persuaded—but he wasn't sure. For his part, Smolla viewed victory as virtually a sure thing.

Listening to the oral arguments, Noronha-Gant realized that this had become about more than him. "It was the first time it registered to me that my report was not just jeopardizing me and Global Witness but also the First Amendment a little bit," he told me. The weight of that felt crushing. He began having trouble sleeping and showing up at work looking bedraggled. He was grinding his jaws so ferociously that the tips of his teeth chipped off.

Six months passed. Then, on a cold, blustery morning in March 2021, Bowman received an email from the clerk of the appeals court. There was a decision in the case.

Bowman opened the attached PDF. It was forty-one pages long. The decision was written by Judge Tatel, whom Bill Clinton had appointed to fill the vacancy created when Ruth Bader Ginsburg joined the Supreme Court in 1994. A civil rights lawyer before he became a judge—who despite being blind was a devoted skier and long-distance runner—Tatel was one of the country's most distinguished judges. Now, writing for himself and Judge Srinivasan, Tatel cut right to the chase: "The First Amendment provides broad protections for speech about public figures, and the former officials have failed to allege that Global Witness exceeded the bounds of those protections." The appeals court had upheld Judge Collyer's decision to dismiss the lawsuit.

Over the ensuing sixteen pages, Tatel dismembered Smolla's arguments. There was no proof, he wrote, that Global Witness had begun its investigation with a preordained conclusion, and, even if it had, that didn't automatically constitute actual malice. The group's comment-seeking letters, and its handling of Tah's and others' replies, were appropriate, Tatel wrote, citing the *Lohrenz* decision that Silberman had long ago signed on to. (A public official's denials are so common that "they hardly alert the conscientious reporter to the likelihood of error.") Nor was Smolla's argument that Global Witness had been out to get Exxon credible or relevant.

"The implications of Tah and McClain's theory are breathtaking," Tatel wrote. "They would find support for an inference of actual malice in a wide swath of investigative journalism that turns out to be critical of its subject."

Bowman turned the page. Silberman had not joined his colleagues' decision. Instead, he had bashed out a dissent, and it was longer than the majority ruling. The first section hinged on the notion that *Catch Me If You Can* falsely accused Tah and McClain of receiving bribes *from Exxon*. This struck Silberman as "ridiculous," because Global Witness had admitted it lacked evidence of Exxon knowing about the $35,000 payments. That, coupled with the officials' denials that the payments were bribes, was enough to persuade the judge that Global Witness had acted with reckless disregard for the truth. (As Tatel had pointed out in his opinion—and as Bowman had repeatedly tried to explain to Silberman during oral arguments—Exxon need not have been the briber. The state oil company, which through the Exxon deal stood to receive millions of dollars, also had a powerful incentive to see the transaction approved, and it was the one that had doled out the bonuses.)

Something about Tatel's opinion had triggered Silberman, whose tone went from logical to frustrated to irate. Any trace of decorum and restraint vanished, as Silberman allowed years of barely pent-up disgust with the judiciary and the media to erupt in an epic conflagration. He trashed Tatel's opinion as "improper," "obviously fallacious," "entirely illegitimate," "dumbfound[ing]," "profoundly troubling," and "procedurally inappropriate." And he was just getting started.

His anger had initially been directed at his two Democrat-appointed colleagues. Now he unfurled an extraordinary broadside against a much bigger target. "After observing my colleagues' efforts to stretch the actual malice rule like a rubber band, I am prompted to urge the overruling of *New York Times v. Sullivan*," Silberman announced. He noted that Justice Thomas, in the *McKee* case, had "already persuasively demonstrated" that the landmark ruling was "a policy-driven decision masquerading as constitutional law." The fifty-seven-year-old *Sullivan* decision had become "a threat to American Democracy. It must go."

Silberman conceded that the court's aim in *Sullivan*, amid the civil rights movement, had been understandable if not justified. But the ruling had imbued the media with enormous power, allowing it "to cast false aspersions on public figures with near impunity." This was an increasingly common argument, one that lawyers like Libby Locke and Charles Harder had been making for years, conveniently ignoring the victories they'd won in and out of court. Now Silberman stamped their questionable premise with the official imprimatur of a judicial opinion.

The reason Silberman found this so upsetting was not so much that people like Christiana Tah, Kathy McKee, or Carey Lohrenz lacked recourse when their reputations were besmirched. It was that he perceived the media as biased in favor of Democrats. "The increased power of the press is so dangerous today because we are very close to one-party control of these institutions," he wrote. He branded the *New York Times* and *Washington Post* as "virtually Democratic Party broadsheets." Large outlets like the *Wall Street Journal*, the Associated Press, the *Los Angeles Times*, the *Miami Herald*, and the *Boston Globe* were liberal, too. "Nearly all television—network and cable—is a Democratic Party trumpet." (He allowed that there were "a few notable exceptions," including Fox News and the *Wall Street Journal*'s editorial page.) Silberman pointed to research claiming that this bias aided Democratic candidates by up to 10 percent in elections.

Even if you accepted Silberman's claims at face value, it was unclear

what business a federal judge had using a court opinion to attack news organizations whose views he happened to disagree with. The whole point
of the First Amendment was that the government shouldn't be able to
suppress speech that its officials disliked. (Not to mention that the news
organizations that Silberman so loathed had nothing whatsoever to do
with this case.)

But that was not how Silberman saw it. "It should be borne in mind
that the first step taken by any potential authoritarian or dictatorial regime is to gain control of communications, particularly the delivery of
news," he said in closing. "It is fair to conclude, therefore, that one-party
control of the press and media is a threat to a viable democracy." The
media was deliberately distorting the marketplace of ideas. And so, he
concluded, "it is a profound mistake to stand by unjustified legal rules
that serve only to enhance the press' power."

Bowman finished reading. He'd known, of course, that Silberman was
against him, but the fury with which he'd written his opinion was jaw-
dropping. So was the fact that he had disregarded the decades of nonpartisan consensus around the *Sullivan* decision, which had long protected
both liberals and conservatives and been embraced by eminent original-
ists like Robert Bork, a close friend of Silberman's who had sat with him
on this same court. (Before Silberman joined the appeals court, Bork had
warned him against taking the job. "You'll be bored to death," Bork had
predicted. "You're too much of an activist.")

Around 11:30 a.m., Bowman emailed his colleagues about the "mostly
good" ruling. "You will hear about Judge Silberman's dissent," he added.
"If a petition to the U.S. Supreme Court was not already all but inevitable given Professor Smolla's position on *Sullivan* and the rightward shift
of the court during President Trump's term, this dissent likely removes
any doubt."

Later that day, Bowman received an email from a top partner at another
law firm asking if perhaps he would like some help with the case, which
surely was headed to the Supreme Court. Bowman politely declined—he
could handle this by himself, thank you!—but it was an indication of just
how hot this case had suddenly become.

Like Bowman, Smolla had been stunned by Silberman's tirade. "I worried his visceral attack on the media and Tucker Carlson–style diatribe would hurt us," Smolla told me. "It makes it seem ideological." (Tah, too, was flummoxed. "I didn't really understand how [Silberman's critique of media bias] related to my case," she said.) Nonetheless, the dissent was practically an invitation to appeal to the Supreme Court, especially since Silberman's friend there had already signaled his desire to overturn *Sullivan*. Smolla gladly accepted the invitation. But in November 2021 the Supreme Court rejected his petition for a writ of certiorari without explanation. (By then, another libel case had attracted the court's attention, as we'll see in the next chapter.)

After more than three years, the litigation was over. But the impact of Silberman's dissent would rapidly ripple outward. His opinions carried immense weight with his legions of admirers, which included former clerks, like Amy Coney Barrett, who sat on some of the country's most powerful courts. "When Silberman speaks, conservative lawyers and judges listen," a *Washington Post* columnist noted. Soon, his dissent would be used to prop up lawsuits and legal opinions that sought to chip away at the First Amendment and to return to the era, before *Sullivan*, in which you had to think twice before publicly criticizing powerful figures—or run the risk of encountering catastrophic legal damages.

For Global Witness, the victory was proud but painful. While the group's insurer absorbed the lion's share of the legal bill, the nonprofit had to shell out a hefty sum to cover the deductible on its insurance policy. And the organization was now fending off another offensive in an unrelated case. Global Witness had issued a report about how Dan Gertler, a mining billionaire, had apparently used a money-laundering network to evade US sanctions. Gertler's side, which denied the allegations, had responded by filing a criminal complaint against Global Witness, and someone was using social media to spread spurious allegations about employees who'd been involved in the project. It was a campaign of intimidation and retribution that made Noronha-Gant's tribulations feel like the opening set at a rock concert.

Not long after the Supreme Court rejected Smolla's petition, Namdjou, Noronha-Gant, and his wife, who had recently given birth to their first child, had a celebratory dinner in London. It was bittersweet. They had won. But Noronha-Gant had stopped doing investigations—like those into suspicious oil deals or the illegal logging contracts that had been denuding Liberia's rainforests—that involved human sources. "I have a family now," he explained. Embarking on investigations that were likely to trigger yearslong wars seemed impractical at best. In the future, he said, "this sort of a story is less likely to be told, at least by me."

A SECOND JUSTICE

O n a rainy Friday in July 2021, about three months after Silberman's fireball of a dissent in the *Global Witness* litigation, the Supreme Court issued its final set of orders for its just-completed term. Once again, the court would make headlines on a case involving libel law.

This time, the case was *Shkëlzen Berisha v. Guy Lawson, et al.*, which pitted the son of Albania's former prime minister against the journalist whose book was the basis for the movie *War Dogs* and whose daughter had been terrified when a stranger showed up at their house in 2017. The lawsuit, filed against Guy Lawson and his publisher, had been part of the tidal wave of litigation and threats that swelled after Trump took office and after Charles Harder, Tom Clare, and Libby Locke had proven the disruptive potential of bare-knuckled legal tactics, even in a world where *Sullivan*'s free-speech protections were the law of the land. Now the case would become a vehicle for rolling back those protections.

The case, in a nutshell, went like this.

Simon & Schuster had published Lawson's *Arms and the Dudes: How Three Stoners from Miami Beach Became the Most Unlikely Gunrunners in History* in 2015. As the subtitle suggested, the book's focus was the bizarre story of childhood friends who had become arms dealers in their twenties. In 2006, their company, run out of an unmarked office in Miami, had won a roughly $300 million Pentagon contract to supply bullets to the Afghan security forces. Through a middleman, they sourced ammo from a supplier in Albania, whose government was trying to dispose of surplus munitions to qualify for NATO membership.

Two of the Miami stoners—Efraim Diveroli and Alex Podrizki—were concerned that the middleman was jacking up the prices they were paying, and so they went to the Albanian capital of Tirana to try to strike a new deal. There they met with a contact inside an office building that was still under construction. A young man, wearing a sweater and a baseball cap and with "sharklike eyes," sat silently in the corner. This, Lawson reported, turned out to be Shkëlzen Berisha, "part of what was known in Albania as 'the family,' the tight-knit and extremely dangerous group that surrounded and lived at the beneficence of the prime minister." (Berisha has denied being at that meeting or having anything to do with corruption or organized crime.)

"Did we just get out of a meeting with the Albanian mafia?" Lawson quoted Podrizki as asking after they left the construction site. "Absolutely," was the response. "Abso-fucking-lutely." At another point, Lawson noted that Diveroli in a recorded phone call had referred to Albanian corruption as reaching up "to the prime minister, to his son."

Other than that, Berisha was barely mentioned in Lawson's 234-page book.

Long before Lawson came along, Berisha had been a controversial figure in Albania, and not just because his father had been the country's strongman, with a reputation for corruption. Local journalists and lawmakers had accused the younger Berisha of responsibility for a 2008 explosion at a munitions facility that killed dozens, sparking a national scandal. Berisha's father had reportedly steered investigators away from his son, and the government inquiry was derailed when a key witness, who had accused both Berishas of involvement in corrupt arms deals, was found dead on a remote Albanian roadside.

None of this was a secret. Lawson had based his descriptions of Berisha on an extensive public record that included leaked diplomatic cables written by the US ambassador to Albania. He'd also relied on previous reports in publications like the *New York Times*, which had published a front-page article in 2008 delving into Berisha's role in problematic weapons sales and quoting someone as describing him as being part of the Albanian mafia.

But at least in his own country, Berisha was accustomed to getting his way with critics. He had successfully sued Albanian media outlets for libel several times. And it seemed like such tactics might work in the United States. When he heard that the *War Dogs* movie was in the works, he hired an American lawyer to send a letter threatening litigation if he were mentioned. Berisha told me that the film producers wrote back promising not to name him or his family. The victory emboldened him.

The lawsuit was filed in federal court in Miami in June 2017. Berisha accused Lawson, Simon & Schuster, and the three arms-dealing stoners of defamation, but it was Lawson who was singled out for especially harsh criticism. "In lieu of reporting an honest story, Lawson played upon the vague prejudices of his readers—the one-dimensional caricature of Albanians as corrupt." Berisha said he'd emailed Lawson after his initial *Rolling Stone* article in the hopes of sharing his side of the story but that Lawson had never replied. (Lawson denied receiving the email but acknowledged not trying to reach Berisha for his version of events.) The lawsuit described Berisha as nothing more than "a father, lawyer, and businessman" and claimed that he had suffered severe reputational damage and was in physical danger because of Lawson's book. He sought $60 million in damages.

The suit made some eyebrow-raising claims, including that Berisha was not a public figure. He "has never held or run for public office, never worked for a political party, nor participated—even indirectly—in government affairs," the suit stated. He was more or less "the quintessential private figure." In case that failed to persuade, Berisha also asserted that Lawson had acted with actual malice: he had conspired with two of the Miami stoners to weave the innocent Berisha into an arms-trafficking scheme, supposedly to boost book sales.

To fend off the lawsuit, Simon & Schuster turned to Liz McNamara, who had previously been one of the publisher's in-house lawyers and now worked at Davis Wright Tremaine, a leading firm representing publishers and media companies. McNamara had years of experience handling such lawsuits, and the details of this one didn't strike her as particularly worrisome. She expected it to get booted out of court at an early stage.

Months of discovery ensued. To Lawson's horror, a team came up to his Dutchess County village to download the contents of his hard drive, some of which would be shared with Berisha's team. The Albanian's US lawyer, Jason Zoladz, issued subpoenas to some of Lawson's sources, who happened to be longtime critics of the Berisha regime. It smacked of intimidation. At one point, a private investigator whose résumé included surveillance work for the notorious spy company Black Cube spent hours lingering outside a dissident's Manhattan apartment, waiting to serve him with one of Zoladz's subpoenas.

In August 2018, McNamara filed a motion for summary judgment, essentially asking the court to rule that the case lacked merit. "This defamation action is a transparent effort to stifle legitimate reporting on Plaintiff's widely publicized involvement in corrupt arms dealing," she and her colleagues wrote. Berisha—a prime minister's son who enjoyed ready access to the media—was clearly a public figure, McNamara argued. But even after a year of discovery yielded nearly twenty thousand documents, not to mention numerous depositions, Berisha "has failed to find a single scrap of evidence" that any of the defendants knew or had reason to believe that what they were publishing was false.

The federal judge presiding over the case, a Bush appointee named Marcia Cooke, issued her ruling just before Christmas in 2018. She agreed with McNamara: Berisha was plainly a public figure, and there was nothing to suggest that Lawson or Simon & Schuster had thought that what he was writing was false. The case was dismissed.

Berisha appealed. What downside was there to keeping the battle alive, in the slim hopes that the plaintiffs might settle or that a different court might reach a more favorable conclusion? Worst-case, he was dragging Lawson and his publisher through an expensive and very unpleasant ordeal, which perhaps would deter journalists from pursuing him in the future. Lawson and his lawyers pondered another possibility: that Berisha was willing to keep throwing good money after bad because he was not the one whose money was being incinerated. They suspected that the litigation was being financed by someone other than Berisha, a secret benefactor, someone like Thiel. When I asked Berisha about this, he said that he paid all of the legal bills for his case. Then he paused and slightly

amended his answer: "If some person for some reason who was supporting a certain philosophy or a certain cause [was helping to finance the
litigation], I don't know." (Zoladz didn't respond to my repeated emails,
phone calls, and text messages.)

In September 2020, the Eleventh Circuit appeals court in Atlanta issued
its ruling. Point by point, the judges validated Cooke's reasoning: Berisha was a public figure, and there was no evidence of Lawson operating
recklessly. His sourcing—a combination of people he had interviewed,
documentary evidence, and the previous work of other journalists—was
solid. "Even if Berisha might nitpick each source for one reason or another," the court found, "this wealth of evidence considered altogether
does not permit a reasonable juror to find clear and convincing proof that
Lawson held serious doubts about the depiction of Berisha in his book."

The appeal was denied. By all rights, the case should have been over.

It was around this time that a lawyer named Roy Katriel had started
trawling through the dockets of the country's thirteen federal appeals
courts, looking for cases that might help him achieve his ambition of
arguing before the Supreme Court.

Katriel had been born in Israel, but his family moved to Venezuela
when he was two. They spent more than a decade there, until, with the
country's economy beginning what would become a long descent, they
moved to Miami in 1983. Katriel was bright and possessed the immi-
grant's zeal to succeed in his adopted homeland. He enrolled at the University of Miami when he was sixteen and, after doubling his course
load, managed to graduate less than two years later with a degree in
physics. He then earned a degree in biomedical engineering. He often
served as an expert witness in personal injury and product liability cases.
"The lawyers I was working with weren't always the sharpest tools in
the shed," he told me. Katriel figured that if they could make a living by
litigating, so could he.

He enrolled in American University's law school, graduated top of his
class, and scored a job at Arnold & Porter, a major law firm, in Washington, DC. Then he hopped to a smaller shop that specialized in class action
lawsuits. For years he'd hoped to run his own law firm, and in 2004 he

took the plunge. The Katriel Law Firm's offices were just down the road from the beach in a San Diego suburb.

Some of Katriel's cases attracted publicity, including a series of lawsuits he filed against Apple for, among other things, allegedly trapping its former customers' text messages when they switched from iPhones to Android devices. But the best path to fulfilling his Supreme Court dreams was to handle high-stakes appeals, and Katriel's only relevant experience in the fall of 2020 was having written a cert petition in a case involving the federal rules of evidence. The court had rejected his petition, but Kannon Shanmugam, one of the country's leading Supreme Court litigators, had emailed Katriel to congratulate him on a brief that was "exceptionally well done." That small act of kindness inspired Katriel to hunt for his next opportunity.

Which was why Katriel had taken to scouring the dockets of the country's federal appeals courts, looking for cases that seemed ripe for review by the Supreme Court. One day, he came across the Eleventh Circuit's rejection of Berisha's appeal. Katriel's initial instinct was that it seemed like an open-and-shut case. Then he remembered having read Thomas's opinion in the *McKee* case. Katriel had been the rare conservative among the mostly liberal army of class action lawyers—"a pink elephant in the room," as he put it—and he considered himself a constitutional originalist, like Thomas. The justice's opinion—in particular his point that the language of the First Amendment didn't protect libelous speech and that libel law therefore was properly the province of state, not federal, law—had resonated. Katriel also found McKee to be a sympathetic figure. The fact that she could get snared in the public figure web suggested to him that the web was too wide.

As he perused the myriad court filings associated with Berisha's lawsuit, it occurred to Katriel that he could use the case to invite the court to do just what Thomas had suggested: reconsider aspects of *Sullivan*. Katriel tracked down Berisha's lawyer, Jason Zoladz, who like him had a solo practice in Southern California. Katriel offered to handle the cert petition for free. The goal was "to have the United States Supreme Court review whether the 'actual malice' standard for defamation cases involving public figures should be reexamined," he emailed Zoladz in

December 2020. "While there is never any assurance that the Supreme Court will accept review of any particular case, Justice Thomas' invitation to consider the question in an appropriate case provides a basis to argue that review should be granted here."

Two weeks passed before Zoladz responded. He wrote that he'd just gotten off the phone with Berisha, "and he's interested in exploring your assistance." Katriel began researching. He stumbled upon a video of Charlie Rose interviewing Antonin Scalia in 2012. The justice, sitting in a dimly lit wood-paneled room at the Supreme Court, brought up the *Sullivan* decision, which, he said, "I abhor." Katriel searched for academic articles and found Justice Kagan's long-ago piece critiquing the *Sullivan* decision. Katriel was pretty sure he was on to something; the voices opposing *Sullivan* and its successor cases were more diverse and more numerous than he'd anticipated.

On February 1, 2021, less than two weeks after Joe Biden was sworn in as the forty-sixth president, Katriel filed his petition for a writ of certiorari. "The question presented is whether this Court should overrule the 'actual malice' requirement it imposed on public figure defamation plaintiffs," it began. Before Katriel even got to the table of contents, he had cited Thomas's opinion in *McKee* and Kagan's old law review article. Sure, he was asking the court to abandon decades of precedents, but he was in good company.

Katriel's goal wasn't to get *Sullivan* itself overturned. He instead trained his sights on a slightly less ambitious target: the Supreme Court's subsequent decisions in *Curtis Publishing v. Butts* and *Gertz v. Robert Welch*, which had applied the actual malice standard to public figures, including marginal ones like Carey Lohrenz. The right to vigorously criticize elected officials was a cornerstone of democracy, Katriel noted. Not so for private citizens who had been dragged unwillingly into the harsh glare of the public spotlight.

Katriel was banking on the resonance of his argument with the court's conservative justices. "This case cleanly and squarely presents the question that Justice Thomas invited the court to review and that other members of the court"—Kagan and Scalia—"have raised," Katriel wrote. The court should "restore the original meaning of the First Amendment."

McNamara's team was surprised by the appeal. They'd never heard of Katriel. They emailed Lawson to tell him about the Hail Mary pass. "Good lord," he replied.

McNamara waived the right to respond to the petition—the same tactic that lawyers for Bill Cosby and countless other parties had used in the hopes that their feigned indifference would undercut petitions for unwanted Supreme Court reviews. Day after day, Katriel checked the Supreme Court website, wondering if the justices would ask McNamara and her colleagues to reply or if the case would wither and die. Weeks passed. Finally, on March 17, Katriel got the news he'd been looking for: the court had requested a response. He was relieved. "We'd thought we were dead," he said.

This time, McNamara wasn't surprised. She knew this was a hot-button issue. It wasn't just Thomas's opinion in *McKee*. Two days after the court asked McNamara to respond to Katriel's petition, the DC appeals court had handed down its decision—including Silberman's dissent—in the *Global Witness* case. Given Silberman's stature among the Supreme Court's conservatives, and the parallels between what he and Katriel were arguing, it was possible the Berisha petition would elicit a similar reaction. The fact that the court wanted her to respond was the first hint of potential trouble. The risks were growing.

McNamara's brief, filed two months later, was straightforward. Katriel had accepted that Berisha was a public figure and that he couldn't prove that Lawson and Simon & Schuster had acted with actual malice; his point was that Berisha shouldn't have to meet such a high bar. McNamara's task, then, was to defend the *Gertz* and *Curtis Publishing* decisions that had created the public figure standards. And so she reminded the justices of the rationale of those long-ago rulings. If you allowed public figures to exact ruinous vengeance whenever a reporter or someone else accidentally got a fact wrong, that would put a deep freeze on such speech. Berisha's goal, she wrote, was simple: "to make it harder to criticize powerful individuals."

And even if the court were inclined to rethink its decades-old precedents, McNamara added, the Berisha case was "an exceedingly poor vehicle" for doing so. If the justices didn't think that someone like Kathy McKee or Carey Lohrenz deserved to be swept up under the actual malice standard, so be it. But Berisha wasn't some random guy trapped in a situation over which he had little control. He was a more conventional public figure—and arguably a public *official*—and he was connected to a scandal involving Pentagon contracting and illicit arms dealing. Surely there was a strong public interest in journalists investigating such controversies, undaunted by the fear of retaliatory litigation.

Now it was up to the justices to decide whether to take the case. McNamara, Katriel, and their clients wouldn't have to wait long to learn their fates.

Two years earlier, David Logan had put the finishing touches on a lengthy article for a law journal. It was the final act of his career, one last chance to make a mark, and it would collide in spectacular fashion with the long-running *Berisha* case.

The way Logan described it, his four decades in academia—as a law professor at Wake Forest and then as a dean and professor at the Roger Williams University School of Law in Rhode Island—had been ho-hum, at least in terms of his output of notable scholarship. Every few years, he would author a paper that would get "zero response," he told me. It often felt like he was shouting into a void. At academic conferences, he'd grown accustomed to people glancing at his name tag and then scurrying away as soon as they realized he didn't work at an elite institution. "They'd see my Roger Williams badge and run," he said. "They didn't want to engage with people who are below them."

Logan was arguably being too hard on himself—he was beloved as a professor—but the inferiority complex had been building for years. The six-foot-nine son of Eastern European immigrants, he'd enrolled at the University of Virginia's law school as a long-haired radical. But a pair of conservative professors, as well as a federal judge whom he later clerked for, left him increasingly skeptical of liberal dogma. In 1981, Logan joined Wake Forest as a law professor. On rare occasions, his work got noticed. Once, Scalia cited an article he'd written about "judicial federalism." Alas, the justice interpreted the piece in the opposite way that Logan had intended.

Logan grew fascinated with the First Amendment and media law. Part of it was familial. His father had worked at what would become Voice of America, reading news reports in his native Slovak for broadcast behind the Iron Curtain. And Logan had once had a stint as a music journalist, reviewing rock albums for *Rolling Stone*.

Around 2000, he got the idea to look at how often media companies and journalists were sued for libel, and how often those suits succeeded. From 1980 through 1996, he found that defendants in libel cases—often but not always news organizations—had prevailed 77 percent of the time. Substantial damages were rare. Logan regarded this as basically a good thing, "a significant victory for those who hoped to rein in, but not destroy, the deterrent effect of the law of libel." He described the Supreme Court's libel decisions as "among the great civil liberties victories of the last half-century."

Not long after the piece was published in the *Virginia Law Review* in 2001, Logan was lured up to Rhode Island to become dean of the Roger Williams law school. One of his goals was to help build the profile of the small school, which had been founded a decade earlier. One year he persuaded Scalia to spend a couple of days on campus, speaking and meeting with students. Five other justices followed, including, in 2013, Elena Kagan. Someone snapped a picture of Logan and Kagan standing in front of a bookshelf of leather-bound legal tomes; he was so much taller than the justice that the top half of his face was cut off in the photo.

The year after Kagan's visit, Logan returned to being a full-time professor. He had always loved teaching, and students fondly recalled his thunderous classroom performances in first-year torts as being akin to revivalist church sermons. Plus, giving up the deanship afforded him more time for research and writing. Soon Trump came to power, and the public square was awash with lies and half-truths that spread virally on social media. Logan thought back to his fifteen-year-old research on the rarity of successful libel lawsuits, and he suspected that helped explain the proliferation of disinformation.

Logan was no fan of Trump. Shortly after the 2016 election, he'd written a blog post calling the incoming president's pledge to open up libel laws "ill-informed" and "ominous" and praising *Sullivan* and its progeny as "powerful protections of zealous reporting." Yet he also thought the media was casting itself as a martyr whenever the president and his allies started braying about "fake news" or suing news organizations for defamation. "There was this sky-is-falling rhetoric," Logan told me. Aside from the fatal but idiosyncratic Gawker verdict, he wasn't aware of any lawsuits doing serious damage to media companies. "I started to see this mismatch between the rhetoric and the data," he said.

Logan soon turned his full attention to producing a paper arguing that, in an era swamped by democracy-decaying misinformation, the media was partly to blame—yet it remained untouchable due to what he concluded was an outdated court decision. He submitted the finished article to dozens of law reviews. The *Ohio State Law Journal* accepted it. The law students who edited the piece suggested that Logan cut a few references to how Trump was simultaneously spreading misinformation and suing news organizations; the article would be more palatable to a wider audience, they argued, if it avoided anything that smelled of politics. Logan agreed.

The article was published in 2020 under an attention-grabbing headline: "Rescuing Our Democracy by Rethinking *New York Times v. Sullivan.*" (Logan dedicated the article to his two University of Virginia professors, who had "urged me to question conventional wisdom.") The bulk of the fifty-six-page paper was devoted to a pair of analytical arguments. First, Logan described how the declining fortunes of the media industry, coupled with the rise of social media, had intensified the pressure on publishers to attract eyeballs at any cost—including by peddling sensationalized news stories or even disinformation. His evidence? Heaps of academic and journalistic research that showed that *social media* (but not traditional news outlets) was swimming in lies. Logan asserted that this was the result of the high threshold that *Sullivan* had erected against defamation lawsuits by public figures.

It was quite a leap. There was no denying that social media was a powerful channel for misinforming citizens and tarnishing reputations. Nor was there any doubt that the purveyors of online lies rarely faced legal consequences. But that reflected the futility of trying to sue an endless procession of mostly anonymous and presumably not-very-wealthy Twitter and Facebook trolls. In addition, social media companies were protected by a law—Section 230 of the Communications Decency Act—that insulated them from liability for what users posted on their platforms. Logan's paper devoted a lone paragraph, on the fifty-third page, to Section 230. How was any of this the fault of *Sullivan*? Logan didn't explain.

Logan's second argument was similarly tortured. To win damages in defamation cases, public figures had to prove that publishers knew that what they were publishing was probably false. "This," Logan asserted, "puts publishers to a hard choice: publishing without verification is the safest legal route, as an attempt to verify that turns up contrary information before publication can constitute reckless disregard for the truth and support liability. As a result, publishers are incentivized to do little or no fact-checking, confident that the more slipshod their investigation, the less likely they are to be guilty of 'actual malice.' In short, under an 'actual malice' regime, ignorance is bliss."

To support this inflammatory hypothesis—that journalists were knowingly publishing questionable information because the act of trying to determine its accuracy would expose them to liability—Logan provided no evidence or examples. Had he spoken to a single reporter, editor, publisher, media executive, or practicing First Amendment lawyer to ascertain whether there was even a kernel of truth to his theory? He told me that he had not. His argument, he said, was based on logic. "It was the product of an academic doing his research," he explained when I pushed him on this. "We don't actually road-test" theories with people who have real-world experience, he added, a bit apologetically, noting that this was why the academy was often referred to as the "ivory tower."

For an ex-journalist, Logan was surprisingly ignorant about how the media operates. Reporters often spend days, weeks, or even months investigating, checking facts, and trying to understand things from multiple perspectives. Their editors interrogate them. Lawyers vet articles before publication. Yes, there was more pressure than ever to move quickly, and mistakes did happen, and there was sometimes reckless or even deliberate misconduct (in which case the journalists could be sued under the actual malice standard). But there was a reason that Logan couldn't muster any examples to support his hypothesis that journalists *deliberately* produced "slipshod" investigations to insulate themselves from lawsuits: it just wasn't true. More often, the opposite happened—news organizations pulled punches to ensure that they were legally bulletproof.

It wasn't until near the end of the paper that Logan presented his most substantive findings. He had analyzed data compiled by the Media Law Resource Center about the frequency and outcome of libel cases. He found that the number of trials involving media companies had declined from an average of twenty-seven a year in the early 1980s to just three in 2017. (He failed to mention that a virtually identical trend had reduced the number of all federal civil trials over the same period. In other words, there was no reason to think this trend was peculiar to libel cases or had anything to do with *Sullivan*.) Media outlets' rate of success in these trials had climbed from 40 percent to 50 percent.

But those rates, Logan asserted, dramatically understated how hard it was for plaintiffs to collect damages. For example, he wrote, less than 10 percent of the time that juries awarded damages in such lawsuits did the payouts survive appeals. "In sum," he concluded, "the threat that defendants today face from libel litigation is virtually nil."

Logan really hoped his piece—his final academic article—would get noticed. He placed an order for dozens of printed copies from Ohio State. He sent them out to academics and other thought leaders. That was normal—the equivalent of reporters sharing a link to their latest story on social media. What was not normal, at least for Logan, was what he did next. He mailed a copy to Clarence Thomas, who a year earlier had made waves with his opinion in the *McKee* case. He sent another copy to Elena Kagan, who had written the law review article questioning *Sullivan* and who had previously visited him at Roger Williams.

Months passed. Aside from a couple of notes from fellow academics, the reaction to his article was "the typical one," Logan recalled. "The sound of a stone falling into the Pacific Ocean."

Then, on the first Friday in July 2021, Logan was in his basement office, where he'd spent the pandemic teaching classes virtually. The windows looked out onto his drizzly backyard. His phone rang. Logan's brother—himself a law professor at Florida State—was on the line, and he sounded excited. "Check this out!" he exclaimed.

"The petition for a writ of certiorari is denied." The Supreme Court would not hear *Berisha v. Lawson*. The journalist had won. The politician's son had lost.

Liz McNamara, the lawyer for Guy Lawson and Simon & Schuster, had taken to constantly refreshing the Supreme Court's website each morning that decisions were due to be announced, waiting to learn whether the court would accept the case. Now she got the answer she was looking for. Her initial reaction was relief. Then she realized there was more to it than the single sentence denying cert—eleven pages more.

Thomas had written a dissent, declaring that he would have taken the case and used it, just as Roy Katriel had suggested, as a medium to reconsider the actual malice standard. To bolster his argument, Thomas cited his own opinion in the *McKee* case and then segued into Silberman's withering dissent in *Global Witness*—a vivid illustration of how judges can quickly create self-sustaining echo chambers.

Thomas had previously argued that *Sullivan* strayed from the original meaning of the First Amendment. Now he took a new tact, pointing to "the doctrine's real-world effects"—namely, that "lies impose real harm." Here, Thomas cited a few examples. One was the 2016 shooting at a Washington, DC, pizzeria that right-wing trolls had baselessly claimed was the headquarters of a pedophilia ring involving Hillary Clinton. "Or," he added, "consider how online posts falsely labeling someone as 'a thief, a fraudster, and a pedophile' can spark the need to set up a home-security system," which was a reference to a *New York Times* article about a Canadian woman who had pursued a decades-long grudge by defaming her perceived enemies online.* The court, Thomas wrote, should no longer "insulate those who perpetrate lies from traditional remedies like libel suits."

Reading the justice's dissent, McNamara felt her frustration building. Thomas didn't even try to explain how *Sullivan* was to blame for

---

* I was the editor of the *Times* article, which was written by my colleague Kashmir Hill.

a vicious conspiracy theory proliferating in the cesspools of social media. In fact, the pizzeria's owner had threatened legal action against Alex Jones and his Infowars site, the foremost purveyors of the sex-ring lies, and those threats had been sufficiently credible that Jones and Infowars had eventually retracted their statements and apologized. (Trying to sue the countless—and mostly anonymous—social media users who were also spreading the "Pizzagate" myth would almost certainly have been futile.)

The case of the Canadian woman also had nothing to do with *Sullivan*. (It wasn't even a matter of American libel law.) After her victims filed libel lawsuits in Canada, a judge there ordered the woman to stop spreading lies. When she disobeyed, the judge deemed her "ungovernable" and found her in contempt of court. But it was up to the victims to get American tech companies to remove her defamatory online posts, and when they refused, there was no recourse: the websites couldn't be held liable because of Section 230.

Did Thomas understand the irrelevance of the examples on which his argument hinged? He must have known that Section 230—not *Sullivan*—was the root cause of many of the problems he decried. In essence, he seemed to be performing a sleight-of-hand, using the unquestionable spread of disinformation on social media as ammunition to roll back safeguards that protected the mainstream media that he loathed.

The real surprise, however, came when McNamara flipped the page. Thomas's opinion had been predictable. But he wasn't the only justice who dissented. Neil Gorsuch had, too.

Gorsuch started off by acknowledging that back in 1964, the Supreme Court had a compelling reason to create the actual malice standard: to shield the handful of national news organizations from crippling libel lawsuits whenever they wrote about powerful people or institutions. But over the ensuing decades, Gorsuch wrote, the media landscape had changed. Major newspapers were whispers of their former selves. Into the void spilled twenty-four-hour cable news and online news platforms that were beholden to virality and clicks, not truth and accuracy.

At the time of the *Sullivan* decision, Gorsuch continued, "many major media outlets employed fact-checkers and editors, and one could argue that most strived to report true stories" because readers would pay more for reliable information. "Less clear is what sway these justifications hold in a new era where the old economic model that supported reporters, fact-checking, and editorial oversight is disappearing."

Where was Gorsuch coming up with this? Primarily, it turned out, from David Logan's article in the *Ohio State Law Journal*, which had found its way to his desk in the months after Logan sent it to Thomas and Kagan. Over the course of his eight-page dissent, Gorsuch cited Logan's piece an extraordinary seventeen times. And when it came to data to support his argument, the justice relied almost entirely on Logan's crunching of the Media Law Resource Center's figures.

At the heart of Gorsuch's opinion was the premise that "the actual malice standard has evolved from a high bar to recovery into an effective immunity from liability." This was not a new argument, but, thanks to Logan, Gorsuch now could marshal data: the average number of media defamation trials had gone from twenty-seven a year to three. Gorsuch was alarmed that even when a plaintiff managed to win damages at trial, those awards withstood appeals only one out of ten times. "The bottom line? It seems that publishing without investigation, fact-checking, or editing has become the optimal legal strategy," Gorsuch wrote, before quoting Logan's "ignorance is bliss" line. It was time, he concluded, to reconsider *Sullivan*.

McNamara and her team were floored. It wasn't only that they disagreed with Thomas and Gorsuch's reasoning. It was that their opinions seemed wholly disconnected from the facts of the case. Thomas was citing online conspiracy theories, which had nothing to do with libel law or *Sullivan*, much less the case at hand. Gorsuch was grumbling about a lack of media fact-checking and how *Sullivan* had made it harder for defamation victims to prevail in court, which was an interesting trend, if it were even true, but had no bearing on the matters at issue here.

Lawson's lawyers emailed him about the result and the two dissenting opinions. He blew up. He was disgusted by how the justices had casually equated the painstaking process of investigative journalism with the slop that far-right trolls were barfing on social media. "Thomas is obviously an angry sad man," Lawson replied to his attorneys. Gorsuch "reads like a pretty dim witted small town lawyer."

The outcome wasn't quite what Roy Katriel had hoped for when he volunteered to take the appeal, but getting a second justice to declare his support for reconsidering *Sullivan* nonetheless felt like a win. His client, Shkëlzen Berisha, agreed. The dissents showed that his lawsuit "was not a baloney thing," he told me.

From his basement office, Logan read Gorsuch's dissent with giddy disbelief. He'd never seen a Supreme Court opinion lean so heavily on a single academic source—much less when that academic was him! The next few days were a blur. Congratulatory calls and emails poured in. One came from Rod Smolla, who wrote that he "was thrilled to see your piece prominently featured" in Gorsuch's dissent and asked permission to include the article in a compendium of First Amendment pieces he was editing. Permission granted!

Logan was invited onto CNN and NPR. He told one radio host that ending *Sullivan* wouldn't doom democracy—after all, England didn't have such vigorous press protections, and "their media seems plenty robust." (He apparently didn't realize that the country had long been the venue of choice for oligarchs and others seeking to quash unfavorable journalism.) Logan reveled in his newfound fame. "It was like lightning striking," he told me over lunch at a Manhattan steakhouse. "How many of us write a law review article that kick-starts a national conversation?"

He was right. While Thomas and Silberman were influential in conservative circles, they were viewed elsewhere as extremists. By comparison, Gorsuch was perceived as a bit more of a moderate. The addition of his voice to the chorus therefore triggered a flurry of news articles, op-eds, TV and radio coverage, academic and political conferences—and, among the proponents of overturning *Sullivan*, rejoicing.

"Sheer brilliance," Libby Locke tweeted about Gorsuch's dissent. She quoted his line about only one in ten jury awards surviving on appeal.

Logan had arrived at that stark ratio by extrapolating from a table in a Media Law Resource Center report that looked at dozens of libel trials. Between 2010 and 2017, there had been twenty-one cases in which juries had awarded damages to plaintiffs that were upheld by the trial court. In only two of those cases—9.5 percent of the total, or one in ten—had judges affirmed the damages on appeal.

But that didn't mean that the damages in the other nineteen cases had been overturned. In fact, eight of those cases were settled prior to any appeal. Four more were never appealed at all. And the appeals in three other cases were pending at the time the report was published. That left just six cases in which higher courts had ruled on damages. In four of those cases, appeals courts had modified the damages awarded by jurors. In the other two, the damages had been affirmed.

Those numbers told a very different story than what Logan had implied and Gorsuch had seized on. It was not true that only one in ten jury awards survived on appeal. The true figure was much higher: one in three. And the ratio was based on a sample size of six, so tiny that it was ridiculous to try to draw any serious conclusions.

Michael Norwick, an attorney at the Media Law Resource Center, had helped compile the data on which Logan had based his article. Five days after the Supreme Court rejected the *Berisha* case, Norwick sent a letter to Gorsuch via the court's public information officer. "I write to point out inaccuracies in the Dissent in hope that you will consider amending it," he wrote, before detailing the problems with the data.

Nobody responded. But a few weeks later, the Supreme Court retroactively altered Gorsuch's dissent. Among other changes, the line about only one in ten awards surviving on appeal became one in three. ("This is the closest I will get in my career to winning a case before the Supreme Court," Norwick joked to friends.) Despite the quiet correction, the false one-in-ten figure would become a potent talking point for lawyers and others seeking to overturn *Sullivan*.

Norwick also sent his letter to Logan. He didn't reply. The professor told me that any mistake in his article "didn't strike me one way or the other as being significant." His article about how the media deliberately avoids the truth wasn't updated or corrected.

STAY OUT OF THE KITCHEN

One evening in October 2021, a crowd gathered at the headquarters of the Heritage Foundation, in a modern, eight-story building a block away from the US Capitol. Within Washington's network of conservative influence peddlers, Heritage, armed with nearly $400 million in assets, stood out as perhaps the most powerful, funneling personnel and ideas into Republican presidential administrations and congressional offices. This day, the foundation had devoted itself to a singular task: celebrating the thirtieth anniversary of Clarence Thomas's ascent to the Supreme Court. Since 8:30 a.m., an all-star lineup of judges, lawyers, academics, and current and former federal officials had been paying tribute to the justice. The main event—when Thomas himself would finally take the stage—was scheduled for 6:30 p.m. Some two hundred people settled into their seats along the curved rows of a windowless auditorium.

To kick off the evening program, the Heritage Foundation was debuting an annual prize: the Justice Clarence Thomas First Principles Award. The inaugural recipient was Larry Silberman. C. Boyden Gray, the former White House counsel who had advised George Bush to pick Thomas for the Supreme Court, had agreed to present the award to Silberman, whom he'd known for decades. Tall and thin, wearing a pinstriped suit and sneakers, Gray hunched over the lectern as he described Silberman's legacy: He had been a loyal right-wing operative since the Nixon presidency. He had done much to advance the conservative legal movement during his years on the bench. But that was not his greatest claim to fame, at least not on this night, with Clarence and Ginni Thomas sitting in the front row.

Silberman and his late wife, Ricky, had been by the Thomases' sides ever since Clarence was at the EEOC. It was Silberman who had encouraged Thomas to become a judge. It was Silberman who had urged Gray to nominate Thomas to the Supreme Court. It was the Silbermans who had defended Thomas and disparaged Anita Hill. "Larry," Gray rasped, "I will say this about you: No one has had more to do with Justice Thomas's extraordinary journey than you, except possibly George H. W. Bush." (Silberman, who would die less than a year later, told the audience that persuading Thomas to become a judge was "the single most important thing I've ever done.")

Before handing the eighty-six-year-old Silberman a large plaque, Gray remarked on just how inseparable the two judges had been. It wasn't simply their long-standing friendship. Their legal philosophies were barely distinguishable, which in part reflected Silberman's mentorship of Thomas as a neophyte judge. "I've often wondered whether they were secretly meeting every day over the last twenty or thirty years," Gray said. "Because there's a certain resonance. And there are many areas that deeply interest me, but one of the ones that gives me the most fun is their shared questions about *New York Times v. Sullivan.*" The audience erupted in appreciative laughter.

It was more than a stray punch line. The conservative movement—including leading politicians, state and federal judges, and a tightly intertwined network of right-wing think tanks—had begun answering Thomas, Silberman, and Gorsuch's calls to arms and taking up the quest to overturn *Sullivan.*

Heritage had been among the first responders. Two years earlier, inspired by Thomas's opinion in the *McKee* case, the foundation had hosted a lopsided debate in which two of the three participants—Libby Locke and a Heritage official—argued that *Sullivan* should be overturned. "Would it be the end of our democratic republic because the press would be out of business, and politicians and the powerful would no longer be held accountable?" Locke had asked, smirking. "No, hardly." Why? Because "the media is largely owned by large, for-profit companies . . . who act in their own economic self-interest."

Indeed, that was what had happened in the early 1960s, when the *New York Times*, facing waves of litigation from L. B. Sullivan and others, had bowed to its economic self-interest and yanked its reporters out of Alabama. Here was a clue as to what an America without *Sullivan* might look like—especially at a time when some of the country's democratic norms and traditions seemed up for grabs. Until the mid-1960s, the media's appetite for aggressively pursuing the country's richest and most powerful people, institutions, and industries had been constrained by, among other things, the realization that doing so might make newspapers and TV broadcasters vulnerable to disastrous damages. There was no particular reason to think that today would be any different. One only had to look to Britain—where the greater risk of litigation had led the media to collectively shy away from covering Lance Armstrong's doping or wrongdoing by sundry Russian oligarchs and Saudi sheikhs, and had made London a destination of choice for libel tourists—to understand what might be in store for the United States.

Large news organizations generally have financial resources and formidable in-house legal departments. But they also have owners, and—regardless of whether they are traditional public-company shareholders, shadowy hedge funds, or billionaires looking to wield influence—owners tend to care about the bottom line. That had been Locke's point: financial incentives would instill discipline. But they also could instill fear. This wasn't simply a matter of outlets paying a price for getting facts wrong. If the burden of proof rested once again with defendants—if it were up to them to prove that they had their facts right, as opposed to being up to plaintiffs to prove that the facts had been wrong—even entirely accurate articles could pose huge financial risks. For many news organizations, the safest bet would be to avoid doing anything to offend the richest and most powerful people, institutions, and industries.

The calculus for smaller outlets and independent journalists would probably be even simpler. Purchasing libel insurance was already expensive. Without the built-in protections of *Sullivan*, it would become more so, since insurance companies set rates according to risk. For the countless news organizations operating on a financial knife's edge, higher insurance prices would mean cutting back in other areas or perhaps foregoing insurance—a perilous roll of the dice. Regardless, their tolerance for taking risks was likely to shrink, which was good news for the local politicians, police chiefs, university presidents, businessmen, and countless others who might otherwise have found themselves under the microscope of their community newspaper.

It was not hard to understand why Locke's clients and Heritage's wealthy donors might welcome a return to such an environment. ("If a small, independent media outlet is publishing a story that is accurate and newsworthy, then they don't have anything to worry about," Locke told me when I asked about this.) The Heritage Foundation's media organ, the *Daily Signal*, amplified Thomas's and Gorsuch's critiques of *Sullivan*, filtering the argument through a nakedly partisan lens. A senior Heritage fellow argued that reversing the long-standing precedent might be the solution to "the outrageous lies and misrepresentations—especially about conservatives—that we see regularly on CNN, MSNBC, and other far-left media organizations."

The Federalist Society followed suit, hosting repeated events about overturning *Sullivan*. At one in Florida, a Clare Locke attorney named Jered Ede—the firm had recently hired him from Project Veritas, the group of conservative provocateurs, where he'd been general counsel—recycled the incorrect data (as well as the "ignorance is bliss" line) that Gorsuch had plucked from David Logan's law review piece, claiming that 90 percent of jury awards in defamation cases were reversed on appeal. The result, Ede declared, is that the media has "virtually a zero percent chance of being found liable" in defamation cases.

The right-wing Claremont Institute jumped in, too. It was backed by some of America's richest families, including two—the Scaife and DeVos clans—that had previously financed or threatened major libel lawsuits. In the 1980s, when Thomas was just starting at the EEOC, he had borrowed a pair of Claremont scholars to help him learn about the Constitution and figure out his personal politics. Since then, the institute and the justice had operated in something approaching lockstep.

By 1999, Claremont's president, Larry Arnn, was hailing Thomas as "the supreme jurist in the land" when it came to promoting original-ism. (Thomas returned the compliment, calling Arnn a "good friend" and noting that he had taken to hiring Claremont fellows to be his Supreme Court clerks.)

In 2019, Thomas's opinion in *McKee* had caught the attention of a Claremont Institute political theorist named Carson Holloway. Hollo-way's day job was being a professor at the University of Nebraska Omaha, but he had procured outside gigs for himself, first at Heritage and then at Claremont. The main requirement of his Claremont sideline was to write occasional pieces that were academically rigorous but were read-able by laypeople and, of course, hewed to the institute's conservative orthodoxy.

This was not a problem for Holloway, a devoted originalist. He'd spent a lot of time thinking about all of the Supreme Court decisions—many of them relics of the Warren Court—that he thought should be over-turned. "There's a lot of things to be cleaned up," as he put it. Holloway had heard Trump periodically ranting about libel laws, but he didn't take the president all that seriously. Thomas was a different matter. His orig-inalist condemnation of *McKee* spoke directly to Holloway. He began re-searching the history of libel law and in 2022 produced a pair of articles building on Thomas's argument, namely that neither the Constitution's framers nor their intellectual forebearers in England intended for libel-ous statements against public officials to enjoy legal protection.

Both pieces—one a Claremont Institute white paper, the other an essay in *American Conservative* magazine—provoked limited public re-action. But they percolated through the conservative firmament. That fall, the James Wilson Institute, another star in the constellation of in-terlinked right-wing think tanks, invited Holloway onto its *Anchoring Truths* podcast to discuss the topic. He used this minor megaphone to urge conservatives to employ the same tactics against *Sullivan* that they had successfully wielded against *Roe v. Wade*. In the abortion wars, he explained, "states pushed the envelope by introducing new abortion regulations that they wanted to see challenged so the issue could come before the Supreme Court again." State legislators should do the same with their libel laws: narrow them to such an extent that they clearly conflicted with *Sullivan.*

"If you were to do that," Holloway proposed, "you would create the possibility of a case that perhaps the court would really need to take."

At 8:45 on a warm Tuesday morning in February 2023, Ron DeSantis arrived at a rented TV studio in Hialeah Gardens, outside Miami. The Florida governor was wearing a navy suit and a patterned, dark red tie. His helmet of thick, brown hair was carefully slicked back and parted. Inside the studio, a makeup artist powdered and primped him, and a producer miked him. Then he walked onto the TV set and parked himself behind a bean-shaped table, flanked on each side by three chairs. Behind him were American and Floridian flags and an electronic screen that flashed "SPEAK TRUTH." The letters were positioned so that in head-on shots of the governor, the cameras captured his face perfectly framed by the word "TRUTH."

Shuffling behind DeSantis onto the stage were guests who'd been handpicked to convey symbolic meaning. There was Nick Sandmann, the teenager who'd been branded on social media as a racist and emerged as a MAGA folk hero. There was a Virginia gun-rights activist who'd been the victim of deceptive editing in a documentary; a lawyer representing a guy who CNN had accused of "selling black market evacuations out of Afghanistan"; and an ex-journalist who asserted that the media's modus operandi was to "push the narrative, facts be damned."

The setup resembled a prime-time cable news show, except that in this case there was a small in-studio audience consisting of the governor's supporters and a specially selected group of conservative journalists and influencers. And the production was being livestreamed on social media, not broadcast on TV.

The event was the latest in a series of showcases to introduce DeSantis—an early if short-lived frontrunner for the Republican presidential nomination—to a national audience. The governor's staff and outside advisers had spent weeks laboring over seating charts, on-screen graphics, and the selection of the panelists who were now seated on either side of DeSantis. A detailed schedule, sometimes down to the minute, tracked the governor's arrival, departure, conversations, and even the weather ("7% chance of precipitation").

Dating back to his years as a congressman, DeSantis had positioned himself as an anti-elitist culture warrior. Like many other conservatives, he viewed the media as biased against Republicans and as easily punchable proxies for the "woke" establishment. His broad goal today was to continue sowing distrust toward this caricatured version of the media, which he described as "probably the leading purveyors of disinformation in our entire society." But there was a narrower focus, too: to build support for making it easier to sue for defamation. He would be the second presidential candidate, after Trump in 2016, to try to transform the seemingly arcane field of libel law into a political weapon.

DeSantis had developed this passion at least a year earlier, in the wake of the *Global Witness* and *Berisha* rulings. In 2022, shortly after C. Boyden Gray bestowed the Heritage Foundation's award on Silberman, a top DeSantis aide, Stephanie Kopelousos, had shared a briefing document and draft of a proposed bill with Republican lawmakers in Tallahassee. The legislation would narrow the legal safeguards that protected news outlets in the "Free State of Florida," as DeSantis liked to call it. It would tighten the definition of who qualified as a "public figure." Statements from anonymous sources would be presumed false, flipping the burden of proof in defamation cases onto the journalists. And it would lower the bar for proving that a news outlet had acted with actual malice.

The goal was to make the media more vulnerable to litigation. But there was a grander ambition as well—the same one that Carson Holloway had articulated. "To the extent these provisions conflict with existing Supreme Court precedent, this legislation aims to invite challenges to such precedent with the goal of restoring the original understanding of the First Amendment," Kopelousos wrote to a top Senate aide.

The bill wouldn't actually be introduced for another year, but it was a clear signal of the governor's intentions. Out of public view, he was being counseled by someone with extensive experience battling the media: Libby Locke. They had met shortly after DeSantis returned from his Navy service in Iraq in 2008. DeSantis's Navy roommate had been a man named Adam Laxalt, who had been Locke's classmate and friend at

Georgetown Law and would later become Nevada's conspiracy-spinning Republican attorney general. After Laxalt introduced them, DeSantis and Locke bonded over their shared Federalist Society worldviews and disdain for the media.

Locke was not just a friend but also an adviser. When DeSantis wanted to send threatening letters to uncooperative news organizations and others, for example, Locke was his woman. She provided some of the services pro bono, explaining to fellow lawyers that she and the governor were pals. (Locke also sent legal threats on behalf of Laxalt when he faced sexual assault allegations in 2018. His campaign paid Clare Locke more than $90,000.)*

DeSantis's defamation infomercial was partly Locke's handiwork. From the outset, it was decided that she and the governor would share the stage—the only question was who else would be invited to participate. Locke provided DeSantis's aides with suggestions. Sandmann was an obvious choice, and she offered to get in touch with him. She also knew how to reach the Virginia gun-rights group. She even suggested a token Democrat: Justin Fairfax, the former Virginia lieutenant governor who had unsuccessfully sued CBS News over its report on his alleged sexual assaults. "Libby says that although he [Fairfax] is on the opposite side of the political isle [sic] from the Governor, she knows him well and says he is very compelling when discussing these issues on defamation," a DeSantis aide noted to colleagues.

DeSantis and his staff, however, wanted hard-core conservatives. As it happened, Daniel Whitehead, the governor's assistant general counsel, had previously worked for both the Claremont Institute and the James Wilson Institute—the two groups that had promoted Carson Holloway's critiques of *Sullivan*. "Daniel says that Carson would be better than some of the other experts Libby recommended," the DeSantis aide wrote. "He is from the Claremont Institute and is more decidedly a right-wing thinker."

Onstage in the Florida TV studio, Holloway and most of the men wore

---

* Locke said my descriptions of her relationships with Laxalt and DeSantis were incorrect, but she wouldn't elaborate.

light shirts and reddish ties. Locke, the only woman, was in a gray dress
and a golden necklace. She was sitting directly to the left of DeSantis,
who introduced her as "an extraordinaire when it comes to First Amendment defamation."

"The problem," Locke told him, the cameras rolling, "is that at every
stage in the legal process, from the moment you file your complaint all
the way through appeal, the thumb is on the scale in favor of the press.
And media defense lawyers come in, and they say 'First Amendment,'
and judges get very nervous about applying the law in a way that is favorable or even evenhanded to a defamation plaintiff. And lives and families
and reputations are ruined as a result."

This could happen to anyone, Locke claimed. Someone with a social
media account could be a public figure, with no recourse if someone
started spreading lies about them. (Actually, federal courts have ruled
that merely posting something on social media doesn't magically transform private people into public figures.) A belly dancer could be one
if she chose to perform in public. "A female Navy pilot is considered a
limited purpose public figure," Locke continued, pausing for emphasis,
"because she chose to be a pilot and a woman." She rolled her eyes.
DeSantis and the other panelists chuckled. (When I told Carey Lohrenz
that she had been invoked as part of DeSantis's antimedia campaign,
she became angry. "Mr. Book Burner," she spat, "keep my name out of
your mouth.")

Holloway chimed in. The solution was the reversal of *Sullivan*. "What
we seem to have is a culture of impunity on the part of the press that
now needs to be re-addressed by perhaps the Supreme Court revisiting
the case," he explained.

DeSantis asked what the odds were of that happening. "I think it's fair
to say that five years ago or ten years ago nobody would be talking about
New York Times v. Sullivan being revisited, but now you have some heavy
hitters," Holloway replied. He said he was optimistic that Thomas and
Gorsuch could persuade some of their colleagues to overturn *Sullivan* on
originalist grounds. With the court's six-to-three conservative majority,
"I think most of the justices are sympathetic to that kind of argument."

DeSantis began wrapping up the event after an hour; he had a meet and greet with the conservative influencers his staff had invited, and then he had to scoot to another event.

"It's our view in Florida that we want to be standing up for the little guy against these massive media conglomerates," the governor declared. "It would contribute to an increase in the ethics in the media and everything if they knew, 'You know what, you smear somebody, you know it's false, and you didn't do your homework, you're going to have to be held accountable for that.'" Hopefully, he added, "you'll see more and more of that across the country."

The legislation that DeSantis's allies had introduced in Tallahassee, with the goal of sparking a Supreme Court reckoning about *Sullivan*, was foiled by opposition from right-wing broadcasters and radio hosts who warned that the bill would "be the death of conservative talk throughout the State of Florida," as the owner of a local Fox affiliate put it. (A different version of the legislation would be introduced in 2024 as well.) In other quarters, though, the campaign was gathering force.

Two months after DeSantis's roundtable, ProPublica reported that Clarence Thomas had accepted luxury vacations paid for by a billionaire friend, Harlan Crow. Thomas had already been under an ethical cloud, and the latest exposé let loose a downpour of criticism. Not since his confirmation battle thirty-two years earlier had he faced such controversy. Once again, his supporters rallied around him. This time, they could draw on a point that Thomas himself had begun articulating in the *McKee* case four years earlier—and that people like Neil Gorsuch, Larry Silberman, Libby Locke, David Logan, Carson Holloway, and Ron DeSantis had subsequently refined, expanded, and popularized.

"Make no mistake: this is defamation," Senator Mike Lee, a Utah Republican, wrote in a Twitter post that would be viewed more than a million times. "The media gets away with it only because Justice Thomas is a public figure, and under a Supreme Court ruling from 1964, public figures have essentially no recourse when they're defamed by the media." Here was a tidy encapsulation of why so many wealthy and powerful people—those who generally had the most to lose from intense media scrutiny—were so eager to see *Sullivan* rolled back.

Not surprisingly, lawyers for Donald Trump were happy to use a variation of the same argument as the former president continued his long-running habit of spraying the court system with libel lawsuits. He sued the Pulitzer Prize board. He sued the *New York Times*. He sued ABC News and George Stephanopoulos. His social media company sued the *Washington Post*. And he sued CNN, seeking more than $475 million in damages for supposedly comparing Trump to Hitler. The beginning of the CNN lawsuit was devoted in large part to reciting Silberman's opinion in *Global Witness*, quoting his warnings that "one-party control of the press and media is a threat to a viable democracy." The actual malice standard, Team Trump wrote, "does not—and should not—apply" if the media outlet is politically biased.

This was not, of course, how courts had repeatedly interpreted the First Amendment, and the lawsuit was soon thrown out. But across the country, more judges were voicing support for doing away with *Sullivan*. (Trump's lawsuits against the Pulitzer board and ABC survived motions to dismiss and were allowed to proceed to the discovery stage—further proof that the threshold for success in libel cases was not nearly as insurmountable as critics claimed.)

In the Florida Panhandle, a Republican judge heard a case in which a city councilman had sued a woman for defamation because she had stood outside Town Hall and told passersby that he was in the pocket of local real estate developers. The judge dismissed the suit but complained that *Sullivan* "was wrongfully decided and was not grounded in the history or text of the First Amendment." He spent several pages extensively quoting from the *McKee*, *Berisha*, and *Global Witness* opinions.

In Michigan, a judge with a passion for breeding horses and pushing religion into the public square used a lawsuit against an ESPN reporter as an opportunity to attack *Sullivan* and align himself with Thomas and Gorsuch. The judge claimed that the actual malice standard had become "nearly insurmountable"—even though in this very case he and his colleagues concluded that the plaintiff had cleared that bar.

In Pennsylvania, a Democratic federal judge with an unusually narrow view of the First Amendment—he'd previously ruled that people lacked the right to film police officers in public—added his voice to the growing chorus when a defamation case landed in his courtroom. "We join several jurists in questioning the continued viability of the actual malice doctrine," he wrote. He quoted Gorsuch's claim that *Sullivan* incentivized people to publish defamatory statements without checking facts or trying to ascertain the truth—an un-fact-checked assertion that came straight from David Logan.

And in South Florida, there was the strange case of Alan Dershowitz and his $300 million lawsuit against CNN. Dershowitz, the prolific author, TV talking head, and Harvard Law professor, had represented Trump in his first impeachment trial in 2020. Dershowitz's lawsuit claimed that CNN, in its impeachment coverage, had defamed him by wrongly telling viewers that he'd said that a president was legally free to do essentially whatever he wanted, including committing crimes. Dershowitz asserted that CNN's falsehoods "resulted in my cancellation." For example, he told me that the *New York Times* had stopped quoting him or publishing his opinion pieces. "I was cut off completely," he said. (That was not entirely true; the *Times* has quoted Dershowitz more than a dozen times since then.) Long before the TV segments in question, Dershowitz's reputation had been soiled by his affiliations with Trump and the sexual predator Jeffrey Epstein, but he said that he had retained access to the mainstream media until CNN mischaracterized his remarks about presidential immunity.

The federal judge overhearing the case was Raag Singhal, and he had sympathy for Dershowitz. A Federalist Society member, Singhal had been appointed by Trump, and he seemed to have little respect for CNN, whose coverage of Dershowitz, the judge wrote, was marked by "foolishness, apathy, and an inability to string together a series of common legal principles." Yet that wasn't nearly enough for a public figure to win a defamation case, in part because Dershowitz, despite having had the opportunity to fish through CNN's files and depose its employees, hadn't presented any evidence that the network knew that what it was reporting was wrong. There was no actual malice. It wasn't a close call, Singhal told me: "The evidence just wasn't there." Nor was there much indication that Dershowitz had been injured. "He's on Fox News all the time. He's published a book," the judge said. "I don't see how he's been harmed." In

2023, Singhal granted CNN's motion for summary judgment and closed the case.

But Singhal for years had been growing distressed with the way that lies proliferated on social media, a development that he, like Justice Thomas, blamed in part on *Sullivan*. Plus, as Gorsuch had written, he suspected that *Sullivan* and its successor cases tended "to discourage a proper level of investigation" by journalists. *Sullivan*, he wrote, "is a great example of how bad facts can contribute to the making of unnecessary law." (Other examples included the notorious *Dred Scott* decision—in which the Supreme Court in 1857 preserved slavery—and *Roe v. Wade*, which Singhal blamed for causing "deep-rooted political and emotional turmoil.")

This was not a line of argument that at first blush seemed likely to appeal to Dershowitz, a renowned constitutional law scholar. In 1964, as a Supreme Court clerk, he'd helped Justice Arthur Goldberg write his concurring opinion in the *Sullivan* case. It argued that Brennan's sweeping majority opinion hadn't gone far enough; Goldberg believed that publishers should generally have complete immunity when they wrote about public officials, even if the publishers intentionally got facts wrong. In other words, the actual malice standard was too narrow.

Of course, that was Goldberg's opinion, not necessarily Dershowitz's. But in 2014, on the fiftieth anniversary of the *Sullivan* decision, Dershowitz had spoken about the case—and his role working on Goldberg's concurrence—at an event at the National Constitution Center. Dershowitz told the sold-out audience that the inevitable result of *Sullivan* and its progeny was that public figures sometimes had to endure blows to their reputations. He noted that he'd personally been subjected to all manner of nasty lies but that his hands were essentially tied.

"It's horrible," Dershowitz said, leaning forward in his armchair. "That's the price of *New York Times v. Sullivan*. And it's a price worth paying. Because if you think of what the opposite would be, everyone in politics is pretty thin-skinned," and the resulting gusher of lawsuits "would really weaken the Constitution considerably. So, it's a cost worth paying. And if you don't like the heat, stay out of the kitchen."

Nine years later, Dershowitz was still lingering in the kitchen but apparently no longer cared for the rising temperature. Like so many others during the Trump era, he had reconsidered his steadfast commitments to press freedoms. (CNN wasn't the only outlet Dershowitz had gone after. In 2019, he'd hired multiple law firms to send threatening letters to *The New Yorker* as it was preparing a less than glowing profile of him.) What had changed since his rousing 2014 defense of *Sullivan*, Dershowitz said, was "cancel culture, which today is the biggest threat to free speech." We were speaking in February 2024, and Dershowitz that night was giving a speech at the University of Miami. He said it was one of the only academic events to which he'd been invited to speak in the past four years.

When Dershowitz appealed Singhal's dismissal of his CNN lawsuit, he embraced the judge's argument as his own. "The public no longer trusts the press because the press habitually engages in irresponsible, often malignant, behavior and then hides behind *Sullivan* and battalions of expensive lawyers to avoid responsibility for the damage they cause," Dershowitz's lawyers wrote. His goal now, Dershowitz said, was to get higher courts to make it easier for public figures like him to satisfy the actual malice threshold.

If that didn't work, he was gunning for the Supreme Court, he told me, snatches of salsa music audible as he walked along a Miami boulevard. "I'm gonna fight this case to the very end."

THE SLUR

A s groups like the Heritage Foundation and Claremont Institute made their cases against *Sullivan*, like-minded lawyers and activists in towns and cities across America took up the fight as their own. One of them was Matthew Fernholz. A lawyer in Wisconsin, he was contacted in the fall of 2021 by a businessman named Cory Tomczyk, who was furious with a community news outlet in Marathon County, in the north of the state. Tomczyk was looking for an attorney, and Fernholz agreed to take his case.

Tomczyk was burly and bearded, his white hair receding in a sharp widow's peak. He'd held positions in the local Republican Party and school board, and lately he'd become a regular on local talk radio. In the early days of the pandemic, he'd offered up his recycling and shredding company, IROW, as a venue for protests against the governor's stay-at-home orders. The events attracted thousands of angry Wisconsinites, some carrying guns and Confederate flags. Later Tomczyk helped organize rallies against masks and vaccines, which he saw as part of the "Covid scamdemic." He had his eye on state elected office.

In 2020, following the nationwide convulsions over police violence and racial injustice, officials in Marathon County had proposed a resolution designating the area "a Community for All." The purely symbolic proclamation provoked bitter controversy. Liberals thought the resolution was a no-brainer to advertise the county's multiculturalism (Marathon had many residents of Southeast Asian heritage) and to signal support for people from all walks of life. Conservatives thought it unnecessarily sowed divisions. The debate raged for more than a year. By the summer of 2021, supporters were warning of economic disaster if the resolution didn't pass, while opponents claimed it was the first step toward "the end of private property."

Marathon's board of supervisors held a series of meetings to let people sound off, and on August 12, 2021, dozens crammed into a dreary room in the courthouse in Wausau, the county seat, for the latest session. Tomczyk was one of the resolution's loudest critics—"I thought it set up the opportunity for some liberal people to enforce their viewpoints and their values on other people within the community," he explained—and he'd been a regular at these gatherings. On this sunny afternoon, he found a seat in the second row, next to a conservative radio host whose show he'd been on. Directly in front of Tomczyk was a thirteen-year-old and his mother, Norah Brown.

About fifteen minutes after the meeting began, an audience member, who appeared to be transgender, stood up to speak. "There's fag number one," Brown heard the man behind her mutter. She swiveled in her seat and glared at him. He looked her in the eye and nodded in the direction of Brown's son. "The second fag," he said.

Brown sent a Facebook message to her friend Christine Salm, who was also in the audience. "The man behind me just referred to the speaker and then to my son as a f**. I am in tears and livid," she typed, shaking her head in disgust.

"I'm so sorry," Salm replied. "His name is Corey Tomczyk he owns IROW."

A few days after the meeting, Brown decided that other people needed to know what had happened. And so she got in touch with a local journalist named Shereen Siewert.

Siewert was the editor of the *Wausau Pilot & Review*. She'd founded the outlet in 2017 after growing frustrated working at other local news organizations. The city's traditional daily paper, the *Wausau Daily Herald*, was owned by the Gannett chain, and it seemed to be constantly downsizing. An alternative weekly struck Siewert as mainly interested in puff pieces. Many evenings, Siewert returned home grumbling about her job. "Why don't you start your own thing?" her husband finally suggested, tired of all the complaining.

That was not as crazy as it sounded. Siewert knew someone with money—lots of it. A high school friend, Paul White, had hit the jackpot in the Powerball lottery, taking home more than $50 million after taxes. He'd told Siewert that if she ever came up with a business idea, she should pitch him, and maybe he'd bankroll it. Well, now she had an idea.

She called White, and he came to Wausau to talk it over. Siewert told him that her best guess was she'd need $50,000 to get her online newspaper started. Would he consider lending her the money? The next day, White came back with his answer: forget about a loan. His foundation would *give* her $50,000 a year. Siewert thought he was joking. White persuaded her he was serious by writing a check on the spot.

One day not long after she launched the *Pilot*, Siewert was eating lunch in a Wausau restaurant when she saw emergency vehicles racing down the street. She flipped on the police scanner she kept in her car. A gunman had opened fire at several nearby locations, killing four people before getting shot by police. Siewert, who'd been a police reporter at the *Daily Herald*, got home and started writing. She didn't stop for twelve hours. Readers flocked to the *Pilot*'s website and devoured the breaking news. "It's terrible to say that a tragedy gave us a boost, but it did," she told me.

The momentum kept building. Over the next couple of years, she published exposés about a local real estate developer, about toxic pollution, about contaminated drinking water. Siewert's initial goal was for the *Pilot* to attract a couple thousand visitors a day. Before long, the traffic was ten times that. She hired a few employees and freelance reporters.

Then, in August 2021, Siewert received an email from Norah Brown, who urged the *Pilot* to cover the next Marathon County board meeting. The previous session, she said, had gotten out of hand. "An individual sitting behind us even referred to one of the other speakers and to my son using a slur (f**)," Brown wrote.

Siewert assigned a reporter to monitor the live video feed of the next meeting, on August 19. Brown stood up and told everyone that an audience member a week earlier had used "an extremely offensive slur."

Another resident, Lisa Ort-Sondergard, also complained that "a local businessman called a young teen a 'fag.'" Two days later, the *Pilot* ran an article about the unidentified businessman's use of the slur.

A week later, the *Pilot* published another piece. This one was about how the fight over the Community for All resolution, which the county board would go on to reject, was tearing the community apart. A proponent had attacked a local official as a "racist pig" and a "redneck." An opponent had warned officials that if they voted for the resolution, they were condoning pedophilia. It wasn't until near the end of the article that the *Pilot* mentioned Cory Tomczyk. It quoted him calling county board members "fools." And the article reported that he had been "widely overheard" calling a thirteen-year-old a "fag."

Before deciding to name Tomczyk in the article, Siewert had spoken with Brown, who told her about her contemporaneous Facebook messages with Salm. Siewert knew and trusted Salm, who confirmed Brown's version of events. Siewert reviewed the messages that the two women had exchanged at the hearing. She also examined social media posts from other attendees who said they'd heard Tomczyk's remark, and she watched video of the hearing to pinpoint the moment at which Tomczyk allegedly used the slur and Brown turned around to glare at him; immediately afterward, Brown could be seen typing something on her phone. That sealed it for Siewert.

For all of her diligence, the *Pilot* had failed to take a rudimentary step: it hadn't contacted Tomczyk beforehand to ask for his version of events. The article also was imprecise on a small but important point. It said that Ort-Sondergard had witnessed the local businessman using the slur, though she would later say that she had only heard about him using it afterward.

When Tomczyk learned what the *Pilot* had written, he was incensed. He had his eye on elected office, and being known as the guy who hurled an offensive epithet at a teenager was probably suboptimal. He denied using the slur at the meeting. He wanted to sue. An acquaintance referred him to Matthew Fernholz.

• • •

Fernholz was a rising star among Wisconsin Republicans. After graduating from Milwaukee's Marquette University Law School in 2010, he'd spent years networking among the state's conservatives, even as his legal practice was devoted to generally mundane commercial disputes. He'd slowly gained notice among Wisconsin's power brokers. In 2014, the Republican governor, Scott Walker, appointed him to a government commission; two years later, the conservative state Supreme Court named him to another. He became the chairman of the Federalist Society's Milwaukee chapter.

Fernholz's big splash came in 2020, when he represented a businessman who sued to overturn the statewide mask mandate imposed by Wisconsin's Democratic governor. The state Supreme Court ruled for Fernholz and his client in March 2021. (The national Federalist Society celebrated the triumph by producing a documentary about the lawsuit.) That same month, Fernholz filed another lawsuit for the same businessman, this one challenging Wisconsin's use of drop boxes for absentee ballots. And just three months after that, Fernholz had filed a libel lawsuit on behalf of a conservative weekly newspaper, the *Lakeland Times*—a virtually unheard-of instance of a news organization being a plaintiff in such a case. The suit was against the liberal owner of a local brewery, who had badmouthed the *Lakeland Times* on Facebook, calling its publisher a "crook," among other false accusations. (Fernholz would eventually win a $750,000 judgment against the brewer, the largest-ever defamation award in Wisconsin.)

Fernholz had first become fascinated by libel and the First Amendment more than a decade earlier, as a budding originalist at Marquette. In a constitutional law class, the professor had spent a day teaching defamation law and the *Sullivan* decision. To Fernholz, this seemed like yet another Warren Court ruling manufactured out of whole cloth, with no connection to the text or meaning of the Constitution. He said as much in class, which led to a brief but vigorous debate, with the professor and other students on one side, and Fernholz alone on the other.

After that, Fernholz hadn't thought much about *Sullivan* until 2019, when Thomas had issued his opinion in *McKee* and two years later when Silberman dissented in the *Global Witness* case. *I wasn't crazy!* Fernholz thought to himself as he read the opinions of these two conservative lions. By the fall of 2021, when Tomczyk approached Fernholz, cases like Shkëlzen Berisha's against Guy Lawson, ChemRisk's against Cherri Foytlin, Jacob Smith's against the *Carroll Times Herald*, Alan Dershowitz's against CNN, and Donald Trump's against just about everyone had become part of an unmistakable trend: all over the country, people with axes to grind against news organizations large and small were rushing to the courts, often aided by lawyers with ideological agendas. Attorneys and other experts on both sides of the debate agreed that the volume of actual or threatened libel suits had soared to what appeared to be unprecedented heights.

Now Fernholz and Tomczyk joined this parade. First, Fernholz dashed off some threatening letters. One went to Lisa Ort-Sondergard. The *Pilot* had quoted her public statement that an unidentified local businessman had used the homophobic epithet. Now Fernholz accused Ort-Sondergard of having falsely fingered Tomczyk, which was not what had happened or what the *Pilot* had reported. "This letter constitutes your notice that your statements attributing this quote to Mr. Tomczyk are defamatory and slanderous, which subjects you to civil and potentially criminal penalties," Fernholz wrote, giving her one week to notify the *Pilot* that her supposed assertions had been false. Ort-Sondergard wrote to Siewert that she had not witnessed the businessman using the slur; she'd heard about it later.

The *Pilot*, however, was Tomczyk's real target. In late September, Fernholz sent Siewert a letter via certified mail. It stated that Tomczyk did not use the slur at the meeting. "Because of the explosive nature of the quote you have attributed to him, this letter constitutes notice that this article in your paper is defamatory and libelous," he wrote. Absent a formal retraction, "my client will consider appropriate legal action."

Unlike major publishers, the *Pilot* didn't have libel insurance—and not for lack of trying. Siewert had previously contacted insurance agents, but nobody would offer her coverage; they kept saying the *Pilot* was too young and too small. Only a month or two earlier, she'd finally found a company that would at least permit her to *apply* for insurance. But her application hadn't been approved yet. And now it was too late. If she got sued, she wouldn't have financial backup to cover her legal fees. The *Pilot*'s future was on the line.

The timing was not ideal. Siewert had health problems. So did her parents. Her sister Krista was dying of cancer. Krista was furious about the lawsuit and urged Siewert to fight. Siewert drew strength from that. She was confident that Tomczyk had used the F word. She refused to retract the article. Hopefully Fernholz was bluffing.

About six weeks later, in early November, she realized that he wasn't. Fernholz filed a libel lawsuit in the Marathon County court on behalf of Tomczyk and his company, IROW. The suit denied that Tomczyk had used the epithet. It mentioned that Ort-Sondergard had not personally heard his client say it. "Defendants' attempts to disparage the Plaintiffs were done intentionally and with an intent to harm Plaintiffs' reputation in the community," the complaint claimed, adding that Tomczyk and IROW "have suffered reputational and financial harm." As evidence, it cited a Facebook post by a Wausau alderman that urged local governments to stop doing business with the company.

Siewert needed a lawyer. She searched for pro bono legal help but came up empty. She eventually contacted the Wisconsin law firm of Godfrey & Kahn, which had a well-known practice defending news organizations and journalists. A Milwaukee-based litigator there, Brian Spahn, agreed to take the case. The firm couldn't represent her for free, but it could be flexible; pay what you can when you can, even a few hundred dollars here and there, Spahn told her.

Spahn already knew of Fernholz, thanks to his high-publicity lawsuit against the liberal brewery. He explained to Siewert that this was part of a nationwide trend of people weaponizing libel laws, and it was especially prevalent in Wisconsin, because unlike dozens of other states, it didn't have an anti-SLAPP law to deter people from filing suits designed to stifle public debate. Just recently, in fact, Godfrey & Kahn had defended the *Wausau Daily Herald*, where Siewert had previously worked, in a seemingly open-and-shut libel lawsuit that had dragged on for nearly three years before it was finally dismissed.

Even after that marathon, though, Spahn thought Tomczyk's lawsuit against the *Pilot* would be short-lived—especially because Siewert informed him that she knew of other people who were willing to testify that they'd heard Tomczyk use the slur. Spahn figured that once Fernholz learned of this, he'd abandon the litigation.

He was wrong. Tomczyk was on a mission—not just to win, it seemed, but also to inflict pain. In an email to an acquaintance shortly after the lawsuit was filed, he noted that Siewert had hired a pricey law firm and predicted that the *Pilot* "will go down." (Fernholz told me that while Tomczyk's main goal "was clearing his name," he also hoped to extract "a pound of flesh.")

Thus began a yearslong brawl. Thousands of pages of internal emails and other documents changed hands in the discovery process. Sworn affidavits were filed, depositions recorded and transcribed, and an endless cycle of motions, objections, replies, and court orders devoured many, many billable hours. At one point, even though she'd been making periodic payments to Spahn's firm, Siewert's outstanding bill hit $158,000. She could have asked her friend Paul White for help, but she felt sheepish. She hadn't even told him she'd been sued. (He eventually learned of it through mutual friends.)

The good news was that the facts appeared to be falling in the *Pilot*'s favor. In addition to Norah Brown, three other witnesses had said under oath that they'd heard Tomczyk use the slur at the now-infamous meeting. It was clear that Siewert and the *Pilot* had tried to confirm the facts before publishing the article. And while Tomczyk remained steadfast that he hadn't said "fag" in that setting, he did acknowledge in a deposition that he had used it, "out of joking and out of spite," toward his gay brother and friends.

In the spring of 2023, nearly eighteen months after the complaint was filed, a Marathon County judge dismissed it. The judge, Scott Corbett, was a self-described conservative and constitutional originalist. He concluded that Tomczyk was a public figure, at least in the context of the debate about the Community for All resolution, and that Siewert and the *Pilot* had taken numerous steps to confirm that Tomczyk used the slur. "On this record, it is not possible to find that the defendants had serious doubts about the truth of the publication," he wrote.

Spahn emailed the news to Siewert, who was in her home office. She wept—and then fixed herself a stiff martini. But the relief was temporary. Barely a month later, Fernholz declared his intention to appeal on the grounds that Tomczyk was a private citizen and therefore should only have been required to show that the *Pilot* acted negligently, not with actual malice. Yes, he'd spoken up at the county meeting, but so had plenty of others. "This act of basic citizenship should not be used to transform unsuspecting private citizens into public figures," Fernholz wrote. The appeal was informed in part by the arguments espoused by Thomas, Gorsuch, Silberman, the Claremont Institute, and others: that *Sullivan*'s web entrapped too many private citizens whose reputations had been damaged and lacked a clear way to fight back, people like Carey Lohrenz and Kathy McKee.

Yet Fernholz was pursuing the appeal on behalf of someone who was no longer a private figure: despite his claims of a ravaged reputation, Tomczyk had been elected to the state senate in 2022.

The prospect of months or years more of this sapped Siewert.* By now, she'd lost her stepfather to Covid and her sister to cancer. The *Pilot* was still going, although some advertisers and donors had fled, apparently in solidarity with Tomczyk. Siewert estimated that she'd lost at least $15,000 a year in revenue as a result. "Every time I write a major story today, I have to think twice about the risk I'm taking," she told me. "Knowing that anyone could sue me at any time for just about anything, I've often questioned why I continue to do this work."

On a broiling morning in August 2023, a small group of legislators gathered inside the state Capitol in Madison. Melissa Agard, the top Democrat in the Wisconsin Senate, had called a press conference to unveil a new piece of legislation: an anti-SLAPP bill to deter the filing of lawsuits intended to quash public debate.

"Politicians and public officials have begun turning to the legal system as a way to express their displeasure with media outlets," Agard said, standing before a green marble fireplace in a room lined with dark

---

* In September 2024, a state appeals court upheld Judge Corbett's dismissal of the lawsuit.

wood paneling. She pointed to Trump's recent $475 million lawsuit against CNN and Tomczyk's ongoing action against the *Pilot*, which became big news in Wisconsin after the *New York Times* wrote about it. "I think that we can all agree that the media's ability to report on matters of public concern without undue legal pressure is vitally important to maintaining a well-informed citizenry as well as a functioning democracy," Agard said.

The goal of the bill was to discourage people like Tomczyk from pursuing such litigation in the future; his lawsuit wouldn't be affected. The bill stipulated that not only would abusive speech-suppressing lawsuits be quickly thrown out of court but that the plaintiffs could also be compelled to pay the defendants' legal fees in certain circumstances. Seven years earlier, a similar anti-SLAPP law in Massachusetts had helped Cherri Foytlin and Karen Savage defeat the libel lawsuit that Clare Locke had filed on behalf of ChemRisk.

A handful of other states—including deep red ones like Kentucky and liberal strongholds like New Jersey—had recently adopted their own anti-SLAPP laws, often with virtually unanimous support from lawmakers. (More than thirty states had such laws as of 2024.) Liberal groups like the ACLU supported the rules; so did conservative ones like the National Right to Life Committee. "This has not been a partisan issue in other states," Agard noted at the press conference. "This should not be a partisan issue in the state of Wisconsin."

The problem was that her bill's cosponsors were all Democrats, who were in a minority in the state legislature. And Tomczyk was now striding the halls of the Capitol in Madison, sponsoring legislation to complicate the use of absentee ballots, to conduct election audits, to require that the "In God We Trust" motto be displayed in classrooms. His mere presence among the lockstep GOP conference meant all but certain death for the anti-SLAPP bill that his lawsuit had inspired. Republicans "have their guy's back," Agard told me, acknowledging the bill's low odds of passage. Fernholz was more succinct: "It's dead."

A similar situation had transpired in Iowa. Steve Holt, a Republican state representative, had introduced an anti-SLAPP bill after hearing about the police lawsuit against Jared Strong and the *Carroll Times Herald*, which despite winning in court had been financially imperiled. Holt called Doug Burns, the paper's owner at the time, and discussed the matter with him, as well as Iowa's Democratic attorney general. At the very least, empowering judges to quickly pull the plug on meritless lawsuits would help minimize the pain for cash-strapped local media. "We want to prevent local news organizations from being driven out of business," he said.

The bill passed the Iowa House by a vote of ninety-four to one. It went to the Senate, where a subcommittee recommended its passage. Then it died at the hands of a single Republican senator, Julian Garrett, who was an enthusiastic Trump supporter and doubted the necessity of such a law. "He has this idea it will protect CNN or something like that," Holt told me.

New Hampshire was another state without an anti-SLAPP law—a relic of a mid-1990s advisory opinion by the state Supreme Court that such legislation would probably violate the state constitution. And that gave Eric Spofford, a wealthy businessman, a potential opening as he plotted vengeance against the radio station that had reported on his alleged history of sexual misconduct.

JUST THE BEGINNING

L auren Chooljian first heard of Eric Spofford when a nurse sent a tip to New Hampshire's public radio station: a local rehab center was not taking appropriate precautions to prevent the spread of Covid-19.

It was the summer of 2020, and the Green Mountain Treatment Center was far from the only business struggling to deal with the fast-spreading coronavirus. But Chooljian's curiosity was piqued when she and a fellow reporter at New Hampshire Public Radio started sniffing around. Some cursory internet research revealed that the rehab facility was owned by Spofford. Hulking and heavily tattooed, he was a recovering heroin addict who had built a personal brand in part by regaling anyone who would listen—including his hundreds of thousands of social media followers—with salacious tales of his drug-addled past. After getting sober, he had built one of New England's largest networks of treatment facilities, called Granite Recovery Centers. He eventually became known as an addiction expert. The internet was filled with testimonials about how Spofford and his treatment centers had saved lives. He had appeared before Congress and had a strong relationship with New Hampshire's governor, Chris Sununu, whose state was on the front lines of the national opioid epidemic.

Chooljian and her colleague, Jason Moon, eventually wrote a story about a Covid outbreak at the unprepared Green Mountain center. At that point, Chooljian would have moved on, except that the article elicited a new, more shocking allegation: that Spofford had a history of sexual misconduct involving patients who were recovering from addiction.

Chooljian, who had a thick head of wavy blondish hair and exuded hipster vibes, had grown up in New Hampshire—her father had been a legendary high school wrestling coach—and after a pit stop in Chicago she'd returned. She'd landed a job as a political reporter at NHPR. Like any good journalist, Chooljian had a knack for irritating powerful people. In 2019, her podcast *Stranglehold*, which critically examined New Hampshire's first-in-the-nation presidential primaries, had pissed off a healthy cross section of the state's political and media elites.

Now, in possession of an explosive tip about a prominent businessman, Chooljian started making phone calls to see what more she could learn. She mostly worked out of a makeshift office in her dimly lit basement, surrounded by incense, dried flowers, and recording equipment. She eventually interviewed dozens of current and former workers and patients at Spofford's rehab centers. It became clear to her that Spofford's behavior was an open secret throughout New Hampshire's recovery community. One person after another told Chooljian that he had tried to sleep with patients, who were in a uniquely vulnerable situation as they struggled to remain sober. Chooljian also heard that Spofford had sexually assaulted an employee.

It was painstaking work. Chooljian needed to corroborate—through documents and on-the-record interviews—what her sources were confidentially telling her. It took more than a year. Before publication, she presented her findings to Spofford and sought his comment. His lawyer at the time, Mitch Schuster, responded with the equivalent of a brushback pitch in baseball. He called Chooljian's editor, Daniel Barrick, to sow doubt about Chooljian's motives and credibility. Then he wrote in a letter that Spofford "vehemently denies any alleged misconduct" and that his client was prepared "to pursue all of his legal rights and remedies based on your disingenuous reporting and malicious conduct."

Chooljian's investigation first aired on the radio and on NHPR's website on March 22, 2022. In the radio piece, a former Granite Recovery patient, identified by her middle name, described how Spofford repeatedly sent her inappropriate chat messages. A former employee said Spofford had sexually assaulted her. Several other ex-employees spoke on the record about what they said was Spofford's misconduct. One,

Piers Kaniuka, Granite Recovery's former director of spiritual life, said he resigned in 2020 after an employee told him that Spofford had attacked her. The piece also quoted Spofford's vigorous denials.

Chooljian let some of her sources know that this was by no means the end of her reporting. She was planning to expand it into a podcast, building on the success of *Stranglehold*, that would hopefully run nationwide.

Chooljian and her colleagues recognized that Spofford wasn't the type to let something like this go. It wasn't just his lawyer's tough-talking letter. The more people Chooljian had talked to during her reporting, the scarier the stories had become—and the more nervous she had grown about her own safety. Spofford had talked openly about his past brushes with violence, and he remained tight with men who had long, ugly rap sheets. "People warned me to be careful," Chooljian told me.

She was right to be worried. Spofford was about to join the procession of powerful people exploiting the legal system to protect their secrets. And his allies were going to deploy even more aggressive means to intimidate Chooljian and her colleagues.

In late 2021, Spofford had sold Granite Recovery for what he said was $115 million, and his Instagram and YouTube pages were filled with shots of him on yachts and private jets and in his new waterfront mansion in Miami. He had money to burn, and the day after Chooljian's piece ran, he initiated what would become a long-running, multifront counteroffensive. Before any lawsuit was filed, Spofford would pour hundreds of thousands of dollars into this endeavor. Politicians like DeSantis and lawyers like Locke liked to say that rolling back First Amendment protections would primarily benefit a theoretical "little guy"—and, sure, they could point to scattered examples of Average Joes harmed by reckless media coverage—but the main beneficiaries would be the people like Spofford who had secrets to hide and the financial resources to hound their critics.

The first stage of Spofford's campaign was a barrage of formal letters, written by his lawyers, putting NHPR journalists and their sources on notice that they might get sued. The letters instructed the recipients to preserve any emails, documents, or other materials related to Chooljian's exposé. Investigative reporters are accustomed to letters like this. Chooljian's sources were not. They were normal people who'd had the courage to speak up about what they saw as wrongdoing by a powerful man. That hadn't been an easy decision for them—or an easy journalistic feat for Chooljian to persuade them to go public. Quite a few of her sources were speaking openly about their addictions for the first time; others were revealing the most traumatic moments of their lives. Now, as they weighed whether to continue cooperating with Chooljian, they had to add another big risk to the equation: the prospect of getting dragged into litigation. Would they be compelled to testify under oath? Would their reputations be wrecked? Would they have to hire lawyers? How would they pay?

Step two for Spofford was to try to get at least one of Chooljian's sources to recant. Piers Kaniuka was an obvious target. He'd known Spofford for years—the two men had even coauthored a book about overcoming addiction—and yet Kaniuka had been quoted in the NHPR piece comparing his old comrade to Harvey Weinstein. Now Spofford's lawyers presented him with what they said was the draft of a lawsuit that would soon be filed against him. As part of a subsequent settlement, Kaniuka agreed to write a notarized letter that apologized to Spofford for, among other things, the Weinstein comparison. Importantly, though, Kaniuka didn't back away from his statement that he'd resigned from Granite Recovery after learning of Spofford's alleged assault.

Spofford posted Kaniuka's letter on Facebook, saying it showed that NHPR's investigation "was not credible and filled with lies." One of Spofford's lawyers, Benjamin Levine, then sent the Kaniuka letter to Chooljian's sources, falsely claiming it was a retraction and even proposing language for them to send Chooljian cutting off contact. Some of the sources told Chooljian that they were unnerved. They feared Spofford, and they saw hundreds of comments on his Facebook post egging him on in his fight with NHPR.

NHPR's outside lawyer, Sigmund Schutz, had been representing news organizations for a long time, and he'd never witnessed such an onslaught. "It's very unusual for sources to be targeted, especially in such a methodical fashion with the clear goal of having the sources retract their stories," he told me.

Levine also shared Kaniuka's supposed retraction with NHPR's board of trustees and demanded that the outlet immediately remove the article from its website. Otherwise, Levine wrote, "Eric would have no choice but to file suit."

Because New Hampshire lacked an anti-SLAPP law, there was effectively no deterrent to someone like Spofford using such litigation as a weapon. Even if a court eventually concluded that the suit was a transparent effort to suppress legitimate speech, his opponents would have to endure months, maybe years, of litigation. Regardless of the outcome, Spofford wouldn't be stuck covering their legal bills. In other words, he didn't have much to lose, aside from what he was already shelling out for his lawyers.

One morning in April 2022, weeks after her investigation was published, Chooljian was on vacation in Telluride, Colorado. It was the first break she'd taken since her baby had been born about a year earlier. She was preparing breakfast in their Airbnb when she received a text from her mother in New Hampshire. The message said she needed help picking out a security camera. "Sadly," she wrote, "we had something happen at the house last night and need one."

"Oh no mom what happened," Chooljian typed.

Her mother described the scene. When she'd woken up that morning, she'd noticed it was unusually cold inside. She'd gone downstairs and seen that a ground-level window was broken. She figured maybe a bird had crashed through it. Then she and her husband saw a softball-size rock inside the house. This was vandalism, not nature. When they went outside to inspect the damage, they both gasped: someone had spray-painted "CUNT" in bright red on one of their white garage doors.

Growing up, Chooljian had not been allowed to say things like "shut up" or "sucks," much less utter a curse word, and so she had no trouble imagining her straightlaced parents' horror at their house being defaced with such a vulgarity. She immediately assumed the vandalism was because of her reporting on Spofford. Her parents told her it was probably just some kid. Chooljian wasn't convinced. She called Daniel Barrick, her editor, to alert him. He had been a steady presence by Chooljian's side throughout the reporting process, including when he fielded the angry call from Spofford's lawyer. When Chooljian reached him, Barrick was in the car with his two children, preparing to go on a family bike ride. Pacing around a pool table in the basement of the Airbnb, Chooljian explained what had happened.

"They hit my house, too," Barrick whispered, trying not to let his kids hear the fear in his voice. The same red profanity had been scrawled in red across a glass storm door. Like Chooljian's parents, he had dismissed the incident as nothing more than a high school prank. Now that looked like wishful thinking.

Chooljian began to cry. "I'm so sorry, Dan," she stammered.

The next day, she was sitting on the porch of the Telluride rental, alternately gazing at a mountain and scrolling through emails. Her goal was to relax, to salvage some of this much-needed vacation. In the best of times, Chooljian was not a naturally calm person—"She's always vibrating," Barrick told me—and now she was having trouble thinking about anything other than the attacks on her parents' and colleague's homes. Then she came across an email from a listserv in Hanover, New Hampshire, where she and her husband, Matt Baer, had lived several years earlier. A neighbor, the message said, "had been the victim of a nighttime crime." The same nasty word had been sprayed on the front door, and a brick had smashed the living-room window. It was Chooljian's old house.

"Matt," she said, "Hanover got hit, too."

By now, Chooljian had zero doubt that the vandalism was tied to her reporting. There simply was no other plausible explanation. Her parents felt similarly, and they were scared. They urged their daughter to reconsider whether she should pursue this story. "Whoever these people are, they obviously have no moral compass and are very unstable," her father told her.

Over the ensuing weeks, while the fear was fresh, Spofford's lawyers ratcheted up the pressure. In addition to threatening to sue unless the radio station removed and apologized for the article, they demanded that NHPR publish Kaniuka's "retraction." Schutz, the radio station's lawyer, replied to Spofford's attorney, Benjamin Levine, defending the article and pointing out that Kaniuka had not recanted. If Spofford sued, Schutz predicted, "he will run into a buzzsaw called the First Amendment."

On the morning of May 20, Schutz spoke by phone with Levine and Spofford's other lawyers. They described their client as distraught. Schutz replied that NHPR's editors were willing to hear out Spofford's side if they wanted to propose a compromise, but under no circumstances was the article coming down. Nor were they going to apologize. The two sides were at an impasse.

Around 3:30 that afternoon, Tucker Cockerline pulled into the parking lot of the Loop shopping center in Methuen, Massachusetts, a small city along the New Hampshire border. After a long pandemic, customers were returning to the Loop's movie theater, restaurants, and retail outlets. Cockerline, however, wasn't looking to kick back.

The thirty-one-year-old walked into Home Depot and made his way to its garden center. Row after row of plants, tools, lawn furniture, and sacks of soil and mulch were stacked on shelves so high that only an employee-operated forklift could fetch them. Cockerline had come to buy some bricks, and the garden center offered a surprising variety. There were red bricks and gray bricks, cement bricks and clay bricks, bricks with holes, even old, reclaimed mill bricks. Cockerline selected two solid, reddish ones. They cost about a dollar each.

Cockerline was five foot nine and had green eyes, a stubbly face, and a long rap sheet. There were drug, assault, and forgery charges, and he had the honor of having once been named by the US Marshals Service as New Hampshire's "Fugitive of the Week." His record suggested a certain haplessness. Back in 2008, for example, when he was eighteen, Cockerline and two other men had made a quick $900 selling a quarter pound of what they claimed were psychedelic mushrooms but in reality were ordinary shiitakes that they had dyed blue. Unfortunately, it was a sting operation, and when the police nabbed Cockerline minutes later, his fingertips were stained with blue food coloring. "I realize I'm making bad decisions in my life," Cockerline told the judge, who sentenced him to up to three years in prison.

Now, armed with a pair of bricks, he was about to make another bad decision.

During a prison stint, Cockerline had gotten to know a man named

Eric Labarge. Labarge had a history of violence. Once, he'd allegedly stabbed someone six times in a brawl in a motel bathroom. (Charges, including assault to murder, were dropped after the victim disappeared.) Another time, he had beaten his girlfriend senseless while driving down the interstate and was apprehended after an hours-long standoff with dozens of cops and a SWAT team.

Labarge and Eric Spofford were close, having traveled in similar circles in New Hampshire's recovery world.

Early that spring, Labarge had called Cockerline and offered him a way to make hundreds of dollars. Cockerline had been game and, along with another guy, proceeded to vandalize the homes of Chooljian's parents and editor and what they'd wrongly thought was the journalist's house in Hanover. Now Cockerline was going to try again. Because his previous accomplice was unavailable—he'd been locked up on unrelated charges in the weeks since the April vandalisms—he enlisted an acquaintance named Michael Waselchuck. "Wanna make sum cash?" Cockerline had texted. "Lil spray paint nd brick through a window $500."

"I'm down to do that," Waselchuck replied. They settled on a plan: Cockerline would target Chooljian's parents; Waselchuck would pay a visit to Chooljian's actual house in the Boston suburb of Melrose.

Cockerline struck first. At 12:54 a.m., he threw one of the Home Depot bricks at the parents' house. True to form, he missed the window, and the projectile bounced harmlessly off the beige siding, coming to rest in some mulch. Undaunted, Cockerline once again spray-painted "CUNT" across the garage door.

About five hours later, it was Waselchuck's turn. By the time he arrived in Melrose, around 5:45 a.m., it was well past sunrise, and the sky was a pale gray. A light rain was falling, and the tall, slender Waselchuck pulled up the hood on his blue raincoat. He approached Chooljian's house on a quiet parkway. He sprayed his own message across the side of the house. Then he launched Cockerline's second brick through a picture window and sprinted away.

"Come thru when you want your paycheck," Cockerline messaged Waselchuck a few hours later, after collecting $1,000 in cash from Labarge.

• • •

Chooljian, her husband, and their daughter were in Chicago when she was awoken by a text message from her father. Heavy thunderstorms had plowed through the city overnight, and lingering rain clouds smothered the rising sun. "The house was vandalized again last night," he wrote.

"WHAT," Chooljian responded, not bothering with punctuation. "What the fuck dad I'm so sorry." Chooljian relayed the news to Baer, then rolled out of bed to fetch their daughter, who was beginning to stir. Baer reached for his phone. There were a bunch of automated alerts from their home-security company. Motion had been detected outside their house, and their doorbell camera had captured videos. Baer had a bad feeling: *I'm about to see things that I don't want to see.* Timestamped barely an hour earlier, the videos revealed a hooded man with sunken cheeks shuffling around and then winding up and hurling a brick. The doorbell cam picked up the sound of glass shattering.

"Lauren, it happened to our house, too," Baer announced.

Chooljian had been bracing for this for weeks. What she lacked in surprise, she made up for in anger. She and Baer had bought their house in December 2020, at the height of the pandemic, and it had been a refuge not just from Covid but also during the early months of parenthood. Chooljian and her baby girl had spent innumerable hours parked on the living room sofa, enjoying the sunshine that poured in through the large picture window, her daughter propped up so she could peer at passing cars. Now that window was broken, their sofa prickled with shards of glass.

From Chicago, Chooljian and Baer divided the phone calls—to Daniel Barrick, Chooljian's parents, the Melrose police, even the FBI. When the cops arrived, they discovered that the vandal had done more than break the window. He had also painted an ominous message in red: "JUST THE BEGINNING!"

The doorbell footage had shown that moments after Waselchuck fled, three pedestrians had passed the house. Back in Melrose a couple days after the vandalism, Baer went out searching for the passersby, who he had heard went on a walk every morning around 6 a.m. He eventually found them. "Hey, I'm Matt," he said. "I live at the house across the street." He asked if they might be able to help identify the perpetrator. The walkers said they couldn't.

"Tell your wife to be more careful next time," one muttered.

Baer recounted the brief but disconcerting chat to me one evening a year later as he, Chooljian, and I sat at their dining room table, eating chicken and pasta that he had prepared us. Small gouges from the brick and broken glass were still visible on the inner windowsill. A framed poster with the words "Ask More Questions" hung nearby. Outside, video cameras, driveway alarms, and motion sensors surveilled the house, and the spot where Baer had painted over Waslechuck's red warning remained visible. Chooljian flipped through her phone, showing me photos of the shattered glass on her sofa and "CUNT" spray-painted on her parents' garage. Her hands quivered.

At its offices in Concord, NHPR installed heavy, reinforced doors, upgraded its security cameras, and added panic buttons in the newsroom. Public radio is not a cash-rich business, and to foot the bill for all the extra security at the office and its journalists' homes, the station had needed to go hat in hand to donors.

Money was not the only challenge. Chooljian was continuing to work on what would eventually become a podcast, *The 13th Step*, about her investigation into Spofford. She needed her sources not only to keep sharing information but also to let their voices be recorded for the podcast. Many were already scarred by the abuse they'd suffered. Now they learned about what had happened to Chooljian and her family and colleague's homes, and they were spooked. "This is obviously making my job more difficult," Chooljian told me. "I think it's safe to assume that was the goal."

Spofford denied that he'd had anything to do with the vandalism, and authorities haven't accused him of being involved. He publicly speculated that—who knows?—maybe the perpetrator was one of Chooljian's unhinged sources. He allowed that it was also possible that the attacks had been carried out by an ally of his, but it certainly wasn't his fault. "Many people in recovery have credited me with saving their lives. Perhaps one of them felt compelled to do these acts in a misguided attempt to defend me. I would never condone it, but I have no control over what other people do." Around then, Spofford posted on social media a photo of himself and Eric Labarge, with the caption #duespaid.

Cockerline, Waselchuck, Labarge, and a fourth man, Keenan Saniatan, were eventually arrested and criminally charged, done in by the long trail of electronic records—Google searches, phone records, video footage, even payments for the two bricks at Home Depot—that they'd left in their wake. (All four pleaded guilty. Cockerline, the first to be sentenced, received twenty-seven months in prison.) The men might not have been criminal geniuses, but Waselchuck's message in red had proven apt: the legal assault was just beginning.

In the fall of 2022, Spofford's lawyers filed a ninety-page libel lawsuit against the radio station, Chooljian, and others, including some of the sources in the article. The suit, in state court in New Hampshire, claimed that NHPR had knowingly relied on untrustworthy sources. It said Chooljian was "tainted by a selfish ambition for personal acclaim." It even asserted that an article that NHPR had run about Chooljian's house being vandalized—in which a freelance reporter had quoted local authorities saying they would probably interview Spofford as part of their investigation—"knowingly weaponized a conspiratorial connection between Eric and the alleged vandalism as a means for the NHPR defendants to deflect from their suppression of the Kaniuka retraction."

These were not strong claims. Chooljian had persuaded numerous sources to go on the record; listeners could hear their voices for themselves. She had meticulously vetted and verified their stories. She had sought and included comments from Spofford. And Spofford's insistence that Piers Kaniuka had retracted his comments to Chooljian was simply false.

NHPR sought to dismiss the lawsuit. Sigmund Schutz, the station's lawyer, pointed out that Spofford's national prominence made him a public figure and that "beyond clichéd smears (woman with 'blinding ambition' tries to take down powerful man) he offers not a hint of factual support for his claims" that Chooljian acted with actual malice. What's more, NHPR's article was factual and correct. "This kind of lawsuit has a real chilling effect," Schutz noted at a court hearing. "The objective of this litigation is that just by filing, win or lose, is to silence critics."

After seven months of wrangling, a judge on New Hampshire's Superior

Court granted NHPR's motion. The complaint "fails to allege that the NHPR defendants acted with actual malice in their reporting," wrote the judge, Dan St. Hilaire, a Republican appointed by Governor Sununu. But he said he would give Spofford time to file an amended complaint that did a better job of establishing the necessary facts. Spofford's team said they would refile a beefed-up version. First, though, the lawyers argued, they needed access to some of NHPR's files, including Chooljian's notes and audio recordings of her interviews with certain sources.

Normally, in order to get to the discovery stage of the legal proceedings, a plaintiff's complaint has to survive the motion to dismiss. That hadn't happened here, so there was no reason to think that Spofford's request would gain traction with St. Hilaire. Schutz also pointed out in a court filing that giving someone like Spofford access to NHPR's files would violate the protections of the First Amendment. "A key reason we have the actual malice standard is to protect speakers from the expense and chilling effect of potential litigation," he wrote.

St. Hilaire wasn't about to let Spofford and his team go fishing through all of NHPR's files. But he thought Spofford's side might have a point; how could they prove that NHPR had acted recklessly without seeing some of the raw materials Chooljian was working with? So St. Hilaire struck a compromise. Instead of ordering NHPR to share its materials with Spofford, he instructed the outlet to provide some of the requested files to the court. St. Hilaire would privately examine them—in what is known as an "in camera" review—to see whether they could potentially be helpful to the plaintiffs.

Chooljian and her colleagues were upset. They had no doubts about the integrity of their journalism. But the materials the judge was demanding included transcripts of her interviews with sources, some of whom had spoken to her on the condition that she keep their identities under wraps because they were terrified, seemingly with good reason, of the potential repercussions if Spofford learned that they were talking. Yet NHPR had no choice but to obey. In October 2023, the radio station handed over nearly three thousand pages of notes, transcripts, and electronic communication between Chooljian and some of her sources and colleagues.

St. Hilaire cruised through the materials, and shortly before Christmas he issued his ruling. The voluminous records, he wrote, "reflect professional and diligent reporting and are totally devoid of any evidence that the NHPR defendants had reason to doubt the truth of their publication." The judge added that there was "absolutely no evidence" that the allegations NHPR aired were false. "Spofford has no viable basis to sue the NHPR defendants or their sources for defamation." St. Hilaire rejected Spofford's requests to see the documents himself. Spofford remained free to file a revised version of the lawsuit within the next month. But, the judge concluded, based on the documents he'd reviewed, doing so "will likely be futile."

St. Hilaire's compromise had been scary for NHPR, but it had played to the journalists' advantage, because their reporting had been responsible. The judge's unequivocal validation of NHPR's work apparently persuaded Spofford's side to throw in the towel. He didn't refile the lawsuit. By then NHPR's *13th Step* podcast had been released to rave reviews. In 2024, Chooljian and her colleagues were finalists for a Pulitzer Prize.

Spofford, however, wasn't about to slink out of the spotlight or entirely give up his fight. Someone started sending bogus requests to Google to remove NHPR's articles about him from its search results, falsely claiming the articles infringed on copyrighted works. (Such requests are a popular new tool for people looking to hide unflattering information online.) And about a week after the Pulitzers were announced, Spofford hosted a one-day event at his Miami mansion. Attendees paid $1,500 to be coached on how to build a business and "A Massive & Profitable Personal Brand." (For an extra $1,000, they could enjoy a "VIP sunset yacht dinner.") In case anyone stumbled across the allegations that Spofford had sexually harassed and assaulted women, his website included a prominent link to the legal complaint against Chooljian and NHPR. Even after it had been eviscerated by a judge, the lawsuit was still doing its job.

THE CASE OF THE CENTURY

About three weeks after the 2020 election, Tom Clare was preparing for Thanksgiving when he got a phone call from a potential client. He and Libby Locke were in their five-thousand-square-foot town house in Old Town Alexandria, which they had bought earlier that year. The property, built in 1794, might have been vast, but school was out, and holiday chaos reigned inside. Clare walked down the hill to his law offices so that he could have a quiet conversation.

The phone call would prove to be seminal. Clare Locke, whose founders claimed that it had become virtually impossible to hold the media to account, was about to play a key role in holding one of the country's most powerful media outlets to account. In doing so, the law firm would present a compelling case as to why there was no need to abandon decades of legal precedent in order to counter the flow of damaging lies and misinformation.

On the phone with Clare was a representative of Dominion Voting Systems, which made the software and other technology that operated the machines on which voters in twenty-eight states had cast ballots in the recent election. Conspiracy theorists were flooding the airwaves and social media with false accusations that Dominion was to blame for Donald Trump's supposedly illegitimate defeat. Trump allies like Sidney Powell, Rudy Giuliani, and Mike Lindell were wrongly claiming that the company had changed or canceled people's votes and was controlled by the Venezuelan government. Outlets like Fox News and One America News were amplifying the disinformation.

The lies were outlandish to the point of being funny, except for one thing: people were believing them. Dominion's business was under siege, and its employees were facing threats. "You're all fucking dead," a caller warned in one of many menacing messages left on the company's customer support line. "Your fucking days are numbered. You better enjoy your Thanksgiving because you'll never see another one."

Luckily for Dominion, Clare and his law firm had a playbook at the ready—the same one that they had used countless times on behalf of men like Oleg Deripaska and families like the Sacklers who were seeking to quash public criticism. Clare agreed to take Dominion on as a client. "We recognized right away just how momentous an issue this was, not only for Dominion, but for the entire country and the integrity of elections," he would say.

Clare and his colleague Megan Meier soon began sending cease-and-desist letters warning Trump's lawyers, his favorite anchors, and media companies like Fox, OAN, and Newsmax that they were spreading defamatory lies. A fifteen-page missive to Sidney Powell catalogued "your reckless disinformation campaign." A letter to Fox News' general counsel urged the network to stop providing platforms to people like Powell. "We are currently drafting a defamation complaint against Ms. Powell and two other defendants," Clare and Meier wrote. "We prefer to focus on holding Ms. Powell and her network of liars and conspiracy theorists accountable, rather than adding Fox News, Fox Business, or its journalists to that complaint."

The goal was twofold: to get the outlets and individuals to stop smearing Dominion and, failing that, to create a paper trail showing that these potential defendants had been put on notice but refused to comply.

Yet liars like Powell and Mike Lindell—the pillow salesman who was an unwavering advertiser on Fox News' oft-boycotted prime-time shows—kept appearing on the network, and the falsehoods about Dominion kept spreading. Ever since calling the race for Biden, Fox News had been losing viewers to far-right cable networks like OAN and Newsmax, and Fox hosts and executives appeared to be so determined to stop the bleeding that they underestimated the potential long-term legal and financial repercussions of allowing their guests to peddle disinformation and their hosts to repeat and endorse the baseless claims.

On January 8, 2021—two days after a mob, intoxicated from a two-month bender of election lies, attacked the Capitol—Clare Locke filed a $1.3 billion lawsuit against Powell, followed by similar actions against Giuliani and Lindell. (Lindell, who a year earlier had hired Charles Harder to sue the *Daily Mail* for reporting about his supposed affair with an actress, now adopted the mantle of victim. "These defamation cases are damaging free speech," he sniffed. "People are afraid to speak out.")

The work for Dominion would quickly become the highest-profile assignment Clare Locke had ever handled. It would inspire others to use defamation lawsuits to combat antidemocratic disinformation. Yet it would ultimately cause such turmoil within Clare Locke that it would imperil the future of the firm.

In 2019, Rachel Goodman had left her job as a lawyer at the ACLU, where she focused on challenging discriminatory housing policies, to take up what felt like a more urgent fight. She joined a young but fast-growing nonprofit called Protect Democracy, founded by veterans of the Obama White House but staffed by lawyers and experts from across the political spectrum. As its name implied, the group's goal was to counter America's increasingly authoritarian tendencies through advocacy, research, and litigation.

Goodman, who had freckles and short, reddish hair, was responsible for a team fighting election-related disinformation. Even before violence engulfed the Capitol, she and her colleagues had been brainstorming ways to confront the proliferation of lies that seemed tailor-made to undermine confidence in the election's integrity. When they read about Clare Locke's work for Dominion—both the flurry of cease-and-desist letters and the suits that the firm had begun to file—something clicked.

Until then, Goodman had associated such tactics with powerful people seeking to silence their critics. Now it occurred to her and her colleagues that there had been a smattering of previous attempts to use libel lawsuits to combat conspiracy theories. There was the letter that the owner of Comet Ping Pong had sent to Alex Jones before a gunman shot up the

Washington pizzeria. There was another defamation lawsuit, also against Jones, filed by the families of children massacred at Sandy Hook Elementary School in Connecticut. (In 2022, a judge and jury awarded the families more than $1 billion in damages.) Now there was Dominion.

Libel law, it seemed to Goodman, was a potentially powerful weapon in the fight against corrosive public lies. Not only could Protect Democracy hold these super-spreaders of disinformation accountable for the damage they caused, but the group could also send a public message that there would be heavy costs associated with spewing damaging falsehoods in the future. "This part of the media ecosystem has been the Wild West, and these suits are like a sheriff showing up in town," she explained.

For that deterrent message to resonate loudly, the litigation would need to get noticed inside the echo chambers that tended to spawn disinformation. That meant going after the worst, highest profile offenders. Goodman and her colleagues began scouting for candidates.

Protect Democracy's first foray came in the summer of 2021 in a lawsuit on behalf of a postmaster in Erie, Pennsylvania. The defendant was Project Veritas—the right-wing group known for entrapment and out-of-context videos—which had accused him of tampering with mail-in ballots. (The suit ended with Project Veritas acknowledging that the allegations were false.)

Next, two election workers in Atlanta sued the Gateway Pundit (a popular far-right conspiracy website), Giuliani, and others for concocting lies about them supposedly pulling fraudulent ballots out of suitcases. (A jury awarded the election workers nearly $150 million in damages from Giuliani. The Gateway Pundit case was awaiting trial as of fall 2024.) Election-related libel lawsuits against MAGA stars like Dinesh D'Souza and Kari Lake would follow in the years ahead.

Virtually overnight, defamation suits seeking to stanch the flow of disinformation—actual, honest-to-goodness disinformation, as opposed to articles or radio segments or books that the subject simply didn't like—seemed to have become all the rage. "It's definitely a brand-new trend," marveled RonNell Anderson Jones, a University of Utah professor and nationally recognized expert on libel law. Even lawyers who defended media companies for a living voiced cautious support for this new phenomenon. Protect Democracy's early victories suggested that the barriers to bringing successful defamation lawsuits were not nearly as insurmountable as Justice Gorsuch and others liked to say. Such suits could "effectively rebut the recent contentions that the *Sullivan* regime doesn't work as intended," the longtime First Amendment attorney Lee Levine noted.

That created a quandary for the lawyers who had been pushing to reconsider *Sullivan*—and who would now be working for Dominion.

In early December 2020, Rod Smolla heard from an attorney named Mitch Langberg. Langberg's father had been a prominent defamation lawyer who had teamed up once or twice with Smolla, and so the men knew each other. Now the younger Langberg approached Smolla with an unusual question: was he a Trump supporter? No, Smolla replied, he had voted for Biden.

Well before the election, Langberg's firm had been providing legal assistance to Dominion. As the lies began spreading, and before Clare Locke came aboard, he had dashed off an early cease-and-desist letter to Fox. Now, at Dominion's request, Langberg was trying to build out the team. Would Smolla be interested in joining? As a starting point, the longtime professor could offer advice on the intricacies of libel and the First Amendment. Later on, he could help draft briefs and argue motions before the courts, bringing his gravitas and academic reputation to bear on Dominion's behalf.

Smolla agreed to join, at an hourly rate of $750.

By early 2021, with Fox and other outlets refusing to stand down, it had become clear that litigation would be Dominion's only recourse. And that meant bigger guns would need to be brought on. Clare Locke was small; it had only six partners at the time. Plus, its lawyers were charging by the hour. While some discounts had been baked into the contract, the monthly bills were already piling up, adding to the financial pressures on Dominion. So the company enlisted a larger firm, Susman Godfrey, to take the lead on the planned lawsuits against Fox and the other media outlets. Susman agreed to work on a contingency basis, meaning it wouldn't get paid unless Dominion collected damages or a settlement.

The complaint against Fox was filed in March 2021 in state court in Delaware, where Dominion and Fox were both incorporated. Including exhibits, it ran to 441 pages. It accused Fox of knowingly providing a platform for guests to lie about Dominion, and it accused hosts, including Tucker Carlson, Maria Bartiromo, and Lou Dobbs, of endorsing and repeating those lies. Dominion sought $1.6 billion in damages.

There was plenty of evidence that Fox and its hosts, not to mention some of its unhinged guests, were airing disinformation. The question was their intent. Did they know the conspiracy theories about Dominion were false? In other words, were they lying?

Dominion executives and their lawyers had a pretty strong hunch that the answers to those questions were yes. But to prove it, they would need to be able to dig through Fox's internal records and depose its employees under oath. And to do that, they would need to survive the cable network's motion to dismiss the lawsuit.

Fox asked the Delaware court to boot the lawsuit on the grounds that its news and business channels were simply reporting on the attempts by Trump and his allies to challenge the election results. Surely explaining the president's arguments to viewers was protected by the First Amendment, even if some of those arguments turned out to be bogus. The lawsuit, Fox's lawyers wrote, "threatens to stifle the media's free-speech right to inform the public about newsworthy allegations of paramount public concern." The problem with this argument was that Fox hadn't been operating in a vacuum. The network's producers, anchors, and executives knew or should have known that what they were saying was false, which, of course, was the test for determining actual malice under *Sullivan*.

Smolla and a Susman Godfrey lawyer teamed up to oppose this motion and defend their lawsuit. They explained to the judge that there was a wealth of publicly available information—some of it even coming from inside the Trump administration—that authoritatively debunked the baloney that people like Powell and Giuliani were serving up and that Fox hosts kept sharing with their audiences. And Dominion's advisers, both its lawyers and its public relations firm, had bombarded Fox with detailed letters seeking to set the record straight, to no avail.

At this stage of the lawsuit, the plaintiffs only had to demonstrate that they had a good chance of being able to win. In December 2021, the Delaware Superior Court judge handling the case, Eric Davis, concluded that Dominion had done so, writing that "it is reasonably conceivable that Dominion has a claim for defamation." The case was allowed to move into the discovery stage.

For Dominion and its lawyers, this was where the fun began. As discovery got underway, both sides agreed on search terms that they would use to scour their electronic systems—as well as the phones and computers of their employees—for records that would have to be turned over to the other side. Fox lawyers initially claimed that the vast majority of what those searches turned up were privileged or irrelevant. Twice a week for months on end, a Susman Godfrey partner, Davida Brook, pushed the court's so-called special master, who'd been assigned the task of adjudicating discovery disputes, to force Fox to hand over the materials. "Every single thing that Fox could fight about, they did," Brook later told the journalist Brian Stelter.

The victories accumulated, and hundreds of thousands of emails, text message chains, and other materials were turned over. As Dominion's lawyers began sifting through the documents, they were stunned by what they saw.

Fox News, it turned out, had an internal research operation, known as the "Brainroom," that had concluded that the allegations about Dominion were "100% false." Producers and executives had repeatedly written to one another about the lies their network was peddling. Hosts had privately admitted that they knew that what they were broadcasting was false. "Sidney Powell is lying," Tucker Carlson had written to his producer in November 2020, even as Fox kept putting her on air.

This kind of black-and-white documentation was like manna for the Dominion team. It made even the infamous *Rolling Stone* rape article—in which the magazine had admitted to all sorts of terrible screw-ups and which Clare Locke often pointed to as the holy grail of irresponsible journalism—look like a nuanced, borderline case. Excited messages whizzed back and forth among Dominion's lawyers. The threshold for what constituted a surprising revelation kept rising. "I'm not sure I'll ever see that type of evidence again," Clare later remarked.

At the same time, both sides were preparing for depositions. Susman Godfrey would handle most of the hundred or so involving Fox personnel, but Clare Locke grabbed a few juicy witnesses, including Lou Dobbs and Tucker Carlson.

Clare and Megan Meier conducted the Carlson deposition together on a Friday in August 2022. The interview would take place remotely. Carlson was at one of his homes. Clare and Meier sat together in his brick-walled office, staring into separate computer screens. The evening before, Fox had inundated the Dominion team with a trove of internal Carlson-related documents—apparently trying to delay the deposition or overwhelm the lawyers—and Meier had stayed up most of the night poring over them and prepping a detailed question-by-question game plan for Clare. During the deposition, he got Carlson to acknowledge that the claim that Dominion's software had altered votes was unsubstantiated and that he had been aware that certain guests on his show were likely to keep lying. Over and over, Carlson was asked about his views about the 2020 election, his misogynistic language toward women, even where he was domiciled. The TV host suspected he was being accused of tax evasion. He repeatedly had to stop himself from responding to Clare's questions with a simple "fuck you."

Later that day, after he filmed his prime-time show from his in-home TV studio, Carlson raged to his producers about his inquisitor. "That slimy little motherfucker," he said, wiping makeup off his face. "It was so unhealthy, the hate that I felt for that guy. . . . He triggered the shit out of me."

It was around that time that Locke began voicing misgivings about the case. From the outset, she hadn't been enthusiastic, noting on a few occasions that she doubted the strength of Dominion's claims of having been defamed. Gradually, her complaints grew more vociferous. The firm was devoting countless hours to the Dominion case, yet it wasn't in the driver's seat. On multiple occasions in 2022 and early 2023, Clare told his colleagues that he was inclined to grant Locke's wish to get the firm off the case. (Clare and Locke disputed this. "The firm did not want to get off the case, and it did not," they said. "To the contrary, Tom and Libby were pushing for the firm to have an even larger role." When I asked them to explain what that meant, they would not elaborate.)

Ostensibly, at least, Locke's concerns were centered on money. The fee arrangement that Clare Locke had negotiated with Dominion included discounted hourly rates and put a cap on the total amount that could be billed, a limit that was fast approaching. Locke stated that the firm would need to stop working as soon as that cap was hit, even if it happened in the middle of the trial.

Meier and another Clare Locke partner, Dustin Pusch, spent hours trying to persuade Clare to push back against his wife. This was the most important case of their careers. What was more, they warned, ditching Dominion would be a public embarrassment; everyone would assume the company had fired them. (In that case, Clare replied, the firm would have to come up with a plan to rebut that misperception.)

While Clare eventually backed down, and the firm kept representing Dominion, that didn't put the matter to bed. Clare Locke lawyers were deeply distressed that their bosses had come so close to jettisoning their years of work. Some of them doubted that finances had been at the root of Locke's concerns. More likely, they thought, the problem was that her law firm and her husband were in secondary roles and that she personally was barely involved. Daniel Watkins, a Clare Locke partner, said that Locke would change the subject whenever he and his colleagues began excitedly discussing what they regarded as the case of the century. "She was upset when things didn't revolve around her," Watkins told me. ("This is demonstrably false and absolutely ridiculous, not to mention completely sexist," Clare and Locke responded.)

But there was another possible explanation. Fox's defense at trial was going to rely on the argument that *Sullivan* protected the media's right to unflinchingly cover public issues. "I was gonna try to clothe the case in the First Amendment," Dan Webb, one of Fox's lawyers, later explained. (Never mind that the network's biggest star, Tucker Carlson, had publicly endorsed Locke's calls to overturn *Sullivan*.) That was causing heartburn among lawyers who defended media companies. If Fox prevailed, they feared that it might add decisive momentum to the campaign to overturn *Sullivan*. After all, if a plaintiff couldn't overcome the actual malice barrier in an open-and-shut case like this, maybe the standard's critics had a point about it being too onerous. Conversely, if Dominion won, that would provide a compelling retort to people like Locke: in instances of egregious lies, the media could be held to account, notwithstanding the protections afforded by *Sullivan* and its successors.

This left Locke in a potential pickle. If her firm won, it would gain bragging rights, but her arguments for overturning *Sullivan* might lose traction. If her firm lost, it would be embarrassing, but the loathsome libel precedents might be on borrowed time. Maybe it was safer to just quit.

The trial was due to begin in April 2023. About two weeks beforehand, the Dominion team descended on Wilmington. They were staying at the DoubleTree next to the court complex. The hotel was drab but functional. Entire floors were booked for the lawyers and witnesses. The food there was not the best, so the Susman Godfrey lawyers negotiated a provision in the hotel contract to allow them to order outside delivery.

Clare was one of the few Dominion lawyers not stationed in Wilmington. He spent most of the first half of April in the Turks and Caicos, where he and Locke had a property. His teammates at Clare Locke and Susman Godfrey groused that while they were cooped up at the dreary DoubleTree, Clare seemed to be lounging in paradise. "It was insane that he was in the Caribbean," one lawyer told me. While Clare said he was fully plugged in from the Turks and Caicos, he arrived in Wilmington only the day before the trial was initially set to begin.

By then, Judge Davis had preemptively ruled that Fox had been peddling false information about the company and the 2020 election, giving Dominion a clear upper hand heading into jury selection. The trial would hinge on actual malice and damages.

The two sides had held settlement talks in the past, but they had been far apart on money and the question of whether Fox would admit to and apologize for having spread lies. As lawyers haggled over which twelve jurors to empanel, Davis pushed both camps to try to hash out a deal one last time. That weekend, a mediator, who happened to be on a cruise of the Danube River in Hungary, was called in to help, and a resolution slowly began coming into focus.

Opening statements were scheduled to get underway on Tuesday, April 18. Lawyers for both sides were in the crowded, overheated courtroom, silently rehearsing their openings. The judge kept delaying the jury's return. Something was afoot. Finally, Davis announced to the stunned courtroom that Dominion and Fox had reached a settlement. The victorious Dominion lawyers marched outside for a press conference, where they disclosed the jaw-dropping deal: Fox had agreed to pay $787.5 million. It appeared to be the largest-ever penalty in an American defamation case.

That night, dozens of Dominion executives, lawyers, and their guests gathered at the Columbus Inn, a short drive from the court. The restaurant's roots traced back to the late 1700s; it was once a hangout for Buffalo Bill. A local lawyer who was helping the Dominion squad had managed to book a large room in the back at the last minute. Most of the furniture had been removed, save for leather banquettes along the sides and tables piled high with food. The space soon became crowded and rowdy. Lawyers toasted each other late into the night. Though they'd been working together for more than two years, it was the first time that many of them had spent time together socially.

At one point, a lawyer dialed Rod Smolla. He'd been planning to travel to Wilmington in the days ahead; now, though, he was in Vermont, giving a talk at his local church. "Let's raise a glass for Rod," someone shouted. Over the speakerphone, Smolla could hear the revelry in the background. The settlement struck him as bittersweet. He was happy for Dominion, but he couldn't help feeling a twinge of disappointment; he'd hoped to one day argue the case before the Supreme Court.

Locke had come to Wilmington to catch the start of the trial, and, to the surprise of some attorneys, she showed up at the Columbus Inn. It was awkward; the team had spent two years in the trenches together. Locke hadn't been part of it—in fact, she'd been quietly waging a rearguard action against her firm's involvement. Yet here she was, enjoying the party.

"Celebrating tonight," Locke emailed me at 10:55 that evening. "It's a bit crazy here on our end." She didn't know the half of it.

Going forward, Clare and Locke would use the Dominion case to drape themselves in the banner of patriotism. "It was an important case for democracy," Clare boasted five days after the settlement. Libel law wasn't for bullying journalists; it was about defending the republic from a rising tide of disinformation.

Clare and Locke's partners, however, had been nursing a growing list of grievances. They thought they deserved more money; they wanted more control. They resented Locke's treatment of subordinates; the story of her cease-and-desist letter years earlier to the administrative staffer who'd called her crazy continued to circulate inside the firm. They had chafed when the firm hired Jered Ede from Project Veritas without consulting the partners. They remained concerned that Locke's reputation as a conservative warrior—and her tendency to share her views on outlets like Fox News—was alienating prospective clients.

But it was Locke's efforts to pull the firm off Dominion that had rankled the most. By the time of the settlement, four partners—Meier, Pusch, Daniel Watkins, and Andy Phillips—had decided to quit to start a rival law firm. They secretly incorporated it weeks later. Like Clare Locke, the new firm would focus on defamation lawsuits, but the plan was to avoid positioning themselves as active enemies of the media. Meier publicly endorsed the *Sullivan* decision. Watkins had a framed copy of the famous "Heed Their Rising Voices" ad hanging in his office.

One morning in August 2023, the four partners gathered in a conference room in Clare Locke's Alexandria offices. The firm's two founders joined the meeting via Zoom. After a week in the Caribbean, they had just flown to Georgia, the site of their sprawling house, complete with a saltwater pool with a swim-up bar, on the shore of Lake Oconee. Meier spoke first. She told Clare and Locke that they were about to issue a press release announcing the creation of their new firm. They expected to take some associates and clients with them. Their departures would leave just one partner at the firm other than Clare and Locke.

On the wall-mounted monitor, the two founders seemed stunned.

Clare said he wasn't sure that the firm would be able to continue operating. Locke questioned when the departures were effective. "Twenty
minutes ago," Watkins responded.*

The meeting ended. The departing lawyers handed in their laptops
and walked to a nearby hotel, where they had readied a makeshift war
room to start breaking the news to their clients and professional acquaintances.

Clare Locke put on a brave face, issuing a public statement that promised an orderly transition. "An expanded plaintiff-side defamation bar
with the ability to hold the press accountable benefits society as a whole,"
the three remaining partners said. The firm soon began replenishing
its ranks, promoting some lawyers and hiring others (including another
refugee from Project Veritas). There would be more than enough defamation cases to go around.

---

* Clare and Locke told me that "there was *never* a moment when anyone thought or said that
the firm would not survive." They accused me of relying on sources with a financial interest
in harming Clare Locke. They said the four partners' true motivation for leaving was to
snatch a multi-million-dollar fee on a case that they had filed at Clare Locke and then took
with them to their new firm.

GUNNING FOR *SULLIVAN*

On a sunny Monday in November 2023, a group of lawyers made their way through Foley Square, the plaza outside the federal, state, and county courthouses in Lower Manhattan. The scene was chaotic. The New York attorney general's fraud trial against the Trump Organization was underway, and Donald Trump was scheduled to be on the stand that day. Protesters, camera crews, and law enforcement swarmed the area. Helicopters buzzed overhead.

These lawyers, however, weren't here for Trump. Instead, they walked into the federal Thurgood Marshall Courthouse and rode the elevator to the seventeenth floor, the home of the Second Circuit Court of Appeals. Led by Shane Vogt, who seven years earlier had successfully tried Hulk Hogan's case against Gawker, they were about to argue a libel case that, though it wasn't generating much fanfare compared to the Trump circus, had potentially greater ramifications. Filed as part of the initial wave of libel lawsuits following Trump's election, and after years of twists, turns, and delays, the litigation had become one of the leading vehicles for attacking *New York Times v. Sullivan*.

The saga dated back to the spring of 2016. Two weeks after the Florida jury ordered Gawker to pay Hogan $140 million, Vogt received an unsolicited call from an aide to Sarah Palin. In the years since John McCain selected her as his bomb-throwing, Tea Party–inspiring running mate in 2008, the former Alaska governor had been fading back into obscurity. Palin had tried various tactics to arrest this fall, including reality-TV cameos. Now, the aide explained to Vogt, Palin wanted to file a libel lawsuit. Her intended target was the rapper Azealia Banks. Days earlier, Banks had come across an online article purporting to quote Palin saying that "Negroes loved being slaves and they were doing just fine under our rules." Banks hadn't realized that the article, which was spreading via social media, was from a satirical website and that the quotes were fake. She took to Twitter and unloaded on Palin, suggesting in profane terms that she be forced to have sex with large Black men.

It seemed like a golden opportunity for the ex-governor to shoehorn herself back into the headlines. She issued a statement to *People* magazine: "I've had enough of the unanswered threats and attacks against my family and me. So, for the first time I'm going to enjoy the only retribution some protected 'celebrities' seem to understand—I'm suing Azealia Banks and can't wait to share my winnings with others who have gone defenseless against lies and dangerous attacks far too long." *People* quoted an unnamed "source in the Palin camp" as saying that the former governor was "in discussions with attorneys" about the planned lawsuit.

Vogt wasn't one to shy away from a fight with long odds. Growing up in the Tampa area, he'd been a standout basketball player despite standing just five foot ten on a good day. He'd been the first in his family to go to college. "There's a chip on my shoulder," Vogt told me, and it motivated him to work extra hard. He had found the experience in the Gawker case—of staring down Harvard-educated lawyers who had clerked for Supreme Court justices—to be invigorating. "It shows that you're on that level, even though you didn't go to those places and don't have those connections," he said.

The problem, as he informed Palin's aide, was that her proposed lawsuit against Banks did not seem promising, not least because the rapper had quickly deleted and apologized for her over-the-top tweets. And so Palin decided not to sue.

That was the end of the matter—at least for the following year. Then, early on a Wednesday morning in June 2017, James Hodgkinson, a Trump-hating leftist armed with a semiautomatic rifle and a handgun, opened fire on Republican lawmakers at a baseball practice in Alexandria, Virginia. Six people were injured. The near-tragedy would provide Palin with another opportunity to sue for libel—and Vogt with a chance to challenge the *Sullivan* decision.

Elizabeth Williamson, an editorial writer at the *New York Times*, had initially heard the news of the shooting on the radio. She'd been working in Washington, covering Congress and politics, since 2003, and she'd previously met some of the lawmakers who'd come under fire that morning. She emailed her colleagues on the editorial page in New York and proposed that they write a quick opinion piece about the attack. After a bunch of back-and-forth, they decided that the focus should be on "the rhetoric of demonization and whether it incites people to this kind of violence," as Williamson's boss, James Bennet, put it in an email.

Williamson, Bennet, and their colleagues knew that this was not the first time that a lawmaker had been attacked by a crazed gunman. In 2011, Jared Lee Loughner had killed six people, including a federal judge and a young girl, and injured thirteen, including Representative Gabby Giffords, in Tucson, Arizona. Loughner was later diagnosed as suffering from paranoid schizophrenia, and no evidence ever emerged that he had been motivated by politics. But in the shooting's immediate aftermath, many observers had assumed otherwise—and they had blamed Palin. The prior year, as she tried to whip up Tea Party fervor, her political action committee had posted on Facebook a map with rifle crosshairs over twenty Democratic congressional districts, including Gifford's. "It's time to take a stand," the ad had implored. Critics, including Giffords, had worried that the use of the crosshairs could incite violence, especially at a time when Palin was urging her supporters on with messages like "Don't Retreat, Instead Reload!" It had been easy—but wrong—to attribute Loughner's shooting spree to Palin's map.

Six years later, Williamson got to work writing her editorial about this latest spasm of violence. She finished the piece around 4:45 p.m. It linked both the Loughner and Hodgkinson shootings to "rage . . . nurtured in a vile political climate" and noted that Loughner's act was preceded by Palin's crosshairs map, though Williamson did not draw a direct causal connection.

Editors read Williamson's piece, and they weren't satisfied. Its central argument felt muddy. Bennet, as the head of the editorial page, was one of the *Times*' highest-ranking journalists. He also happened to be the brother of a Democratic senator from Colorado. He picked up Williamson's draft a little after 5 p.m. He agreed; it wasn't in great shape. The newspaper had an 8 p.m. deadline, and rather than give Williamson feedback and ask her to revise the editorial, Bennet decided to sharpen it himself. He would have to move fast.

Around 7:20, he sent the new version to Williamson, who was working from her home in Washington's Palisades neighborhood. "I really reworked this one," he wrote. "I hope you can see what I was trying to do. Please take a look. Thank you for the hard work today and I'm sorry to do such a heavy edit."

Williamson skimmed the edited piece. She trusted Bennet. "Looks great," she responded.

This turned out to be a disastrous oversight—responsibility for which was shared with the small team of *Times* editors and fact-checkers who were supposed to serve as a backstop against errors. Bennet had changed the description of the Loughner shooting to say that "the link to political incitement was clear. Before the shooting, Sarah Palin's political action committee circulated a map of targeted electoral districts that put Ms. Giffords and 19 other Democrats under stylized cross hairs." He also noted that in that day's Virginia shooting, there had been "no sign of incitement as direct as in the Giffords attack." Bennet would later say that he hadn't intended for the editorial to suggest that the crosshairs map provoked Loughner's shooting spree, but he had drawn what looked like a straight line between the two.

The editorial, headlined "America's Lethal Politics," went up on the *Times* website at 9:45 p.m. Fifty minutes later, Ross Douthat, a *Times* columnist, emailed Bennet "to express [his] bafflement at the editorial." He noted that there was "no evidence that Jared Lee Loughner was incited by Sarah Palin or anyone else, given his extreme mental illness and lack of any tangible connection to that crosshair map, the Tea Party or other right-wing cause."

"Thanks," Bennet replied a half hour later. "I'll look into this tomorrow." But he was worried and logged on to Twitter right then. He immediately saw that others were leveling the same criticism: that the *Times* had falsely blamed the Loughner shooting on the Palin map.

By then it was approaching midnight. "Are you up?" Bennet texted Williamson. "The right is coming after us over the Giffords comparison. Do we have it right?" (It wasn't just conservatives. Liberals were pointing out the mistake, too.)

Williamson had already turned in for the night. Bennet, however, was too anxious to sleep. A little after 5 a.m., he emailed Williamson and another colleague. "I don't know what the truth is here," he wrote. "I'd like to get to the bottom of this as quickly as possible this morning and correct the piece if needed."

Bennet and Williamson then talked on the phone, with Bennet sounding "crestfallen." "I feel lousy about this one," he texted her after they spoke. "I just moved too fast. I'm sorry." He went on to ask her for "a rock-solid version of what we should say" if she determined that the *Times* had to issue a correction.

"On it," Williamson confirmed. "We'll do the right thing." She quickly concluded that the piece indeed needed to be corrected.

Inside the *Times*' Renzo Piano–designed headquarters a block from Times Square, journalists were scrambling to clean up the mess. The *Times* might publish a thousand pieces in a week; mistakes are not uncommon, but they are taken seriously. A group of editors got to work figuring out how exactly to fix the editorial and drafting language to publicly acknowledge the error. A team charged with monitoring social media reported to colleagues that they were seeing a tidal wave of criticism online. By midmorning, both Bennet and the *Times*' official spokeswoman were receiving queries from other news organizations that were working on stories about the botched editorial.

At 11:15 a.m.—about fourteen hours after the editorial went online— the *Times* issued a correction, saying that the editorial "incorrectly stated that a link existed between political rhetoric and the 2011 shooting. . . . In fact, no such link was established." The *Times* tweeted the correction to its tens of millions of followers, acknowledging that "we got an important fact wrong. . . . We're sorry about this and we appreciate that our readers called us on the mistake."

Palin's camp had not reached out to the *Times* to request a correction or apology. But thirty-two minutes after the *Times* fixed its error, Palin shared her own message on social media. It consisted of a screenshot of two paragraphs from an obscure website called *Blasting News*. "Palin has not been in the public eye recently," the snippet read. "The irony would be all too delicious if she returned to the national stage by taking the New York Times to court and suing it for the attempted assassination of her character." To that text, Palin added her own note: "am talking to attorneys this AM and exploring options."

This time, when the same Palin aide reached out, Shane Vogt thought the former governor had a case.

As a politician, Palin had mastered two very effective tactics, ones that Trump would supercharge when he burst onto the political scene years later. First was a knack for spreading falsehoods, such as her claim that President Obama's health plan used "death panels" to ration medical care. Second was a constant thrum of attacks designed to delegitimize the "lamestream media" that kept calling her out.

No news outlet presented a more inviting target than the *Times*. Palin derided the newspaper on the campaign trail, on TV, and in interviews. At one point, she'd even taunted the *Times* for renting out part of its headquarters. "I ain't saying you a golddigger," she wrote on Facebook, butchering the Kanye West lyrics, "but there's a reason you messin' with broke, broke, broke."

Now, with Trump assailing the *Times* and the rest of the "fake news" media from the White House, Palin saw a chance to go mano a mano with her old nemesis. Vogt did, too. He spent days researching the members of the *Times* editorial board, reading everything they'd written about Palin and about the Loughner shooting back in 2011, and it persuaded him that he could build a case that these liberals not only didn't like Palin but also had every reason to know that her crosshairs map was not connected to the Arizona massacre. (Vogt at this point didn't even realize the central role that Bennet—the brother of a prominent Democrat—had played behind the scenes.)

Less than two weeks after the *Times* ran and corrected its editorial,

Vogt filed a lawsuit in federal court in Manhattan. Calling her "a devoted wife, mother and grandmother," the complaint explained that "Mrs. Palin brings this action to hold The Times accountable for falsely stating to millions of people that she . . . is part of a pattern of 'lethal' politics and responsible for inciting an attack." The suit accused the editorial writers of engaging in "a purposeful avoidance of the truth," noting that the newspaper in other instances had correctly stated that there was no evidence connecting the Loughner shooting to the Palin map. And it claimed that the editorial had caused "damage to her reputation, humiliation, embarrassment, mental suffering, shame and emotional distress." The suit sought damages "far in excess of $75,000," the threshold required to ensure that a civil action remained in federal rather than state court.

The *Times* was accustomed to such lawsuits. Barely a month earlier, for example, a coal company had sued over a different editorial. (Murray Energy would abandon that suit a year later.) The newspaper had a fleet of lawyers at the ready to deal with such claims. Their record was impeccable. The *Times* hadn't been on the losing end of a libel lawsuit in the United States since the early 1960s, when L. B. Sullivan and his good ol' boys had taken advantage of Alabama's racist courts to punish the paper for covering the civil rights movement.

After being served with Palin's lawsuit, the *Times*' in-house lawyers contacted their counselors at Ballard Spahr (the same law firm that had represented Global Witness when Rod Smolla sued on Christiana Tah's behalf). The lawyers assigned to this case would include Lee Levine, a pillar of the First Amendment bar, and Jay Ward Brown, a journalist-turned-lawyer with a quarter of a century of experience representing the *Times* and other news organizations.

The lawsuit struck Brown as flimsy—the newspaper had swiftly corrected and apologized for the editorial—but he and his colleagues suspected that its raison d'être was a whole lot more than recovering damages for the former governor. Their bet was that, like Vogt's Gawker case, this one was being bankrolled by a deep-pocketed donor, presumably someone with animus toward the *Times*, the *Sullivan* decision, or both. If that were the case, the plaintiffs were probably aiming to drag things out and ultimately get the case to the Supreme Court.

The case was assigned to an iconoclastic and blunt-talking federal judge named Jed Rakoff. A former prosecutor whom Clinton appointed to the bench in 1996, he had developed a reputation for doing things his way. Instead of rubber-stamping legal settlements between the government and Wall Street firms, he'd invalidated them as overly lenient. He'd publicly lambasted the Justice Department for not holding more executives accountable for the 2008 financial crisis. Some of his headline-grabbing decisions—including a ruling that the federal death penalty was unconstitutional—had been swiftly overturned. "If you're never reversed on appeal," he once explained, "you probably have taken too narrow a view of the law." That was the attitude he would bring to the Palin case, and it would play right into the former governor's hands.

In July, Brown submitted a motion to dismiss the lawsuit. Even if its claims were taken at face value, he argued, they did not show that the *Times* had acted with actual malice. The editorial had been sloppy but not a deliberate smear.

In order to decide whether Palin and Vogt's claims were plausible, Rakoff wanted to better understand how the editorial had come to be. So he asked Bennet to testify at what's known as an evidentiary hearing. This was a break from normal procedure. A judge is supposed to evaluate a motion to dismiss based on what's alleged in a lawsuit, not on evidence that he collects elsewhere. But Rakoff wasn't one to be hemmed in by tradition. At the hearing in August 2017, he and lawyers for both parties quizzed Bennet about what he meant by the words he wrote, about his state of mind, about grammar and sentence structure.

"What I *wasn't* trying to say was that there was a direct causal link between this map and the shooting," Bennet explained at one point. He said he didn't recall reading prior pieces in the *Times* or *The Atlantic* magazine—where he'd been the top editor at the time of the Loughner attack—that made clear that there was no known connection between the shooting and the crosshairs map.

Less than two weeks later, Rakoff ruled. "What we have here is an editorial, written and rewritten rapidly in order to voice an opinion on an immediate event of importance, in which are included a few factual inaccuracies somewhat pertaining to Mrs. Palin that are very rapidly corrected," he wrote, repeatedly citing Bennet's testimony. That was not actual malice. The lawsuit was dismissed.

But nobody thought the fight was over. Two days before Thanksgiving, Vogt notified the court that Palin intended to appeal—and that he had called in some backup: Libby Locke and Tom Clare.

For Brown and his colleagues, this was another sign that the lawsuit was about more than repairing Palin's reputation. He presumed that Locke was interested in the case because it represented an alluring way for her to attack not only the country's paper of record but also the *Sullivan* decision.

Oral arguments in the appeal took place nearly a year later at the towering Thurgood Marshall Courthouse. It was the first day of fall in 2018, warm but cloudy. Locke, who had given birth to a girl twelve weeks earlier, spoke first. She argued that Rakoff had wrongly relied on Bennet's testimony in dismissing the case. "It was improper for the district court to credit Mr. Bennet's testimony that he didn't remember reading these *Atlantic* articles or these *New York Times* articles," she said. Her husband stood at the back of the courtroom in jeans and a sweater, wearing their infant in a BabyBjörn.

The Second Circuit Court of Appeals judges—two appointed by Republican presidents, one by a Democrat—were openly skeptical of Rakoff, with one deriding the "tremendously unusual" nature of his evidentiary hearing.

"Your honor," Lee Levine said when it was his turn to speak, "I understand you are quite troubled by the evidentiary hearing. We didn't ask for it, and I acknowledge it was quite unusual." But even without Bennet's testimony, he said, Rakoff would have been right to throw out the lawsuit, because Palin's claim that Bennet acted with actual malice was farfetched. "You have this tale about a long-simmering personal animosity against Mrs. Palin that supposedly arises from the fact that she endorsed his brother's political opponent for office," Levine deadpanned. "He then sits on this simmering animosity for seven years and does nothing. And during this same period, he's publishing all these articles in *The Atlantic* and the *New York Times* that exonerates her from any responsibility for the Loughner shooting. And then suddenly he decides he's going to slip into the middle of this editorial a reference to political incitement . . . and get his long-awaited revenge. . . . And then he promptly corrects it!"

Eleven months later, in 2019, the appeals court published its decision. The three judges ruled that Rakoff should not have heard, much less relied upon, Bennet's testimony. Based on the facts put forward in the lawsuit, "the assertion that Bennet knew the statement was false, or acted with reckless disregard as to whether the statement was false, is plausible."

The case was sent back to Rakoff with instructions to let discovery get underway.*

Thus began another two-plus years of legal wrestling and waiting. This was an unpleasant proposition for the *Times*, which had to dredge up and preserve voluminous records, make employees available for depositions, and pay a squadron of top-shelf lawyers to handle discovery, deal with an avalanche of legal motions, and prepare for trial. An outlet with less money and fewer employees might have folded.

The *Times* lawyers still believed that someone was secretly financing this lawsuit; they doubted Palin, whose income by this point derived in large part from creating personalized videos for strangers on the Cameo platform, would be able to afford the seven-figure bill for a yearslong case. In early 2020, the lawyers sent Palin's team a list of formal questions known as interrogatories. The eighth query: "Please identify anyone other than yourself with any financial interest in this litigation, and any third party otherwise providing financial support for the fees and costs of this litigation."

In a court filing, Vogt refused to answer, calling the request "a fishing expedition that seeks information totally irrelevant to the claims and defenses at issue." When I asked him about this, he refused to discuss his fee arrangements but said that "there's no third-party financing or anything like that. Palin is the person responsible for paying the fees." In a subsequent conversation, he implied that Palin hadn't been able to pay all of those fees but that he wasn't going to walk away from her. "We don't always get full payments from our clients for everything," he said.

---

* Clare Locke's website lists the win against the *Times* as one of the firm's greatest victories.

Regardless of who was bankrolling the litigation, Palin's side was no longer hiding its ultimate purpose: overturning *New York Times v. Sullivan*. Vogt filed a motion urging Rakoff to preemptively rule in Palin's favor on the grounds that she shouldn't be subjected to the actual malice standard. Not because she wasn't a public figure—she obviously was—but because *Sullivan* "was judicially-imposed to solve problems peculiar to a bygone era, long-before the Internet and social media took hold of American society," Vogt argued. "It has become clear that the rule is obsolete and unworkable, incapable of consistent application, and holds no footing in the modern speech landscape."

A federal judge couldn't buck a higher court's precedent, but by complaining about *Sullivan* early on, Vogt could create a paper trail that might be useful if the case were to reach the Supreme Court—which, he told me, he "would like it to." He said he never would have tried this approach had it not been for Thomas's opinion in *McKee* the year before. Without cover from a Supreme Court justice, the anti-*Sullivan* argument would have seemed farfetched and frivolous. Now, though, it felt reasonable. "Thomas opened that door," Vogt explained.

As expected, Rakoff rejected Palin's plea, as well as one from the *Times* to rule in the newspaper's favor. The case would go to trial in early 2022, more than four and a half years after the editorial had been published.

That January, Jay Brown drove six hours to New York from his home in the foothills of Virginia's Blue Ridge Mountains. The whole Ballard Spahr team would be staying at the dingy Four Points hotel in Lower Manhattan. It was a brisk fifteen-minute walk from the Daniel Patrick Moynihan Courthouse and would serve as the trial team's base of operations. Brown had lodged there before, and he knew the hotel's shortcomings. In addition to boxes of evidence, he had packed his Toyota RAV4 with several lamps to supplement the hotel rooms' dim lighting.

The pandemic was easing, but federal courts were still taking precautions. Lawyers and witnesses were required to show proof of vaccination or present a negative Covid test result before entering the twenty-seven-story courthouse. The day before the trial was scheduled to begin, Palin tested positive. (Barely a month earlier, Palin had said she'd get the vaccine "over my dead body.") That delayed the start by another week.

The trial finally got underway on February 3. As they entered the court that morning, the lawyers had to navigate through a mighty media scrum on the lookout for Palin. It was so hectic that, going forward, Brown and his team decided they would sneak through back alleys on their approach to the courthouse.

The courtroom, with windows overlooking the Manhattan and Brooklyn skylines, was specially designed to allow for social distancing and to inhibit the spread of germs. Even so, it was packed with lawyers, clerks, security, journalists, supporters of the governor, and a sketch artist. Once the jury was seated, Vogt stood to present his opening statement. He'd spent the past week holed up in a room at the Millennium hotel across from the World Trade Center complex. He, his colleagues, and Palin were staying there after having abandoned their initial lodgings, which had been perfumed with the overpowering smell of marijuana.

"We come into this case with our eyes wide open and keenly aware of the fact that we're fighting an uphill battle" in terms of Palin's reputation in a heavily Democratic city, Vogt began, addressing the jury of five women and four men. "To be clear, we're not here trying to win your votes for Governor Palin or any of her policies. We're here to prove a libel case to you, and that case involves a very specific false narrative about Governor Palin that is particularly horrific and was debunked back in 2011." He concluded by saying that Bennet was biased and had set out to smear Palin. "What they did to Governor Palin was malicious."

Despite his years of experience arguing before the country's highest courts, Brown had only tried two jury cases in his career. So he'd enlisted a colleague, Dave Axelrod—who as a former federal trial lawyer had more than a dozen jury cases to his name, including a victory in a recent insider-trading trial in Rakoff's courtroom—to take the lead with the jury. (Brown would handle legal arguments with the judge.) The *Times* made a mistake, Axelrod explained. It learned of its mistake. It fixed its mistake—all by the following morning. What's more, Axelrod said, Palin's reputation hadn't been harmed one bit.

Over the course of the ten-day trial, two witnesses would stand out as pivotal: Bennet and Palin. Bennet went first. By now, he had left the *Times* and landed at *The Economist*, where he was an editor. To keep germs at bay, the witness stand was enclosed in plexiglass. Once inside, Bennet, wearing a dark suit, removed his black KN95 mask—a face covering that, until now, had enabled him to keep his anger about what he saw as a bogus case largely invisible to the jury. With previous witnesses, including other *Times* employees, Vogt had deployed a folksy, courteous demeanor. Now, with Bennet, there was an edge to his voice. He cast Bennet as a creature of the establishment, "born to privilege and raised in a family with a strong Democrat tradition," as Vogt had put it in a court filing. He ticked through Bennet's private-school pedigree, then got him to confirm for the jury that he had campaigned and even edited speeches for his brother, Senator Michael Bennet, in 2010, around the time that SarahPAC published its crosshairs map.

One of the challenges for Vogt was to convince the jury that the *Times'* swiftly issued correction did not make up for its initial malicious act. The correction hadn't mentioned Palin by name, instead simply stating that the newspaper had wrongly drawn a connection between the shooting and political incitement. The *Times* owed the defamed governor an apology, Vogt maintained.

"Did you reach out to Governor Palin to apologize?" he asked Bennet.

"I didn't, because I learned that our policy was not to do that. And I raised my concerns about that policy, but it remained in place."

"And are you still working at the *Times*?" Vogt pushed.

"No, I'm not," Bennet acknowledged, his bald head reflecting the courtroom's overhead lights.

It was clear where Vogt was heading. "Since you left the *Times*, have you reached out to Governor Palin to apologize to her?" he asked.

"No, I haven't." It was the closest Vogt came to landing a punch, but Bennet had managed to keep his cool. And the blow was slightly lessened when Bennet testified to the *Times* lawyers that he'd figured Palin would interpret any apology as an effort to wriggle out of the lawsuit.

Bennet left the stand. Palin replaced him.

That morning, to the delight of the waiting photographers, she had shown up at court in a pink coat and sunglasses, holding hands with her boyfriend, former New York Rangers star Ron Duguay. In the courtroom, an audience had gathered in anticipation of fireworks.

Vogt asked her what impact the editorial had had on her. "Well," she replied, "it's hard to lay your head on the pillow and have restful nights when you know that lies are told about you, a specific lie that was not going to be fixed. That causes some stress anyone would feel. So yes, tough to get a good night's sleep."

"Was it hard for you, when this was published, to deal with how you felt about it?"

"It was, because there I was up in Wasilla, Alaska, with that frustration of knowing that, you know, you're up against those who buy ink by the barrel, and I had my No. 2 pencil [in] my kitchen in Alaska, and I knew it was going to be tough to deal with, and I would probably have to deal with it on my own."

Before the defense cross-examined her, Rakoff tried to ease the tension. In his spare time the judge had taken up ballroom dancing with his wife, whirling around a dance floor in a tuxedo and top hat. When Palin's daughter was on the reality-TV show *Dancing with the Stars*, the former governor had confessed on camera that she didn't know how to dance. "You are missing one of the great joys in life," Rakoff now told her. "I would encourage you to reconsider. There is, seated in the courtroom, a beautiful lady who is my wife who is an expert in ballroom dancing. So after this is all over, I encourage you to take lessons."

"I need help," Palin agreed.

"Very good," Rakoff said approvingly.

Playtime ended. Palin returned to the stand. Axelrod asked if she had ever sought a correction from the *Times*.

"No," she said. "They just accused me of inciting murder. I didn't think I was going to get a friendly response." (By the time Palin started tweeting about the editorial, the *Times* was already rushing to correct it.)

What about the harm that she had suffered? Had any of her family members asked about the editorial or expressed dismay?

Your parents? "I don't recall."

Your sister? "I don't recall specifically."

Your other sister? "Same answer."

Your brother? "No."

Your kids? "At some point," though it might have been "months later," after she had filed the lawsuit. This did not sound like someone who had endured severe emotional distress.

A rotating cast of reporters, lawyers, Palin supporters, and other curious onlookers cycled through the courtroom on various days. One of the regulars was Charles Harder. He'd had a trial scheduled that week on the East Coast, but it had been delayed, and so, with time to kill, he'd decided to observe this rare instance of the *New York Times* having to publicly defend itself in a libel case. "It was like I was going to the World Series, but better," he told me. He sat in the gallery taking notes.

Closing arguments began on Friday, February 11. It was sixty degrees and sunny, the type of winter day in New York that might convince even hardened skeptics that the planet was overheating. Vogt's law partner, Ken Turkel, spoke first. "What this dispute is about, in its simplest form, is really power and lack of power," he began. "And I know that may seem not easy to take in when you're dealing with someone who was, in 2008, on the international stage, but the truth of the matter is, in 2017, Sarah Palin is a consultant and a speaker; she's a mother and a grandmother." He harped on the *Times*' lack of direct apology to Palin, which he said was "indicative of an arrogance and a sense of power that's uncontrolled and for which Governor Palin's only remedy is to use our system here, our judicial system."

Turkel wrapped up after an hour and forty-five minutes. He invited the jury to award what it saw fit—even if that was just $1. "Having one of the largest newspapers in the word call you a murderer . . . maybe it's worth something," he suggested. "All they had to do was dislike her a little less, and we are not sitting here today."

Then it was Axelrod's turn. If Bennet had been trying to defame Palin, would he have reacted so quickly when Ross Douthat first flagged the problem with the editorial? Would he have immediately texted Williamson or sent marching orders at five o'clock in the morning? "Does that make any sense?" Axelrod asked. "No, of course not."

The defense rested its case by reminding jurors about the stakes. This wasn't just about Sarah Palin, James Bennet, and the *New York Times*. "At bottom, this case is about whether a newspaper can publish stories and express opinions that are critically important without fear that a powerful person will seize on an honest mistake that was corrected almost immediately and tie up the paper in litigation and potential liability," Axelrod concluded. "Freedom of the press and freedom of speech are fragile things."

That Friday afternoon, the jury retired to its meeting room and began deliberating.

Before the case was submitted to the jury, Jay Brown had filed what's known as a Rule 50 motion. It asked the judge to decide that, based on the evidence presented during trial, no reasonable jury could find for Palin because there was insufficient evidence that Bennet or the *Times* had acted with actual malice. With the jurors out of the courtroom, Rakoff had heard arguments from both sides about whether he should grant the motion and essentially short-circuit the lawsuit.

The judge had enjoyed presiding over this case. The personalities were colorful, the questions of law important, and the national attention intense. Rakoff recognized that the matter might one day land on the docket of the Supreme Court. After the jurors started their deliberations, he spent the weekend contemplating the Rule 50 motion. On Monday he told the lawyers that he would reveal his decision but also would let the jurors work toward reaching a verdict. That way, in the event of an appeal, higher courts would have the benefit of both his and the jury's determinations. "I think this is an example of very unfortunate editorializing on the part of the *Times*," Rakoff explained to the mostly full courtroom (minus the jurors). "But having said that, that's not the issue before this court. My job is to apply the law. The law here sets a very high standard for actual malice. And in this case, the court finds that that standard has not been met." He had ruled for Bennet and the *Times*.

Rakoff noted that he would not formally issue his ruling until after a verdict was handed down by the jury, which "of course will not know about my decision." But he had just divulged it in open court. Within minutes, news outlets had issued alerts announcing that Rakoff planned to throw out Palin's suit. That evening, Rakoff wished the jurors a happy Valentine's Day and reminded them not to read any news about the case.

The next day, the jury reached its verdict. The nine men and women were ushered back into the courtroom. The verdict envelope was passed to the clerk and then to Rakoff. He put on his glasses and read the enclosed slip. "Mr. Foreman, please rise," the clerk instructed. "As to the plaintiff's libel claim, you the jury find the defendant liable or not liable, you say?"

"Not liable." The verdict was unanimous. Brown and Axelrod wrapped Bennet in a hug.

The CEO of the New York Times Company celebrated the verdict as "a good day for the free press." Outside the Moynihan courthouse, Palin grumped to reporters that she was "disappointed." If she, Vogt, or anyone else had hoped for a repeat of Gawker, they were out of luck. Yet the disappointment was tempered by the knowledge that they would appeal—a plan that was soon reinforced by events back in the courthouse.

Before the jurors left the building, Rakoff's clerk had conducted routine exit interviews, asking them if there was anything that could have been done differently or more clearly during the trial. Rakoff regarded this as an important way to make him a better judge, and his clerks had done similar interviews in hundreds of other cases. This time, something unexpected came up: a few jurors mentioned that they'd seen the news alerts about Rakoff's plan to dismiss the case. The jurors insisted that they hadn't been swayed by the alerts, but it was impossible to know if the news had subtly, perhaps even subconsciously, colored the deliberations.

Rakoff was at Columbia University teaching a class that evening, and so he didn't learn about what the jurors had said until the following morning. When his clerk broke the news, the judge was surprised and upset. Rakoff was seventy-eight and, by his own admission, far from tech-savvy. It hadn't occurred to him that jurors might see the news pop up on their locked phone screens. He informed the lawyers for both sides about what his clerk had learned. There had been little doubt that Palin would appeal the verdict. Now there was none.

· · ·

Vogt's appeal to the Second Circuit asked for a new trial. It faulted Rakoff for not allowing Palin's side to present evidence of Bennet's supposed political bias and his knowledge—including in the form of *Atlantic* articles that ran while Bennet edited the magazine—that the crosshairs map did not spur the Arizona shooting. It blamed the judge for prematurely announcing his Rule 50 decision. And it took issue with some of Rakoff's instructions to the jury.

The appeal also trained its sights on *Sullivan*. Vogt again argued that the 1964 decision was outdated. He even claimed that Palin—a former governor and vice presidential nominee who had taken pains to keep herself in the limelight—didn't meet the Supreme Court's original understanding of a public figure. By then, Justice Thomas had doubled and tripled down on his calls to reverse *Sullivan* and its progeny, complaining in dissents whenever his colleagues refused to hear cases that might test the court's long-standing precedents. His fellow justices showed little interest in budging. In fact, in a 2023 case unrelated to libel—it concerned a Colorado man sending threatening messages to a prominent singer—a majority of the court had embraced the logic behind *Sullivan*. Some lawyers saw that as evidence that the landmark ruling was safe, at least for the time being.

Oral arguments in the Palin case were held in the same Thurgood Marshall Courthouse that had been the venue for the previous appeal years earlier. Vogt navigated through the crowds that had gathered in anticipation of Trump's appearance at his fraud trial. Inside the ornate seventeenth-floor courtroom, he and Jay Brown faced three Republican-appointed judges. "We're back before this court on the same issue that we were here for just about five years ago, which is actual malice," Vogt said. "We think the times have changed so significantly since that rule was created by an unelected branch of our government sixty years ago that it has no place in the modern speech landscape."

Judge John Walker, who'd also heard Palin's previous appeal, interrupted: "Why isn't that a question for the Supreme Court to decide?" When Vogt kept pushing, Walker again broke in. "I think you're wasting time," he rasped.

That was the low point for Vogt. Going forward, the judges seemed to be taking his and Palin's side. They wondered aloud whether the push alerts announcing Rakoff's Rule 50 decision had "tainted" the jury. Judge Reena Raggi said she was "concerned" and "perplexed" by Rakoff's jury instructions. The third judge, a Trump appointee, also asked pointed questions.

Vogt and Brown had both come into court that morning recognizing the high stakes. At the very least, a costly and protracted retrial was on the line. At most, a crucial First Amendment precedent was up for grabs.

By the time oral arguments ended after an hour, the stakes hadn't changed, but the playing field had. Vogt walked into Foley Square. The sky had grown overcast, the air chilly. It was almost exactly a year before the 2024 presidential election, and protesters were waving signs and shouting about the dangers that Trump posed to democracy. Vogt wasn't bothered. Things seemed to be unspooling just as he had hoped.

His confidence would prove well founded. In August 2024, the appeals court handed down its decision. The three judges faulted Rakoff for wrongly excluding evidence, giving incorrect instructions to the jury, and prematurely announcing his Rule 50 findings. Rakoff's mistakes, the judges wrote, "impugn the reliability" of the jury's verdict in favor of the *Times*. The only solution, they concluded, was a retrial.

Palin was pumped. And why not? A new trial guaranteed that this seven-year legal war would extend into at least 2025, keeping her name in the news and—who knows—maybe even winning her some money in the process. Vogt, too, was thrilled. His mission hadn't changed. He wanted to beat the *Times* in Rakoff's courtroom, of course, but regardless of which side prevailed at trial, a fresh cycle of appeals was all but inevitable. And that was where the real pay dirt might lie: another opportunity to invite the Supreme Court to reconsider *Sullivan* and make it legally and financially riskier for people to criticize or question the rich, famous, and powerful.

EPILOGUE: A MISOGYNIST AND A SNAKE

I n the spring of 2024, I was working on an article for the *New York Times* about the exodus of partners from Clare Locke. Libby Locke and Tom Clare had repeatedly ignored or turned down my requests for interviews, and so I sent them a list of dozens of questions covering everything that was likely to be in the article. This is standard operating procedure in investigative journalism—a "no surprises" letter, we call it. Having spent a lot of time researching the hardball legal tactics that Clare Locke and others often employed, I felt like I knew what to expect. Instead, I was about to get a personal demonstration of just how far some lawyers would go to prevent certain information from seeing the light of day.

Clare Locke's initial salvo arrived a few days later in the inbox of the *Times'* lawyer, David McCraw. Instead of answering any of my questions, Clare sought to undermine my credibility. He questioned whether I was really working on a piece for the *Times* and accused me of engaging in "improper and unethical" conduct by using "the threat of [a] New York Times article to coerce engagement for his book." He also suggested that I was using the possibility of an article to pressure his law firm and one of its clients, Project Veritas, to settle a pending lawsuit against the *Times*. He warned of "enormous legal risk" for me, the *Times*, and my book publisher.

The next day, after I assured Clare that my questions were indeed for an upcoming article and reiterated my willingness to meet with him and Locke, they doubled down. Clare insisted to McCraw that "it is just not credible that all the questions he emailed us last week are really for a New York Times article." (They were!) He and Locke protested my unwillingness to let them provide information off-the-record (which would mean the *Times* couldn't publish it).

When McCraw responded by urging them to speak with me, Locke shot back in an email: "Enrich is a misogynist and a snake. (You can quote me on that!)"

Two days later, Clare and Locke sent me and McCraw a forty-page document. It disputed some of the information that I had asked about. It laced into former Clare Locke partners, describing their romantic relationships and spending habits and divulging snippets from their internal reviews. It included screenshots of chat messages in which lawyers had praised Locke's appearances on Tucker Carlson's show. And it assailed me as sexist and malicious. My editors and I incorporated their responses into the story.

Then came a letter that Clare Locke wrote on behalf of Project Veritas, falsely claiming that I had tried to extract information about the organization from its former lawyers. The letter asserted that my supposed conduct violated a 2021 court order that barred the *Times* from trying to obtain attorney-client-privileged materials about Veritas.

I was more perplexed than worried about this latest argument, but hours before the article was scheduled to publish, a final letter arrived, and this one accomplished its apparent mission: it unnerved me.

As I skimmed the nine-page letter on my phone, I saw that it included screenshots of text messages and emails between me and Megan Meier, one of the partners who had left Clare Locke to start her own firm. My heart felt like it skipped a beat. How on earth did Clare Locke get those messages? I slowed down and read the full letter, which explained that Meier and her colleagues had provided Clare Locke with all of their electronic communications with me. I was shocked.

It wasn't a secret that the ex-partners had spoken to me. They'd all agreed to talk about certain topics on the record, and I had asked Clare and Locke to respond to some of their comments. Clare and Locke, I later learned, had turned around and threatened their former partners with legal action for supposedly leaking confidential information to me. My written communications with the ex-partners had been brief and innocuous—mostly involving things like arranging meetings or phone calls—and so the four had apparently not seen any harm in handing over our messages to their former bosses. Now Clare and Locke were using these messages to cast me as dishonest and corrupt.

One of the texts that I'd sent to Meier, for example, had asked her to call me so that I could "give you a heads up on something." The reality was prosaic. I was preparing to send my initial detailed list of questions to Clare and Locke, and I suspected that it might prompt them to accuse their former partners of leaking to me. I didn't want Meier to be blindsided.

Clare and Locke, however, framed the message as evidence of my ulterior motives. I hadn't been aware of it at the time, but their firm had recently approached the *Times*' outside lawyers to discuss the possibility of Project Veritas dismissing its lawsuit against the *Times*. Two days later, I'd sent my "heads up" text to Meier. In their letter, Clare and Locke implied that I had been alerting Meier to the potential dismissal of the Veritas lawsuit. The letter stated unequivocally that "the timing and content" of the forthcoming *Times* article was "related to the Project Veritas litigation." It was a serious—and false—accusation of unethical behavior.

The *Times* didn't flinch. McCraw gave the green light, and the article was published the following morning. For the thousandth time, I felt blessed to work for an institution with the resources and appetite to stand up to such onslaughts.

Still, I wondered how Clare and Locke had thought this would unfold. Had they truly doubted that I was working on a piece for the *Times*? Did they really think I was trying to weaponize a newspaper article to harm their client in its litigation against my employer? Did they expect their allegations against me to lead the *Times* to kill the article? To water it down?

My best guess: Clare Locke had previously tried variations of these intimidation tactics so many times, and with such resounding success, that they figured it was worth a shot when it was their reputations, not those of their clients, on the line. It was all part of an effort, as one lawyer described it to me, to "use words to change reality." They were trying to murder the truth.

. . .

One afternoon shortly before my Clare Locke article was published, the
Claremont Institute's Carson Holloway arrived at the University of Notre
Dame to speak about *Sullivan*. Since publishing his initial critique of the
ruling in 2022, Holloway had gained prominence in conservative circles.
He'd dashed off numerous essays attacking the decision and had happily
accepted invitations to speak at gatherings sponsored by groups like the
Federalist Society. Now, addressing a group of students and faculty inside one of Notre Dame's Gothic-style buildings, Holloway gave a brief
history of public attitudes toward the sixty-year-old *Sullivan* decision. A
litany of other Supreme Court cases in the 1960s and '70s—none more
so than *Roe v. Wade*—had instantly provoked the ire of the right. Not
Sullivan. Instead, "the case became rather revered as a landmark ruling,"
Holloway explained. It was a relatively new addition to many conservatives' hit lists, having "become controversial in recent years in a way that
it wasn't for a long time."

That was an understatement. Especially relative to the long-running
controversies engulfing hot-button issues like abortion and school prayer,
the onset of hostility toward *Sullivan* felt abrupt, like someone had
suddenly flipped a switch inside the conservative hive mind. What had
started in 2016 with Donald Trump's vow "to open up our libel laws"
had rapidly metastasized into a political and legal movement, gaining
the support of at least two Supreme Court justices and many other judges
and lawmakers—not to mention the bevy of lawyers like Libby Locke
and activists like Carson Holloway.

Would this crew quickly accomplish its mission? Perhaps not. Holloway urged conservatives to borrow from the playbook that antiabortion
activists had relied on to get the Supreme Court to reverse *Roe*. It had
taken five decades for conservatives to win that war. By that standard, the
campaign to reinterpret the Constitution to restrict press freedoms could
be in its early stages.

Indeed, the fates of the current crop of lawsuits designed to kneecap
the *Sullivan* precedent—such as Sarah Palin's action against the *Times*
or Alan Dershowitz's against CNN—might not be known for years. Per-

haps they will fail. Maybe they will only partially succeed. For instance, it is not hard to envision the Supreme Court substantially narrowing the scope of who classifies as a public figure or even ruling that the actual malice standard should only apply to government officials.

The consequences of such a shift—much less an outright reversal of *Sullivan*—are likely to be stark: a damper on investigative journalism, especially into companies, universities, religious institutions, and their leaders. Greater legal risks and higher insurance costs—and therefore lower odds of survival—for community newspapers and upstart media outlets. New dangers for anyone who speaks up about wrongdoing by authority figures or big businesses. In short, a substantial erosion of the ability of the media (and everyone else) to inform the public and hold the powerful to account.

If that sounds far-fetched, consider what is happening in Mississippi, where a former Republican governor, Phil Bryant, sued a nonprofit news outlet, *Mississippi Today*, for its prize-winning articles about how the state government misspent tens of millions of dollars in federal grants intended for Mississippi's poorest residents. The lawsuit, which is seeking more than $1 million in damages, didn't challenge the facts in the article, but it demanded that the journalists provide Bryant's lawyers with their notes, internal communications, and sources. *Mississippi Today* refused. In June 2024, a state judge appointed by Bryant's Republican successor ordered the news organization to comply. More appeals are pending, but the outlet's leaders and journalists face the prospect of jail time and crippling fines if they are found in contempt of court, as Bryant's lawyers are advocating. "It is not difficult to see how the lawsuit against us could become part of a broader effort to dismantle press freedoms for journalists across the nation," Adam Ganucheau, the editor of *Mississippi Today*, warned.

Or consider that in the days before and after he won the 2024 presidential election, Trump managed to intensify his already-fierce rhetoric against the media. He joked about journalists getting shot. He decried TV networks as "the enemy camp." He blocked reporters from attending an Election Day event because they had written what he perceived as negative articles. He filed a $10 billion lawsuit against CBS and threatened to subpoena its records. Many of his supporters—including billionaires like

Elon Musk—piled on, alternating between ridiculing the mainstream media as irrelevant and branding reporters as dangerous propagandists. The climate was so hostile that news organizations began preparing for the once-unthinkable possibility that the federal government might try to yank networks' broadcast licenses, revoke certain news outlets' nonprofit tax statuses, or even jail journalists.

Finally, consider the ethical clouds hanging over two conservative Supreme Court justices. A flag associated with the January 6 uprising was flying outside a house owned by Samuel Alito just as he was poised to hear a high-stakes case about the attempted insurrection. And Clarence Thomas for years failed to disclose that he was accepting luxury trips and other valuable gifts from a billionaire friend. Both scandals came to light because of investigative journalism, and both prompted the justices' ideological allies to claim that the left-wing media was sowing misinformation in order to thwart conservatives—the same critique that Larry Silberman had articulated when he argued for overturning *Sullivan* in 2021.

It had been more than thirty years since Thomas was first engulfed in scandal. Back then, even after narrowly surviving his Senate confirmation, he had been a junior justice on a relatively moderate court, so humiliated or angry that he rarely uttered a word from the bench. Today, the tables have turned. Thomas is ascendant on a staunchly conservative court that has shown its willingness to toss long-standing precedents out the window. The media is still tormenting him, but now he and his colleagues just might be able to do something about it.

ACKNOWLEDGMENTS

I'm not sure that this book would exist were it not for my colleagues at the *New York Times*. On more occasions than I can count, their reporting about everyone from Russian oligarchs to Britney Spears's business manager was met with threatening letters from Clare Locke, Harder LLP, and their ilk. I began to wonder how such legal threats were affecting smaller news organizations and independent journalists. My attempt to answer that question was the beginning of this project.

Members of my investigative team in the *Times* Business section—Jessica Silver-Greenberg, Emily Steel, Jesse Drucker, Rebecca Robbins, Jim Stewart, and John Carreyrou—all provided advice or assistance and/or tolerated me when I was distracted, cranky, or absent. Ryan Mac, Kirsten Grind, Ken Vogel, Rob Copeland, Emma Goldberg, Rebecca O'Brien, Kashmir Hill, Katie Baker, Katie Robertson, and Katie Rosman offered me information, stories, and suggestions. Jessica Silver-Greenberg and Rachel Abrams gave invaluable feedback on the manuscript.

Ellen Pollock allowed me to pursue this project, encouraged my reporting, and generally put up with me, sometimes at a normal decibel. I'm also grateful to Mohammed Hadi, Pui-Wing Tam, Joe Plambeck, Virginia Hughes, Kitty Bennett, Sharon O'Neal, Dave Schmidt, Noreen Malone, Preeta Das, and Kevin McKenna. Higher up the *Times* food chain, Matt Purdy, Jim Yardley, Kirsten Danis, Sam Dolnick, Michael Slackman, Monica Drake, Carolyn Ryan, and Joe Kahn encouraged and otherwise supported me. So did A. G. Sulzberger, whose stewardship of the *Times* and belief in the importance of a free press have inspired me and many others.

David McCraw deserves special recognition. The *Times*' unflappable in-house lawyer has enabled more high-impact journalism than anyone who doesn't work at the *Times* can imagine. He has been a crucial resource for me since I arrived in 2017, and that continued as I researched and wrote this book.

One of the pleasures of this project was talking to dozens of journalists around the country and world. They made me proud of my profession. Among many others, thank you to Conrad Swanson, Jared Strong, Shereen Siewert, Rachel Ehrenfeld, Guy Lawson, Jonathan Gant, David Marchant, Laurie Brown, Scott Stedman, Cherri Foytlin, Karen Savage, Doug Burns, Monika Bauerlein, Julia Black, Mike Masnick, Skyler Swisher, Lachlan Cartwright, Keach Hagey, Patrick Radden Keefe, Erik Wemple, and a troupe of still-scarred Gawker refugees. Lauren Chooljian and her colleagues at New Hampshire Public Radio were especially generous with their time.

My agent Dan Mandel believed in this book from the get-go. At Mariner Books and HarperCollins, my editor, Matt Harper, offered excellent advice. Kyran Cassidy expertly vetted the manuscript from a legal standpoint. Mark Steven Long copyedited. Maureen Cole drummed up publicity. Thanks as well to Peter Hubbard and Liate Stehlik.

A handful of close friends have made me a happier, saner person: Saúl, Pete, Dominic, Kevin, Ray, Vanessa, Dan, Emily, Mimi, Carolina, and Tom. Jen, Walter III, Walter IV, and William lent us their home in London. Jason, Brad, Matt, Ed, and Red survived a long weekend in Vegas without me so that I could finish this book.

Thank you to my parents, Peggy and Peter Enrich, for their steadfast encouragement and for once again providing advice on the manuscript.

This book is dedicated to my siblings. My sister Liza is probably the most patient, caring, empathetic person I have ever met. My brother Nick has been a wonderful friend my entire adult life (even when I whip him on the pickleball court). I love you both. Jay and Jords, thank you for being you. Hazel and Zander, thank you for making me even more of a Swiftie.

Jasper and Henry: Thank you for tolerating my nights and weekends of work. I am so proud of your hard work, your passion, your intelligence, your athleticism, your creativity, your sensitivity—everything except for

Jasper's support of Man City and Henry being a Yankees fan. A special shout-out to Milkshake, who spent countless hours sitting on my lap or curled around my feet as I wrote this book.

Finally, thank you to Kirsten: my travel companion, my drinking buddy, my first reader whose blunt advice always improves my books and who takes on so much to give me the time and space to report and write. Shame on Aubrey Plaza for trying to steal your vibe. I love you.

NOTES

PROLOGUE: A PANICKED PHONE CALL

1 *knocked the neighborhood:* Guy Lawson interview with author.

1 *"holding corrupt motherfuckers to account":* Lawson email to author.

1 *sold clothes by the pound:* Lawson interview.

1 *towering ginkgo tree:* Maria Ricapito, "Maya Kaimal & Guy Lawson Renovate a Rhinebeck Victorian," *Upstate House*, Winter 2018.

2 *pay his own way:* Lawson interview.

2 *"Get the fuck away":* Lawson interview.

3 *the cover sheet read:* Shkëlzen Berisha v. Guy Lawson, Case 1:17-cv-22144, "Summons in a Civil Action," June 8, 2017.

3 *$60,000,000:* Berisha v. Lawson, "Civil Cover Sheet," June 8, 2017.

3 *the most secretive and ritualized proceedings:* Supreme Court Historical Society, "How The Court Works—The Justices' Conference."

3 *about eighty cases:* University of Michigan Law Library, "U.S. Supreme Court Research Guide," March 26, 2024.

3 *twice the prior month:* US Supreme Court docket report for No. 20–1063.

4 *fifty-four-page list of orders:* US Supreme Court Order List, July 2, 2021.

4 *settled by duels:* Anthony Lewis, *Make No Law: The Sullivan Case and the First Amendment* (New York: Vintage Books, 1992), p. 154.

4 *the offender's tongue:* Mike Allen, "Reform of Libel Laws Is Continuing Issue," *Richmond Times-Dispatch*, March 30, 1989.

5 *continuing through 2024:* Donald Trump speech in Rome, Georgia, March 9, 2024.

5 *the idea of jailing reporters:* George Packer, "Is Journalism Ready?" *The Atlantic*, January–February 2024.

6 *exacerbated a crisis:* Penny Abernathy, "The State of Local News," Northwestern University Medill School of Journalism, June 29, 2022.

7 *murder the truth:* Reed Albergotti, "Some Russian Oligarchs Are Using U.K. Data Privacy Law to Sue," *Washington Post*, March 31, 2022.

CHAPTER 1: CLARENCE THOMAS'S CLEAREST ANSWER

11 *ninety-six degrees:* Weather Underground, "Arlington, VA Weather History," for September 16, 1991.

11 *sinking of the* Titanic: US Senate, "Kennedy Caucus Room," senate.gov.

11 *leather-upholstered chair:* Richard L. Berke, "Thomas Accuser Tells Hearing of Obscene Talk and Advances," *New York Times*, October 12, 1991.

12 *paid his own way:* Clarence Thomas, *My Grandfather's Son: A Memoir* (New York: Harper, 2007), p. 132.

12 *on the final day:* Thomas, *My Grandfather's Son*, p. 132.

12 *"how dependent she is":* Juan Williams, "A Question of Fairness," *The Atlantic*, February 1987.

12 *received hate mail as a result:* Thomas, *My Grandfather's Son*, pp. 132–33.

12 *two minimum-wage jobs:* Karen Tumulty, "Sister of High Court Nominee Traveled Different Road," *Los Angeles Times*, July 5, 1991.

12 *was soon slotted:* Williams, "A Question of Fairness."

13 *enforcement of antidiscrimination laws:* Williams, "A Question of Fairness."

13 *lacked a cohesive worldview:* Emma Brown and Rosalind S. Helderman, "For John Eastman and Clarence Thomas, an Intellectual Kinship Stretching Back Decades," *Washington Post*, December 23, 2022.

13 *a proper conservative:* Ken Masugi, "The New American Slave Revolt, Led by Clarence Thomas," *American Greatness*, July 2, 2022.

13 *Thomas would recall:* Brian Lamb, "Q&A: Clarence Thomas," C-SPAN, October 3, 2007.

13 *Thomas wrote years later:* Thomas, *My Grandfather's Son*, pp. 184–85.

13 *she was with him:* Susan Baer, "Common Threads Link Virginia Thomas to the Supreme Court Nominee," *Baltimore Sun*, September 27, 1991.

13 *nearly two decades:* Oral History Project of the Historical Society of the District of Columbia Circuit, "Honorable Laurence H. Silberman," p. 82.

13 *He recommended Thomas:* Ken Foskett, "Thomas Building Conservative Judicial Legacy," *Palm Beach Post*, July 6, 2001.

14 *"a job for old people":* Thomas, *My Grandfather's Son*, pp. 193–94.

14 *"if you don't like it":* Thomas, *My Grandfather's Son*, pp. 193–94.

14 *showed his new colleague the ropes:* Jane Mayer and Jill Abramson, *Strange Justice: The Selling of Clarence Thomas* (Boston: Houghton Mifflin, 1994), p. 162.

14 *"became my judicial mentor":* Thomas, *My Grandfather's Son*, p. 204.

14 *introducing Thomas around town:* Mayer and Abramson, *Strange Justice*, p. 154.

14 *Silberman was on it:* Silberman DC Circuit oral history, see n. 34, pp. 191–92.

14 *seven-days-a-week task:* Mayer and Abramson, *Strange Justice*, pp. 210–11; John C. Danforth, *Resurrection: The Confirmation of Clarence Thomas* (New York: Viking, 1994), pp. 21–24.

14 *came across as "wooden":* Mayer and Abramson, *Strange Justice*, p. 219.

14 *"as little as possible":* Thomas, *My Grandfather's Son*, pp. 232–33.

15 *hadn't given much thought:* Mayer and Abramson, *Strange Justice*, pp. 218–19.

15 *a fresh topic:* US Government Printing Office, Transcript of Day 5 of Thomas confirmation hearings, pp. 417, 458.

15 *virtually no media attention:* The lone reference, as far as I can tell, was a short paragraph at the end of a *St. Louis Post-Dispatch* article summarizing the day's testimony. William H. Freivogel, "Thomas Looks Likely to Win Confirmation," *St. Louis Post-Dispatch*, September 17, 1991.

15 *394 copies a day:* Lewis, *Make No Law*, p. 9.

16 *"a dangerous undertaking":* Samantha Barbas, "The Enduring Significance of *New York Times Co. v. Sullivan*," Knight First Amendment Institute, March 18, 2024.

16 *like Henry Ford and James Fisk:* Barbas, "The Enduring Significance."

16 *roughly $3 million in damages:* Lewis, *Make No Law*, pp. 11–13.

16 *barely profitable newspaper:* Lewis, *Make No Law*, pp. 7, 107.

16 *"weapon to intimidate the press":* Lewis, *Make No Law*, pp. 7, 36.

16   *attention was causing trouble:* Barbas, *Actual Malice*, pp. 34–36.

17   *were sufficiently bloodied:* Judge Frank Johnson, Order in *US v. Knights of Ku Klux Klan*, June 2, 1961; Barbas, *Actual Malice*, pp. 43–49.

17   *"not our policy":* US Commission on Civil Rights, *Justice: 1961 Commission on Civil Rights Report*, pp. 32, 186.

17   *trying to delegitimize the media:* Barbas, *Actual Malice*, pp. 34–36.

17   *"white man's justice":* Lewis, *Make No Law*, pp. 25–26.

17   *apparently was a pedophile:* Barbas, *Actual Malice*, pp. 104–5.

17   *toting pistols:* Barbas, *Actual Malice*, p. 107.

17   *largest libel judgment:* Lewis, *Make No Law*, pp. 33–36.

18   *damages totaling nearly $300 million:* Lewis, *Make No Law*, p. 37.

18   *not to write articles:* Barbas, *Actual Malice*, p. 87.

18   *what he was writing was false:* Lewis, *Make No Law*, p. 120.

18   *dove into the history:* Lewis, *Make No Law*, pp. 49–51.

19   *was evidence to Wechsler:* Lewis, *Make No Law*, p. 115.

19   *King showed up:* Barbas, *Actual Malice*, pp. 188–89.

20   *even broader interpretations:* Lewis, *Make No Law*, p. 150.

20   *by some counts:* Richard A. Epstein, "Was *New York Times v. Sullivan* Wrong?" *University of Chicago Law Review*, 1986, p. 783.

21   *along with factors:* Leonard Downie Jr., "Forty Years After Watergate, Investigative Journalism Is at Risk," *Washington Post*, June 7, 2012.

21   *Nixon blamed* Sullivan: Anthony Lewis, "Nixon and a Right of Reply," *New York Times*, March 24, 1974.

22   *Much of the coverage:* William Boot, "The Clarence Thomas Hearings," *Columbia Journalism Review*, January–February 1992.

22   *fiddled with a pen:* "Thomas Senate Judiciary Committee Hearing, Day 5, Part 2," C-SPAN, September 16, 1991.

22   *had been hard for Thomas:* Danforth, *Resurrection*, p. 16.

23   *he and Ginni hid out:* Thomas, *My Grandfather's Son*, p. 253.

23   *blamed the national media:* Boot, "The Clarence Thomas Hearings."

23   *writhing in agony:* Danforth, *Resurrection*, p. 106.

23   *Luttig later put it:* Danforth, *Resurrection*, p. 108.

23   *photographers trained their lenses:* Danforth, *Resurrection*, p. 57.

23   *Hill spent seven hours:* Berke, "Thomas Accuser Tells Hearing."

24   *"with all guns blazing":* NYU Institute of Judicial Administration, "Hon. Laurence H. Silberman: An Interview with Paul D. Clement," *Oral History of Distinguished American Judges*, May 17, 2017.

24   *"high-tech lynching":* Berke, "Thomas Accuser Tells Hearing."

24   *wiping away tears:* Maureen Dowd, "In an Ugly Atmosphere, the Accusations Fly," *New York Times*, October 12, 1991.

24   *a serial liar:* John Harwood and Jackie Calmes, "Defense of the Nominee Uses Two-Pronged Attack," *Wall Street Journal*, October 14, 1991; Dowd, "In an Ugly Atmosphere."

24   *lesbian who was "acting out":* David Brock, *Blinded by the Right: The Conscience of an Ex-Conservative* (New York: Three Rivers Press, 2002), p. 104.

24   *more no votes:* R. W. Apple Jr., "Senate Confirms Thomas, 52–48, Ending Weeks of Bitter Battle," *New York Times*, October 16, 1991.

24   *the narrowest margin:* Susan Page, "Amid Supreme Pomp, Clarence Thomas Is Sworn In," *Newsday*, October 19, 1991.

24   *had sided with him:* Boot, "The Clarence Thomas Hearings."

24   *dwelled on the negative:* Boot, "The Clarence Thomas Hearings."
24   *"suggest others do the same":* Clarence Thomas, Speech at National Center for Policy
      Analysis, C-SPAN, September 6, 1996.

CHAPTER 2: THE FIGHTER PILOT

25   *the phone rang:* Elaine Donnelly interview with author.
25   *funeral at Arlington National Cemetery:* PBS Frontline, "Navy Blues," 1996.
26   *didn't want that to happen:* Donnelly interview.
26   *appointed Donnelly to federal commissions:* Donnelly interview.
26   *a sympathetic receptacle:* Judge Judith W. Rogers, Opinion of US Court of Appeals for
      DC Circuit, *Carey Lohrenz v. Elaine Donnelly, et al.*, Case 02–5294, December 12, 2003.
26   *happened to meet Hultgreen:* Donnelly interview.
26   *the women had not been qualified:* Judge Royce C. Lamberth, "Memorandum Opinion,"
      Carey Lohrenz v. Elaine Donnelly, et al., Case 1:96-cv-00777, August 16, 2002.
27   *substantiate his allegations:* Donnelly interview.
27   *the concessions that had been granted:* Donnelly interview; Lamberth, "Memorandum
      Opinion."
27   *She asked the senator:* Complaint in *Lohrenz v. Donnelly*, April 24, 1996.
27   *record had been above average:* Lamberth, "Memorandum Opinion."
27   *appeared to have benefited:* Lamberth, "Memorandum Opinion."
27   *they assured her:* Lamberth, "Memorandum Opinion."
27   *shrugged this off:* Donnelly interview.
27   *published a report:* Center for Military Readiness, "Special Report on Double Standards
      in Naval Aviation," April 1995.
28   *pretending to be aviators:* Carey D. Lohrenz, *Fearless Leadership: High-Performance
      Lessons from the Flight Deck* (Minneapolis: Alke Publishing, 2014), p. 19.
28   *her hopes were rekindled:* Carey Lohrenz interview with author.
28   *six-feet-tall:* Evan Thomas and Gregory L. Vistica, "Falling out of the Sky," *Newsweek*,
      March 17, 1997.
28   *with honors:* Rogers, DC Circuit Court Opinion.
28   *third in her class:* Jane Pauley, "Top Gun," *Dateline NBC*, July 3, 1996.
28   *designation of naval aviator:* Rogers, DC Circuit Court Opinion.
28   *call sign: "Vixen":* Thomas and Vistica, "Falling out of the Sky."
28   *premier fighter jet:* Thomas and Vistica, "Falling out of the Sky."
28   *military's newfound progressivism:* Rogers, DC Circuit Court Opinion.
28   *To the irritation:* Thomas and Vistica, "Falling out of the Sky."
28   *on a recruiting poster:* Lamberth, "Memorandum Opinion."
28   *told the* Green Bay Press Gazette: Lamberth, "Memorandum Opinion."
28   *"women can do this":* Lamberth, "Memorandum Opinion."
29   *54,000-pound:* Pauley, "Top Gun."
29   *$38 million:* Michael E. Ruane, "F-14 Crashes, Killing Female Combat Pilot," *Charlotte
      Observer*, October 27, 1994.
29   *a terrifying thrill:* Lohrenz, *Fearless Leadership*, p. 3.
29   *could kill dozens of people:* Pauley, "Top Gun."
29   *twenty-six-year-old Lohrenz:* Tony Perry, "'Controlled Crashes' in the Night," *Los An-
      geles Times*, February 17, 1995.
29   *hard enough for Lohrenz:* Ruane, "F-14 Crashes"; Thomas and Vistica, "Falling out of
      the Sky."

29   *front-page articles about it:* Lamberth, "Memorandum Opinion."

29   *onboard the USS Lincoln:* Lohrenz interview, August 24, 2023; Thomas and Vistica, "Falling out of the Sky."

29   *"everyone had a copy of it":* Lohrenz interview.

29   *self-confidence began slipping away:* Thomas and Vistica, "Falling out of the Sky"; complaint in *Lohrenz v. Donnelly.*

29   *performance in training exercises deteriorated:* Thomas and Vistica, "Falling out of the Sky."

29   *The day before:* Complaint in *Lohrenz v. Donnelly.*

29   *"Skipper wants to see you":* Thomas and Vistica, "Falling out of the Sky."

29   *overseeing the base's recycling program:* Lohrenz interview.

29   *"the price of cardboard":* Thomas and Vistica, "Falling out of the Sky."

30   *a leading advocate:* Richard Goldstein, "Rosemary Mariner, Pathbreaking Navy Pilot and Commander, Is Dead at 65," *New York Times,* February 1, 2019.

30   *"You need help":* Lohrenz interview.

30   *had repeatedly sued:* Karen Bowers, "Longform: Susan Barnes," *Westword,* January 29, 1998.

30   *a strong legal case:* Lohrenz interview.

30   *Scared and angry:* Donnelly interview.

30   *She shelled out:* Donnelly interview.

31   *resigned from the Navy:* Lohrenz interview.

31   *wanted advice:* Rod Smolla interview with author.

31   *could help with research and other tasks:* Smolla interview.

31   *defended* Hustler *magazine's right:* Rod Smolla, *Deliberate Intent: A Lawyer Tells the True Story of Murder by the Book* (New York: Crown Publishers, 1999), p. 62.

31   *CNN offered him a gig:* Smolla interview.

31   *participate in his mock Supreme Court sessions:* Nat Hentoff, "The Scorned Law Professor," *Village Voice,* February 1, 2000.

32   *"financially destitute":* Smolla, *Deliberate Intent,* p. 237.

32   *roughly $500,000 in fees:* Smolla interview.

32   *first original movie:* Susan King, "True Hit-Man Case Basis of First FX Movie," *Los Angeles Times,* August 4, 2000.

32   *"Smolla is a turncoat":* Liptak, "A How-To Manual."

32   *the judge tossed the case:* Lamberth, "Memorandum Opinion."

32   *Donnelly felt vindicated:* Donnelly interview.

32   *one of the best in America:* Sylvia Rector, "The Lark in West Bloomfield to Close in December," *Detroit Free Press,* September 9, 2015.

32   *like she'd been violated:* Lohrenz interview.

32   *"the best, strongest case":* Lohrenz interview.

32   *His plan was to:* Smolla interview.

33   *"question the party line":* Donnelly interview.

33   *left ninety-two people dead:* Judge Abner Mikva, Opinion in *Dameron v. Washington Magazine Inc.,* Case 84–5056, December 24, 1985.

33   *drenched his dress shoes:* Smolla interview.

33   *of keen interest:* Smolla interview.

34   *Dameron was settled precedent:* Rowan Scarborough, "Libel-Suit Ruling Seen by Year's End," *Washington Times,* September 23, 2023.

34   *It occurred to Smolla:* Smolla interview.

34   *"no reasonable juror":* Rogers, DC Circuit Court Opinion.

34   *Smolla was surprised:* Smolla interview.

34 *There were Republican politicians: Miller v. Nestande*, 192 Cal. App. 3d 191 (1987); *Conroy v. Spitzer*, 70 Cal. App. 4th 1446 (1999).

34 *accused of defaming: Farrakhan v. N.Y.P. Holdings*, 168 Misc. 2d 536 (1995).

35 *should be dismissed:* Judge Kenneth Starr, Opinion for the DC Circuit Court in *Ollman v. Evans and Novak*, December 6, 1984.

35 *a love letter to* Sullivan: Judge Robert Bork, Concurring Opinion in *Ollman v. Evans and Novak*, December 6, 1984.

35 *"a plaintiff who has not sought publicity":* Petition for a writ of certiorari in *Lohrenz v. Donnelly*, March 10, 2004.

35 *rejected the appeal:* US Supreme Court Order List, May 17, 2004.

CHAPTER 3: FUNDING EVIL

36 *"whatever you want to say":* Video of Rachel Ehrenfeld speech at SPEECH Act celebration, September 20, 2010.

36 *a bone-chilling Friday:* Weather Underground, "New York City Weather History," for January 23, 2004.

36 *coined the term "narcoterrorism":* Dominic Kennedy, "Libel and Money: Why British courts Are Choice of the World," *The Times* (London), May 19, 2005.

36 *her apartment in midtown Manhattan:* Rachel Ehrenfeld interview with author; Rachel Ehrenfeld, "A Legal Thriller in London," *Newsweek*, June 7, 2010.

37 *roughly $3 billion:* Kennedy, "Libel and Money."

37 *gold-plated bathroom fixtures:* Douglas Martin, "Khalid bin Mahfouz, Saudi Banker, Dies at 60," *New York Times*, August 27, 2009.

37 *had repeatedly described:* Complaint in *Ehrenfeld v. Bin Mahfouz*, Case 04-cv-9641, December 8, 2004.

37 *She'd noted that:* Rachel Ehrenfeld, *Funding Evil: How Terrorism Is Financed—and How to Stop It* (Lanham, Maryland: Taylor Trade Publishing, 2003), pp. 26, 46.

37 *"substantial award of damages":* Plaintiff's Memorandum of Law in Opposition to Motion to Dismiss, *Ehrenfeld v. Mahfouz*, June 10, 2005.

38 *"a town called sue":* Sarah Lyall, "Britain, Long a Libel Mecca, Reviews Laws," *New York Times*, December 11, 2009.

38 *paid him £300,000:* Press Association, "Lance Armstrong Settles with *Sunday Times*," *The Guardian*, August 25, 2013.

38 *finally admitted to doping:* Juliet Macur, "Armstrong Admits Doping, and Says He Will Testify," *New York Times*, January 14, 2013.

38 *"cannot afford it":* Lyall, "Britain, Long a Libel Mecca."

38 *in the wake of such warnings:* Sarah Lyall, "Are Saudis Using British Libel Law to Deter Critics?" *New York Times*, May 22, 2004.

38 *had backed down:* "Saudi Jihad on Free Speech," *Investor's Business Daily*, August 7, 2007.

38 *gleeful running tally:* Wayback Machine archive of binmahfouz.info from May 16, 2022.

39 *the more she loved America:* Ehrenfeld interview.

39 *an early Army court martial:* Jeffrey M. Winn, "Ripened Reflections of a Lucky Vietnam Draftee," *New York Law Journal*, April 19, 2023.

39 *Kornstein and Ehrenfeld had met years earlier:* Daniel Kornstein interview with author.

39 *sued Ehrenfeld for defamation:* Plaintiff's memorandum in *Ehrenfeld v. Mahfouz*.

39 *"to gag the media":* "Mr Justice Eady, Defender of the nation's privacy," *Telegraph*, November 13, 2008.

39   *damages and legal fees:* Brief on Behalf of Plaintiff-Appellant to New York Court of Appeals, August 24, 2007.

40   *wrote in a court filing:* Plaintiff's memorandum in *Ehrenfeld v. Mahfouz.*

40   *Steve Brogan:* Larry Neumeister, "NY Court: Saudi Billionaire Can Pursue British Claims in the US," Associated Press, March 3, 2008.

40   *included the bin Laden family:* David Enrich, *Servants of the Damned: Giant Law Firms, Donald Trump, and the Corruption of Justice* (New York: Mariner Books, 2022), p. 108.

40   *"misusing the courts":* Ivry, "Seeking US Turf."

40   *"to pay my lawyers":* Toobin, "Let's Go."

40   *had suddenly grown wary:* Ehrenfeld interview.

40   *jurisdiction over bin Mahfouz:* Judge Richard Casey, Order in *Ehrenfeld v. Mahfouz,* April 26, 2006.

40   *told the* Weekly Standard*:* Duncan Currie, "The Libel Tourist Strikes Again," *Weekly Standard,* August 20, 2007.

40   *"directed to the legislature":* Ciparick opinion.

41   *issue to champion:* Rory Lancman interview with author.

41   *"hangs in the balance":* Elizabeth Samson, "Last Stop on the Libel Tour," *New York Jewish Week,* December 5, 2007.

41   I found a winner: Lancman interview.

41   *a name meant to ensure:* Lancman interview.

41   *"free speech capital of the world":* US Fed News, "Assemblyman Lancman, Sen. Skelos Introduce Bill to Protect American Authors," January 14, 2008.

42   *felt like she wasn't alone:* Ehrenfeld interview.

42   *"need to twist arms":* Lancman interview.

42   *Rachel's Law:* Adam Cohen, "'Libel Tourism': When Freedom of Speech Takes a Holiday," *New York Times,* September 15, 2008.

42   *began pushing lawmakers:* Ehrenfeld interview.

42   *enacted similar laws:* Ehrenfeld, "A Legal Thriller in London."

42   *a lobbyist named Brett Heimov:* Brett Heimov interview with author; Open Secrets, "Client Profile: Rachel Ehrenfeld: 2009."

42   *He introduced her:* Ehrenfeld interview.

42   *watched the surprise:* Heimov interview.

42   *a group of Vermont librarians:* Ehrenfeld and Heimov interviews.

42   *"gonna get this done":* Heimov interview.

43   *scuttle the whole thing:* Heimov interview.

43   *a heart attack in Jeddah:* Martin, "Khalid bin Mahfouz, Saudi Banker."

43   *handed each lawmaker a copy:* Ehrenfeld and Kornstein interviews.

43   *In the media:* Arlen Specter and Joe Lieberman, "Foreign Courts Take Aim at Our Free Speech," *Wall Street Journal,* July 19, 2008.

43   *one version of the proposed legislation:* Congress.gov, "H.R. 5814–Free Speech Protection Act of 2008," introduced on April 16, 2008.

43   *bulwark against libel tourism:* Andrew C. McCarthy, "Can Libel Tourism Be Stopped?" *Commentary,* September 2008.

43   *issued a news release:* Office of Sen. Jeff Sessions, "Congress Passes Sens. Leahy-Sessions Free Speech Bill," July 29, 2010.

43   *"It's done":* Heimov interview.

44   *Ehrenfeld paid for the catering:* Ehrenfeld interview.

44   *"something to celebrate":* Video of Sessions speech at SPEECH Act celebration, September 20, 2010.

44   *become the first senator:* Eli Stokols, "Sen. Jeff Sessions Endorses Trump," *Politico*, February 28, 2016.

CHAPTER 4: TRUMP'S BIZARRE VOW

48   *"like you've never got sued before":* "Trump Vows Newspapers Will 'Have Problems' If He's Elected," *Washington Post*, February 26, 2016.

48   *his failed $500 million action:* Anthony Lewis, *Make No Law*, p. 206.

48   *There were his threats:* Ashley Parker and Josh Dawsey, "Trump's Effort to Stop Publication of Scathing Book Is a Break from Precedent," *Washington Post*, January 4, 2018.

48   *won only once:* Emily Bazelon, "Billionaires vs. the Press in the Era of Trump," *New York Times Magazine*, November 22, 2016.

49   *dismiss a libel lawsuit against him:* Memorandum of Law in Support of Defendants' Motion to Dismiss, *Jacobus v. Trump*, June 27, 2016.

49   *a New York court agreed:* Judge Barbara Jaffe, New York State Supreme Court ruling in *Jacobus v. Trump*, January 9, 2017.

49   *"most important address of his administration":* Spiro Agnew speech to Midwest Regional Republican Committee, November 13, 1969.

49   *Some seventy million people:* Richard Nixon Foundation, "11.3.69," nixonfoundation.org, November 3, 2009.

50   *"core values of reporting":* Matthew Pressman, *On Press: The Liberal Values That Shaped the News* (Cambridge, Massachusetts: Harvard University Press, 2018), p. 6.

50   *for nearly thirty minutes:* Audio of Agnew speech available at americanrhetoric.com /speeches/spiroagnewtvnewscoverage.htm.

50   *poured in from all over the country:* Thomas Alan Schwartz, "He Was Trump Before Trump," *The Conversation*, November 8, 2019.

50   *"the Magna Carta":* Chris Lehmann, "The Eyes of Spiro Are Upon You," *The Baffler*, April 2001.

50   *continuously pummeled the "elite media":* "Spiro Agnew with Brains," *Newsweek*, November 27, 1994.

51   *as retribution:* "Spiro Agnew with Brains."

51   *was running low on money:* Tim Alberta, "The Deep Roots of Trump's War on the Press," *Politico*, April 29, 2018.

51   *"Newt, Newt, Newt!":* Thomas Fitzgerald, "Gingrich Scores with Voters by Socking 'Big Media,'" *Philadelphia Inquirer*, January 22, 2012.

51   *widely attributed:* Rich Lowry, "The Media Is Trump's Evil Empire," *Politico*, August 23, 2017; Peters, "Gingrich Bets on Attack Mode."

51   *Gingrich later explained:* Alberta, "The Deep Roots of Trump's War on the Press."

51   *"bad people":* Nancy Benac and Jonathan Lemire, "Trump's Contempt for the Media Is Calculated," Associated Press, June 15, 2016.

51   *revoked press credentials:* Benac and Lemire, "Trump's Contempt for the Media."

51   *"THE LIBERAL MEDIA!":* Alberta, "The Deep Roots of Trump's War on the Press."

52   *"He wants to be very aggressive":* Benac and Lemire, "Trump's Contempt for the Media."

52   *one journalist wrote:* Rich Lowry, "Trump's Evil Empire," *National Review*, August 25, 2017.

52   *"rather than an anomaly":* Alberta, "The Deep Roots of Trump's War on the Press."

CHAPTER 5: STARTING A REVOLUTION

53 *doubling as a fundraiser:* Manu Raju, "Tester rocks with Pearl Jam," *Politico*, September 30, 2012.

53 *sold out in fifteen minutes:* Raju, "Tester Rocks with Pearl Jam."

53 *working his way up:* Maximillian Potter, "Down and Dirty," *Esquire*, January 2017.

54 *exposing the rickety finances:* Gabriel Sherman, "The Worldwide Leader in Sextapes," *GQ*, January 19, 2011.

54 *Brett Favre's alleged sexual harassment:* A. J. Daulerio, "'Brett Favre Once Sent Me Cock Shots': Not a Love Story," Deadspin, August 4, 2010.

54 *traffic nearly quadrupled:* Potter, "Down and Dirty."

54 GQ *credited him:* Sherman, "The Worldwide Leader in Sextapes."

54 *editor of* Gawker *itself:* Potter, "Down and Dirty."

54 *abusing substances:* Steve Martorano, "From Hulk Hogan's Lawsuit to Struggles with Substance Abuse, AJ Daulerio's Been There," *Behavioral Corner Podcast*, interview with Daulerio, February 6, 2021.

54 *"still broke all the time":* Daulerio interview with Martorano.

54 *battling a cold:* Jessica Letkemann, "Pearl Jam Rocks for Montana Senator," *Billboard*, October 2, 2012.

54 *rasped to the cheering crowd:* Raju, "Tester Rocks with Pearl Jam."

54 *"dumb enough to try it":* YouTube video of concert, at 1:02 mark, youtu.be/mZRZKTco YUA?si=sUCFlUOyvEXGGmkq.

54 *strolled the ancient campus:* Aron D'Souza interview with author.

55 *always researched people:* D'Souza interview.

55 *though not publicly:* Peter Thiel, "The Online Privacy Debate Won't End with Gawker," *New York Times*, August 15, 2016.

55 *Gawker had documented:* J. K. Trotter, "This Is Why Billionaire Peter Thiel Wants to End Gawker," Gawker, May 26, 2016.

55 *financial struggles and tax avoidance:* Owen Thomas, "Give Me Liberty or Give Me Taxpayer Money," Gawker, May 6, 2009.

55 *women getting the right to vote:* Owen Thomas, "Facebook Backer Wishes Women Couldn't Vote," Gawker, April 28, 2009.

55 *"freedom and democracy are compatible":* Peter Thiel, "The Education of a Libertarian," *Cato Unbound*, April 13, 2009.

55 *causing investors to pull money:* Max Chafkin, *The Contrarian: Peter Thiel and Silicon Valley's Pursuit of Power* (New York: Penguin Press, 2021), pp. 133–34; Ann Coulter, "Peter Thiel Brings Down Gawker," *UNSAFE* podcast, April 26, 2024.

55 *rival tech reporters as "toothless":* Chafkin, p. 123.

55 *"should be described as terrorists":* Connie Loizos, "Peter Thiel on Valleywag," *PE Hub*, May 18, 2009.

55 *hire private investigators:* Chafkin, *The Contrarian*, p. 127.

56 *"Basically run a proxy war":* D'Souza interview.

56 *"Ten million":* D'Souza interview.

56 *put their plot in motion:* D'Souza interview.

56 *Manhattan-based terrorist organization:* Coulter, "Peter Thiel Brings Down Gawker."

56 *even hacking the company's computers:* Chafkin, *The Contrarian*, p. 194.

56 *Then someone mentioned:* D'Souza interview.

56 *"You don't want a superstar":* D'Souza interview.

57   *registered Democrat:* Jacob Pierce, "How Charles Harder Went from UCSC Democrat to Trump's Top Lawyer," *Good Times* (Santa Cruz), November 6, 2018.

57   *Hollywood hatchet man:* Ryan Mac and Matt Drange, "Hulk Hogan's Lawyers Have Made Suing Gawker Their 'Bread and Butter,'" *Forbes*, May 30, 2016.

57   *was the first stop:* Michael Cieply, "Guard Dog to the Stars (Legally Speaking)," *New York Times*, May 21, 2011.

57   *a larger, cushier:* Charles Harder email to author.

57   *Harder's specialty:* Eriq Gardner, "Ailes Media Litigator Charles Harder on His Improbable Rise," *Hollywood Reporter*, September 22, 2016.

57   *"Eastwood" chairs:* Matthew Belloni, "Clint Eastwood Sues Furniture Company for Selling 'Eastwood' Chairs," *Hollywood Reporter*, April 7, 2012.

57   *diamond-encrusted watches: Sandra Bullock v. Toy Watch USA*, complaint filed in LA County Superior Court, June 19, 2012.

57   *Brooks Brothers–style wardrobe:* Alexander Nazaryan, "Meet Charles Harder, the Gawker Killer Now Working for Melania Trump and Roger Ailes," *Newsweek*, October 14, 2016.

57   *"cog in the Hollywood machine":* Jason Zengerle, "Charles Harder, the Lawyer Who Killed Gawker, Isn't Done Yet," *GQ*, November 17, 2016.

57   *asked him to help write:* Harder email to author.

57   *in early 2012:* Ryan Holiday, *Conspiracy: Peter Thiel, Hulk Hogan, Gawker, and the Anatomy of Intrigue* (New York: Portfolio/Penguin, 2018), pp. 59–60.

57   *some very rich individuals:* D'Souza interview.

57   *"a strong negative impression":* Harder email to author.

57   *"straight for the jugular":* D'Souza interview.

57   *Thiel liked the idea:* Coulter, "Peter Thiel Brings Down Gawker."

58   *to win a crippling verdict:* Holiday, *Conspiracy*, pp. 71–72.

58   *a vehicle for retribution:* D'Souza interview.

58   *hooked on scoops:* Potter, "Down and Dirty."

58   *"like an addict needs their next fix":* Sherman, "The Worldwide Leader in Sextapes."

58   *boasting about his sexual exploits:* Fabio Bertoni, "The Stakes in Hulk Hogan's Gawker Lawsuit," *New Yorker*, March 23, 2016.

58   *"thought it was newsworthy":* Nick Madigan, "Gawker Editor's Testimony Stuns Courtroom in Hulk Hogan Trial," *New York Times*, March 9, 2016.

58   *"a blockbuster":* Daulerio interview with Martorano.

58   *about seven million page views:* Anna M. Phillips, "Ringside Seat Battle Begins," *Tampa Bay Times*, March 2, 2016.

58   *would remain online:* Holiday, *Conspiracy*, pp. 104–5.

59   *about twenty employees:* D'Souza interview.

59   This is it: D'Souza interview.

59   *Houston accepted the offer:* Harder email to author, October 11, 2023; Holiday, *Conspiracy*, pp. 106–7.

59   *"tolerated by a civil society":* Holiday, *Conspiracy*, p. 109.

59   *volunteered to help them sue:* D'Souza interview; Harder email to author.

59   *he helped organize:* Ryan Mac, "Behind Peter Thiel's Plan to Destroy Gawker," *Forbes*, June 7, 2016; Harder email to author.

59   *seemed to dissemble:* Holiday, *Conspiracy*, pp. 148–50.

60   *at least $500 an hour:* Harder email to author.

60   *would stick with him:* D'Souza interview.

60   *celebrities in publicity cases:* Doug Mirell interview with author.

60 *suboptimal for Mirell:* Mirell interview.

61 *a couple of high-profile right-of-publicity cases:* Charles Harder, *Gawker Slayer: The Professional and Personal Adventures of Famed Attorney Charles Harder* (self-published, 2021), p. 149.

61 *"law firm is built around" Peter Thiel:* Holiday, *Conspiracy,* p. 191.

61 *"set up a whole law firm":* Coulter, "Peter Thiel Brings Down Gawker."

61 *said that was inaccurate:* Harder email to author.

61 *should just move on:* Julia Marsh, "Gawker's Internal Emails Show Callous Response to 'Rape' Victim," *New York Post,* March 11, 2016.

61 *Nobody thought there'd be a trial:* Daulerio interview with Martorano.

62 *"No four-year-old sex tapes":* Sarah Kaplan, "Gawker on Trial," *Washington Post,* March 11, 2016.

62 *representing the parents:* Anita Kumar, "Judge to Decide Fate of Comatose Woman in 2 Weeks," *Tampa Bay Times,* January 29, 2000.

62 *more than any other judge:* "Trial Judge in Hulk Hogan-Gawker Case Is Most Reversed in Pinellas," *Tampa Bay Times,* March 25, 2016.

62 *routinely sided with Hogan:* Charles Harder, "Hulk Hogan's Lead Lawyer Explains How His Team Beat 'Arrogant,' 'Defiant' Gawker," *Hollywood Reporter,* April 5, 2016.

62 *Thiel later boasted:* Coulter, "Peter Thiel Brings Down Gawker."

62 *it cautioned:* Tom Kludt, "Hulk Hogan Taunts Gawker on Twitter at Start of Trial," CNN, March 1, 2016.

62 *audiovisual bells and whistles:* D'Souza interview.

63 *he was peeing next to:* D'Souza interview.

63 *that it was monochromatic:* Kludt, "Hulk Hogan Taunts Gawker."

63 *embarrassed by his baldness:* Steven Perlberg, "Hulk Hogan Takes the Stand in $100 Million Suit Against Gawker," *Wall Street Journal,* March 7, 2016.

63 *never tried a case in front of a jury:* Shane Vogt interview with author.

63 *high school with Hogan:* Vogt interview.

63 *"It was power":* Tom Kludt, "Hulk Hogan's Lawyer Says Gawker Posted Sex Tape to 'Harm' Him," CNN, March 7, 2016.

63 *belatedly recognized the high stakes:* Jonathan Mahler, "Gawker's Moment of Truth," *New York Times,* June 12, 2015.

63 *valued at $83 million:* Tom Kludt, "Hulk Hogan Jury Hears Gawker's Plea for Mercy," CNN, March 21, 2016.

63 *to cover the legal bills:* Perlberg, "Hulk Hogan Takes the Stand."

63 *"to hold elites accountable":* Kaplan, "Gawker on Trial."

64 *"what Gawker had to say":* Nick Madigan, "Hulk Hogan Takes the Stand in His Trial Against Gawker," *New York Times,* March 8, 2016.

64 *"not safe for work":* Tamara Lush, "Hulk Hogan Says He Was 'Completely Humiliated' by Sex Video," Associated Press, March 7, 2016.

64 *"when speech is suppressed":* Julia Marsh and Bruce Golding, "'I Don't Have a 10-Inch Penis,'" *The Sun,* March 8, 2016.

64 *"part of the show":* Tom Kludt, "Hulk Hogan Trial Testimony Gets Raunchy," CNN, March 8, 2016.

64 *"had to be an entertainer":* Kludt, "Hulk Hogan Trial Testimony Gets Raunchy."

64 *"ten-inch penis":* Marsh and Golding, "'I Don't Have a 10-Inch Penis.'"

64 *trying not to laugh:* Kludt, "Hulk Hogan Trial Testimony Gets Raunchy."

64 *stitched together clips:* Vogt interview.

64 *dropped the notebook:* Vogt interview.

64 *didn't betray any emotions:* Tom Kludt, "Gawker Editor Says He Found Hulk Hogan Sex Tape 'Amusing,'" CNN, March 9, 2016.

64 *life had seemed to consist:* Claire Zulkey, "A Surprising Gift," *Inbox Collective*, July 12, 2023.

65 *"joining a roller derby league":* Daulerio interview with Martorano.

65 *his terrible sobriety:* Daulerio interview with Martorano.

65 *"No, not at all":* Tom Kludt, "Gawker Editor Defends Hogan Sex Tape as Journalism," CNN, March 14, 2016.

65 *"when two people have sex":* Kludt, "Gawker Editor Defends Hogan Sex Tape."

65 *Jurors were appalled:* "Jurors in Hulk Hogan v. Gawker Trial Say They Made 'Absolutely Correct' Decision," ABC News, March 24, 2016.

65 *"playing God":* Tom Kludt, "Hulk Hogan Jury Has Reached Verdict in $100 Million Gawker Suit," CNN, March 18, 2016.

65 *"worse off as a result":* Kludt, "Hulk Hogan Jury Has Reached Verdict."

65 *one juror later said:* Chris Spargo, "Defiant Gawker Founder Nick Denton Says He Has No Remorse," *Daily Mail*, March 24, 2016.

66 *another juror explained:* "Jurors in Hulk Hogan v. Gawker Trial."

66 *less than six hours:* Kludt, "Hulk Hogan Jury Has Reached Verdict."

66 *hugged his lawyers:* Vogt interview; Harder, "Hulk Hogan's Lead Lawyer Explains."

66 *who was "ecstatic":* D'Souza interview.

66 *dried tears remained visible:* Tom Kludt, "Hulk Hogan Awarded $115 Million in Gawker Sex Tape Case," CNN, March 18, 2018.

66 *"tears of joy":* Harder, *Gawker Slayer*, pp. 18–19.

66 *to celebrate their landmark victory:* Vogt interview.

66 *$27,000 in student loans:* Tom Kludt, "Hulk Hogan Jury Adds $25.1 Million to Gawker's Liability in Sex Tape Case," CNN, March 21, 2016.

66 *would be greatly reduced:* Brian Stelter and Tom Kludt, "Gawker's Nick Denton Certain He Will Still Beat Hulk Hogan," CNN, March 22, 2016.

66 *weren't told about that, either:* Stelter and Kludt, "Gawker's Nick Denton Certain"; Spargo, "Defiant Gawker Founder."

67 *prepared for this eventuality:* D'Souza interview.

67 *"act of destruction":* Nick Denton, "How Things Work," Gawker, August 22, 2016.

67 *flown in from Japan:* D'Souza interview.

67 *D'Souza told him:* D'Souza interview.

67 *briefly relapsed:* Daulerio interview with Martorano.

67 *$1,505.78 in his Chase checking account:* Matt Drange and Ryan Mac, "Former Gawker Editor Lashes Out at Peter Thiel," *Forbes*, August 18, 2016.

67 *placed on his account:* Ryan Holiday, "A. J. Daulerio on Recovery and Finding Peace with Stoicism," *Daily Stoic Podcast*, June 8, 2021.

67 *had used similar tactics:* Samantha Barbas, *Actual Malice: Civil Rights and Freedom of the Press in* New York Times v. Sullivan (Oakland, California: University of California Press, 2023), p. 127.

CHAPTER 6: VANQUISHING THE DARK SIDE

69 *an important new backer: Peter Thiel:* Ben Jacobs, "Peter Thiel, PayPal Co-founder, to Be Delegate for Donald Trump," *The Guardian*, May 10, 2016.

69 *more than $1 million:* David Streitfeld, "Peter Thiel to Donate $1.25 Million in Support of Donald Trump," *New York Times*, October 15, 2016.

69   *Ryan Mac and Matt Drange outed Thiel:* Ryan Mac and Matt Drange, "This Silicon Valley Billionaire Has Been Secretly Funding Hulk Hogan's Lawsuits Against Gawker," *Forbes*, May 24, 2016.

69   *unable to resist:* Ann Coulter, "Peter Thiel Brings Down Gawker," *UNSAFE* podcast, April 26, 2024.

69   *Thiel explained:* Andrew Ross Sorkin, "Peter Thiel, Tech Billionaire, Reveals Secret War With Gawker," *New York Times*, May 25, 2016.

70   *"our mystery benefactor":* Charles Harder, *Gawker Slayer: The Professional and Personal Adventures of Famed Attorney Charles Harder* (self-published, 2021), p. 27.

70   *"a really nice chess set":* Harder, *Gawker Slayer*, pp. 33–34.

70   *an hour-long interview:* Staff, "A Transcript of Donald Trump's Meeting with the 'Washington Post' Editorial Board," *Washington Post*, March 21, 2016.

71   *thought it might be a prank:* Harder, *Gawker Slayer*, pp. 84–85.

71   *must have recommended him:* Charles Harder email to author. Thiel didn't respond to my requests for comment.

71   *The* Hollywood Reporter *called him:* Eriq Gardner, "Ailes Media Litigator Charles Harder on His Improbable Rise," *Hollywood Reporter*, September 22, 2016.

71   *spending lots of time with the Trumps:* Harder, *Gawker Slayer*, p. 86.

71   *held in the Trump Tower offices:* Harder, *Gawker Slayer*, pp. 88–89.

71   *switched his California voter registration to nonpartisan:* Beth Reinhard and Emma Brown, "Trump Family Relies on Nemesis of Free-Speech Advocates in Legal Battles," *Washington Post*, July 25, 2018.

72   *counseling Jared Kushner:* Gabriel Sherman, "Jared Kushner Adds Charles Harder to Legal Team as West Wing Pressure Mounts," *Vanity Fair*, October 17, 2017.

72   *Stormy Daniels and* People *magazine:* Reinhard and Brown, "Trump Family Relies on Nemesis."

72   *Douglas Brinkley said:* Ashley Parker and Josh Dawsey, "Trump's Effort to Stop Publication of Scathing Book Is a Break from Precedent," *Washington Post*, January 4, 2018.

72   *"crush the media":* Parker and Dawsey, "Trump's Effort to Stop Publication."

73   *"a racist, misogynist, and xenophobe":* Redacted email reviewed by author.

73   *renamed Harder LLP:* Harder, *Gawker Slayer*, pp. 160–61.

73   *$4.4 million in fees:* Federal Election Commission records reviewed by author.

73   *"to conquer evil":* Harder, *Gawker Slayer*, p. 23.

73   *"the Dark Side" of journalism:* Harder, *Gawker Slayer*, pp. 8–9.

74   *threaten* New York *magazine:* Matthew Garrahan, "Ailes Hires Hollywood Libel Lawyer to Take on New York Magazine," *Financial Times*, September 5, 2016.

74   *that Ailes might sue:* Sydney Ember and Stacy Cowley, "Roger Ailes Hints at Suit Against *New York* Magazine," *New York Times*, September 5, 2016.

74   *"legally responsible for those damages":* Jodi Kantor and Megan Twohey, *She Said: Breaking the Sexual Harassment Story That Helped Ignite a Movement* (New York: Penguin Press, 2019), pp. 162–65.

75   *"preparing the lawsuit now":* Emily Smith, "Harvey Weinstein Plans to Sue New York Times for $50M," *New York Post*, October 5, 2017.

75   *"his personal animus":* Harder email to *New Yorker*, reviewed by author.

75   *lawsuits against a blogger:* J. K. Trotter, "Trump's Personal Attorney Has a History of Taking Aim at Reporters' Anonymous Sources," *Insider*, March 28, 2019.

75   *a suit against a reporter for* The Deal: Trotter, "Trump's Personal Attorney."

75   *existed in various forms before he came along:* Ryan Mac, "Behind Peter Thiel's Plan to Destroy Gawker," *Forbes*, June 7, 2016.

76   *"right side of the law":* Mike Masnick, "Techdirt's First Amendment Fight for Its Life,"
        Techdirt, January 11, 2017.

76   *"FAKE NEWS":* Tweet by @va_shiva, February 19, 2017.

76   Will I get sued over this?: Mike Masnick, keynote speech at Personal Democracy Forum,
        June 12, 2017.

76   *declined by a third:* Mike Masnick interview with author.

76   *dismissed Ayyadurai's lawsuit:* Mike Masnick, "Case Dismissed: Judge Throws Out
        Shiva Ayyadurai's Defamation Lawsuit Against Techdirt," *Techdirt*, September 6, 2017.

76   *No money changed hands:* Mike Masnick, "Our Legal Dispute With Shiva Ayyadurai Is
        Now Over," *Techdirt*, May 17, 2019.

76   *into the indefinite future:* Masnick interview.

76   *still struggled to speak:* Masnick interview.

76   *told an audience in 2017:* Masnick speech.

CHAPTER 7: A COUPLE OF WORKHORSES

77   *"perhaps the greatest threat":* Jason Zengerle, "Charles Harder, the Lawyer Who Killed
        Gawker, Isn't Done Yet," *GQ*, November 17, 2016.

77   *wanted to be a lawyer:* Libby Locke, "Alumni Spotlight Panel: Women in and of the
        World," New York University video on YouTube, February 16, 2016.

78   *liked to tell the story:* Locke on NYU panel.

78   *the same Georgia high school:* David Lat, *Original Jurisdiction* podcast with Tom Clare
        and Libby Locke, April 26, 2023.

78   *the diving team:* NYU Athletics, "2000/2001 Women's Swimming and Diving Roster:
        Elizabeth Locke."

78   *one friend said:* Jason Kander interview with author.

78   *president of the law school's Federalist Society chapter:* Libby Locke profile on Kirkland
        & Ellis website, accessed via Internet Archive.

78   *he'd had since college:* Tom Clare and Libby Locke, letter to author and *New York Times*,
        April 5, 2024.

79   *a series of front-page apologies:* Alix M. Freedman and Rekha Balu, "How Cincinnati
        Paper Ended Up Backing Off from Chiquita Series," *Wall Street Journal*, July 17, 1998.

79   *not to bestow awards:* Geanne Rosenberg, "Tom Yannucci: On the Attack," *Columbia
        Journalism Review*, September 2000.

79   *lawyers such as Ken Starr:* Lat, *Original Jurisdiction* podcast with Clare and Locke.

79   *"dedication to her work and clients":* Clare and Locke letter, April 5, 2024.

79   *defending an insurance company:* Locke's Kirkland profile.

79   *"I was hooked":* Lat, *Original Jurisdiction* podcast with Clare and Locke.

80   *the last thing Kirkland needed:* Lat, *Original Jurisdiction* podcast with Clare and Locke.

80   *beers after work:* Lat, *Original Jurisdiction* podcast with Clare and Locke.

80   *"less talented female lawyers":* Clare and Locke email to author, May 15, 2024.

80   *"Kirkland did retaliate against Libby":* Clare and Locke email.

81   *"do this on our own?":* Lat, *Original Jurisdiction* podcast with Clare and Locke.

81   *breeding Labrador retrievers:* Erik Larson, "Conservative Power Couple Wage Legal
        War on Stolen-Election Myth," *Bloomberg News*, February 26, 2021.

81   *it felt natural:* Lat, *Original Jurisdiction* podcast with Clare and Locke.

81   *Locke would reminisce:* Lat, *Original Jurisdiction* podcast with Clare and Locke.

81   *"their work wasn't good enough":* Clare and Locke email.

81   *wishing them well:* Clare and Locke letter, April 5, 2024.

82   *had insisted to employees:* Megan Meier interview with author; Andy Phillips interview with author.

82   *"abandoned the marriage relationship":* Clare's wife's divorce filing, Circuit Court of Arlington County, Virginia, December 30, 2015.

82   *denied abandoning the marriage:* Thomas Clare, "Answer to Complaint for Divorce," Circuit Court of Arlington County, March 8, 2016.

83   *an ugly picture of UVA:* Sabrina Rubin Erdely, "A Rape on Campus," *Rolling Stone*, November 19, 2014.

83   *had barely fact-checked:* Sheila Coronel, Steve Coll, and Derek Kravitz, "*Rolling Stone* and UVA: The Columbia University Graduate School of Journalism Report," *Rolling Stone*, April 5, 2015.

83   *a $1.65 million settlement:* Rod Smolla interview with author; Sydney Ember, "*Rolling Stone* to Pay $1.65 Million to Fraternity over Discredited Rape Story," *New York Times*, June 13, 2017.

83   *she had hired Clare Locke:* Zoe Tillman, "Key Figures in *Rolling Stone* Controversy Seek Legal Advice," *New York Law Journal*, December 15, 2014.

84   *"what the facts were":* Alanna Durkin Richer, "Attorneys Make Final Pitch to Jurors in *Rolling Stone* Trial," Associated Press, November 2, 2016.

84   *told a local TV station:* Tribune News Services, "Jury Finds Against *Rolling Stone* in Lawsuit over Rape Story," *Chicago Tribune*, November 4, 2016.

CHAPTER 8: A FORM OF EXTREMISM

85   *consulting firm had concluded:* Barry Meier, "Criticized in Print, Consultant Takes On Defiant Foes," *New York Times*, October 12, 2015.

85   *BP had invited her:* Cherri Foytlin interview with author.

86   *recited a quiet prayer:* Foytlin interview.

86   *She, too, was outraged:* Karen Savage interview with author.

86   So much for ChemRisk being independent: Savage interview.

86   *article in the* Wall Street Journal: Peter Waldman, "Study Tied Pollutant to Cancer; Then Consultants Got Hold of It," *Wall Street Journal*, December 23, 2005.

87   *Their article questioned:* Cherri Foytlin (with Karen Savage), "ChemRisk, BP and Purple Strategies: A Tangled Web of Not-So-Independent Science," *Huffington Post*, October 14, 2013.

87   *to attract much notice:* Savage and Foytlin interviews.

87   *"any and all corrective measures":* Richard Keil email to Stuart Whatley (*Huffington Post* editor), October 14, 2013, reviewed by author.

87   *Neither woman had been sued before:* Foytlin and Savage interviews.

87   *representative of ChemRisk wrote to Foytlin:* Foytlin and Savage interviews.

87   *consulted a law professor:* Bill Quigley (Loyola professor) email to author.

88   *she looked up online:* Savage interview.

88   *firsthand experience:* George W. Pring and Penelope Canan, *SLAPPs: Getting Sued for Speaking Out* (Philadelphia: Temple University Press, 1996), p. ix.

89   *"the future of representative democracy":* Pring and Canan, *SLAPPs*, p. 2.

89   *paperwork to terminate the lawsuit:* Massachusetts Superior Court, Memorandum & Order in *Cardno ChemRisk v. Cherri Foytlin & another*, July 20, 2016.

90   *his legal fees from ChemRisk:* Massachusetts Supreme Judicial Court ruling in *Cardno ChemRisk v. Cherri Foytlin & another*, February 14, 2017.

90   *about $150,000:* John Reichman interview with author.

90   *"need a lot of protection":* John R. Ellement, "Blog Criticism of Company Protected, SJC Rules," *Boston Globe*, February 15, 2017.

90   *sexual predator Peter Nygard:* Tom Clare emails to *New York Times*, February 2020, reviewed by author.

90   *There was Elon Musk:* Joe Palazzolo and Khadeeja Safdar, "Elon Musk's Boundary-Blurring Relationships With Women at SpaceX," *Wall Street Journal*, June 11, 2024.

90   *"creating a biased narrative":* Tom Clare letter to *New Yorker*'s Fabio Bertoni, reviewed by author.

91   *helped pay for billboards:* Jesse Marx, "Idaho Billionaire Who Once Opposed Same-Sex Marriage Sponsors Desert AIDS Project Fundraiser," *Desert Sun*, September 28, 2016.

91   *"an appropriate lifestyle":* Clara Jeffery and Monika Bauerlein, "We Were Sued by a Billionaire Political Donor," *Mother Jones*, October 8, 2015.

91   *some significant errors in the piece:* Stephanie Mencimer, "Pyramid-Like Company Ponies Up $1 Million for Mitt Romney," *Mother Jones*, February 6, 2012.

92   *"disavow our reporting":* Monika Bauerlein interview with author.

92   *threw out the lawsuit on* Sullivan *grounds:* Judge Darla Williamson, Order Granting the *Mother Jones* Defendants' Motion for Summary Judgment, *VanderSloot v. Foundation for National Progress*, October 6, 2015.

92   *more than $600,000:* Monika Bauerlein, "The Legal War Against Mother Jones Keeps Getting More Intense," *Mother Jones*, November 2, 2021.

92   *soared to $150,000:* Monika Bauerlein email to author.

92   *"a significant financial hit":* Bauerlein email to author.

92   *"mudslinging advertised as journalistic fearlessness":* Williamson, order granting summary judgment.

92   *"totally vindicated":* Frank VanderSloot, "VanderSloot Vindicated in *Mother Jones* Lawsuit," EastIdahoNews.com, October 6, 2015.

92   *who faced allegations:* Matthew Hill, "Diamond's Atlas Mara Said in Talks to Buy Finance Bank Zambia," Bloomberg News, June 23, 2015.

92   *as Mahtani put it at the time:* Rajan Mahtani news release, "Zambia Reports May Be Shut Down Permanently, Dr. Rajan Mahtani Takes Action!" Newswire.com, August 11, 2015.

93   *hundreds of posts about Mahtani:* James Kimer letter to Rajan Mahtani, December 22, 2017, reviewed by author.

93   *suspected it was one of his political rivals:* Kenneth Kakompe, "Mahtani's Success Continues as Sakwiba Sikota of Zambia Reports Chokes with Envy," *Zambian Watchdog*, December 21, 2015.

93   *built an automated system:* David Marchant interview with author.

93   *skimmed the document and then posted it:* Marchant interview.

93   *Marchant received an email:* Joseph Oliveri letter to Marchant, March 13, 2018, reviewed by author.

94   *"So . . . thanks!":* Marchant letter to Ehrenfeld, "Praising ACD," American Center for Democracy.

95   *"to our worldwide readership":* Marchant email to Oliveri, March 13, 2018, reviewed by author.

95   *never heard back:* Marchant interview.

95   *"do something about it":* Julie Hirschfeld Davis and Michael M. Grynbaum, "Trump Intensifies His Attacks on Journalists and Condemns F.B.I. Leakers," *New York Times*, February 24, 2017.

95   *the White House blocked:* Davis and Grynbaum, "Trump Intensifies His Attacks."

95 *violence against journalists:* Emily Cochrane, "'That's My Kind of Guy,' Trump Says of Republican Lawmaker Who Body-Slammed a Reporter," *New York Times*, October 19, 2018.

95 *"a sham and a disgrace":* Michael M. Grynbaum, "Trump Renews Pledge to 'Take a Strong Look' at Libel Laws," *New York Times*, January 10, 2018.

96 *"That is absolutely right":* "Report: WH Considers Changing Libel Laws," *CNN Newsroom*, May 1, 2017.

97 Mother Jones *reporter whose article:* Mencimer, "Pyramid-Like Company Ponies Up $1 Million."

97 *"take no prisoners" lawyer:* Erik Wemple interview with author.

CHAPTER 9: COORDINATED CAMPAIGNS OF HARASSMENT

98 *had once orchestrated the arrests:* David Carr, "Media Executives Arrested in Phoenix," *New York Times*, October 19, 2007.

98 *"a truly sadistic man":* First Amendment Watch at New York University, "Ex-Sheriff Seeking $147.5 Million in Defamation Suit Against NY Times," October 24, 2018.

98 *sued CNN, the* Huffington Post, *and* Rolling Stone: First Amendment Watch at New York University, "Federal Judge Dismisses $300 Million Defamation Suit Against Three Media Companies Brought by Former Arizona Sheriff Joe Arpaio," November 4, 2019.

99 *A procession of federal judges ruled:* Chief Judge Roger Gregory, US Court of Appeals for Fourth Circuit, opinion in cases 22–1198, 22–1207, and 22–1326, February 22, 2023.

99 *sued Gizmodo:* Katherine Krueger, "Court Docs Allege Ex-Trump Staffer Drugged Woman," Splinter News, September 21, 2018.

99 *it was fair game:* Eriq Gardner, "Gizmodo Beats Jason Miller Defamation Lawsuit," *Hollywood Reporter*, August 28, 2019.

99 *"no idea" who was financing the litigation:* Judge Mark A. Roberts, Order Regarding Defendants' Motion to Compel Third-Party Funding Discovery Requests, *Anthony Nunes Jr., et al., v. Ryan Lizza and Hearst Magazine Media*, Case 20-cv-4003-CJW, October 26, 2021.

99 *accused him of sexual assault:* Grace Segers, "Justin Fairfax Accuser Vanessa Tyson: 'In My Ideal World, I'd Want Him to Resign,'" CBS News, March 31, 2019.

100 *began publicly complaining:* Laura Vozzella, "Appeals Court Backs Dismissal of Virginia Lt. Gov. Justin Fairfax's Defamation Suit," *Washington Post*, June 23, 2021. "Just because someone is an elected official doesn't mean they should have less rights under the law," Fairfax's spokeswoman, Lauren Burke, told me.

100 *he emailed an acquaintance:* "Statement of Undisputed Material Facts in Support of Plaintiff's Motion for Summary Judgment," *Michael E. Mann v. National Review*, Superior Court of the District of Columbia, Case 2012-CA-008263, January 22, 2021.

100 *"legal liability for defamation":* Isabel Vincent, "Harvard Board Facing Probe over Claudine Gay Cover-Up," *New York Post*, January 9, 2024.

100 *"without proper attribution":* Emma Green, "Why Some Academics Are Reluctant to Call Claudine Gay a Plagiarist," *New Yorker*, January 5, 2024.

100 *"dark money" from liberal nonprofits:* Kenneth P. Vogel and Shane Goldmacher, "Democrats Decried Dark Money. Then They Won With It in 2020," *New York Times*, January 29, 2022.

100 *he tweeted:* Jerry Dunleavy, "Democratic Lawyer Marc Elias Questions Press Freedoms After NYT Article on 'Dark Money,'" *Washington Examiner*, January 31, 2022.

101   *when the tip came in:* Jared Strong interview with author.

101   *the layoffs:* Michael Gartner, "In Des Moines, Gannett's Cuts Are Devastating," Niemen Watchdog, June 25, 2011.

101   *for nearly a century:* "Carroll, Jefferson Newspapers Remain with Iowa Family Under New Ownership," *Editor & Publisher*, November 30, 2022.

101   *to see what was happening:* Transcript of Jared Strong deposition in *Smith v. Strong and Herald*, March 16, 2018.

101   *remarked to a local TV station:* Todd Magel, "Naked Man Found Trapped in Chimney Pleas to Trespassing Charge," KCCI, May 19, 2016.

101   *basketball star accused of rape:* Jared Strong and Matthew Rezab, "Star Player Still on Court Despite Alleged Rape," *Carroll Times Herald*, December 11, 2015.

101   *readers objected:* Strong interview.

102   *two-to-one margin:* Carroll County Election Summary Report, carrrollcountyiowa.gov, November 15, 2016.

102   *the enemy of the people:* Doug Burns interview with author.

102   *failed to share exculpatory evidence:* Jason Clayworth and Luke Nozicka, "Confusion About 'Liars List' May Be Depriving Suspects of Fair Trials," *Des Moines Register*, May 15, 2019.

102   *accused of threatening to kill:* Jared Strong, "Officer Resigns For Contact with Minor," *Carroll Times Herald*, June 15, 2021.

102   *was summoned for a meeting:* Strong interview.

102   *her rival's Ford Fusion:* "Felony Criminal Mischief Charge Reduced to Misdemeanor Offense for Carroll Woman," KCIM News, November 17, 2017.

103   *messages to a sixteen-year-old girl:* Jared Strong, "Carroll Cop Who Courted Teenage Girls Resigns," *Carroll Times Herald*, July 18, 2017.

103   *"People shouldn't judge":* Jared Strong, "Police Chief Was Slow to Address 'Problem Officer,'" *Carroll Times Herald*, May 25, 2018.

103   *anytime they wished:* Caitlin Yamada, "Truth Wins: How One Paper Defended a Libel Claim," *Iowa State Daily*, April 10, 2019.

103   *even threats:* Strong interview.

103   *the third generation of his family:* "'Give More to the Community Than You Take,'" *Carroll Times Herald*, January 31, 2020.

103   *a legitimate news story:* Burns interview.

103   *colleagues grumbling about Strong:* Jacob Smith interview with author.

103   *that the conversation be off-the-record:* Strong deposition.

103   *Smith questioned the motive:* Smith interview.

103   *threatened to fire him:* Smith interview.

104   *"it finally happened":* Strong interview.

104   *a terse email:* Burns interview.

104   *sued Buzzfeed News:* Stephanie Taylor, "Officers File Defamation Suit," *Tuscaloosa News*, March 9, 2019.

104   *for an article:* Katie J. M. Baker, "A College Student Accused a Powerful Man of Rape. Then She Became a Suspect," *Buzzfeed News*, June 22, 2017.

104   *as a federal judge ruled:* Judge David Proctor, opinion in *Adam Jones et al. v. Buzzfeed et al.*, Case 7:19-cv-00403, March 15, 2022.

104   *dogged by long-running litigation:* Jayme Fraser, "Court Overturns Libel Verdict Against Fort Bend Star," *Houston Chronicle*, December 23, 2014.

104   *personal injury and family law:* Van Dyke Law Office, "About Us," accessed via Internet Archive.

104 *take this case on contingency:* Smith interview.

105 *the supposed "untruths":* "Former Carroll Police Officer Sues Local Publisher," KCIM News, July 20, 2017.

105 *"We're in trouble, huh?":* Strong interview.

105 *glaring at him:* Strong interview.

105 *a rate of about two per week:* Penny Abernathy, "The State of Local News 2022," Northwestern University Medill School of Journalism, June 29, 2022.

105 *"news deserts":* Abernathy, "The State of Local News 2022."

106 *politics polarize:* McKay Coppins, "A Secretive Hedge Fund Is Gutting Newsrooms," *The Atlantic*, October 14, 2021.

106 *taxes go up:* Abernathy, "The State of Local News 2022."

106 *voter turnout wanes:* Jay Jennings and Meghan Rubado, *Newspaper Decline and the Effect on Local Government Coverage*, November 2019.

106 *Misinformation spreads:* David Ardia et al., "Addressing the Decline of Local News, Rise of Platforms, and Spread of Mis- and Disinformation Online," UNC Center for Media Law and Policy, December 2020.

106 *not enjoyed in a century:* Abernathy, "The State of Local News 2022."

106 *began yanking their business:* Burns interview; "Carroll, Jefferson Newspapers Remain with Iowa Family."

106 *since the Great Depression:* "Carroll, Jefferson Newspapers Remain with Iowa Family."

106 *Burns said no:* Burns interview; "Iowa Newspaper in Financial Peril Turns to Social Media to Raise $140,000," *The Gazette*, October 11, 2019.

106 *"hill you're willing to die on":* Brian Ross, "Iowa Newspaper Paying the Price for Investigative Journalism," Law & Crime Trial Network, November 1, 2019.

106 *she'd just been fired:* Strong, "Police Chief Was Slow to Address 'Problem Officer.'"

106 *he and March parted ways:* Strong interview.

107 *March ghosted him:* Strong interview.

107 *"at my request":* Brad Burke email to Strong, reviewed by author.

107 *in stunned silence:* Strong interview.

107 *police department said was insubordination:* "Insubordination and Violation of 'Last Chance Agreements' Basis for Firing," KCIM News, February 19, 2018.

107 *to discredit the outlet:* Burns interview.

107 *stress-drinking:* Strong email to author.

108 *the judge wrote:* "Judge dismisses former officer's lawsuit against Daily Times Herald," *Carroll Times Herald*, May 22, 2018.

108 *print the paper only twice a week:* Burns interview.

108 *told the* Washington Post: Meagan Flynn, "A Small-Town Iowa Newspaper Brought Down a Cop," *Washington Post*, October 10, 2019.

109 *he contemplated suicide:* Douglas Burns, "Suicidal Thoughts, Resilience in a Small-Town Iowa Newspaper's Fierce Last Stand," *Iowa Mercury*, October 11, 2022.

109 *"worst day of my life":* Burns interview.

109 *"did not pay off at all":* Strong interview.

109 *Originally named* Out West: O'Dell Isaac, "From *Out West* to *The Gazette*: A Timeline of Colorado Springs' Newspaper," *The Gazette*, March 18, 2022.

109 *hundreds of other awards:* Isaac, "From *Out West* to *The Gazette*."

109 *journalists had cheered the deal:* John Schroyer, "Phil's *Gazette*, Chapter 1," philsgazette.blogspot.com, January 22, 2017.

110 *the owner's business or political interests:* John Schroyer, "Phil's *Gazette*, Chapter 2," philsgazette.blogspot.com, January 24, 2017.

110   *an antidrug activist:* Corey Hutchins, "*Gazette* Publisher in Colorado Defends Contro-
      versial Marijuana Series," *Columbia Journalism Review*, March 25, 2015.

110   *quit in disgust:* Jason Salzman, "Spiked: A Conservative 'Shadow' Hangs over Colorado
      Newspapers Owned by GOP Billionaire Phil Anschutz," *Colorado Times Recorder*, July
      27, 2023.

110   *More journalists resigned:* John Schroyer, "Phil's *Gazette*, Chapter 3," philsgazette.blog-
      spot.com, January 25, 2017; Salzman, "Spiked."

110   *the sour vibes:* Conrad Swanson interview with author.

110   *smelled a story:* Vince Bzdek interview with author.

110   *"Do you want to look into this?":* Swanson interview.

110   *1,500 tons of ore per day:* Gold Hill Mesa, "Golden History," goldhillmesa.com.

110   *used arsenic and other chemicals:* Conrad Swanson, "Rich History of Gold Mining Left
      Problems Within Its Wake," *The Gazette*, August 25, 2019.

111   *fourteen million tons of toxic dregs:* Rich Laden, "Regulators Approve Environmental
      Plan for Gold Hill Mesa Development," *The Gazette*, October 25, 2016.

111   *two hundred feet of slurry:* Thomas A. Terry et al., "Geology of Colorado Springs,"
      Engineering Geology in Colorado: Contributions, Trends, and Case Histories, Colorado
      Geological Survey, 2007.

111   *Few structures stood:* Rich Laden, "Former Gold Milling Site to Be Colorado Springs,
      Colo., Urban Development," *The Gazette*, January 24, 2004.

111   *persuaded the city:* Laden, "Former Gold Milling Site."

111   *trucked in as a buffer:* Laden, "Regulators Approve Environmental Plan."

111   *city officials hadn't considered:* Conrad Swanson, "City Halts New Building Phase at
      Gold Hill Mesa," *The Gazette*, August 25, 2019.

111   *other customers couldn't eavesdrop:* Swanson and Hannah Polmer interviews.

112   *The house had even been featured:* "Home Not Effectively Green, Lawsuit Says," *Colo-
      rado Springs Business Journal*, September 3, 2013.

112   *the allure had faded:* Bill Rudge and Hannah Polmer interview with author.

112   *"I need the City to assure me":* Swanson, "City Halts New Building."

112   *rinky-dink violations:* Letters from Gold Hill Mesa Neighborhood representative to
      Rudge and Polmer, June–July 2015, reviewed by author.

112   *stigmatizing the development:* Gold Hill Mesa letter to residents, August 2015, reviewed
      by author.

112   *deserted Rudge's legal practice:* Rudge and Polmer interview.

112   *intimidating neighbors:* Heather Kelly email to author.

113   *buying back their home:* Rudge and Polmer interview.

113   *promised not to disparage the development:* Letter from Jeffrey S. George (Hogan Lovells
      lawyer) to Hannah Polmer, December 4, 2018, reviewed by author.

113   *Now she worried:* Polmer interview.

113   *He spent months:* Swanson interview.

114   *came to* The Gazette*'s office:* Bzdek interview.

114   *increasing the risk of sliding:* Swanson, "Rich History of Gold Mining."

114   *until more testing could be done:* Swanson, "City Halts New Building."

114   *"article was fundamentally flawed":* Kelly email.

115   *"irresponsible and libelous recent articles":* Richard Hanes email to Chris Reen, August
      27, 2019, reviewed by author.

115   *already in the pipeline:* Swanson interview.

115   *enough to crack buildings:* Conrad Swanson, "Agency Finds Sinking at Gold Hill Mesa,
      Calls for More Testing," *The Gazette*, September 22, 2019.

116 *"yellow journalism at its worst"*: Hanes letter to Steven Zansberg, September 11, 2019, reviewed by author.

116 *"to evaluate potential litigation"*: Monte McKeehen letter to Vince Bzdek, September 14, 2019, reviewed by author.

116 *"'bet-the-company' trial firm"*: "Gold Hill Mesa Hires Denver Law Firm to Assess Claims Against the Gazette," Gold Hill Neighborhood LLC, September 20, 2019.

116 *signed a bipartisan law:* Melissa Wasser, "Colorado Becomes 31st Jurisdiction with Anti-SLAPP Protections," Reporters Committee for Freedom of the Press, June 5, 2019.

117 *Now Swanson was called:* Swanson interview.

117 *"scorn in the neighborhood"*: Conrad Swanson, "Gold Hill Mesa Residents Fear Retribution from Community After Reporting Problems," *The Gazette*, October 6, 2019.

117 *drafts of the articles:* Article drafts reviewed by author.

117 *viewed them as "ancillary"*: Bzdek interview.

117 *"false rumors" about the housing development:* Laura A. Hass letter to Sean Wells (lawyer for Rudge and Polmer), December 23, 2014; Jeffrey George letter to Wells, August 12, 2015; George letter to Wells, March 2, 2016. Letters reviewed by author.

118 *attorneys sought access:* CORA request submitted by John Cook, May 25, 2020, reviewed by author.

118 *"in ongoing or potential litigation"*: Internal CGS emails, November 1, 2019, reviewed by author.

118 *"way more fact-based"*: Erinn Callahan, "Testing Could Ease Limbo at Gold Hill Mesa," *Colorado Springs Business Journal*, February 14, 2020.

118 *a spokeswoman noted ominously:* Callahan, "Testing Could Ease Limbo."

118 *allowed Gold Hill Mesa:* Mary Shinn, "State Gives Gold Hill Mesa Expansion Green Light After Reviewing Soil Report Paid for by Developer," *The Gazette*, August 8, 2020.

118 *help defray the costs:* Breeanna Jent, "Council Approves City Funding for Gold Hill Mesa," *The Gazette*, October 24, 2023.

CHAPTER 10: CLARENCE THOMAS CHANGES HIS MIND

119 *well over four hundred others:* US Supreme Court Order List, February 19, 2019.

119 *Los Angeles in 1963: Kathrine McKee v. William Cosby*, Amended Complaint, Case 3:15-cv-30221-MGM, July 1, 2016.

120 *Doris Day and Elizabeth Taylor:* Kathy McKee interview with author.

120 *McKee told prospective employers:* McKee interview.

120 *Sammy Davis Jr.'s father:* McKee interview; Jennie Miller, "Former Vegas Showgirl Reflects on Wild Youth," C&G Newspapers, July 7, 2010.

120 *a couple of kisses onstage:* McKee interview.

120 *"we were lovers"*: Nancy Dillon, "Exclusive: Bill Cosby Accused of Raping Ex-girlfriend of Sammy Davis Jr.," New York *Daily News*, December 22, 2014.

120 *one of the first episodes of* Saturday Night Live*:* McKee interview; David Henry and Joe Henry, "*Saturday Night Live* and Richard Pryor: The Untold Story Behind *SNL*'s Edgiest Sketch Ever," *Salon*, November 3, 2013.

120 *short-lived* Bill Cosby Show: McKee petition for writ of certiorari, April 19, 2018.

120 *with Cosby's wife, Camille:* Amended complaint in *McKee v. Cosby*.

121 *Pine Knob amphitheater:* McKee interview; "Bill Cosby Took Advantage of Me in Detroit Hotel: Actress," New York *Daily News*, December 22, 2015.

121 *to see family:* Dillon, "Bill Cosby Accused."

121 *the elegant Hotel St. Regis:* McKee interview.

121 *their relationship was platonic:* "Bill Cosby Took Advantage."

121 *bathrobe and wool cap:* Amended complaint in *McKee v. Cosby.*

121 *shut the door:* "Bill Cosby Took Advantage."

121 *he raped her:* Amended complaint in *McKee v. Cosby.*

121 *the essence of a dead man:* McKee interview.

121 *blocking her exit:* McKee interview.

121 *McKee drove him:* "Bill Cosby Took Advantage."

121 *she turned on CNN:* McKee interview.

122 *"our collective understanding of Bill Cosby":* Tom Scocca, "Who Wants to Remember Bill Cosby's Multiple Sexual-Assault Allegations?" Gawker, February 4, 2014.

122 *"America's Dad":* "Bill Cosby Faces Sexual Assault Allegations," *CNN Newsroom,* November 15, 2014.

122 *nauseated her:* McKee interview.

122 *She recognized:* McKee interview.

123 *more than a dozen women:* Lorne Manly and Graham Bowley, "Cosby Team's Strategy: Hush Accusers, Insult Them, Blame the Media," *New York Times,* December 28, 2014.

123 *to dig up dirt:* Stacy Brown, "Cosby's Investigators 'Dig Up Dirt' on Rape Accusers," *New York Post,* December 28, 2014.

123 *threaten women with defamation lawsuits:* Manly and Bowley, "Cosby Team's Strategy."

123 *fired off a letter:* Martin D. Singer letter to Cyna J. Alderman and Nancy Dillon, December 22, 2014, reviewed by author.

123 *"Dissemination Is Prohibited":* Singer letter to Alderman and Dillon.

123 *leaked to the* Hollywood Reporter: Austin Siegemund-Broka, "Bill Cosby's Lawyer Threatens New York Daily News over 'Defamatory' Rape Story," *Hollywood Reporter,* December 23, 2014.

123 *including snippets from the Singer letter:* Amended complaint in *McKee v. Cosby.*

124 *with a cousin:* McKee interview.

124 *he and McKee could wring:* Bill Salo interview with author.

125 *"protected by the First Amendment":* Judge Mark G. Mastroianni, Memorandum and Order Regarding Defendant's Motion to Dismiss, *McKee v. Cosby,* February 16, 2017.

125 *"This is outrageous":* Salo interview.

125 *"immunizing them from defamation liability":* Judge Sandra Lynch, First Circuit Court of Appeals ruling in *McKee v. Cosby,* Case 17–1256, October 18, 2017.

126 *"we're going to appeal":* Salo interview.

126 *suspended for a year:* New York Appellate Division, "Matter of Salo—Opinion of the Court," July 27, 2010.

126 *because she was a Black woman:* Salo interview.

126 *victimizing her again:* McKee interview.

126 *are prescribed:* US Supreme Court Clerk's Office, "Memorandum to Those Intending to Prepare a Petition for a Writ of Certiorari," January 2023.

126 *turned to Time's Up:* McKee and Salo interviews.

126 *worked with Sandra Bullock:* Eriq Gardner, "'Gawker Slayer': A Time's Up Referral and a Lawyer's Journey from Hollywood to Trumpland," *Hollywood Reporter,* March 3, 2021.

127 *Harder would get a cut:* Salo interview.

127 *he'd been "honored":* Charles Harder, *Gawker Slayer: The Professional and Personal Adventures of Famed Attorney Charles Harder* (self-published, 2021), p. 103.

127   *"too stringent":* Eriq Gardner, "Ailes Media Litigator Charles Harder on His Improbable Rise," *Hollywood Reporter,* September 22, 2016.

127   *"the standard is so high":* Jason Zengerle, "Charles Harder, the Lawyer Who Killed Gawker, Isn't Done Yet," *GQ,* November 17, 2016.

127   *an Irish bar in Manhattan:* Salo interview.

129   *"If we win this case":* Salo interview.

129   *who was beginning to realize:* McKee interview.

129   *the court asked Cosby's side:* US Supreme Court docket report for No. 17–1542.

129   *another ten times:* Supreme Court docket report.

130   *the justices might be reluctant:* Charles Harder email to author.

130   *she'd written a piece:* Elena Kagan, "A Libel Story: Sullivan Then and Now," *Law and Social Inquiry,* 1993.

130   *hard to pin down:* Transcript of Kagan testimony to Senate Judiciary Committee, June 30, 2010.

130   *he'd written a short memo:* John Roberts memo to Fred Fielding, August 28, 1985, via Reagan Presidential Library, reaganlibrary.gov/public/digitallibrary/smof/counsel/roberts/box-066/40_485_6909456_066_004_2017.pdf.

130   *"gosh,* fifty, sixty *years":* Transcript of Gorsuch testimony to Senate Judiciary Committee, March 21, 2017.

131   *anything the Ku Klux Klan could have inflicted:* Ken Foskett, "The Public Profile and Inner Pain of Clarence Thomas," Cox News Service, August 12, 2001.

131   *"none of whom knew me":* Clarence Thomas, *My Grandfather's Son: A Memoir* (New York: Harper, 2007), p. 154.

131   *devoted to Thomas's perspective:* Ernest Holsendolph, "Skills, Not Bias, Seen as Key for Jobs," *New York Times,* July 3, 1982.

131   *denied that ever happened:* Richard Prince, "Justice Holds News Media in Contempt," *Journal-isms,* September 1, 2011.

131   *"poisonous snakes and speaking in tongues":* Thomas, *My Grandfather's Son,* p. 225.

131   *an article in the* Los Angeles Times*:* David G. Savage, "Thomas' Church a Center of Anti-Abortion Activity," *Los Angeles Times,* July 11, 1991.

132   *"a few hundred dollars":* Thomas, *My Grandfather's Son,* p. 225.

132   *the* New York Times *drily noted:* Maggie Haberman and Annie Karni, "Trump Meets with Hard-Right Group Led by Ginni Thomas," *New York Times,* January 26, 2019.

134   *an expansive view of the First Amendment: Citizens United v. FEC* and *Reed v. Town of Gilbert;* Lee Levine and Stephen Wermiel, "What Would Justice Brennan Say to Justice Thomas?" *Communications Lawyer,* Spring 2019.

135   *wrote Rod Smolla:* Rod Smolla, "Look to Bill Cosby Case as Proof That American Defamation Law Needs a Review," *Delaware Online,* March 12, 2019.

135   *"He speaks out for rape survivors":* Amul Thapar, *The People's Justice: Clarence Thomas and the Constitutional Stories That Define Him* (Washington: Regnery Gateway, 2023), p. 213.

135   I've seen men like that*:* McKee interview.

136   *"a slap in my face":* McKee interview.

CHAPTER 11: THE OLIGARCHS' REVENGE

139   *more than $1,200 an hour:* Clare Locke letter to Kytch, November 29, 2021, filed as exhibit in *Clare Locke v. Kytch,* Case 1:24-cv-00545, April 30, 2024.

139   *buy himself an Aston Martin:* Tom Clare and Libby Locke letter to author and *New York Times,* April 5, 2024.

140   *Notre Dame's varsity fencing team:* Clare and Locke email to author, May 15, 2024.

140   *"takes seriously the art of war":* Daniel Watkins interview with author.

140   *"a story of fire and ice":* David Lat, *Original Jurisdiction* podcast with Tom Clare and Libby Locke, April 26, 2023.

140   *honeymoon in the Seychelles:* Tom Clare post on Facebook, May 5, 2018.

140   *"It's really problematic":* Federalist Society, "The Future of Libel Law," 2017 National Lawyers Convention, November 17, 2017.

140   *public figures have limited recourse:* Libby Locke, "How It Feels to Be Falsely Accused," *Wall Street Journal*, October 4, 2018.

140   *Carlson gushed: Tucker Carlson Tonight*, Fox News Channel, September 27, 2018.

141   *hadn't instigated a fight:* Sarah Mervosh and Emily S. Rueb, "Fuller Picture Emerges of Viral Video of Native American Man and Catholic Students," *New York Times*, January 20, 2019.

141   *"they can bring defamation claims": Tucker Carlson Tonight*, Fox News Channel, January 23, 2019.

141   *the law firm's internal Slack channel:* Clare and Locke letter to author.

141   *Clare Locke hired the husband:* Locke appeared on *The Ingraham Angle* in February 2019. Clare Locke hired James O'Toole—whose wife, Elisa Cipollone, is a producer on the Fox show—in August 2019, according to his LinkedIn profile. Cipollone's father is Pat Cipollone, who was Trump's White House counsel and had previously worked with Clare and Locke at Kirkland & Ellis.

141   *endorsed Sandmann's libel lawsuit:* Michael M. Grynbaum and Eileen Sullivan, "Trump Attacks The *Times*, in a Week of Unease for the American Press," *New York Times*, February 20, 2019.

141   *He'd suggested "retribution":* "Clarence Thomas Backs Trump's Call for Changing Defamation Law to Ease Suits Against Media," Fox News, February 19, 2019.

141   *"a true ENEMY OF THE PEOPLE":* Grynbaum and Sullivan, "Trump Attacks The *Times*."

142   *"Us being the media": Tucker Carlson Tonight*, Fox News Channel, February 20, 2019.

142   *a "corpse-filled struggle":* Andrew Higgins and Kenneth P. Vogel, "Two Capitals, One Russian Oligarch," *New York Times*, November 4, 2018.

143   *ordering a contract killing:* Andrew E. Kramer, "Praise for the Mueller Report, from an Unlikely Source: Oleg Deripaska," *New York Times*, April 3, 2019.

143   *emerged as a character:* Kramer, "Praise for the Mueller Report."

143   *one of several Russian oligarchs:* As recently as 2021, Clare Locke represented Mikhail Fridman, Petr Aven, and German Khan in their lawsuit against the private intelligence company Fusion GPS, according to legal filings.

143   *sent an unsolicited letter:* Tom Clare letter to David McCraw, January 15, 2019, reviewed by author.

143   *"acting as a public relations counsel":* US Department of Justice, "Protecting the United States from Covert Foreign Influence," September 2020.

144   *"I do not act in that capacity":* Clare email to Ken Vogel, February 20, 2019, reviewed by author.

144   *its mandate was limited:* Redacted letter from DOJ's Brandon Van Grack, July 23, 2019; Tom Clare wrote in an email to Vogel in March 2022 that the letter was to Clare Locke and concerned its representation of Deripaska. Letter available at justice.gov/nsd-fara /page/file/1234531/download.

144   *"the representations in your letters":* Van Grack letter.

145   *Stedman was a news junkie:* Scott Stedman interview with author.

145 *grades had taken a drubbing:* Scott Stedman interview.

145 *about $3,000 a month:* Scott Stedman interview.

145 *"virtually a ghost":* Natasha Bertrand, "Senate Intelligence Committee Summons Mysterious British Security Consultant," *Politico*, June 5, 2019.

146 *tracked down records:* Scott Stedman and Jess Coleman, "Walter Soriano: The Covert Operative for Russian and Israeli Elite," *Forensic News*, July 14, 2019.

146 *electronic surveillance and hacking:* Stedman and Coleman, "Walter Soriano."

146 *regularly went after journalists:* Lord Justice Warby, Court of Appeal ruling in *Soriano v. Forensic News, et al.*, Case CA 2021–000484, December 21, 2021.

146 *"We will not delete this story":* Stedman and Coleman, "Walter Soriano."

147 *This article described the connections:* Scott Stedman and Robert J. DeNault, "Israeli Spy Companies Show Critical Link Between Flynn, Deripaska, and Senate Intelligence Committee Target Walter Soriano," *Forensic News*, June 16, 2020.

147 *cease his reporting:* In re Application of Forensic News LLC, "Memorandum of Law," Case 1:22-mc-00993-KAM, March 31, 2022.

147 *"the actual sources of these false claims":* Clare letter to Scott Stedman, June 11, 2020, reviewed by author.

148 *the article deadpanned:* Stedman and DeNault, "Israeli Spy Companies Show Critical Link."

148 *spreading "malicious falsehoods":* Soriano v. Forensic News, Particulars of Claims, August 16, 2020.

148 *"established within the United Kingdom":* Soriano v. Forensic News, Particulars of Claims.

149 *"You almost got shot, dude!":* John Stedman interview with author.

149 *"This is from Mr. Soriano":* Scott Stedman interview.

149 *"contact me if serious":* Gibson Dunn attorney's email to Scott Stedman, reviewed by author.

149 *allowed the libel claims to stand:* Mr. Justice Jay, Approved Judgment in *Soriano v. Forensic News*, January 15, 2021.

150 *"renders unenforceable":* In re Application of Forensic News LLC, Memorandum of Law.

150 *data-protection claims were reinstated:* Warby, Court of Appeal ruling.

150 *a British lawmaker said:* Reed Albergotti, "Some Russian Oligarchs Are Using U.K. Data Privacy Law to Sue," *Washington Post*, March 31, 2022.

150 *they grew worse:* Scott Stedman interview; John Stedman interview.

151 *"when you're in the right":* John Stedman interview.

151 *Stedman's rapidly dwindling savings:* Scott Stedman interview.

151 *the latest threatening letter:* Andrew Brettler letter to Scott Stedman and others, March 10, 2022, reviewed by author.

152 *Rechtschaffen had once asked him:* Shlomo Rechtschaffen email to Scott Stedman, June 8, 2020, reviewed by author.

153 *"what lawfare looks like":* Scott Stedman testimony to Commission on Security & Cooperation in Europe, "Confronting Oligarchs, Enablers, and Lawfare," April 6, 2022.

153 *"based on circumstantial and inadequate evidence":* Robert J. Denault post on Twitter, June 30, 2022, available via Internet Archive.

154 *Stedman folded:* Scott Stedman email to David Marchant, March 2, 2023, reviewed by author.

154 *"I kindly request":* Stedman email to Marchant.

154 *Marchant replied tartly:* Marchant email to Stedman, March 2, 2023, reviewed by author.

154 *"wanted that information documented":* Huntington Police Department report, July 17, 2023, reviewed by author.

154 *explained on social media:* Post by @ScottMStedman on Twitter, March 30, 2023.

CHAPTER 12: TRIGGERING A FEDERAL JUDGE

155 *about a third of the time:* NYU Institute of Judicial Administration, "Hon. Laurence H. Silberman: An Interview with Paul D. Clement," Oral History of Distinguished American Judges, May 17, 2017.

155 *Republicans and right-wing causes:* David G. Savage and Tom Hamburger, "Few Impartial on Panel Co-Chair," *Los Angeles Times*, February 11, 2004.

155 *laying the legal groundwork:* Emily Langer, "Laurence Silberman, Titan of Conservative Jurisprudence, Dies at 86," *Washington Post*, October 3, 2022. The five-to-four Supreme Court decision was *District of Columbia v. Heller*, in which the court for the first time recognized an individual's right to bear arms, unrelated to their service in a militia.

156 *to pursue the "Troopergate" scandal:* David Brock, *Blinded by the Right: The Conscience of an Ex-Conservative* (New York: Three Rivers Press, 2002), p. 159.

156 *opposed the renaming of military bases:* Ryan Grim, "Federal Judge Lambasts Amendment to Rename Confederate Bases as 'Madness,'" *The Intercept*, June 15, 2020.

156 *a behind-the-scenes adviser:* Brock, *Blinded by the Right*, p. 105.

156 *"a largely illegitimate institution":* Oral History Project of the Historical Society of the District of Columbia Circuit, "Honorable Laurence H. Silberman," p. 194.

156 *"jeopardize the whole judiciary":* "Hon. Laurence H. Silberman: An Interview with Paul D. Clement."

156 *Yoo attributed Silberman's attitude:* John Yoo interview with author.

156 *his performance didn't disappoint:* Lawrence L. Knutson, "Federal Appeals Judge Attacks News Media, Jurists," Associated Press, June 13, 1992.

157 *a "landmark" speech:* John Fund, "The Limits of 'Growth,'" *Wall Street Journal*, December 10, 2003.

157 *their fiftieth wedding anniversary:* Silberman DC Circuit oral history, p. 238.

157 *fruitful and very leaky relationships:* Lee H. Hamilton (chairman), *Joint Report of the Task Force to Investigate Certain Allegations Concerning the Holding of American Hostages by Iran in 1980*, 1993, p. 62.

157 *claimed to an interviewer:* Silberman DC Circuit oral history, pp. 263–64.

157 *this was nonsense:* David Savage and Tom Hamburger emails to author.

158 *There was an exposé:* "Signing Their Lives Away: Liberia's Private Use Permits and the Destruction of Community-Owned Rainforest," Global Witness, September 3, 2012.

158 *cancel the contracts and arrest:* Jonathan Paye, "Liberia: Ex-forestry Boss Arrested for Corruption," Associated Press, February 22, 2014.

158 *had bribed Liberian legislators:* Global Witness, *Curse or Cure? How Oil Can Boost or Break Liberia's Post-War Recovery*, September 2011.

158 *a multipart transaction:* Global Witness, *Catch Me If You Can: Exxon's Complicity in Liberian Oil Sector Corruption and How Its Washington Lobbyists Fight to Keep Oil Deals Secret*, March 2018, pp. 7, 20.

158 *The source eventually provided:* Noronha-Gant interview.

158 *paid $35,000 apiece:* Global Witness, *Catch Me If You Can*, p. 30.

159 *Noronha-Gant's immediate thought:* Noronha-Gant interview.

159 *appeared to have come:* Global Witness, *Catch Me If You Can*, p. 30.

159 *from a government bank account:* Defendants' Motion to Dismiss, *Christiana Tah, et al. v. Global Witness Publishing*, Case 1:18-cv-02109, November 9, 2018.

159 *"was most likely a bribe":* Complaint in *Tah v. Global Witness*, September 10, 2018.

159 *had not come from Exxon:* Global Witness, *Catch Me If You Can*, p. 30.

159 *She was "appalled"*: Complaint in *Tah v. Global Witness*.
159 *dialed back some of the wording*: Nicola Namdjou interview with author.
160 *sent copies of the report*: Complaint in *Tah v. Global Witness*.
160 *didn't expect things to escalate*: Noronha-Gant interview.
160 *all the more baffling*: Christiana Tah interview with author.
161 *"I needed to seek redress"*: Tah interview.
161 *suggested Rod Smolla*: Tah interview.
161 *told his new client*: Smolla interview.
161 *agreed to work on contingency*: Tah interview.
161 *"the trivialization of free speech"*: Rodney A. Smolla, *Suing the Press: Libel, the Media, and Power* (New York: Oxford University Press, 1986), p. 257.
162 *Smolla explained*: Smolla interview.
162 *other reputable news organizations*: Festus Poquie, "Liberian Panel Wants Ex-President Sirleaf's Son Prosecuted," Bloomberg News, May 30, 2018.
162 *"misuse of public money"*: Poquie, "Liberian Panel Wants Ex-President Sirleaf's Son Prosecuted"; Motion to Dismiss, *Tah v. Global Witness*.
163 *a substantial amount of money*: Namdjou and Tah interviews.
163 *anxiety wasn't helping*: Noronha-Gant interview.
164 *petrified of appearing in court*: Smolla interview.
165 *at the dining room table*: Smolla interview.
166 *furiously zapping messages*: Namdjou and Noronha-Gant interviews.
168 *"punch him in the nose"*: Silberman DC Circuit oral history, p. 189.
168 *looking bedraggled*: Namdjou interview.
168 *tips of his teeth chipped off*: Noronha-Gant interview.
168 *devoted skier and long-distance runner*: Jerry de Jaager, "Judge David Tatel, '66," University of Chicago Law School, April 18, 2023.
171 *a close friend of Silberman's*: "Hon. Laurence H. Silberman: An Interview with Paul D. Clement."
171 *"too much of an activist"*: "Hon. Laurence H. Silberman: An Interview with Paul D. Clement."
171 *"likely removes any doubt"*: Chad Bowman email reviewed by author.
172 *the Supreme Court rejected his petition*: US Supreme Court Order List, November 1, 2021.
172 *carried immense weight*: "A Judge for First Principles," editorial, *Wall Street Journal*, October 25, 2021.
172 *"When Silberman speaks"*: Ruth Marcus, "Trump's Attacks on the Press Were Bad. What This Federal Judge Did Was Worse," *Washington Post*, March 21, 2021.
172 *deductible on its insurance policy*: Namdjou interview.
172 *used a money-laundering network*: "Undermining Sanctions," Global Witness, July 2, 2020.
172 *campaign of intimidation and retribution*: "Intimidation and Scare Tactics Won't Work on Us," Global Witness, July 7, 2020.
173 *celebratory dinner in London*: Namdjou interview, August 2, 2023.
173 *"I have a family now"*: Noronha-Gant interview.

CHAPTER 13: A SECOND JUSTICE

174 *an unmarked office in Miami*: C. J. Chivers, Eric Schmitt, and Nicholas Wood, "Supplier Under Scrutiny on Arms for Afghans," *New York Times*, March 27, 2008.

175 *to qualify for NATO membership:* Chivers, Schmitt, and Wood, "Supplier Under Scrutiny."

175 *"Abso-fucking-lutely":* Guy Lawson, *Arms and the Dudes: How Three Stoners from Miami Beach Became the Most Unlikely Gunrunners in History* (New York: Simon & Schuster, 2015), pp. 173–76.

175 *a reputation for corruption:* Anthony J. Blinken, "Public Designation of Albanian Sali Berisha Due to Involvement in Significant Corruption," US Department of State, May 19, 2021.

175 *steered investigators away from his son:* Guy Lawson affidavit in *Berisha v. Lawson, et al.*, Case 1:17-cv-22144, August 9, 2018.

175 *was found dead:* Nicholas Kulish, "Whistle-Blower's Death Provides Focus for Albanians' Suspicions About Authority," *New York Times*, October 8, 2008.

175 *had based his descriptions:* Lawson affidavit.

175 *part of the Albanian mafia:* Chivers, Schmitt, and Wood, "Supplier Under Scrutiny."

176 *successfully sued Albanian media outlets:* Shkëlzen Berisha interview with author; Judge Marcia Cooke, Order Granting Defendants' Motion for Summary Judgment, *Berisha v. Lawson*, December 21, 2018.

176 *The victory emboldened him:* Berisha interview.

176 *singled out for especially harsh criticism:* Complaint in *Berisha v. Lawson*, June 8, 2017.

176 *sharing his side of the story:* Berisha interview.

177 *To Lawson's horror:* Guy Lawson interview with author.

177 *issued subpoenas:* Gary Kokolari interview with author; proof of service on subpoena issued to Kokolari, June 21, 2018, reviewed by author.

177 *résumé included surveillance work:* Ronan Farrow, "The Black Cube Chronicles: The Private Investigators," *New Yorker*, October 7, 2019.

177 *spent hours lingering:* Kokolari interview; Kokolari subpoena proof of service.

177 *a transparent effort to stifle:* Defendants' Motion for Summary Judgment, *Berisha v. Lawson*, August 8, 2018.

177 *nearly twenty thousand documents:* Defendants' Motion for Summary Judgment, *Berisha v. Lawson*.

177 *The case was dismissed:* Cooke, Summary Judgment Order.

177 *pondered another possibility:* Lawson interview.

178 *validated Cooke's reasoning:* Eleventh Circuit Court of Appeals ruling in *Berisha v. Lawson*, Case 19–10315, September 2, 2020.

178 *moved to Miami in 1983:* Roy Katriel interview with author.

178 *graduated top of his class:* Katriel interview; Katriel profile on LinkedIn.

179 *trapping its former customers' text messages:* Jonathan Stempel, "Apple Must Face U.S. Lawsuit over Vanishing iPhone Text Messages," Reuters, November 11, 2014.

179 *"exceptionally well done":* Kannon Shanmugam email to Katriel, reviewed by author.

179 *inspired Katriel:* Katriel interview.

179 *"pink elephant in the room":* Katriel interview.

180 *"should be granted here":* Katriel email to Jason Zoladz, December 7, 2020, reviewed by author.

180 *"exploring your assistance":* Zoladz email to Katriel, December 22, 2020, reviewed by author.

180 *"I abhor":* Charlie Rose, "Antonin Scalia," charlierose.com, November 27, 2012.

181 *"Good lord":* Lawson interview.

181 *requested a response:* Supreme Court docket for Case 20–1063.

181 *"thought we were dead":* Katriel interview.

182 *the final act:* David Logan interview with author.

182 *a long-haired radical:* Logan interview.

182 *Scalia cited:* Scalia opinion in *City of Richmond v. J. A. Croson Co.*, January 23, 1989.

183 *about "judicial federalism":* David A. Logan, "Judicial Federalism in the Court of History," *Oregon Law Review*, 1987.

183 *in the opposite way:* Logan interview.

183 *reading news reports:* Logan interview.

183 *77 percent of the time:* David A. Logan, "Libel Law in the Trenches: Reflections on Current Data on Libel Litigation," *Virginia Law Review*, May 2001.

183 *"among the great civil liberties victories":* Logan, "Libel Law in the Trenches."

183 *Five other justices followed:* Bruce M. Selya, "Skivvies and All," *Roger Williams University Law Review*, Summer 2023.

183 *cut off in the photo:* Photo reviewed by author.

183 *akin to revivalist church sermons:* Rebekkah Ruth Nardi Stoeckler, "Logan Church," *Roger Williams University Law Review*, Summer 2023.

183 *Logan thought back:* Logan interview.

184 *"protections of zealous reporting":* David A. Logan, "Logan on Trump and Libel Law," Roger Williams University School of Law, January 3, 2017.

184 *suggested that Logan cut:* Logan interview.

185 *"ignorance is bliss":* David A. Logan, "Rescuing Our Democracy by Rethinking *New York Times Co. v. Sullivan*," *Ohio State Law Journal*, 2020.

186 *a virtually identical trend:* Michael Norwick, "The Empirical Reality of Contemporary Libel Litigation," Media Law Resource Center, March 2022.

186 *He mailed a copy:* Logan interview.

187 *"Check this out!":* Logan interview.

187 *"petition for a writ of certiorari is denied":* US Supreme Court Order List, July 2, 2021.

187 *a reference to a* New York Times *article:* Kashmir Hill, "A Vast Web of Vengeance," *New York Times*, January 30, 2021.

188 *had been sufficiently credible:* Andy Kroll, *A Death on W Street: The Murder of Seth Rich and the Age of Conspiracy* (New York: Public Affairs, 2022), pp. 115–16.

188 *found her in contempt of court:* Hill, "A Vast Web of Vengeance."

190 *"an angry sad man":* Email reviewed by author.

190 *felt like a win:* Katriel interview.

190 *with giddy disbelief:* Logan interview.

190 *came from Rod Smolla:* Email reviewed by author.

190 *"seems plenty robust":* Kimberly Atkins Stohr and Stefano Kotsonis, "The Case for Rethinking American Libel Law," *On Point*, WBUR, July 12, 2021.

190 *"Sheer brilliance":* Libby Locke post on Twitter, July 2, 2021.

191 *a very different story:* Letter from MLRC's Michael Norwick to Justice Gorsuch, July 7, 2021, reviewed by author.

191 *altered Gorsuch's dissent:* Supreme Court comparison of revised opinion, July 29, 2021, available at supremecourt.gov/opinions/20pdf/20-1063diff_dc8e.pdf.

191 *joked to friends:* Michael Norwick interview with author.

CHAPTER 14: STAY OUT OF THE KITCHEN

192 *nearly $400 million in assets:* Heritage Foundation 2022 financial statement.

192 *Some two hundred people:* The Heritage Foundation, "Justice Thomas' Thirty-Year Legacy on the Supreme Court," YouTube, October 22, 2021.

192   *debuting an annual prize:* "A Judge for First Principles," *Wall Street Journal*, October 25, 2021.

193   *to nominate Thomas to the Supreme Court:* Oral History Project of the Historical Society of the District of Columbia Circuit, "Honorable Laurence H. Silberman," pp. 191–92; Jane Mayer and Jill Abramson, *Strange Justice: The Selling of Clarence Thomas* (Boston: Houghton Mifflin, 1994), p. 154.

193   *erupted in appreciative laughter:* Heritage Foundation, "Justice Thomas' Thirty-Year Legacy."

194   *"their own economic self-interest":* "Libel Laws and the Press," video of Heritage Foundation event, C-SPAN, October 3, 2019.

195   *amplified Thomas's and Gorsuch's critiques:* Hans von Spakovsky, "Thomas Fires Warning Shot at Media, Organizations That Lie About Conservatives," *Daily Signal*, June 28, 2022.

195   *recycled the incorrect data:* The Federalist Society, *"New York Times v. Sullivan,"* 2023 Florida Young Lawyers Summit, YouTube, video, September 1, 2023, youtube.com/watch?v=m50o66JN2kA.

195   *the Scaife and DeVos clans:* Katherine Stewart, "The Anti-Democracy Think Tank," *The New Republic*, September 2023.

195   *financed or threatened major libel lawsuits:* In the 1980s, Richard Mellon Scaife spent $2 million financing a landmark defamation case that retired general William Westmoreland brought against CBS. (George Lardner Jr., "Pittsburgh Millionaire Financed Westmoreland's Suit Against CBS," *Washington Post*, February 28, 1985.) Richard DeVos, meanwhile, threatened a $500 million libel lawsuit against the *Detroit Free Press* after it revealed a long-running tax scam involving his company, Amway. (Jane Mayer, *Dark Money: The Hidden History Behind the Rise of the Radical Right* (New York: Anchor Books, 2016), p. 371.)

196   *"the supreme jurist in the land":* Larry Arnn speech at Claremont Institute's Annual Lincoln Day Dinner, C-SPAN, February 9, 1999.

196   *Thomas returned the compliment:* Clarence Thomas speech at Claremont Institute's Annual Lincoln Day Dinner, C-SPAN, February 9, 1999.

196   *first at Heritage and then at Claremont:* Carson Holloway profile at University of Nebraska Omaha.

196   *"a lot of things to be cleaned up":* James Wilson Institute, "'Rethinking Libel, Defamation, and Press Accountability' with Carson Holloway," *Anchoring Truths* podcast, October 21, 2022.

196   *a Claremont Institute white paper:* Carson Holloway, "Rethinking Libel, Defamation, and Press Accountability," Claremont Institute Center for the American Way of Life, September 21, 2022.

196   *essay in* American Conservative *magazine:* Carson Holloway, "Overturn *New York Times v. Sullivan*," *American Conservative*, September 9, 2022.

196   *this minor megaphone:* Holloway on *Anchoring Truths* podcast.

197   *powdered and primped him:* Executive Office of the Governor of Florida, advance notes for defamation roundtable, undated, obtained by author via public records request.

197   *"facts be damned":* Governor Ron DeSantis's panel discussion, Facebook, video, February 7, 2023, facebook.com/watch/live/?ref=watch_permalink&v=1833236057055722.

197   *conservative journalists and influencers:* Governor's office advance notes.

197   *spent weeks laboring:* Governor's office advance notes.

198   *"leading purveyors of disinformation":* DeSantis at panel discussion.

198   *shared a briefing document:* Skyler Swisher, "Records: DeSantis' Office Eyed Bill to Alter Libel Laws," *Orlando Sentinel*, May 18, 2022.

198 *"aims to invite challenges":* Swisher, "Records: DeSantis' Office Eyed Bill."

198 *They had met:* David Lat, *Original Jurisdiction* podcast with Tom Clare and Libby Locke, April 26, 2023.

199 *Laxalt introduced them:* Daniel Watkins (a former Clare Locke partner) interview with author.

199 *sexual assault allegations in 2018:* Grant Stern, "Nevada AG's Extortion Letter," *The Stern Facts*, October 26, 2018.

199 *more than $90,000:* Nevada Secretary of State campaign finance records.

199 *she and the governor would share the stage:* Executive Office of the Governor of Florida, list of possible formats for defamation panel, undated, obtained by author via public records request.

199 *DeSantis aide noted to colleagues:* Executive Office of the Governor of Florida, briefing notes for defamation roundtable, undated, obtained by author via public records request.

199 *the Claremont Institute and the James Wilson Institute:* Federalist Society profile page of Daniel T. Whitehead.

199 *"more decidedly a right-wing thinker":* Governor's office briefing notes.

200 *federal courts have ruled:* Elizabeth McNamara, Brief in Opposition to Petition for Writ of Certiorari, *Berisha v. Lawson*, May 17, 2021.

201 *he had a meet and greet:* Governor's office advance notes.

201 *foiled by opposition:* Ken Bensinger, "Right-Wing Media Splits from DeSantis on Press Protections," *New York Times*, April 3, 2023.

201 *the owner of a local Fox affiliate put it:* James W. Schwartzel (owner of WFSX-FM) email to Florida lawmakers, March 17, 2023, reviewed by author.

201 *"this is defamation":* Twitter post by @BasedMikeLee, April 18, 2023.

202 *the CNN lawsuit:* Trump v. CNN, Case 0:22-cv-61842-AHS, complaint filed October 3, 2022.

202 *judge dismissed the suit:* Judge Brad Thomas, *Mastandrea v. Snow*, Florida District Court of Appeals, per curiam, February 2, 2022.

202 *passion for breeding horses:* Judge Mark T. Boonstra, profile page on Michigan Courts website, courts.michigan.gov.

202 *religion into the public square:* Dustin Bass, "Michigan Judge Appeals to Americans for Morality Reform," *Epoch Times*, April 29, 2023.

202 *"nearly insurmountable":* Judge Mark Boonstra, *Reighard v. ESPN*, Michigan Court of Appeals, May 12, 2022.

202 *lacked the right to film police officers:* Jonathan Turley, "Federal Court: First Amendment Does Not Generally Protect Public Filming of Police in Public," jonathanturley. org, February 24, 2016.

203 *"questioning the continued viability":* Judge Mark Kearney, opinion in *Ralston v. Garabedian*, Case 2:19-cv-01539, August 26, 2022.

203 *his $300 million lawsuit against CNN:* Alan Dershowitz v. CNN, Case 0:20-cv-61872, September 15, 2020.

203 *reputation had been soiled:* Niraj Chokshi, "Alan Dershowitz Says Martha's Vineyard Is 'Shunning' Him over Trump," *New York Times*, July 3, 2018.

203 *he had sympathy for Dershowitz:* Raag Singhal interview with author.

203 *Federalist Society member:* Raag Singhal's Senate Judiciary Committee questionnaire.

203 *"foolishness, apathy, and an inability":* Judge Raag Singhal, Order in *Dershowitz v. CNN*, April 4, 2023.

204 *"discourage a proper level of investigation":* Singhal interview.

204 *helped Justice Arthur Goldberg write:* Alan Dershowitz interview with author.

204 *spoken about the case:* Alan Dershowitz speech at the National Constitution Center, You-Tube, March 27, 2014.

205 *threatening letters to* The New Yorker: Dershowitz interview; Fabio Bertoni (*New Yorker* lawyer) interview with author.

205 *less than glowing profile of him:* Connie Bruck, "Alan Dershowitz, Devil's Advocate," *New Yorker,* July 29, 2019.

205 *Dershowitz's lawyers wrote: Dershowitz v. CNN,* appeal to Eleventh Circuit, Case 23–11270, July 11, 2023.

CHAPTER 15: THE SLUR

206 *agreed to take his case:* Matthew Fernholz interview with author.

206 *carrying guns and Confederate flags:* Reid J. Epstein, "In Wisconsin, Virus Creates New Front in Long-Simmering Partisan Wars," *New York Times,* April 23, 2020.

206 *"Covid scamdemic":* Cory Tomczyk deposition, October 4, 2022.

206 *provoked bitter controversy:* Reid J. Epstein, "A 'Community for All'? Not So Fast, This Wisconsin County Says," *New York Times,* May 18, 2021.

207 *"the end of private property":* Epstein, "A 'Community for All'?"

207 *one of the resolution's loudest critics:* Defendants' Brief in Support of Motion for Summary Judgment, *Cory Tomczyk, et al., v. Wausau Pilot and Review Corp., et al.,* Marathon County Circuit Court, Case 21-CV-625, December 2, 2022.

207 *"it set up the opportunity":* Tomczyk deposition.

207 *"fag number one":* Norah Brown deposition, November 1, 2022.

207 *sent a Facebook message:* Brief of Defendants-Respondents, *Tomczyk v. Wausau Pilot,* Wisconsin Court of Appeals, November 8, 2023.

207 *founded the outlet:* Shereen Siewert interview with author.

208 *more than $50 million after taxes:* "Ham Lake Man Wins Portion of Powerball Lottery," North Metro TV, August 8, 2013.

208 *writing a check on the spot:* Paul White interview with author; Siewert interview.

208 *didn't stop for twelve hours:* Siewert interview.

208 *traffic was ten times that:* Siewert interview.

208 *an email from Norah Brown:* Email to *Wausau Pilot & Review,* August 18, 2021, reviewed by author.

209 *the* Pilot *ran an article:* Damakant Jayshi, "As Diversity Decision Nears Conclusion, an Adult Dismisses a Slur Against 13-Year-Old, Saying 'Get Over It!'" *Wausau Pilot & Review,* August 21, 2021.

209 *would go on to reject:* Damakant Jayshi, "Marathon County Rejects 'Community for All' Resolution," *Wausau Pilot & Review,* August 25, 2021.

209 *had spoken with Brown:* Shereen Siewert deposition, September 21, 2022.

209 *Siewert reviewed the messages:* Brief of Defendants-Respondents.

209 *That sealed it for Siewert:* Defendants' Summary Judgment Motion.

209 *hadn't contacted Tomczyk beforehand:* Siewert deposition.

209 *he was incensed:* Fernholz interview.

210 *appointed him to a government commission:* Gov. Scott Walker appointed him to the state board overseeing architects, engineers, designers, and land surveyors.

210 *named him to another:* Wisconsin Office of Lawyer Regulation, District Committee Six.

210 *Supreme Court ruled for Fernholz:* Jason Calvi, "Wisconsin Supreme Court Strikes Down Statewide Mask Mandate," FOX 6, March 31, 2021.

210 *a documentary about the lawsuit:* Federalist Society, *Pandemic Powers: Wisconsin's State of Emergency*, YouTube, May 5, 2023.

210 *drop boxes for absentee ballots:* Riley Vetterkind, "Businessman Files Lawsuit Challenging Ballot Drop Boxes," *Wisconsin State Journal*, March 17, 2021.

210 *had filed a libel lawsuit:* Chris Rickert, "Publisher Libel Suit Flips the Script," *Capital Times*, June 11, 2021.

210 *largest-ever defamation award in Wisconsin:* Daniel Bice, "Progressive 'Bernie Brew' Owner Ordered to Pay Record $750,000 for Defaming Conservative Publisher," *USA Today*, October 30, 2023.

210 *as a budding originalist at Marquette:* Fernholz interview.

211 *Fernholz thought to himself:* Fernholz interview.

211 *One went to Lisa Ort-Sondergard:* Fernholz letter to Ort-Sondergard, September 24, 2021, reviewed by author.

211 *Ort-Sondergard wrote to Siewert:* Ort-Sondergard letter to *Wausau Pilot & Review*, October 1, 2021, reviewed by author.

211 *"will consider appropriate legal action":* Fernholz letter to Siewert, September 24, 2021, reviewed by author.

211 *didn't have libel insurance:* Siewert interview.

212 *Hopefully Fernholz was bluffing:* Siewert interview.

212 *it could be flexible:* Brian Spahn interview with author.

212 *Spahn already knew of Fernholz:* Spahn interview.

213 *"will go down":* Tomczyk deposition.

213 *outstanding bill hit $158,000:* Siewert and Spahn interviews.

213 *learned of it through mutual friends:* White interview.

213 *three other witnesses:* Brief of Defendants-Respondents.

213 *"out of joking and out of spite":* Tomczyk deposition.

213 *Marathon County judge dismissed it:* Judge Scott Corbett, Decision on Summary Judgment, April 28, 2023.

213 *conservative and constitutional originalist:* "County Circuit Court Race," *Star News* (Medford, WI), March 16, 2021.

214 *fixed herself a stiff martini:* Siewert interview.

214 *"This act of basic citizenship":* Appellants' brief in *Tomczyk v. Wausau Pilot*, October 9, 2023.

214 *lost at least $15,000 a year:* Siewert email.

214 *"a way to express their displeasure":* "News Conference: Senate Agard and Legislative Democrats to Introduce Anti-SLAPP Legislation," *Wisconsin Eye*, August 23, 2023.

215 *the* New York Times *wrote about it:* Jeremy W. Peters, "Report on Anti-Gay Slur Could Put Local News Site out of Business," *New York Times*, August 15, 2023.

215 *A handful of other states:* Dan Greenberg, David Keating, and Helen Knowles-Gardner, "Anti-SLAPP Statutes: 2023 Report Card," Institute for Free Speech, November 2, 2023.

215 *virtually unanimous support from lawmakers:* David Keating (president of Institute for Free Speech) interview with author.

215 *complicate the use of absentee ballots:* Wisconsin Assembly Bill 1037.

215 *conduct election audits:* Wisconsin Senate Bill 736.

215 *displayed in public school classrooms:* Wisconsin Assembly Bill 778.

216 *Holt called Doug Burns:* Steve Holt interview with author; Doug Burns interview with author.

216 *"We want to prevent":* Holt interview.

216 *an enthusiastic Trump supporter:* "'Everybody Get Out': Trump Urges Voters to Turn
      Out on Caucus Night Amid Frigid Temperatures," WMUR 9 (ABC affiliate), January
      14, 2024.

216 *doubted the necessity of such a law:* State Rep. Megan Srinivas interview with author;
      Carol Hunter, "Why Iowa Needs a Law to Protect Your Right to Free Expression," *Des
      Moines Register*, July 10, 2022.

216 *probably violate the state constitution:* New Hampshire Supreme Court, opinion of the
      justices at the request of the Senate, May 11, 1994.

CHAPTER 16: JUST THE BEGINNING

217 *curiosity was piqued:* Lauren Chooljian interview with author.

217 *tales of his drug-addled past:* Anthony Pompliano interview with Eric Spofford,
      "Shocking Story of Former Drug Addict Turned CEO," *The Pomp Podcast*, January
      9, 2023.

217 *had a strong relationship:* Lauren Chooljian, "Sununu Calls Allegations Against Spof-
      ford 'Serious,'" New Hampshire Public Radio, March 23, 2022.

217 *eventually wrote a story:* Lauren Chooljian, "Clients, Staff Say Major N.H. Addiction
      Treatment Center Mishandled COVID Outbreak," New Hampshire Public Radio, De-
      cember 14, 2020.

217 *a new, more shocking allegation:* Chooljian interview.

218 *high school wrestling coach:* Dave Dyer, "End of an Era: Chooljian Built Wrestling Dy-
      nasty," *The Eagle-Tribune*, September 16, 2019.

218 *had pissed off:* Marc Tracy, "'Losing Friends' over How She Covers the New Hampshire
      Primary," *New York Times*, February 9, 2020.

218 *She eventually interviewed dozens:* Chooljian interview.

218 *He called Chooljian's editor:* Daniel Barrick interview with author.

218 *"disingenuous reporting and malicious conduct":* Mitchell Schuster letter to Lauren
      Chooljian, March 11, 2022, reviewed by author.

218 *Chooljian's investigation first aired:* Lauren Chooljian, "He Built New Hampshire's
      Largest Addiction Treatment Network. Now, He Faces Accusations of Sexual Miscon-
      duct," New Hampshire Public Radio, March 22, 2022.

219 *by no means the end of her reporting:* Chooljian interview.

219 *Chooljian and her colleagues recognized:* Chooljian and Barrick interviews.

219 *for what he said was $115 million:* Marketing for Eric Spofford's "Miami Mansion Mas-
      termind" class, available at cashflowiskingmastermind.com/reserve-your-spot-now.

219 *the day after Chooljian's piece ran:* Mitchell Schuster "litigation hold" letter to Chool-
      jian source, March 23, 2022, reviewed by author.

219 *hundreds of thousands of dollars into this endeavor:* Screenshot of deleted Spofford
      Facebook post, May 26, 2022, reviewed by author.

219 *letters instructed the recipients:* Schuster letter to Chooljian source; Benjamin Levine
      letter to Sigmund Schutz (NHPR's outside lawyer), June 9, 2022.

220 *coauthored a book:* Eric Spofford and Piers Kaniuka, *Real People Real Recovery: Over-
      coming Addiction in Modern America* (Plantation, Florida: J. Ross Publishing, 2019).

220 *a subsequent settlement:* Deleted Spofford Facebook post.

220 *letter that apologized to Spofford:* Piers Kaniuka letter to NHPR, May 17, 2022.

220 *"not credible and filled with lies":* Deleted Spofford Facebook post.

220 *cutting off contact:* Misty Marris letter to Chooljian source, May 18, 2022, reviewed by
      author.

220 *they were unnerved:* Chooljian interview; screenshot of Chooljian text message with source, reviewed by author.

221 *on vacation in Telluride, Colorado:* Chooljian interview; Matt Baer (Chooljian's husband) interview with author.

221 *"had something happen at the house":* Text message reviewed by author.

221 *a softball-size rock:* Criminal complaint, *USA v. Tucker Cockerline, Keenan Saniatan, and Michael Waselchuck,* Case 1:23-mj-08245, June 15, 2023.

221 *they both gasped:* Barry Chooljian interview with author.

221 *say things like "shut up" or "sucks":* Chooljian interview.

222 *Barrick was in the car:* Barrick interview.

222 *"I'm so sorry, Dan":* Chooljian interview.

222 *"the victim of a nighttime crime":* Listserv email reviewed by author.

222 *"Hanover got hit, too":* Chooljian and Baer interviews.

222 *her father told her:* Barry Chooljian interview.

222 *"a buzzsaw called the First Amendment":* Sigmund Schutz letter to Benjamin Levine, May 19, 2022, reviewed by author.

223 *Schutz spoke by phone:* Levine letter to Schutz, May 23, 2022, reviewed by author.

223 *Around 3:30 that afternoon:* Federal grand jury indictment of Eric Labarge, Keenan Saniatan, Tucker Cockerline, and Michael Waselchuck, *USA v. Cockerline, et al.*, Case 1:23-cr-10245, September 7, 2023.

223 *had come to buy some bricks:* Complaint in *USA v. Cockerline, et al.*

223 *about a dollar each:* Homedepot.com list of bricks for sale.

223 *green eyes:* "In Brief," *New Hampshire Union Leader,* February 14, 2013.

223 *There were drug, assault:* "New Hampshire Police Logs," *Eagle-Tribune,* May 28, 2015.

223 *forgery charges:* "Rock. Sheriff Department Arrest Logs," *Foster's Daily Democrat,* January 14, 2016.

223 *"Fugitive of the Week":* "In Brief," *New Hampshire Union Leader.*

223 *blue food coloring:* Jason Schreiber, "Fungus Fakeout Gets Trio Arrested," *New Hampshire Union Leader,* November 13, 2008.

223 *"I'm making bad decisions":* Jason Schreiber, "Man Sentenced in Sale of Fake Hallucinogen," *New Hampshire Union Leader,* June 29, 2009.

223 *Cockerline had gotten to know:* Complaint in *USA v. Cockerline, et al.*

224 *brawl in a motel bathroom:* Clynton Namuo, "Police: Man Stabbed 6 Times over Drugs," *New Hampshire Union Leader,* October 5, 2010.

224 *after the victim disappeared:* "Motel Stabbing Charges Dropped," *Daily News of Newburyport,* January 14, 2011.

224 *beaten his girlfriend senseless:* Doug Ireland and Jo-anne Mackenzie, "Danville Standoff Ends Peacefully," *Eagle-Tribune,* October 26, 2012.

224 *make hundreds of dollars:* Complaint in *USA v. Cockerline, et al.*

224 *locked up on unrelated charges:* Complaint in *USA v. Cockerline, et al.*

224 *"Wanna make sum cash?":* Federal grand jury indictment of Labarge, Saniatan, Cockerline, and Waselchuck.

224 *Cockerline struck first:* Complaint in *USA v. Cockerline, et al.*

224 *sprinted away:* Chooljian's doorbell cam video of vandalism.

224 *$1,000 in cash from Labarge:* Federal grand jury indictment of Labarge, Saniatan, Cockerline, and Waselchuck.

225 *smothered the rising sun:* Weather Underground, "Chicago, IL Weather History," May 21, 2022.

225 *"The house was vandalized again":* Chooljian text messages, reviewed by author.

225 *Baer had a bad feeling:* Baer interview.
225 *"it happened to our house, too":* Chooljian and Baer interviews.
225 *divided the phone calls:* Chooljian and Baer interviews.
225 *"JUST THE BEGINNING!":* Photo reviewed by author.
225 *"Hey, I'm Matt":* Baer interview.
226 *He publicly speculated:* Spofford statement issued by one of his lawyers, Misty Marris, May 26, 2022.
227 *a ninety-page libel lawsuit:* Eric Spofford v. NHPR, et al., Case 218–2022-cv-00803, September 20, 2022.
227 *These were not strong claims:* Judge Daniel I. St. Hilaire, Order Following In Camera Review, December 13, 2023.
227 *sought to dismiss the lawsuit:* Defendants' Memorandum in Support of Motion to Dismiss, Spofford v. NHPR, et al., October 14, 2022.
227 *"has a real chilling effect":* "Spofford's Attorney Tells Judge NHPR Engaged in 'Reckless Disregard' of Facts," NH Journal, January 31, 2023.
228 *Schutz also pointed out:* Defendants' Opposition to Motion for Limited Discovery, Spofford v. NHPR, et al., May 8, 2023.
228 *St. Hilaire struck a compromise:* Judge Dan St. Hilaire, Order on Motion for Limited Discovery, Spofford v. NHPR, et al., May 30, 2023.
228 *were upset:* Chooljian interview.
228 *nearly three thousand pages:* St. Hilaire, Order Following In Camera Review.
229 *issued his ruling:* St. Hilaire, Order Following In Camera Review.
229 *sending bogus requests:* Lumen.com database of copyright complaints, available at lumendatabase.org/notices/search?sort_by=&term-exact-search=true&term=%22Eric+Spofford%22.
229 *a popular new tool:* BBC, "How Fake Copyright Complaints Are Muzzling Journalists," March 1, 2023.
229 *"Massive & Profitable Personal Brand":* Spofford's Miami Mansion Mastermind website.

CHAPTER 17: THE CASE OF THE CENTURY

230 *bought earlier that year:* Property records via Redfin.
230 *walked down the hill:* David Lat, Original Jurisdiction podcast with Tom Clare and Libby Locke, April 26, 2023.
230 *have a quiet conversation:* Tom Clare on So to Speak podcast with Lee Levine, May 9, 2023.
231 *"You're all fucking dead":* Tom Clare and Megan Meier email to Fox News general counsel Lily Fu Claffee, December 22, 2020, reviewed by author.
231 *"We recognized right away":* Andrew Goudsward, "Lawyers Win Big in $787.5 Million Fox Defamation Case," Reuters, April 20, 2023.
231 *sending cease-and-desist letters:* Erik Larson, "Conservative Power Couple Wage Legal War on Stolen-Election Myth," Bloomberg News, February 26, 2021.
231 *"reckless disinformation campaign":* Clare and Meier letter to Sidney Powell, December 16, 2020.
231 *letter to Fox News' general counsel:* Clare and Meier email to Claffee.
231 *to create a paper trail:* Clare on So to Speak podcast.
231 *an unwavering advertiser:* Jeremy Barr, "Fox News and Mike Lindell's MyPillow Are Taking a Break," Washington Post, January 12, 2024.

231 *so determined to stop the bleeding:* Jim Rutenberg, Michael S. Schmidt, and Jeremy W. Peters, "Missteps and Miscalculations: Inside Fox's Legal and Business Debacle," *New York Times*, May 27, 2023.

232 *"afraid to speak out":* Ed Pilkington, "Groups Increasingly Use Defamation Law to Ward Off US Election Subversion," *The Guardian*, November 18, 2023.

232 *a more urgent fight:* Rachel Goodman interview with author.

232 *something clicked:* Goodman interview.

232 *had sent to Alex Jones:* Andy Kroll, *A Death on W Street: The Murder of Seth Rich and the Age of Conspiracy*, (New York: PublicAffairs, 2022), pp. 115–16.

233 *families of children massacred:* Elizabeth Williamson, "Truth in a Post-Truth Era: Sandy Hook Families Sue Alex Jones, Conspiracy Theorist," *New York Times*, May 23, 2018.

233 *more than $1 billion in damages:* Elizabeth Williamson, "With New Ruling, Sandy Hook Families Win over $1.4 Billion from Alex Jones," *New York Times*, November 10, 2022.

233 *"these suits are like a sheriff":* Goodman interview.

233 *Protect Democracy's first foray:* Complaint in *Robert Weisenbach v. Project Veritas, et al.*, Court of Common Pleas of Erie County, PA, Case 10819–21, August 13, 2021.

233 *acknowledging that the allegations were false:* Statements from Project Veritas and James O'Keefe, February 5, 2024.

233 *two election workers in Atlanta sued:* Reid J. Epstein, "Two Election Workers Targeted by Pro-Trump Media Sue for Defamation," *New York Times*, December 2, 2021.

233 *stars like Dinesh D'Souza and Kari Lake:* Protect Democracy, "Litigation"; *Stephen Richer v. Kari Lake, et al.*; *Mark Andrews v. Dinesh D'Souza, et al.*

233 *"a brand-new trend":* RonNell Anderson Jones interview with author.

234 *Lee Levine noted:* Jeremy W. Peters, "First Amendment Scholars Want to See the Media Lose These Cases," *New York Times*, March 13, 2022.

234 *the men knew each other:* Rod Smolla interview with author.

234 *an hourly rate of $750:* Smolla interview.

234 *Dominion's only recourse:* Lat, *Original Jurisdiction* podcast with Clare and Locke.

234 *were already piling up:* Lawyers and others familiar with the arrangement, in interviews with author.

235 *ran to 441 pages:* Complaint in *US Dominion Inc., et al., v. Fox News Network*, Superior Court of Delaware, Case N21C-03–257 EMD, March 26, 2021.

235 *"paramount public concern":* Defendant's Brief in Support of Motion to Dismiss, *Dominion v. Fox*, May 18, 2021.

236 *"it is reasonably conceivable":* Judge Eric Davis, Opinion in *Dominion v. Fox*, December 16, 2021.

236 *Twice a week:* Alaina Lancaster, "How Susman's Davida Brook Unearthed Key Documents," *The Recorder*, October 30, 2023.

236 *"that Fox could fight about":* Brian Stelter, *Network of Lies: The Epic Saga of Fox News, Donald Trump, and the Battle for American Democracy* (New York: One Signal Publishers, 2023), pp. 228–29.

236 *hundreds of thousands:* Stelter, *Network of Lies*, p. 238.

236 *stunned by what they saw:* Lawyers involved in the case, in interviews with author.

236 *"100% false":* Amanda Terkel, Jane C. Timm, and Dareh Gregorian, "Here's What Fox News Was Trying to Hide in Its Dominion Lawsuit Redactions," NBC News, March 29, 2023.

236 *"Sidney Powell is lying":* Dominion's Brief in Support of Motion for Summary Judgment, *Dominion v. Fox*, January 17, 2022.

236 *Excited messages:* Interviews with lawyers involved in the case.

237 *Clare later remarked:* Clare on *So to Speak* podcast.

237 *a simple "fuck you":* Matt Gertz, "Tucker Carlson on Getting 'Triggered' by Dominion's Deposition Lawyer," Media Matters for America, May 3, 2023.

237 *raged to his producers:* Gertz, "Tucker Carlson on Getting 'Triggered.'"

237 *inclined to grant Locke's wish:* David Enrich, "How a Case Against Fox News Tore Apart a Media-Fighting Law Firm," *New York Times*, April 10, 2024.

238 *happened in the middle of the trial:* Interviews with Daniel Watkins (former Clare Locke partner) and others; Enrich, "How a Case Against Fox News."

238 *assume the company had fired them:* Interviews with Watkins and others; Enrich, "How a Case Against Fox News."

238 *"clothe the case in the First Amendment":* Dan Webb on *So to Speak* podcast with Lee Levine, May 9, 2023.

239 *to order outside delivery:* Interviews with lawyers involved in the case.

239 *in the Turks and Caicos:* Flight records for Clare Locke jet; Enrich, "How a Case Against Fox News."

239 *Davis had preemptively ruled:* Jeremy W. Peters and Katie Robertson, "Fox News Suffers Major Setback in Defamation Case," *New York Times*, March 31, 2023.

240 *began coming into focus:* Jeremy W. Peters, Jim Rutenberg, and Katie Robertson, "How Hard Lines in Fox-Dominion Deal Talks Suddenly Softened," *New York Times*, April 20, 2023.

240 *overheated courtroom:* Jim Rutenberg, *New York Times* live briefing on Dominion trial, April 18, 2023.

240 *a hangout for Buffalo Bill:* Terry Conway, "A New Vibe," *The Hunt*.

240 *toasted each other late into the night:* Attendees at the party, in interviews with author.

240 *a lawyer dialed Rod Smolla:* Smolla interview.

240 *showed up at the Columbus Inn:* Enrich, "How a Case Against Fox News."

241 *boasted five days after the settlement:* Lat, *Original Jurisdiction* podcast with Clare and Locke.

241 *without consulting the partners:* Enrich, "How a Case Against Fox News."

241 *secretly incorporated it weeks later:* Washington, DC, incorporation records, June 6, 2023.

241 *publicly endorsed the* Sullivan *decision:* Meier post on LinkedIn, March 2024.

241 *had just flown to Georgia:* Flight records for Clare Locke jet.

242 *the three remaining partners said:* Sara Merken, "Clare Locke Partners Split to Form New Firm After Dominion Win," Reuters, August 3, 2023.

242 *another refugee from Project Veritas:* Julia Witt. Her profile page on Clare Locke's website said her previous job, as a lawyer at Veritas, was at "a journalism organization."

CHAPTER 18: GUNNING FOR *SULLIVAN*

243 *made their way through Foley Square:* Shane Vogt interview with author.

243 *including reality-TV cameos:* Emily Yahr, "Sarah Palin and Family's Long, Complicated History with Reality TV," *Washington Post*, April 3, 2014.

243 *the aide explained to Vogt:* Vogt interview.

244 *from a satirical website:* "Palin: 'Even the French Understand That Slavery Wasn't Our Fault, Because the Negroes Liked It," NewsSlo, March 31, 2016, accessed via Internet Archive.

244 *sex with large Black men:* Ashley Rae, "Exclusive: Rapper Calls for Sarah Palin to be Gang Raped," Media Research Center, April 4, 2016.

244 *a statement to* People *magazine:* Lindsay Kimble and Tierney McAfee, "Sarah Palin Says She Will Sue Azealia Banks," *People*, April 5, 2016.

244 *five foot ten on a good day:* Vogt interview.

244 *as he informed Palin's aide:* Vogt interview.

245 *put it in an email:* James Bennet email to colleagues, June 14, 2017, disclosed in *Sarah Palin v. New York Times Company* (hereinafter *Palin v. NYT*), Case 1:17-cv-04853.

245 *paranoid schizophrenia:* Marc Lacey, "Suspect in Shooting of Giffords Ruled Unfit for Trial," *New York Times*, May 25, 2011.

245 *the ad had implored:* Jeff Muskus, "Sarah Palin's PAC Puts Gun Sights on Democrats She's Targeting in 2010," *Huffington Post*, January 9, 2011.

245 *Critics, including Giffords:* Frank Rich, "No One Listened to Gabrielle Giffords," *New York Times*, January 15, 2011.

245 *"Don't Retreat, Instead Reload!":* David Weigel, "Explaining Sarah Palin's 'Don't Retreat, Reload' Comment," *Washington Independent*, March 26, 2010.

245 *finished the piece around 4:45 p.m.:* Elizabeth Williamson trial testimony, *Palin v. NYT*, February 4, 2022.

245 *a direct causal connection:* Brief for Defendants-Appellees, *Palin v. NYT*, Second Circuit Court of Appeals, Case 22–558, December 8, 2022.

246 *decided to sharpen it himself:* James Bennet trial testimony, *Palin v. NYT*, February 9, 2022.

246 *working from her home:* Elizabeth Williamson deposition, *Palin v. NYT*, May 19, 2020.

246 *"really reworked this one":* Bennet email to Williamson, June 14, 2017, disclosed in *Palin v. NYT*.

246 *She trusted Bennet:* Williamson trial testimony.

246 *"Looks great":* Williamson email to Bennet, June 14, 2017, disclosed in *Palin v. NYT*.

246 *Bennet would later say:* Bennet trial testimony.

246 *"to express [his] bafflement":* Ross Douthat email to Bennet, June 14, 2017, disclosed in *Palin v. NYT*.

247 *"Do we have it right?":* Bennet text to Williamson, June 14, 2017, disclosed in *Palin v. NYT*.

247 *too anxious to sleep:* Bennet trial testimony.

247 *"don't know what the truth is here":* Bennet email to Williamson, June 15, 2017, disclosed in *Palin v. NYT*.

247 *"I'm sorry":* Williamson trial testimony.

247 *journalists were scrambling:* Bennet trial testimony.

247 *At 11:15 a.m.:* Brief for Defendants-Appellees, *Palin v. NYT*.

247 *"no such link was established":* "America's Lethal Politics," *New York Times*, June 14, 2017.

247 *tweeted the correction:* @nytopinion tweet (retweeted by @nytimes), June 15, 2017.

248 *obscure website called* Blasting News*:* Mark Whittington, "New York Times Revives Lie About Sarah Palin and the Shooting of Gabby Giffords," *Blasting News*, June 15, 2017.

248 *added her own note:* @SarahPalinUSA tweet, June 15, 2017.

248 *former governor had a case:* Vogt interview.

248 *"death panels":* Jim Rutenberg and Jackie Calmes, "False 'Death Panel' Rumor Has Some Familiar Roots," *New York Times*, August 13, 2009.

248 *"lamestream media":* David Carr, "How Sarah Palin Became a Brand," *New York Times*, April 4, 2010.

248 *"messin' with broke, broke, broke":* Palin Facebook post, December 19, 2016.

248 *Palin saw a chance:* John F. Harris, "The Cynical Spectacle of Sarah Palin's Lawsuit Against the *New York Times*," *Politico*, February 10, 2022.

248 *it persuaded him:* Vogt interview.

249 *Vogt filed a lawsuit:* Complaint in *Palin v. NYT*, June 27, 2017.

249 *had sued over a different editorial:* Murray Energy, "Murray Energy Corporation Sues the *New York Times* For False and Defamatory Article," PR Newswire, May 5, 2017.

249 *would abandon that suit:* Amanda Reilly, "Murray Drops Defamation Suit Against the *Times*," *E&E News*, May 29, 2018.

249 *hadn't been on the losing end of a libel lawsuit:* George Freeman (former lawyer for *New York Times*) interview with author; Liz Spayd, "A Rare Libel Suit Against the *Times*," *New York Times*, May 10, 2017.

250 *reputation for doing things his way:* Adam Liptak, "Stern Words for Wall Street's Watchdogs, from a Judge," *New York Times*, December 16, 2013.

250 *"too narrow a view of the law":* David S. Hilzenrath, "Judge Jed Rakoff on Free Love, the Death Penalty, Defending Crooks and Wall Street Justice," *Washington Post*, January 20, 2012.

250 *Bennet explained at one point:* Transcript of Bennet testimony at evidentiary hearing, *Palin v. NYT*, August 16, 2017.

250 *Rakoff ruled:* Rakoff order dismissing *Palin v. NYT*, August 29, 2017.

251 *called in some backup:* Notice of appeal in *Palin v NYT*, November 21, 2017.

251 *warm but cloudy:* Weather Underground, "New York City Weather History" for September 21, 2018.

251 *had given birth to a girl:* Tom Clare and Libby Locke letter to author and *New York Times*, April 5, 2024.

251 *"It was improper":* Audio recording of oral arguments at Second Circuit Court of Appeals, September 21, 2018.

251 *stood at the back of the courtroom:* Clare and Locke letter.

252 *published its decision:* Judge John M. Walker Jr., Second Circuit opinion, *Palin v. NYT*, Case 17–3801, August 6, 2019.

252 *seven-figure bill for a yearslong case:* Dermot Cole, "Candidate Sarah Palin Has Yet to Come Clean with Alaskans," *Anchorage Press*, May 25, 2022.

252 *The eighth query:* Interrogatory reviewed by author.

253 *Vogt filed a motion:* Plaintiff's Memorandum in Support of Motion for Partial Summary Judgment, *Palin v. NYT*, June 19, 2020.

254 *"over my dead body":* Richard Luscombe, "Sarah Palin Says She'll Get Covid Vaccine 'Over My Dead Body,'" *The Guardian*, December 21, 2021.

254 *overpowering smell of marijuana:* Vogt interview.

254 *five women and four men:* Seth Stevenson, "Sarah Palin Wasn't the Point," *Slate*, February 15, 2022.

254 *insider-trading trial in Rakoff's courtroom:* Dave Axelrod interview with author; *Securities and Exchange Commission v. Daryl Payton, et al.*, Case 14-cv-4644.

255 *an edge to his voice:* Sarah Ellison, "James Bennet Testifies as Sarah Palin Trial Raises Questions," *Washington Post*, February 8, 2022.

255 *put it in a court filing:* Plaintiff's Response to Defendants' Local Rule 56.1 Statement of Material Facts, *Palin v. NYT*, July 10, 2020.

255 *and even edited speeches:* James Bennet deposition, *Palin v. NYT*, May 20, 2020.

255 *reflecting the courtroom's overhead lights:* Seth Stevenson, "'I Don't Know What the Truth Is Here,'" *Slate*, February 8, 2022.

256 *holding hands with her boyfriend:* Elahe Izadi and Sarah Ellison, "New York Times Offers Defense in Sarah Palin Libel Trial," *Washington Post*, February 9, 2022.

256   *in a tuxedo and top hat:* Sasha Abramsky, "Jed Rakoff and the Lonely Fight for Wall Street Justice," *The Nation*, June 18, 2014.

256   *didn't know how to dance:* "Sarah Palin Visits *Dancing with the Stars*," ABC News, YouTube, video, September 28, 2010.

259   *"a good day for the free press":* Jeremy W. Peters, "Sarah Palin's Libel Claim Against the *Times* Is Rejected by a Jury," *New York Times*, February 15, 2022.

259   *the knowledge that they would appeal:* Vogt interview.

259   *hadn't been swayed by the alerts:* Brief of Appellant, *Palin v. NYT*, September 19, 2022.

260   *"you're wasting time":* Recording of oral arguments, *Palin v. NYT*, November 6, 2023.

EPILOGUE: A MISOGYNIST AND A SNAKE

263   *a list of dozens of questions:* Author email to Clare and Locke, March 28, 2024.

263   *Clare Locke's initial salvo:* Clare email to David McCraw, April 1, 2024.

263   *they doubled down:* Clare email to McCraw, April 2, 2024.

264   *"a misogynist and a snake":* Locke email to McCraw, April 3, 2024.

264   *a forty-page document:* Clare and Locke letter to McCraw, April 5, 2024.

264   *on behalf of Project Veritas:* Clare and Locke letter to McCraw and Jay Brown (Ballard Spahr), April 8, 2024.

264   *a 2021 court order that barred the* Times: Michael M. Grynbaum and Marc Tracy, "Judge Clarifies Order on *New York Times* Coverage of Project Veritas," *New York Times*, December 14, 2021.

264   *a final letter arrived:* Clare and Locke letter to McCraw and Brown, April 9, 2024.

265   *"heads up on something":* Author text to Megan Meier, March 27, 2024.

265   *the article was published:* David Enrich, "How a Case Against Fox News Tore Apart a Media-Fighting Law Firm," *New York Times*, April 10, 2024.

266   *dashed off numerous essays:* Carson Holloway, "Malice Toward Wall, Defamation for None?" *Law & Liberty*, December 20, 2022; Carson Holloway, "*Sullivan* and the Right to Reputation," *Law & Liberty*, October 30, 2023; Carson Holloway, "Trump Takes Aim at *New York Times v. Sullivan*," Claremont Institute, January 20, 2023.

266   *"revered as a landmark ruling":* Notre Dame Center for Citizenship & Constitutional Government, "*New York Times v. Sullivan* and the Original Meaning of the First Amendment: Carson Holloway," YouTube, March 27, 2024.

267   *didn't challenge the facts in the article:* Adam Ganucheau, "Mississippi Opens the Playbook for Dismantling a Free Press," *New York Times*, June 14, 2024.

267   *"It is not difficult to see":* Ganucheau, "Mississippi Opens the Playbook."

267   *He blocked reporters:* Katie Robertson, "Trump Team Revokes Election Party Access for Some Journalists," *New York Times*, Nov. 5, 2024.

268   *even jail journalists:* Kyle Paoletta, "Trump Wins, the Press Loses," *Columbia Journalism Review*, Nov. 6, 2024.

268   *flying outside a house:* Jodi Kantor, Aric Toler, and Julie Tate, "Another Provocative Flag Was Flown at Another Alito Home," *New York Times*, May 22, 2024.

INDEX